yle

"Boyl ... e focus here. . . . A me ... ything, at great risk, ... ed Frank Lloyd Wrig ... amiliar autobiographical material. He inhabits the space of Wright's life and times with particular boldness. . . . Boyle has been writing his own fascinating, unpredictable, alternately hilarious and terrifying fictional history of utopian longing in America. *The Women* adds a powerful new chapter to this continuing narrative."

—Joanna Scott, *The New York Times Book Review*

"Riveting . . . Despite dozens of writers' attempts to capture Wright's story, it seems safe to say that none has rendered it with more crackling life than Mr. Boyle. . . . Many have noted the paradoxical contrast between Wright's messy personal life and the sublime tranquility of his designs. With Mr. Boyle's rich characterizations and a sober, appreciative eye for Wright's achievements, the author does justice to both."

—Penelope Rowlands, *The Wall Street Journal*

"Move over, Nora Roberts! With this potboiler about the love life of Frank Lloyd Wright, T. C. Boyle, one of America's most inventive writers, bursts feverishly into the realm of romance fiction. . . . True readers of the genre, be warned: It's a romance *only* in spirit. Call it a thinking man's soap opera. . . . The fiery loves that populated the life of America's premier architect make an excellent grist for over-the-top melodrama. . . . Boyle tells all this in garish detail, luxuriating in the considerable opportunity for heated sex and operatic gush such a chronicle of human foibles might offer. . . . So much for the material. But, oh, the writing! Boyle is a marvel at descriptive prose."

—Marie Arana, *The Washington Post*

"Wonderfully entertaining . . . By moving his story backwards in time, Boyle achieves the best and most satisfying type of dramatic irony, in which his readers are privy, in advance, to the fates of his characters. . . . Boyle's portrait of Wright himself is deliciously repulsive. . . . At the same time, he does a brilliant job of exploring Wright's matchless artistic sensibilities. . . . Boyle's ability to write from the perspective of an outraged wife, a reverent acolyte, or a crazed murderer is uncanny. . . . In his inexhaustible capacity to beguile us as a natural storyteller, T. C. Boyle is surely one of our most American novelists since Mark Twain, and one of our very best." —Howard Frank Mosher, *The Boston Globe*

"Boyle's prose moves with equal parts vigor and grace. His rhythmic, turbo-charged sentences virtually leap off the page. . . . Boyle handles the big themes—Wright the genius battling an uncomprehending, philistine world and Wright the man loving and loathing his women—with extraordinary brio."

—Dan Cryer, *San Francisco Chronicle*

"Daredevil artistry . . . The novel seems to rise fully articulated, like one of Wright's own iconic constructs. This is a tale of seductive genius: Who can resist a man who reshapes the world?"

—Cathleen Medwick, *O, The Oprah Magazine*

"Juicy and enjoyable . . . Each woman is memorable, but Miriam steals the show. . . . Boyle is as fearless and up-for-it a writer as any working today. His output so far proves he can do just about anything. It's hard to belt a theme around such a sprawling body of work, but the cause and effect between human appetite—for fame, sex, money, freedom—and folly nearly serves."

—Taylor Antrim, *Los Angeles Times*

"[*The Women*] is extremely readable and deftly builds a portrait of the artist as pure egoist. . . . It proves an effective showcase for Boyle's own strengths as a craftsman. His prose is full of vivid descriptions and turns of phrase that pop with a preternatural precision." —*The New Yorker*

"After reading *The Women*, you may never experience Frank Lloyd Wright's Fallingwater or Guggenheim Museum in quite the same way. With invigorating storytelling, Boyle conjures an intelligent and carefully detailed fictional portrait based on the architect's tumultuous relationships. . . . In Boyle's impressively researched book, the reader is swept along by the force of imagined dialogue and the literary alchemy of fact and supposition."

—Lisa Jennifer Selzman, *The Houston Chronicle*

"At once glowing and irreverent . . . *The Women* uses innovative structures, muscular language and exuberant characterizations as its building blocks. . . . A neatly constructed mix of fact and fiction about Frank Lloyd Wright's way with females."

—Heller McAlpin, *Newsday*

"American egomaniacs fascinate us all—admit it—but few fiction writers have as much fun with them as Boyle does. . . . To see a monument to [Wright], read *The Women*."

—Betsy Willeford, *The Miami Herald*

"Zesty and gorgeously crafted . . . poignant and thought-provoking . . . As art, it's real pleasure, and likely to delight all those who reveled in *Loving Frank*."

—Karen Sandstrom, *The Cleveland Plain Dealer*

"Book by book, yarn by yarn, the novelist T. C. Boyle has been assembling a fabulous and tawdry imaginative history of the United States. . . . This sexy, hilarious page-turner re-creates the rolling storm front created by a charming man and the personal chaos his determination to live outside of conventions created for those who lived within his orbit. . . . *The Women* gives tremendous life to the ladies of its title. The intelligence of Boyle's narrative voice seeps down, in his casual, elegant prose, into the details of their lives."

—John Freeman, *The Kansas City Star*

"A wild and improvisational examination of Frank Lloyd Wright and the women he loved . . . One of the strengths of this book is Boyle's evenhandedness when it comes to gender. Neither Wright nor his loves get short shrift psychologically, and the women are particularly well fleshed out, especially the mercurial, gaudy Maude. . . . Boyle masterfully braids the stories of the main characters to create a weird, eccentric, and provocative family portrait."

—Carlo Wolff, *The Christian Science Monitor*

"Put down your Roth and Bellow for tales of the all-devouring ex-wife, because T. C. Boyle has just checked in with a novel to make all the other episodes of the ex-files sound like *Little Women*. . . . Boyle's best book in ages." —Mark Shechner, *The Buffalo News*

"Engrossing . . . Boyle's profoundly flawed characters are convincing. . . . [They] are clothed in prose so assured you want to bet money on it." —Sarah L. Courteau, *Bookforum*

ABOUT THE AUTHOR

T. C. Boyle is the author of the novels *Talk Talk*, *The Inner Circle*, *Drop City* (a finalist for the National Book Award), *A Friend of the Earth*, *Riven Rock*, *The Tortilla Curtain*, *The Road to Wellville*, *East Is East*, *World's End* (winner of the PEN/Faulkner Award), *Budding Prospects*, *Water Music*, and eight collections of stories. In 1999, he was the recipient of the PEN/Malamud Award for Excellence in Short Fiction. His stories appear regularly in major American magazines, including *The New Yorker*, *GQ*, *Esquire*, *Harper's*, *McSweeney's*, and *Playboy*. A member of the American Academy of Arts and Letters, he lives near Santa Barbara, California. T. C. Boyle's Web site is www.tcboyle.com.

T. CORAGHESSAN BOYLE

THE WOMEN

A NOVEL

PENGUIN BOOKS

PENGUIN BOOKS

Published by the Penguin Group

Penguin Group (USA) Inc., 375 Hudson Street, New York, New York 10014, U.S.A.
Penguin Group (Canada), 90 Eglinton Avenue East, Suite 700, Toronto, Ontario, Canada M4P 2Y3 (a division of Pearson Penguin Canada Inc.) • Penguin Books Ltd, 80 Strand, London WC2R 0RL, England • Penguin Ireland, 25 St Stephen's Green, Dublin 2, Ireland (a division of Penguin Books Ltd) • Penguin Group (Australia), 250 Camberwell Road, Camberwell, Victoria 3124, Australia (a division of Pearson Australia Group Pty Ltd) • Penguin Books India Pvt Ltd, 11 Community Centre, Panchsheel Park, New Delhi – 110 017, India • Penguin Group (NZ), 67 Apollo Drive, Rosedale, North Shore 0632, New Zealand (a division of Pearson New Zealand Ltd) • Penguin Books (South Africa) (Pty) Ltd, 24 Sturdee Avenue, Rosebank, Johannesburg 2196, South Africa

Penguin Books Ltd, Registered Offices:
80 Strand, London WC2R 0RL, England

First published in the United States of America by Viking Penguin,
a member of Penguin Group (USA) Inc. 2009
Published in Penguin Books 2009

3 5 7 9 10 8 6 4 2

Publisher's Note: This is a work of fiction based on real events.

THE LIBRARY OF CONGRESS HAS CATALOGED THE HARDCOVER EDITION AS FOLLOWS:

Boyle, T. C.
The women : a novel / T. Coraghessan Boyle.
p. cm.
ISBN 978-0-670-02041-6 (hc.)
ISBN 978-0-14-311703-2 (pbk.)
1. Wright, Frank Lloyd, 1867–1959—Relations with women—Fiction. I. Title.
PS3552.O932W66 2009
813'.54—dc22 2008042462

Printed in the United States of America
Set in Electra • Designed by Francesca Belanger

For Karen Kvashay

AUTHOR'S NOTE

The following is a fictional re-creation of certain events in the lives of Frank Lloyd Wright, his three wives—Catherine Tobin, Maude Miriam Noel and Olgivanna Lazovich Milanoff—and his mistress, Mamah Borthwick Cheney. While actual events and historical personages are depicted here, all situations and dialogue are invented, except where direct quotes have been extracted from newspaper accounts of the period. I am deeply indebted to Frank Lloyd Wright's many biographers and memoirists, especially Meryle Secrest, Brendan Gill, Robert C. Twombly, Finis Farr, Edgar Tafel, Julia Meech, Anthony Alofsin, John Lloyd Wright and Ada Louise Huxtable, and I would like to thank Keiran Murphy and Craig Jacobsen, of Taliesin Preservation, Inc., for their assistance, and Charles and Minerva Montooth and Sarah Logue for their kindness and hospitality.

Early in life I had to choose between honest arrogance and hypocritical humility; I chose arrogance.

—FRANK LLOYD WRIGHT

PART I OLGIVANNA

INTRODUCTION TO PART I

I didn't know much about automobiles at the time—still don't, for that matter—but it was an automobile that took me to Taliesin in the fall of 1932, through a country alternately fortified with trees and rolled out like a carpet to the back wall of its barns, hayricks and farmhouses, through towns with names like Black Earth, Mazomanie and Coon Rock, where no one in living memory had ever seen a Japanese face. Or a Chinese either. Stop for fuel, a sandwich, a chance to use the washroom, and you'd think a man had come down from Mars and propped himself up on the seat of a perfectly ordinary canary-yellow and pit-of-hell-black Stutz Bearcat roadster. (And what is a bearcat, anyway? Some hybrid monster out of an adman's inventory, I suppose, a thing to roar and paw and dig at the roadway, and so this one did, as advertised.) Mostly, along that route on a day too hot for October, and too still, too clear, as if the season would never change, people just stared till they caught themselves and looked away as if what they'd seen hadn't registered, not even as a fleeting image on the retina, but one man—and I won't take him to task here because he didn't know any better and I was used to it by then—responded to my request for a hamburger sandwich by dropping his jaw a foot and a half and exclaiming, "Well, Jesus H. Christ, you're a Chinaman, ain't ya?"

The whole business was complicated by the fact that the ragtop didn't seem to want to go up, so that my face was exposed not only to the glare of the sun and a withering cannonade of dust, chicken feathers and pulverized dung, but to the stares of every stolid Wisconsinite I passed along the way. The ruts were maddening, the potholes sinks of discolored water that seemed to shoot up like geysers every fifty feet. And the insects: I'd never in my life seen so many insects, as if spontaneous generation were a fact and the earth gave them up like grains of pollen, infinite as sand, as dust. They exploded across the windscreen in bright gouts of filament and fluid till I could barely make out the road through the wreckage. And everywhere the lurching farm dogs, errant geese, disoriented hogs and suicidal cows, one obstacle after another looming up in my field of vision till I began to freeze at every curve and junction. I must have passed a hundred farm wagons. A thousand fields. Trees beyond counting. I clung to the wheel and gritted my teeth.

Three days earlier I'd celebrated my twenty-fifth birthday—alone, on the overnight train from Grand Central to Chicago's Union Station, a commemorative telegram from my father in my suitcase alongside my finger-worn copies of the *Wendingen* edition and the Wasmuth portfolio and several new articles of clothing I felt I might find useful in the hinterlands, denim trousers and casual shirts and the like. I never did bother to unpack them. To my mind, this expedition was a ritual undertaking, calling for formal dress and conventional behavior, despite the rigors of the road and what I can only call the derangement of the countryside. My hair, combed and recombed repeatedly against the buffeting of the wind, was a slick brilliantined marvel of study and composition, and I was dressed in my best suit, a new collar and a tie I'd selected especially for the occasion. And while I hadn't opted for the goggles or cap, I did stop in at Marshall Field's for a pair of driving gloves (dove-gray, in kid leather) and a white silk scarf I envisioned fluttering jauntily in the wind but which in fact knotted itself in a sweaty chokehold at my throat before I'd gone ten miles.

I kept my spine rigid and held to the wheel with one hand and the mysterious gearshift with the other, just as the helpful and courteous man at the automobile agency had demonstrated the previous night in Chicago when I'd purchased the car. It was a 1924 model, used but "very sporty," as he assured me—"in terrific condition, first-rate, really first-rate"—and I paid for it with a check drawn on the account my father had set up for me when I'd disembarked at San Francisco four years earlier (and to which, generously and indulgently, he continued to add on the first of each month).

I have to admit I liked the looks of it as it sat there at the curb, motion arrested, power in reserve, all of that, though I wondered what my father would have thought of it. Inevitably it brought to mind loose women and undergraduates in raccoon coats—or worse yet, gangsters—but the other cars looked ordinary beside it. Funereal, even. There was one black Durant that should have had a mortuary sign in the window, and there must have been a dozen or more Fords sitting there looking as dull as dishwater in the faded paint Henry Ford had dubbed Japan black (and I can't imagine why, unless he was thinking of ink sticks and *kanji*, but then how would he or any of his designers in the remote xenophobic purlieus of Detroit know anything of *kanji*?).

There didn't seem to be any bullet holes in the fenders, not as far as I could see, and the engine spat and roared in a gratifying way. I climbed in, took a turn or two around the block, the salesman at my side shouting out directions, admonitions and beginner's praise, and then I was on my own, creeping out of town as the ratcheting high-crowned Fords and Chevrolets came roaring at me or shot up to overtake me from behind. I didn't give them a second glance, even when my fellow drivers crowed in derision and made rude gestures out the streaming windows. No, I was too busy, gearshift, clutch, brake and accelerator requiring my full and very close attention. (In theory, piloting a car was nothing at all, a mere reflex—anybody could do it, even women—but in practice it was like plunging into a superheated public bath over and over again.)

As for the countryside, the closest I'd come to a rural setting was at Harvard University, where my dormitory room looked out on well-kept lawns, shrubbery and the deep continents of shade cast by the oaks and elms that had brooded over the heads of generations before me. I'd never been to a farm, even to visit, and I found my meat and eggs in the market like anyone else. No, I was a thoroughly urban being, raised in a series of apartments in the Akasaka district of Tokyo and in Washington, D.C., where for six years my father was cultural attaché at the Japanese embassy. Sidewalks appealed to me. Paved avenues. Streetlights and shops and restaurants where you could find a French maitre d' and perhaps even a chef who was familiar with béchamel and sauce béarnaise instead of the ubiquitous brown gravy and mashed potatoes. I traveled by train, streetcar and hackney cab like anyone else and the only animals I saw with any frequency were pigeons. And dogs. On the leash.

And yet here I was, fighting the gearshift and the clutch that was so stiff it all but dislocated my kneecap every time I disengaged it, weaving down a godforsaken unpaved lane in the hinterlands of Wisconsin, immured in an ever-deepening layer of dust and insect parts, frustrated, angry, lost. But not simply lost: irretrievably lost. I'd seen the same farmhouse three times now and counting, the same staved-in wagon with the weeds growing through the spokes of its rusted wheels, the same wedge-faced cows in the same field, gazing at me out of the maddening nullity of their bovine eyes, and I didn't know what to do. Somehow I'd fallen into the trance of the roadway, my limbs working automatically, my brain shut down, and all I could do was turn left and then right and left again till the familiar barn loomed up in front of me and I found myself creeping past it yet again in my growling sleek road machine that had become my purgatory and my prison.

As it happened, I was in possession of a hand-drawn map sent me by one Karl Jensen, secretary for the Taliesin Fellowship, of which I was a new—and charter—member, but it showed a purported road along a purported river that didn't seem to exist. I was wondering where I'd gone wrong, the persistent whine of the engine sending up sympathetic vibrations in my head, when on what must have been my fourth pass, the scene suddenly shifted: there was the barn, there the wagon, there the cows, but now something new had entered the picture. A stout woman in a plain gray shift and apron was stationed at the side of the road, a brindled dog and two small boys at her side. When I came within sight she began windmilling her arms as if we were at sea and she'd fallen over the rail and into the green grip of the tailing waves, and before I could think I was jerking at the gearshift and riding the brake until the car came to a lurching halt some twenty feet beyond her. She waited a moment till the dust had cleared, then came up the side of the road wearing a stoic expression, the boys (they must have been seven or eight, somewhere in that range) dancing on ahead of her while the dog yapped at their heels.

"Hello!" she called out in a breathless delicate voice. "Hello!"

She was at the side of the car now, the boys shying away at the last minute to poise waist-deep in the roadside vegetation and peer up uncertainly at me. I was conscious of the distance between us, of the high-flown seat of my Stutz automobile and the prodigious running slope of its fenders. The weeds, flecked here and there with the rust of the season, crowded the roadway, which wasn't much wider than a cart-path in any case. One of the boys reached down for a stem of grass and inserted it between his front teeth. I couldn't think of what to say.

I watched her expression as she took me in, two pale Hibernian eyes measuring my face, my clothes, the splendor of the automobile. "Are you looking for something?" she asked, but plunged right on without waiting for the answer. "Because you been up this road four times now. Are you lost"—and here she registered the truth of what her eyes had been telling her all along: that is, that I was foreign, and worse, an exotic—"or something?"

"Yes," I said, trying for a smile. "I seem to have—got myself in a bind here. I'm looking for Taliesin?" I made a question of it, though I didn't realize at the time that I was mispronouncing the name, since I'd never heard it spoken aloud. I suppose I must have given it a Japanese emphasis—*Tál-yay-seen* rather than the more mellifluous *Tal-ee-éssin*, because she just stared blankly at me. I repeated myself twice more before one of the boys spoke up: "I think he means Taliesin, Ma."

"Taliesin?" she repeated, and her features contracted round the sourness of the proper noun. "Why would you want to go there for?" she asked, her voice rising to a kind of suppressed yelp on the final (superfluous) syllable, but even as she asked, the answer was settling into her eyes. Whatever the association was, it wasn't pleasant.

"I have a, uh"—the car shuddered and belched beneath me—"an appointment."

"Who with?"

The words were out of my mouth before I knew what I was saying: "Wrieto-San."

The narrowed eyes, the mouth gone rancid all over again, the dog panting, the boys gaping, insects everywhere: "*Who?*"

"Mr. Lloyd Wright," I said. "The architect. Builder of"—I'd pored over the Wasmuth portfolio till the pages were frayed and I knew every one of his houses by heart, but all I could think of in the extremity was the pride of Tokyo—"the Imperial Hotel."

No impression, nothing. I began to feel irritated. My English was perfectly intelligible—and I had sufficient command of it even to pronounce with little effort that knelling consonant that gave my countrymen so much trouble on the palate. "Mr. Lloyd Wright," I repeated, giving careful emphasis to the double *L*.

And now it was my turn for a moment of extended observation: Who was this woman? This farmwife with the unkempt boys and outsized bosom and the chins encapsulating one another like the rings of a tree? Who was she to question me? I didn't know, not at the time, but I suspected she'd never heard of the Imperial Hotel or the unearthly beauty of its design and the revolutionary engineering that enabled it to survive the worst seismic catastrophe in our history with nothing more than cosmetic repairs—for that matter, I suspected she'd never heard of my country either, or of the vast seething cauldron of the Pacific Ocean that lay between there and here. But she knew the name of Lloyd Wright. It exploded like an artillery shell in the depths of her eyes, drew her mouth down till it was closed up like a lockbox.

"I can't help you," she said, lifting one hand and dropping it again, and then she turned away and started back down the road. For a moment the boys lingered, awed by the miraculous vision of this gleaming sporty first-rate yellow-and-black automobile drawn up there on the verge of their country lane and the exotic in command of it, but then they slouched their shoulders and drifted along in her wake. I was left with the insects, the weeds and the dog, which squatted briefly in the dirt to dig at a flea behind one ear before trotting off after them.

As it turned out, I did ultimately find the road to Taliesin, whatever the symbolism of that might imply or portend—if I hadn't, there wouldn't be much point in putting any of this down on paper. At any rate, I sat there a moment, dumbfounded by the kind of show of indifference that might have been usual here but would have been unheard of in my country—*Americans*, I muttered, and I couldn't help thinking of my father, an inveterate rumbler and declaimer whose mounting frustrations during his Washington years seemed almost to have buried him—then jerked my hand to the gearshift and reversed direction. The farmhouse passed by on my left this time and before long I was taking a series of random turns until I found myself discovering new barns, new lanes and new ruts until finally—mirabile dictu—the purported river came into existence and the road along with it. I felt my spirits soar. Things were looking up.

Any minute now, I kept telling myself, *any minute*, but then, in the midst of my mounting joy, my insecurities began to take hold. I had no idea what to expect. While I was confident in my education to this point—after a full course of study at Tokyo Imperial University, I came first to Harvard and then M.I.T. for advanced work because I wanted a modern outlook on architecture, a *Western* outlook, and I was willing to work all day and lucubrate till dawn to get it—I was coming to Taliesin on impulse. It was as simple as this: one afternoon the previous spring I'd been trudging down the hall of the architecture building with a ziggurat of books under one arm and my case of drafting tools in the other, feeling out of sorts and depressed (what the popular musicians call "blue," the true hue of anomie and hopelessness, my inamorata having left me for a Caucasian who played trombone, that most phallic of instruments, my studies repetitive and insipid and as antiquated as the Ionic column and plinth on which they were founded) when I took a bleary, world-weary moment to stand before the notice board outside the dean's office.

An announcement caught my eye. It was exquisitely printed on creamy dense high-fiber paper and it announced the founding of the Taliesin Fellowship under the auspices of Frank Lloyd Wright at his home and studio in Wisconsin, tuition of $675 to include room and board and an association with the Master himself. I went directly back to my room and drafted a letter of application. Five days later Wrieto-San personally wired back to say that I was accepted and that he awaited the arrival of my check.

And so here I was, at the moment of truth. At the crossroads, as it were, and could anyone blame me for being more than a little anxious? I felt like a freshman coming to campus for the first time, wondering where he was going to sleep, what he would eat, how his coevals would view him and whether he'd experience the grace of acceptance and success or sink into disgrace and failure. Unconsciously, I began to increase my speed, the wind seizing my hair, the scarf slapping at my shoulders like a wet towel ripped down the middle, and I can only think it was providence that kept the loping dogs and blundering cows and all the rest off the road and out of the way on that final stretch to Taliesin.

The river ran on and the road with it. Five minutes passed, ten. I was impatient, angry with myself, anxious and queasy all at once—and where was it, where was this architectural marvel I knew only from the pages of a book, this miracle of rare device, the solid heaven where I'd be living for the next year and quite possibly more? Where? I was cursing aloud, the engine racing, the vegetation falling back along the sides of the road as if beaten with an invisible flail, and yet I saw nothing but more of the same. Fields and more fields, stands of corn, hills rising and dipping all the long way through whatever valley I was in, barns, eternal barns—and then, suddenly, there it was. I looked up and it materialized like one of the hidden temples of *The Genji Monogatari*, like a trompe l'oeil, the shape you can't see until you've seen it. Or no, it didn't appear so much as it unfolded itself from the hill before me and then closed up and unfolded and closed up again.

Was I going too fast? Yes. Yes, I was. And in applying the brake I somehow neglected the clutch—and the wheel, which seemed to come to life all on its own—and my Bearcat gave an expiring yelp and skewed across the road in a tornado of dust and flying litter, where it stalled facing in the wrong direction.

No matter. There was the house itself, an enormous rambling place spread wide and low across the hill before me, struck gold under the afternoon sun, a phoenix of a house, built in 1911 and burned three years later, built again and burned again, only to rise from the ashes in all its golden glory. I couldn't help thinking of Schelling's trope, great architecture existing like frozen music, like music in space, because this was it exactly, and this was no mere chamber piece, but a symphony with a hundred-voice chorus, the house of Wrieto-San, his home and his refuge. To which I was invited as apprentice to the Master. All right. I slapped the dust from my jacket, worked a comb through my hair, tried above all to *get a grip*. Then I started up the car and drove off in search of the entrance.

It wasn't as easy as all that. For one thing, in all this

hodgepodge of roads and cart-paths I couldn't determine which one led into the estate, and once I did find what I took to be the right road, wending through the muddy chasm of a hog farm, I was arrested by the proliferation of signs warning against trespass. These could hardly apply to me, I reasoned, and yet an innate uncertainty—shyness, if you will, or call it an inborn cultural reverence for the rules and norms of society—held me back. The automobile shivered in the mud. I jerked the gearshift to the neutral position and stared for a long moment at the nearest sign. Its meaning was quite plain—incontrovertible, in fact. NO, it read, TRESPASSING.

It was just then that I became aware of a figure observing me from behind the slats of a wooden fence on my left periphery. A farmer, as I took it, in spattered overalls and besmeared boots. He was standing ankle-deep in the ordure of the hog yard—right in the heart of it—the very animals nosing around him and giving rise to one of the rawest and most unpleasant odors I'd ever encountered. I watched him watching me for a moment—he was grinning now, something sardonic and judgmental settling into his eyes—and then I raised my voice to be heard over the engine and the guttural vocalizations of the animals. "I wonder if you might—" I began, but he cut me off with a sharp stabbing laugh. "Oh, go on ahead," he said, "—he don't care for nothing like that. That's just for tourists." He gave me a long bemused look. "You ain't a tourist, are ya?"

I shook my head no and then, thanking him with an abbreviated bow, I found the lowest gear and started up the hill, which seemed, unfortunately, to grow ever steeper even as the limestone walls and terraces and broad-hipped roofs of the house drew closer. But there was gravel under the wheels now and the prodigious Bearcat seized it, the wheels churning and the engine screeching like a mythical beast beating its wings and belching fire. Up I went, up and up—till the gravel suddenly deepened into a kind of lithic sludge and the wheels vacillated and then grabbed with a vicious spewing of rock and I thought to apply the brake just as I crested the hill and nosed up to the bumper of the car parked there. I was lit up with excitement, trembling with the exertion, the tension, the glory of it all. So what if I'd mistakenly come up the back road, used only by the tractor and the dray horses? So what if I'd come within an ace of hurtling into the rear bumper of Wrieto-San's Cord Phaeton, the swiftest and most majestic automobile manufactured anywhere on this earth? I was here. I was home.

My first impressions? Of peace, of beauty abounding, of an old-world graciousness and elegance of line. And there was something more too: a deep-dwelling spiritual presence that seemed to emanate from the earth itself, as if this were a holy place, a shrine where the autochthonous tribes had gathered to worship in a time before Wrieto-San's ancestors, the Lloyd Joneses, had come over from Wales, a time before Columbus, a time when Edo was cut off from the world. I felt as if I'd entered one of the temples of Kyoto—Nanzenji, or better yet, Kinkakuji, its gold leaf harboring the light. All my anxiety dissolved. I felt calm, instantly calm.

It was four o'clock in the afternoon. The sun hung above the treetops like a charm on an invisible string. I cut the engine and all the birds in the world began to sing in unison. Almost immediately the exhaust dissipated and I became aware of the lightness and purity of the air. It was scented with clover, pine, the chlorophyll of new-mown grass and the faintest trace of woodsmoke—and food, a smell of cookery that reminded me I hadn't eaten since that ill-fated hamburger sandwich. I took a moment to breathe in deeply, considered lighting a cigarette and then thought better of it. Taliesin awaited me.

I was just stepping out of the car, pulling off my

(sweat-soaked) gloves preparatory to unknotting the scarf, when a figure emerged from one of the garage stalls in the courtyard just beyond the coruscating hood of the Cord. It took me a moment—my eyesight was far superior at a narrower range, the range of the drafting table, that is, than it was at a distance—before I realized, my pulse pounding all over again, that I was in the presence of the Master himself.

I bowed. Deeply. As deeply as I'd ever bowed to anyone in my life, even my reverend grandfather and the regent of Tokyo Imperial University.

He returned my bow with one of his own—abbreviated, a bow of the head and shoulders only, as befitted his position in respect to my own. At the same time he surprised me by offering a greeting in Japanese. "*Konnichi wa*," he said, leveling his eyes on me.

"*Hajimemashite*," I replied, bowing a second time.

Wrieto-San was then sixty-five, though he admitted to sixty-three and looked and acted like a man ten or even fifteen years younger. In his autobiography, which had been published to great acclaim that year, he claimed to be five feet eight inches tall, but he was considerably shorter than that (I stand five feet seven and over the course of the ensuing weeks had the opportunity on a number of occasions to compare height casually with him and I certainly must have had at least an inch on him, perhaps two). He was dressed like an aesthete heading to an art exhibition: beret, cape, high-collared shirt, woolen puttees and the Malacca cane he affected both for elegance and authority. His hair, a weave of thunderhead and cumulus, trailed over his collar.

"*Ogenki desu-ka?*" he asked. (How are you?)

"*Genki desu*," I replied. "*Anata wa?*" (I'm fine. And you?)

"*Watashi-mo genki desu.*" (I'm fine too.)

This seemed to have exhausted his Japanese, because he leaned in against the hood of the Cord, seeking the light as if to get a better perspective on me, and switched to English. "And you are?"

I bowed again, as deeply as I could. "Sato Tadashi."

"Tadashi? I knew a Tadashi in Tokyo—Tadashi Ito, one of Baron Ōkura's group." He gave me an appraising look, taking in the sheen of my shoes, the crease of my trousers, my collar and tie. "Your name means 'correct,' yes?"

I bowed in acknowledgment.

"And do you suit your name? Are you correct, Tadashi?"

I told him I was—"at least at the drafting board"—and he let out a laugh. He was a great one for laughing, Wrieto-San, a repository of playfulness and merriment and a natural soothing charm that only underscored the magnetism of his genius. And, of course, he was famous for his acerbity too, his moods and his temper, especially if he felt he wasn't getting the respect—adulation, worship even—he felt he deserved.

"And proper too?"

Another bow.

He was grinning now, his whole face transformed. "Well, I tell you, Tadashi, I have to say this is one of the features I like best about your people," he said, straightening up and dancing a little circle round me on the paving stones—he could never remain static for long, his enthusiasm inexhaustible, his energy volcanic. "The following of the norms and strictures. I can be like that too," he said, and he gave a wink to preface the sequel, "but I hope you won't be shocked, Sato-San, if I'm *improper* more than I am proper. Wouldn't want to pin a man down, would you? Shackle him with convention?"

I didn't know where the conversation had sailed off to, but I understood that this was a form of banter and that the only answer necessary was a soft murmured, "No."

"But you're the one from Harvard, via the Institute of Technology, isn't that right?"

"Yes."

"My observation"—he was forever making pronouncements, as I would come to learn, and he'd made this one before—"is that Harvard takes perfectly good plums as students and makes prunes of them."

His tone indicated that laughter was called for and so I laughed and told him that he was right. Knowing how deeply he'd been influenced by the architecture of my nation, by the simplicity and cleanness of line of our homes and temples, I bowed again and said, "I simply could not go back to Japan with the sort of classical and ornamental education I was getting at the university . . ."

"So you came to me."

"I wanted a hands-on approach, organic architecture, the use of native materials and the design of buildings that complement rather than dominate nature, all of this, all you've pioneered, in the Robie house, the Darwin Martin, the, the Willits and—"

His expression—and I mean no disrespect at the comparison—was like the drawing-down of a lapdog's features when it's rolled over and stroked. He looked gratified—I'd said the right thing, precisely the right thing—and he was inwardly complimenting himself on his choice of Sato-San as a pupil. "Good," he said, holding up a hand to forestall me. "Excellent. But I warn you, I am no teacher and there will be no instruction here. The Fellowship, as I see it, will offer you an opportunity to work at my disposal, for my purposes, in all phases of supporting my enterprise as a working architect. You do understand that, don't you?"

I said that I did.

"All right, fine. You'll start in the kitchen. Mrs. Wright tells me we need an extra hand there." A bell had begun to ring—it was, as I'd soon learn, a Chinese artifact he'd brought back with him from one of his Far Eastern excursions and it tolled every day at four so that the Fellowship could gather outdoors in the tea circle for afternoon refreshment. He'd already turned and started off in the direction of the sound, when he swung back round on me. "And this car, Tadashi—is it yours?"

"Yes, Wrieto-San."

We both looked to the Bearcat crouched there behind the Cord, its fenders flaring and canary hood aglow despite the layer of dust. Wrieto-San's expression had become sober, judgmental, the sort of look he adopted for discussions of all pecuniary matters, which, sad to say, were at the very heart of his life. To think that a man of his stature—not to mention age, wisdom and genius—should have to scramble continually to make ends meet, struck me then as unconscionable, as it does now, all these years later. And yes, I'd heard the rumors—that he was broke, pitifully few commissions coming in as a result of his misadventures and the scandals that had dogged him through the course of the past twenty years, the Depression drying up the pool of potential clients, his work considered derrière-garde in the face of changing fashion, the Fellowship simply a way of milking money out of those gullible enough to think his aura could communicate anything bankable to them—but still I was shocked to discover how much of the man was involved in simply keeping things afloat. He was tightfisted, no other way to say it. Maybe even something of a confidence man. And what did they call him in Spring Green, the nearest town? *Slow-Pay Frank.*

"Isn't it a bit extravagant?" he wondered aloud. "That is, wouldn't it have been wiser, all the way around, if you'd put your money into the Fellowship? This tuition—it can hardly cover room and board, let alone all the other benefits you'll see here—and I've kept it artificially low in order to get things started, given the difficult times. But really, Tadashi, this is . . . *excessive.*"

It wasn't for me to point out the discrepancy here. Though I will say privately that the Cord must have cost many times what I'd paid—or rather my father had paid—for the Bearcat, which was, I admit, something of an indulgence. But then I liked fine things too—and I'd never before owned an automobile. What I said, however—with a bow—was that the car wasn't what it appeared to be.

"It's a Stutz, isn't it?" he asked, narrowing his eyes.

"*Hai,* Wrieto-San. It is. But this is an old car, eight years old. Used. I bought it used. Yesterday. In Chicago." I attempted a smile, though frankly my mood was in decline. "So that I could be here promptly to join the Fellowship and work under your guidance and direction."

He seemed to consider this a moment. "All right," he said finally. "Fine. But don't expect instruction from me. I am not a pedagogue, not by any means. Remember that." The bell rang once more. Several small birds—swallows, swifts?—darted out from under the eaves and shot across the courtyard. Wrieto-San turned to go, but caught himself. He gave me another long look. "You do cook," he said, "don't you?"

In fact, I didn't cook. Or I cooked in the way any bachelor in any society cooks: minimally. The boiled egg. Beefsteak flipped twice in the pan. Frankfurter on a bun. None of this mattered, however, because my kitchen apprenticeship would consist entirely in chopping cabbage, husking corn and peeling the potatoes the other apprentices had dug out of the manure-enriched earth. The cooks, in fact, were two women of the community, the sisters of one of the workmen Wrieto-San had hired to renovate the Hillside Home School (formerly a progressive boarding school run by Wrieto-San's spinster aunts), which stood on the far southwestern verge of the Taliesin property and was meant to house a portion of the Fellowship, and they had their own view of the Master, a view considerably less awestruck than my own. In any case, on that first evening, as I stood there watching Wrieto-San's squared-up shoulders recede in the distance while he strode briskly away, the cane in constant motion—jumping right and left, twirling in the air like a magician's wand—I didn't have time to reflect on my status. At that moment an absurdly tall and powerfully built young man appeared out of nowhere, flinging himself over the near parapet like an acrobat and striding up to me with his right hand outstretched. He was dressed in overalls, work boots, a very casual flannel shirt with rolled-up sleeves. "Hiya," he said, "you must be the new arrival."

I attempted a bow, but the hand thrust itself at my own for the inevitable handshake, the half-amicable, half-aggressive and thoroughly unsanitary ritual greeting by which the men of this country test and judge one another. His hand enveloped mine—a rough hand, callused and work-hardened—and I tried to exert an equal pressure as we held to each other, sending my message through the flesh as he was sending his. His message was that he held no prejudices though he was nine inches taller than I and outweighed me by a good seventy-five pounds and had been raised in a place where a Japanese face was as rare as an Eskimo's or a Bantu's, and my message was that I was the equal of anyone and prepared for anything the Master might require of me—including kitchen duty.

"Wes Peters," he said, giving one last crushing squeeze (which I resisted with my own not insignificant pressure), before dropping my hand by way of completing the ceremony. "And you are Sato, right?"

I bowed in acknowledgment, but this was an abbreviated bow, a bow reserved for equals. "Call me Tadashi," I said.

"Right," he said, "Tadashi. Glad to meet you. And welcome."

"You're one of the apprentices, I presume?"

"Yes," he said, and he was grinning now. "Our ranks are growing by the day. Mr. Wright says there'll be thirty of us eventually. A whole squad. Including women. Five of them. From Vassar."

I didn't know what to say to this—was thirty a large number? Or small? How much work could there be? I'd envisioned myself laboring side by side with Wrieto-San on drawings of significance, plans for great edifices like Unity Temple, the Fukuhara house or the Larkin Administration Building, my pencil under command of his. And women. I hadn't expected women, not in an architectural enterprise. Distracted, I murmured, "Good. That sounds good." Or perhaps I said, "Capital."

I'd been drawing since childhood, and where my fellow students at the Yasinori Academy might have sketched biplanes or automobiles, I created a private world for myself, doing perspective drawings of invented cities and then peopling them with fully fleshed figures striding down spacious boulevards on their way to the country houses I created for them, replete with sketches, floor plans and elevations. (Floor plans held a special fascination for me because I could so easily manipulate them to the greater good and insurmountable happiness of these blithely striding people for whom I'd devise names and occupations and emotional histories, pulling a wall back here for the billiard room or a sweets room there or a boy's bedroom with a three-tiered bunk bed, ten-gallon hats and mounted bison heads on the walls and a private chute to the street below.) It seemed I always had a pencil in my hand, doodling, sketching, shading and coloring.

I'd sometimes sit for hours dreaming over a sheet of paper till I saw things there no one else could see, compass, protractor and straight edge guiding me, my knees knocking beneath the table in sheer excitement, my whole being groping for coherence. It was incantatory, a form of magic, an electric current running from brain to hand to pencil till the page came to life.

"But listen," Wes was saying, his eyes jumping from mine to the Bearcat and back again, "I think we're going to have to miss the tea circle today because we need groceries, I mean, we *really* need groceries, and I was just wondering if you wouldn't mind . . ." he trailed off. He gave the car a significant look.

It took me a moment—I can be a slow study at times, particularly when I'm fatigued, and I was no more than ten minutes out of the car, my bags still in the rumble seat, impressions washing over me like a tsunami—before I understood. "Oh, yes," I said. "Of course."

"If you don't mind," he repeated in a meliorating tone, the tone of someone who'd got what he wanted, and he was already ambling toward the car with his great scissoring strides even as I fell in beside him. "It's only four miles."

"Oh, no," I said, swinging open the door on the driver's side and peering down the hellish incline to the twisting road and the pig farm in the distance as he squeezed in beside me, "I don't mind. No, no, not at all."

The woman at the grocery gave me—gave *us*—the sort of look the farmwife had impressed on me earlier, the clamped lips and burning eyes, no hint of sympathy or even common humanity, as Wes called for catsup, coffee, tea, flour, sugar, massive sacks of dried beans and rice and all the other necessaries the farm and vegetable gardens at Taliesin were unable to provide. (This look, incidentally, was one I would become inured to in the coming months. It had something to do with my racial difference, of course, but it was leveled almost equally on Wes and Herbert Mohl and just about anyone else associated with Taliesin, and was chiefly due to Wrieto-San's attitude toward paying on account and the reservoir of bad feeling in the immediate environs over his past flings and flirtations and what the deeply conservative local populace considered the immoral way in which he conducted himself. Publicly. Here in the heartland. And he the son and nephew of preachers.) Once Wes had put his signature to the account—the woman livid, overheated, the tendons standing out in her neck, and her eyes flaying the very skin from our bones—we climbed into the Bearcat, our arms laden, and made our way back to Taliesin.

And then I was in the kitchen, peeling onions.

The *chef de cuisine* (Miss Emma Larson, forty-five years old, vigorous and plump, her graying hair bobbed and swept forward in a way that might have been fashionable on a mannequin in a department store window a decade earlier) bent over a blackened cauldron that was vigorously rattling atop the woodstove while her sister Mabel beat eggs with a whisk, and what must have been several pounds of cured meat made the journey from fry pan to platter. After the onions I peeled potatoes, and after the potatoes I peeled carrots. After that I washed dishes, hundreds, thousands of them, for weeks on end. What did I learn from the experience? That Wrieto-San (or Mr. Wright, as everyone, even his enemies among the farmwives and grocers, invariably called him) liked his food plain. He liked whitefish, calf's liver *aux oignons*, stewed vegetables, good honest fried potatoes and berries ripe from the bush and swimming in the cream he was denied as a boy. And I learned that Taliesin was a true and democratic communal undertaking, save for the god in his machine who presided over it all in his freewheeling and unabashedly despotic way, and I saw too that a practicing architect was like the general of an army, like the general of generals, and that a whole host of amenities, civilities and mores had to be sacrificed along the way to the concrete realization of an inchoate design.

He ran our lives, that was the long and short of it. *Daddy Frank*. How many times had I heard one apprentice or another call him that behind his back? *Daddy Frank*, paterfamilias of Taliesin. He stirred the pot continually, interfering in our personal affairs, our amours and disputes and loyalties, even as he squelched our initiative and individualism as fiercely as he'd asserted his own when he was apprentice to Louis Sullivan a generation earlier. Truly, I don't think I'll ever forgive him for coming between me and Daisy Hartnett—or for the loan he inveigled from my father (and, of course, failed to repay).

But I'm not complaining—that's not the purpose of this exercise. Not at all. And I was not of that subset of snickerers and wiseacres who acted as if the Fellowship were some sort of extended summer camp and Wrieto-San an archaic figure out of the dim past, "the greatest living architect of the nineteenth century," as one wag had it. I stayed at Taliesin for nine years, longer than practically any apprentice, if you exclude Herbert Mohl and Wes, who wound up marrying Svetlana, Wrieto-San's stepdaughter, and they marked the defining epoch of a long, fortunate and prosperous life. Nine years. I had a nine-year association with greatness, with the man who could sit down and spin out the design for perhaps the single most significant dwelling of the century as if he'd been born with it in his head—I'm talking of Fallingwater here—even as the exasperated client was en route from Milwaukee and expected to pull into the drive at any moment. I witnessed that. I handed him the paper, sharpened the pencils, hung over his shoulder with half a dozen others in a kind of awe that approached reverence.

I don't mean to exaggerate my importance—I was a cog in his machine for a certain period, one of many cogs, that and nothing more. But I knew him and I knew those who knew him when I was still a boy in short pants a whole continent and an ocean away and Taliesin I was rising out of the mists—men like old Dad Signola, the stonemason, whose mark will be there on the yellow dolomite piers for as long as the house stands, and Billy Weston, master carpenter, who lost half his world in service to the vision of it. I knew Mrs. Wright—Olgivanna, Wrieto-San's third and last wife—and his daughters Svetlana and Iovanna, and I knew the apprentices and the clients and Wrieto-San's four sons and two daughters from his first marriage. But did I know *him*?

There will be complaints, of course—I can foresee that. This is an imperfect process, what with the interposition of the years, the vagaries of memory, the re-creation of scenes the accuracy of which no one now living can affirm or deny. And too, I've had to rely on my co-author and translator (the young Irish American Seamus O'Flaherty, who is husband to my granddaughter, Noriko, and whose as yet unpublished translations of Fukazawa and Shimizu are, I understand, quite novel), many of whose locutions seem, I must confess, rather odd in the final analysis. Still, the question remains: Did I know the man we Japanese revere as Wrieto-San? Who was he, after all? The hero who was paraded through the streets of Tokyo after five years' work on the Imperial Hotel (and cost overruns that nearly bankrupted Baron Ōkura's backers) to triumphant shouts of "*Banzai, Wrieto-San! Banzai!*" as he claims in his autobiography? Or the profligate con artist who had to be removed from the site, the job, the country, in disfavor, if not disgrace? Was he the wounded genius or the philanderer and sociopath who abused the trust of practically everyone he knew, especially the women, especially them?

Tadashi Sato
Nagoya, April 9, 1979

CHAPTER 1: DANCING TO THE DEAD

On the day he met Olga Lazovich Milanoff Hinzenberg, at a ballet performance in Chicago in the fall of 1924, Frank Lloyd Wright* was feeling optimistic, buoyant even. It might have been raining that day—it *was* raining, gray pluvial streaks painting the intermediate distance like a pointillist canvas, stooped figures trudging along the streets beneath the shrouds of their umbrellas, sleet predicted, snow on the way—but his mood was unconquerable. He'd always thought of himself as a genial type, sunny and effervescent, one of those rare people who could transform the mood of an entire room simply by striding through the door, but the emotional upheaval of the past two years—since he'd come back from Japan, at any rate—had worn him down. Miriam was the problem, of course, or the crown and pinnacle of it. There were money woes, certainly. Insufficient commissions, fainthearted clients, and the deep-dwelling ignorance of his countrymen (and cowardice, cowardice too) in the face of the Fauvists, the Futurists, the Dadaists and the Cubists and all the rest of the *ists* and *isms*, Duchamp and Braque and Picasso, and worse yet, the soi-disant International Style of Le Corbusier, Gropius,

* Wrieto-San in the original.

Meyer and Mies—all the movements that had sprung up to make him feel antiquated and embattled. None of that helped. While he was in the Far East, the Europeans had been invading America.

But things were looking up. Miriam was gone now, gone since May, though every time he closed his eyes over a drawing or the pages of a book he saw her face, the tragic one she wore like a mask, rearing up in his consciousness till it dissolved in a swirl of dark bruised spots. Still, she was gone and Taliesin was at peace again. Three young couples—the Neutras, the Tsuchiuras and the Mosers—had been in residence, and there were musical evenings, good fellowship, the quiet of the fireside. And here he was, back in Chicago on business and stamping the rain from his hat and cloak in the vestibule of the theater, ripe for a little recreation.

A friend* had asked him if he'd like to see Karsavina perform selections from "Sleeping Beauty," "La Fille Mal Gardée" and "Les Sylphides" that afternoon and he'd jumped at the chance, though the prima ballerina's best days were long behind her and her supramundane beauty was a whisper of what it had been. He wanted to be seen about town, if only to shake some of the lint off the moth-eaten blanket of rumor and outright lies the scandalmongers had laid over him—he'd be opening an office here again at the first of the year and needed to make his presence felt. All right. Fine. The rain fell in the street, the door swung open and shut on the premonitory breath of winter, people crowded the lobby: men in fancy dress or the suits they'd worn to church, women swathed in furs and pearls, their voices sailing away from them to chime and chirrup like the disquisitions of the

* Unidentified male; perhaps one of his acquaintances from earlier, happier days in Chicago society.

birds in the aviary at the Lincoln Park Zoo. Were people avoiding him? Wasn't that—?

It was. Olivia Westphal, whom he'd once promenaded around Oak Park in his first car (the custom-made Stoddard-Dayton sports roadster that could hit sixty on the straightaway, a car he still dreamed of in the moments before waking, the "Yellow Devil" that had people leaping for the curb and cost him the very first speeding ticket ever issued on those sleepy equine streets), hoping to land a commission to build for her and her new husband (and she'd stabbed him in the back even then, opting to have Patton and Fisher build her an ornamented box of a place that was as insipid as a bowl of Kellogg's Corn Flakes left out overnight. On the counter. In a puddle of soured milk). And what the years had done to her: she was a matron now, gone to fat in the face and upper arms, with a bulky squared-up figure that all but erased the curvilinear contours he'd once found so enticing. She looked him dead in the eye—recognized him, he saw that—and then looked away again.

And how did that make him feel? Belligerent. Angry. Disgusted. Let them ignore him, the prudes and the timid little rodents they were married to, afraid all their lives to break ranks, to live, to make the grand gesture, any gesture . . . but now his companion*

* Call him Albert Bleutick for convenience's sake, a man of median height, median coloring, with a medial swell of paunch and a personality that was neither dominant nor recessive, a companion of the second stripe, one who could be relied upon to pick up the tab at lunch and actively seek out tickets to the ballet, the symphony, the museum. His was the fate of all minor characters in a major life: to perform a function and exit, as colorless as the rain descending on the dreary gray streets on a day that might as well have rinsed itself down the drain for all anyone cared.

had him by the arm and was leading him toward a group of men in the very center of things—was that Robert? Oscar?—and he felt himself swell up till he could hardly keep his cane from pirouetting across the floor. What he didn't notice—nor did his companion—was the tall dark sober-faced young woman slipping in through the door, her ticket clutched in one gloved hand, her purse in the other. She noticed him, though, her gaze roving over the crowd from the place she'd chosen in the corner—both wanting to be seen and at the same time striving for anonymity, unescorted at a matinee, unattached and at odds with her husband, a devotee of the dance and of what Karsavina had once been, a single woman out on a rainy afternoon. Olgivanna saw the same hats, shoulders, furs and jabbering faces he'd seen, a cotillion, a pecking order, society at large, and then all at once he was there and her eyes seized on him.

Her first sensation was the thrill of recognizing a celebrated face in public, a jolt of the nervous system that carried with it a hint of self-congratulation, as if she'd come up with the solution to a puzzle in a flash of inspiration. The second thing she felt was that she absolutely must talk to him—a compulsion so strong she very nearly bolted through the crowd to him, though here she was an utter stranger and unescorted and unintroduced, but she suppressed the impulse out of shyness and a vertiginousness verging on panic: What could she possibly say to him? How would she break the ice? Get him to look at her even? And the third thing, a thought clamoring atop the other two and cloaked in a rush of hormonal flapping, was that he would know her on some deep unfathomable level, as if it were fated, as if they were reincarnated lovers out of the *Mahabharata* or Rice Burroughs—and more: that he would take her to himself, master her in a fierce blend of power and submission.*

Frank† was oblivious. He was the center of attention, preening and performing for the little group that had gathered round him, old friends and fellows-well-met, joking, laughing, carting out one story after another and making his deadpan observations about this couple or that—and let them look, let them—when the start of the program was announced and Albert took him by the arm and they made their way to a box in front. As it happened, Albert slid in first, taking the seat adjoining a vacant one, and Frank settled in on his right. The lights dimmed. The conductor rose from the pit, his arms elevated over the score. And then, at the last minute, Olgivanna drifted gracefully down the center aisle, a moving shadow against the backdrop of the stage. The usher stood aside, the curtain rising now, the audience stirring, and here was her seat, and she barely had time to register the unremarkable figure beside her before the music began and the dancers appeared and she realized with a jolt that *he* was there, right there, one seat over from her.

For his part, Frank had glanced up as she slipped into her seat—a reflex of the human organism: there's a movement, the eye goes to it—just as he would have glanced up at anyone, the cows from the lobby or the

* I knew her at Taliesin as a sour, thin, humorless woman, tubercular in that first year, busy, always busy with the work of the place, scrubbing, hanging out clothes, hoeing in the garden and splitting wood for the stove, the furnace and the seventeen fireplaces we kept going eternally for the poor heat of them in that cavernous edifice, but she was a girl once, and in love. Grant her that.

† Wrieto-San in the original, and ff.

stuffed shirts they were with or even one of his sworn enemies. A glance, that was all, but he liked what he saw. She was hatless, with minimal makeup, her hair parted in the middle and drawn up in a chignon, a lace shawl clinging to her shoulders. He registered that—the simplicity of her dress and style, a kind of purity and faith in her own beauty that stood all the rest of the puffed-up, powdered and behatted matrons on their heads, and the way she'd moved, a tall young woman in her twenties, sliding into a seat at the ballet with a balletic grace all her own. He stole another glance. And then another.

There was movement on the stage now, a burst of applause as Karsavina appeared—her legs good still, her face less so—and its dying fall. He was conscious of silent effort, of women and men twirling and wobbling like bowling pins that won't go down, and he understood immediately that this would be a mediocre performance by an artist in decline. A bore. A wasted afternoon. He bent forward to look past Albert. The young woman—she was a girl, really—sat quietly with her hands folded in her lap, her gaze fixed on the stage. Her carriage was flawless, from the way she held her shoulders to the swell of her breasts to the pronounced lines of her jaw and cheekbone in profile, the beautifully scalloped ear and the pale jewel that glittered at the lobe of it—minimalist, everything about her a studied composition of the minimal. But she wasn't an American girl—he would have bet on it.

Ten minutes into the performance—or perhaps it was longer than that, perhaps it was twenty—he began to fidget. He wanted to get up and leave—they were just going through the motions up on the stage, tired motions, dead motions, and nobody in the audience knew any better—but he had an even stronger impulse to stay and somehow attract this girl's attention because he knew her, knew her just by looking at her, and he wanted more, much more, contact, recognition, a glance, a smile. "They're lifeless," he murmured, leaning into Albert, his friend's startled face hanging there in the glow of the stage like a jack-o'-lantern on a wire. "They're dead," he said, just loudly enough so that she could hear—and she did hear, he could tell from her reaction though she never shifted her eyes from the stage—"dead and dancing to the dead."

At the intermission—at the moment the applause died and before she could get up and wander off by herself—he leaned across Albert and said, "I couldn't help but notice your response—you agree, don't you? That Karsavina might just as well have stayed in London for all the inspiration she's showing here today? That she'd *rather* be in London. Knitting. Or whatever she does there."

She turned her face to him then, her eyes fastening on his. He couldn't know what he was saying, couldn't know how his comment during the dance had echoed one of the dicta of Gurdjieff,* her master, who had striven his whole life to awaken the race from the deadness of the material world and into the consciousness of the mystic truths that lay beyond it, or that she'd been one of Gurdjieff's principal *danseuses*, or that she'd left

* Georgei Ivanovitch Gurdjieff, 1866 (?)–1949. Philosopher, composer, shaman, hypnotist. Magnum opus: *Beelzebub's Tales to His Grandson*. Espoused lifelong doctrine called "The Work," a muddled philosophy of being with its own mythos and cosmology that attracted to him a ring of disciples whom he arbitrarily embraced and cast out of the fold. He was at Taliesin in 1938, I believe it was, a shambling ancient Armenian Turk or Gypsy of some sort with an accent so impenetrable he might as well have been talking through a gag. I remember seeing him off in the distance each morning, a bundle of animated rags conferring with Mrs. Wright while Wrieto-San fumed in the studio.

Paris just three weeks earlier at his insistence after she'd nursed him through the worst of his injuries from the automobile accident that had nearly killed him, or how she'd chopped wood all afternoon every day so that he'd have enough fuel to keep warm through the blasts and contingencies of the winter—or even, on a more elemental level, that she agreed wholeheartedly with his assessment of Karsavina. "Yes," she said, "you are absolutely right. This is a rote performance. An embarrassment."

Her voice captivated him. Soft, rhythmic, the beat of the phrases a kind of music in itself, and what was her accent? Eastern European of some sort—Polish? Romanian? He said, "She's married to a diplomat, isn't she? Running a school now"—he'd gleaned this from the program and added, redundantly—"in London."

"The Royal Academy of Dancing. She helped to found it."

"Yes," he said, talking past Albert's flaming face, "yes, of course. But let me introduce myself—and my friend here, this is Albert Bleutick—"

She dropped her eyes a moment, then came back to him. "But you do not need an introduction," she murmured, and he felt the blood charge through his veins as if a ligature had been loosened. "Certainly, this is the case, no? But I am Olga Milanoff, known to my friends"—and here she paused to let him consider the freight of nuances the association was meant to carry—"as Olgivanna."

Somewhere, somehow, Albert got lost in the shuffle, and Frank couldn't really recall when or where it had happened—on the way to the tea dance to which he'd invited her or after they'd got there? No matter. From the moment the three of them left the theater at intermission till they hustled out into the drenched streets looking for a cab, he could think of nothing but the excitement of the affair at hand, the old libidinous fires restoked,* the quickening pulse of possibility. Was he too old for this sort of thing? Was he wary, considering what he'd been through with Miriam—and before her, Mamah and even Kitty? If the thought crossed his mind, he dismissed it. Age was nothing to him—he was fifty-seven and fit as a farmer—and he was one of those sexually charged men who couldn't live without a woman at the center of his life. Already, since the official break with Miriam, though she'd been dead to him for a year and more, he'd come very close to finding that woman in the bow mouth and satiric eyes of a certain lady novelist,† and when that proved impossible on any number of scores, he'd moved a coed from the University of Wisconsin into Taliesin and his bed. But he wasn't satisfied. Not yet. Not even approximately. He needed—*complication.* Love, yes. Sex, of course. But something more than that, something fraught and embattled, a relation to make the juices flow in every sense.

The sandwiches were soggy, the tea tepid. Albert disappeared. The orchestra played the old songs in the old dreamily civilized way of pre-war London (tango, yes, but delivered up in a rendition that was almost sedate) and stayed away from the jittery nonsense of the speakeasies. They talked for two hours and more. They danced and she was as light in his arms as a feather pillow. He let her know that he didn't smoke or drink and she didn't mind at all, even as so many of the other couples on the dance floor showed the obvious effects of alcohol and every time they

* One of those curious overheated phrases of O'Flaherty-San, which we will let stand.

† Zona Gale, author of popular appeasements such as *Miss Lulu Bett,* who was then at the height of her fame, and more marginally, her beauty. But she kept cats and had claws of her own. And, of course, like all novelists, she had unrealistic expectations.

looked up one man or another was spiking his companion's tea with a clear liquid decanted from a flask. She agreed with him that jazz music was, for the most part, hyperactive. And yes, she did love Bach, one of her earliest musical inspirations when she was a girl in Montenegro.

He must have lifted his eyebrows—*Montenegro?*—because she informed him that this was a kingdom on the Adriatic and that she came from an exalted family of warriors and judges. "We are Serbs," she told him, oversugaring her tea, a cucumber sandwich arrested at her lips. "Do you know Serbs?"

"Oh, yes," he lied, "yes, of course. Hundreds of them." But he was smiling—his flashing eyes, his floating hair—and breezed right past it: "And I'm still waiting for my first Montenegrin commission. You don't think the king over there might want a new palace? In the Prairie Style? Or how about a pleasure dome on the sacred River Alph?" His smile widening to clinch the joke. "Or is that in another part of the world?"

He dropped her that night at the apartment where she was staying with disciples exiled—like her—from Gurdjieff's enclave in Fontainebleau,* and he was there the next morning, flowers in hand, to take her to breakfast. That was the beginning of a more elaborate dance, a waltz in three-quarter time that swept them through the corridors of museums, galleries and concert halls, with side trips to admire the houses he'd built in the city and in Oak Park, and which culminated in the inevitable invitation to Taliesin.

It was December, a week before Christmas. An arctic front had advanced across the Great Lakes and the skies were stripped of color. She packed her bags—a few things only, an outfit or two for jaunts through the coun-

* Officially, the Gurdjieff Institute for the Harmonious Development of Man, an oxymoronic designation, it seems to me.

try, formal wear for dinner—and she came alone on the train through the whitening stubble fields and forlorn villages of Illinois and Wisconsin, having arranged for her daughter to stay behind in Chicago with her estranged husband.* She would remember that journey all her life, the sense of enclosure and security the coach gave her as the snow ran against the windows and she ate the sugared buns she'd brought with her and sipped coffee from the cup of her thermos, the world reduced and tranquil. Though she had a book with her—a bound manuscript Georgei had given her when she left Paris—she never opened it. She hardly noticed the other passengers, didn't speak a word to anyone. She was wrapped up in something complex, something that brought her deep, into the deepest part of herself, and as the coach thumped and jostled and ran smooth over the uninterrupted stretches, she leaned into the window and watched the ghost of her reflection run along with it.

Was she trading one guru for another, was that it? A luminous middle-aged magus of inner sight for an equally luminous middle-aged wizard of outward form and structure? Inner for outer? Was she choosing this man—and she whispered his name aloud: Frank, *Frank*—because he was the supreme deity of the field in which Vlademar was a mere toiler, Vlademar whom she'd married too young, at eighteen, to know any better and who was divorcing her because he refused to allow her to express herself in any way at all? Was going off with Frank Wright any different from going off with Gurdjieff—to dance, to serve, to absorb the radiance with her mouth, her fingers, her heart and mind and spirit? Or was it simply a father she was looking for, a father to replace the one she'd lost? No matter, because there was one surety in all of this, one thing she knew

* Vlademar Hinzenberg. An architect. A Russian.

without stint: he was hers if she wanted him. And this journey, this weekend ahead, would settle that once and for all.

He was there waiting for her at the Spring Green station, his automobile idling at the curb, the exhaust spectral against the backdrop of the new-fallen snow. There was snow in his hair, snow salting his beret and his coat and his long trailing scarf. "Olgivanna," was all he said, and then he was embracing her there on the platform for anyone to see while his chauffeur—one of the workmen from Taliesin, Billy Weston—held open the door of the car for her. She felt the floorboards vibrating beneath her, caught a scent of the exhaust mingled with the soap Frank used, and then Billy Weston put the car in gear and they were moving. In a matter of moments the town fell away behind them and they were out in the countryside, trees heavy with snow, the road paved in white, smoke coiling away from farmhouse chimneys and livestock trampling the yards in dumb display. It was as if they'd gone back in time.

She gazed at Frank. Held tight to his hand. He talked the whole while, the words spilling out of him, every turning in the road or glimpse of a barn's faded red flank a cause for celebration, his voice so melodious and rich it was as if he were singing. She watched his eyes, his lips, the flutter of his tongue against the roof of his mouth: he was singing and she was his audience. She was almost surprised when Taliesin drew into sight, the lake in front of the house capped white atop the ice, and the house itself clinging low to the ground and huddling beneath its own weight of snow and the forest of icicles depending from the eaves. It was like something the ancient Celts might have built, or the barrow men before them: mystical, out of time, as ancient as the dirt it stood upon and the stone pillars that supported it. What did she say as they wound their way up the drive? That it was beautiful, magical? Or no: that it was living art. That was what she called it: living art.

There were introductions—to the Neutras, the Mosers and the Tsuchiuras—and a brisk walk around the courtyard to get a sense of the scope of the place, and all she could think of was a Japanese village set down whole here on the side of a mountain in the hills of Wisconsin. Inside, the place was elaborately decorated for Christmas—wreaths and cuttings and dried flowers, a spangle of silver balls, art everywhere, and cheer, good cheer and tidings of the season.* And then she was installed in one of the guest rooms and changing for dinner while he fidgeted outside the door, talking, always talking, one subject bleeding into another, her snowy journey reminding him of the winter excursions he made back and forth from Fiesole to Berlin in the days when he was putting together his portfolio and how the sun had struck the walls of the villas in Italy and how the amber stone of Taliesin reminded him of it, and how *was* her daughter? Would she be all right without her mother for a few days? When she emerged, he handed her a glass of mulled cider and escorted her through the maze of rooms, showing off the fine things he'd collected—Japanese prints by Hiroshige, Hokusai, Sadahide; Ming vases; marble heads dat-

* Wrieto-San was a great one for holidays—Memorial Day, the Fourth of July, Halloween, Thanksgiving, Christmas—and if there was no holiday in sight he would invent one to suit him, the Fundament of June, Midsummer's Eve, the Pillars of March, the stronger the whiff of paganism the better. He was an inveterate arranger too, forever fussing over his furniture and objets d'art, and he threw himself into holiday decoration with all the fierceness of his unflagging energy (an energy, unfortunately, that often manifested itself in a sort of superhuman volubility that made it difficult to be around him for more than an hour or two at a time).

ing to the Tang Dynasty; Genroku embroidery and Momoyama screens—all the while discoursing on the cleanliness of the Japanese culture and the simple organic elegance of its architecture. "And their sex practices," he said, standing before the fire now in the big low-ceilinged room that commanded views of the hills and valley beyond, "very clean, very civilized. And open."

She wanted to tip her head back, look him in the eye and ask just how he'd managed to acquire his knowledge—there was heat in the air and they'd be together tonight for the first time: that was the unspoken promise that had brought her all the way out here on the train—when the Tsuchiuras entered the room. She'd only had a moment to chat with them when she arrived, an exchange of the formal pleasantries—Kameki was an architect who'd worked with Frank in Japan and Los Angeles both, as she understood it—and now here they were, dressed for dinner and bowing.

"Isn't that right, Tsuchiura-San?" Frank asked, his expression gone sly.

Another bow. There was a burst, as of gunfire, from a knot in one of the logs laid across the fire. "I am sorry, Wrieto-San, but I haven't heard you. We are only now here."

"I was telling Olgivanna of the sexual openness in your country—the clean, healthy view women and men alike take of the amorous functions . . ."

Both the Tsuchiuras—they were young, her age, and the realization came to her in a flash—burst into laughter.

For the first time since she'd met him, Frank seemed at a loss, but he was quick to cover himself. "What I mean is, in contrast to our prudes and puritans, the timid and fearful little people who want to set the rules for everybody else—"

"Like Prohibition, you mean," Olgivanna put in and

she was soaring, already soaring on the heady currents of the place, the company, the conversation.

"Yes, well," Frank said, leaning over to poke at the fire, "you know that I don't approve of drinking—I've seen too many good men ruined by it, carpenters and draftsmen too—"

Again the Tsuchiuras laughed—and she, giddy, joined in. "A dime a dozen, Wrieto-San," Kameki said, hardly able to draw breath he was laughing so hard, "all these drunken draftsmen. But not Tsuchiura Kameki, not a good honorable *Japanese* draftsman—"

"And Prohibition isn't at all such a bad . . ." Frank began, but he looked at the three of them and trailed off, laughing himself now. "But maybe"—he gave a broad wink as he set the poker back down against the unfinished stone of the fireplace—"it's the Swiss and Austrians we have to watch out for, what do you think, Kameki?"

The Neutras and Mosers had just strolled into the room, talking animatedly in German, and Werner Moser, picking up on the last phrase, said, "And what is this we Austrians and Swiss are being accused of?"

"Sex," Kameki said. "Good, clean, open—and what was it, Wrieto-San, civilized?—sex."

More laughter. Laughter all around, though Dione Neutra seemed puzzled until Frank broke in, his expression sober suddenly—or earnest, that was it. Earnest. He'd enjoyed the joke—he was the soul of levity, the single most ebullient man Olgivanna had ever met, and he encouraged jocularity in his associates and apprentices—but now, settling back into the role of the Master, he returned to the point he'd been making. For her benefit. "Now you know perfectly well I was talking of the Japanese—what would you call it?—*freedom* in sexual matters; that is, the acceptance of sex as a vital and necessary function, uncluttered, or, or unencumbered, by the mores of the church and politicians. And so clean.

The kimonos, the celebration of beauty and ceremony—the tea ceremony, for instance. And this spills over into all aspects of society."

"You're speaking of the geisha," Olgivanna heard herself say. All around her the room was held in suspension, the fire radiant, the Christmas wreaths capturing the light, the vast planes of the windows opening onto the night and the drifted snow beneath. *Geisha,* she thought. The courtesans with their clogs and kimonos and lacquered hair. Was that what he wanted?

"Women of the floating world," Kameki said in a soft voice.

Frank moved into her, put an arm round her waist, the heat of him like a second fire, like a movable furnace. "Yes," he said, "the geisha. But not one of them—none I've ever seen, anyway—could match the beauty and grace of you."

And then someone said, "Here, here," and they were all lifting glasses of cider and he was staring her full in the face, swept up in the rapture of the moment. She closed her eyes for the public kiss, the stamp and seal and imprimatur of her new master, and she felt so transported she let the image of Georgei—wizened, pale, sunk into the graying sheets and the fortress of his mind—fade until it was nothing at all.

And then—and then there was dinner, bountiful honest food and the sort of conversation that lifted up the world and all of them but Frank speaking English with an accent, Japanese, German, Montenegrin—and when they gathered round the fire afterward and Dione played her cello and sang Schubert in the voice of an angel descended, she felt so natural, so at home, that she got up and danced for them all. She knew the song* only vaguely, but that didn't matter because there was a deeper

* "The Elf King." And what could be more appropriate?

rhythm at work here, an enchantment that intoxicated her. She let herself go deep into the spirit, the harmonious movement, the trance of the Sufi mystics, everything Georgei had taught her, and she brought it all to the surface of her being, right there, right there in Taliesin in the big room before the fire that snapped and breathed in the crucible of creation—and not for an audience in a theater somewhere, but for him, for him alone.

CHAPTER 2: MIRIAM AGONISTES

None of the doctors could help her in Los Angeles or the provincial outpost of San Diego either, little people all of them, sniveling types, handwringers, an army of effete bald-headed men in spectacles who were mortified of the law—as if this law had any more right to exist than Prohibition, because who was the federal government to dictate what people could and couldn't do with their own bodies, their own minds, their personal needs and wants and compulsions? Were they going to regulate needs, then? Dole them out? Tax them? Miriam* was so furious, so burned up and blistered with the outrage of it that she must have been overly severe with the cabman—the driver with his hat cocked back on his head and his trace of a Valentino

* Maude Miriam Noel, 1869–1930. Southern belle, sculptress, dilettante. Wrieto-San's second wife. I never met her personally, but Billy Weston described her to me in some detail. "She was trouble," he said. And then he used one of those peculiarly apposite American expressions—such a trove, the English language—"She was," and he paused a moment to stare off into the distance, as if his brain, the actual organ, were being radically compressed by the squeezebox of the memory, "real hell on wheels."

mustache—because when they got to the border at Tijuana, he stopped the car, turned round in the seat and demanded payment in full. Insolently. Out of insolent little pig's eyes. "This is as far as I go," he said, and she couldn't place his accent.

She was immovable. She felt her face concretize, the pores sealing up, the muscles round her mouth and eyes going to stone. "Nonsense," she spat. "Drive on."

There was a customs man standing off to the left of the car, a slouching congenital idiot with a lazy eye and bad teeth, and he'd already showed them his smile and waved them on—no searches here, no passports required—and he was giving her a curious look now. As if he'd seen everything in his day, every sort of indecision and cataclysm, women four and five months gone heading down to *la clínica* for the procedure that would make them right again, rumrunners with their empty trucks, day-trippers and ethnologists and rock collectors, but this, this was a new wrinkle altogether.

"No," he said, "no more," and he shoved his way out of the car and tried to pull open the back door, but she held fast to the handle. "Get out," he insisted and it gave her a small pulse of pleasure to hear the tremor in his voice. The war was already won.

"I won't," she said just to savor the words on her lips. "Now, I've paid you to take me to Tijuana, and I won't budge until you fulfill your end of the bargain." She looked round her in growing outrage: the customs man, a river of Mexicans in pajamas and serapes, mules, dogs, Indian eyes, Indian hair, dust, muck, filth, the street vendors and beggars in their cutaway rags—and hanging over it all the heat, the impossible punishing heat that stewed the odor of decay till she could barely breathe. "Move on," she demanded.

He saw the look in her eyes, saw the way her face had set, and he didn't even try to Jew her out of an extra two bits, as any of the rest of them would—he just shrugged, climbed back into the cab and put the car in gear. A moment later they were lurching down the rutted streets, the human circus of Mexican poverty unfolding outside the window like a mural in a moving picture. She was uncomfortable, feeling the heat, dizzy from the stench—she'd sweated through her undergarments and the seat of her dress, and her hair was gummy beneath her parrot-green silk caftan, which she'd chosen expressly to bring out the color of her eyes. But there was no one here to care about the color of her eyes. Just peasants—*campesinos,* isn't that what they called them? And what was pharmacy? A cognate: *farmacia,* wasn't it? She consulted the Spanish/English phrasebook in her purse and found the term under the heading "Useful Phrases": *¿Donde está la farmacia?*

There was a dog dead beside the road, the carcass swollen beneath a second skin of insects, people strolling by as if it were some sort of monument, as if it had been molded of brass and put there by the town council to honor canine achievement. The cab lurched again, in and out of a rut, and the dog was gone. "The *farmacia,*" she said, the cords tightening in her throat. "Take me to the *farmacia,* the first one you see. Quickly, quickly."

He didn't seem to have heard her, so she repeated herself. A scorched minute blistered by. There were birds now, some sort of Mexican birds, exploding up from the road—pigeons, Mexican pigeons. "The *farmacia,*" she said, and she was beginning to feel desperate, all her outrage evaporated in the face of the hopelessness of this place, these peasants, this driver—and he was American, of some sort, a legitimate cabbie from San Diego who'd agreed on a legitimate price here and back, half paid in advance, half when she was restored to her hotel on Coronado Island where the sea breezes stirred themselves each afternoon to neutralize the heat. Peasants she knew. Peasants she'd dealt with in Paris, where they were alternately surly and unctuous, and Tokyo, where they bowed to the floor and laughed behind your back, but these people frightened her. It was dangerous here. She could sense it. See it, see it with her own eyes. Prostitutes. Drunks. That man there—staggering as if he were riding an invisible donkey, his eyes red as some demon's, staring belligerently through the window at her. And there—another unconscious in the dirt and no more a concern than the dog in his jacket of flies. She was about to open her mouth again, about to say she'd had enough, forget it, he could take her back and away from all this, this chaos and filth and the ungodly stink, when the car abruptly came to a halt. "What?" she said. "What is it?"

But the driver—was he Italian, was that it?*—merely pointed a finger. It took her a moment, and then she saw the sign, black script, freehand, on a white background: FARMACIA. She gathered up her purse and the cloth bag she'd brought along, leaned over the front seat and commanded her voice long enough to say, "You wait, now," and then she was out on the street and the sun hit her like an axe. Five steps, a wooden walk, and then the door and the bell that announced her even as the cab jumped into gear and shot away from the curb with a crunch of tires and a rat-tat-tat of exhaust. She felt the fear seize her

* Of course, O'Flaherty-San is flexing his imagination here, trying to see things as Miriam would have seen them. I suspect the driver was what is known as a Chicano, a U.S. citizen of Mexican descent—or, perhaps, as my Spanish dictionary has it, a *caudillo*, a member of the Latin American ruling class whose blood remains relatively undiluted, making for fairer skin, but one wonders what such a man would be doing behind the wheel of a cab. On the other hand, he may have been Italian, after all.

then, a cold hand laid on the back of her neck. She was going to die here, she was sure of it, lost and abandoned in a place where her French was no use to her or her Southern charm either—and her children would never know, her friends, Frank . . . no obsequies, no sepulcher, nothing. She'd be like that dog lying bloated at the side of the road . . .

At that moment—as the bell sounded and the door swung back and she stood there frozen while the taxi receded down the street—two women in mantillas came up the walk behind her, their black hair braided and their eyes ducking away from hers, and what did they want? They wanted to go through the door, that was it, and she was in their way and they were waiting for her. Politely. Respectfully. She came to her senses then, murmured an apology (illogically, in French: *Pardon*) and stepped into the store. It was close and dark, hotter even—if that was possible—than the street outside. Slowly, as her eyes began to adjust, the features of the place started to take on shape. There were jars everywhere, a cornucopia of jars, and in the jars various dried herbs and potions, and there were folded browning sheaves of plants suspended from the ceiling to dry, the smell of them musty and bitter and sweet all at once. And the counter. The counter behind which stood a man identical to the spineless physicians and pharmacists of Los Angeles and San Diego counties, right down to the spectacles and the bald dome of his head, except that his skin was the color of the varnish on a very old chest of drawers—and what was that in the jar at his elbow, chicken's feet? She thought of the apothecary's shop in *Romeo and Juliet*, the mad mixer of potions, and what was the word she wanted, the word she'd practiced all the way down here in the cab? *Un dormidero*, that was it. *Un dormidero*.

But then the man behind the counter smiled at her, a broad, winning, helpful and welcoming smile—

anything can be purchased here, Señora, anything at all, that was what his smile said—and the word flew right out of her head. He said something then, something she didn't catch and couldn't be expected to, but the gist of it was obvious: How may I help you?

Feeling better now, feeling herself again—or nearly herself—she straightened up and approached the counter, giving him his smile back even as the two women who'd followed her in browsed among the jars and their mysterious contents. What she said then was contained in a single word, a word she hadn't had to memorize: "*Morfina.*"

She watched his eyes. "Do you understand?"

His smile widened. He nodded.

"I want," she said carefully, "*morfina.*"

She didn't wait till she was back at the hotel, though certainly that would have been more pleasant, because she'd been feeling ill and run-down and light-headed all morning—and her stomach, her stomach was cramping and her bowels weren't right and no amount of bicarbonate of soda could even begin to help. The man behind the counter—the little brown pharmacist who'd suddenly become her best friend in the world—had given her what she wanted, *all* she wanted, the only limiting factor the number of dollars she laid out on the tin countertop, dollars outweighing pesos here (and that was funny, since *dollar* was some sort of nonsense word as far as she knew and *peso* was a measure of weight, of gravity itself), and she'd filled her cloth bag with a dozen tubes of morphine sulfate hypodermic tablets (1/4 gr.) and ten of the diamorphine hydrochloride (1/6 gr.). And she got herself some new pravazes as well, the needle she carried in her very clever little kit (it was made to resemble an outsized cigarette lighter, with room for two tubes and the hypodermic itself) having become blunted through use and unpleasant in the extreme. When the purchase was completed, the two women in shawls watching her surreptitiously and the pharmacist smiling till she thought his head would burst, she gave him another word, which might have been Spanish—or maybe it was Latin: "Taxi."

"Taxi," he repeated, as if she'd just supplied the one term that would make his life complete. "Taxi, *sí*," and he shouted something toward a tumbled nest of straw baskets where a striped Mexican blanket concealed a doorway behind the counter. In the next moment, a boy with his eyes still asleep emerged, took one look at her and ran out into the street shouting the magic word.

The driver knew not a syllable of English, but San Diego was not an Anglican designation and the dollars she waved at him immediately bridged any difficulties of interpretation. The sun hammered her briefly and then she was in the back of the car, everyone grinning now—the pharmacist and the two customers who'd followed her out into the street, the boy and the taxi driver and even the random passerby, a whole world of dedicated grinning. The door shut on her, the car a Tin Lizzie, a flivver, a rattrap of the worst and flimsiest construction—and ancient, the first sedan ever made—but it had a roof, and, apparently, an engine. The thing jolted and bumped as if it were pitching headlong down the side of a cliff, the smells assaulted her all over again, the heat crouched atop her, right under the caftan (and she wouldn't take it off, wouldn't show her hair and the sweat and the fright she must have been), but none of that mattered for long because immediately she was dissolving a tablet in water and drawing it into her pravaz and between bumps finding a vein high up on her right thigh beneath the rolled-up sweat-soaked hem of her dress.

After that, the breezes blew and the smells dissipated. The man at the border waved them on without a second glance, the world took on a metallic sheen—the sheen of the high seas as seen from a deck chair on the

SS *Paris*—and she wasn't in Mexico anymore. She wasn't in the bleached brown desert of San Diego either, not on land at all. She was on a cruise, perched high up on the rail with the wind in her face and the birds wheeling overhead, on her way back to France.

As it turned out, she didn't get to Paris that year or the following year either. She went up to San Francisco for a while, but the place bored her—too far out of the way, too cold, too bright, what with the sun painted like a thin layer of glue over all those rows of gingerbread houses Frank would have hated till he ground his teeth to dust—and then she came back to Los Angeles for an extended stay with Leora Tisdell,* who'd just lost her husband. For a while, through the spring and into the summer of 1925, she set up a kiln in the back of Leora's guesthouse and with her friend's encouragement she began to work in clay again, just to see if she could recover her eye. (Leora had artistic aspirations of her own, and now, as she put it, that she was out from under the heel of her husband, she meant to do up California in oils.)

In the first week, Miriam produced a bust of Leora and Leora produced a portrait of Miriam. The portrait was meant to be naturalistic but it was so ineptly done it might have been an abstract by Picasso or Miró, and the only feeling Miriam derived from it was sadness. "You know, don't you, that when I was in Paris I concentrated

* Née Caruthers, 1870–? A friend of Miriam's youth in Memphis. They remembered each other's birthdays and corresponded frequently, but never more voluminously or passionately than in the first few years of Miriam's marriage—at fifteen—to Emil Noel, scion of a distinguished Southern family, who took her off to Chicago where he became a decidedly inartistic functionary at Marshall Field's.

on distinct parts of the human body rather than busts, because they're so utterly conventional, and I worked almost exclusively in marble," Miriam told her friend one afternoon as they sipped Singapore slings and sat regarding the clay bust, which, in retrospect, could have been worked a bit more around the nose and the orbits of the eyes and hadn't really taken the glaze well at all. "I had a pair of folded hands accepted for the permanent collection in the Louvre, you know," she added, and the thought buoyed her, took her off her friend's sofa, out of the house and Los Angeles with its irritating faux-Spanish décor and drooping palms and all the way back to the day she first walked through the doors of the museum and saw them there, her hands, mounted for display, and people—*Parisians*—gathered there to admire them. It was a towering moment, fueled by the Singapore sling cocktail and the dose of *morfina* she'd taken for her digestion and to control the tremor that had begun to recur in the back of her neck—all along her spine, really—but the sensation didn't last. A few days later she took a cast of Leora's hands, with the thought of buying a block of Carrara marble and getting back into the game, doing something significant and lasting, but the impulse seemed to fade as the sun rose and set and rose again and again and again till it burned all the ambition out of her.

She was feeling vaguely out of sorts—betwixt and between, that was it—thinking she might go to her daughter, Norma, in Chicago, or maybe back up to San Francisco for a few days, or Mexico, down the coast somewhere, where it was clean and you could get a decent meal that wasn't all wrapped up in those half-burned little pancakes they seemed to serve with everything, even steak, when a man came to the door asking for her. Leora's servant—a Chinese in a white coat and faintly greasy black tie—found her in the yard, where she was stretched out on a chaise longue beside the pool reading

*La Noire idole** for the third time. She put on a wrap and padded barefoot through the dark corridors to the front door.

The man was nobody she knew—ferret-faced, lithe as a twig, with an insinuating expression. "Yes?" she said, looking down at him from beneath the high conical towel she'd wrapped round her hair.

"Maude Miriam Noel Wright?" he said, his shoulders slithering inside his jacket as if he were molting, a twitch at the left corner of his mouth.

"Yes," she said, and she was going to add "I am she" or "I'm her," she couldn't decide which, when he handed her a finger-smudged envelope, turned abruptly on one heel the instant she took it from him and sauntered off down the walk.

Inside was a divorce summons and attached notice stating that Frank Lloyd Wright had initiated proceedings against her on grounds of desertion. That was it, nothing more. No explanation, no word from *him*, no prior warning or even the most cursory and two-faced attempt at reconciliation. And what did she feel—in that moment, the towel wrapped round her head, her toes clenching the abrasive hemp of the doormat and her

* *La Noire idole, Étude sur la Morphinomanie*, by Laurent Tailhade. Paris: Leon Vanier, 1907. A defense and celebration of morphine, written to counter the sensationalism of Maurice Talmeyr's *Les Possédés de la morphine*, which chose to view the use of this medicinal drug in what Tailhade considered an erroneous and negative light. In Miriam's defense, it should be said that during her days in Paris—roughly 1904–1914—the use of morphine was widespread, particularly in fashionable and artistic circles, and was considered, on the whole, no more remarkable in a young woman than smoking, wearing trousers or imbibing cocaine-infused beverages like the wildly popular Vin Mariani.

right hand held out rigid before her, the black type of the summons staring back at her as if each letter were a miniature face and each face reduced suddenly to a pair of spitting lips? Rage, that was what. Not disappointment, not surprise, not heartbreak, but just that: rage.

Yes, she'd left him. Of course she had. Anyone would have. A saint—even the martyrs in their hair shirts and bloody rags. He was impossible, the single most infuriating human being she'd ever met, what with his God complex and his perfectionism, fussing over every last detail as if the world depended on it, his snoring, his *musical* evenings, the utter soul-crushing desolation of rural Wisconsin where he all but kept her prisoner and every overfed housewife and goggling rube staring at her as if she had the letter A sewed to the front of her dress. Of course she'd left him. But that didn't mean she didn't love him still.

Before she knew what she was doing she'd balled the summons in her fist and she was tearing it to pieces and flinging those pieces—sad defeated little flakes of paper like shed skin—into the flowerbed. She was in the house next, not the main house but the bungalow out back, and she had a lamp in her hand—Leora's lamp, a hand-me-down, rubbish from the rubbish shop, no antique—and she was methodically beating it against the white plaster wall. Which was crumbling, right there before her, in an accumulating avalanche of white powder.

It was Leora who discovered her—she must have been crying out, the Chinese popping his head in the door like a jack-in-the-box and in the next moment Leora rushing into the room and calling out her name over and over, as if to remind her who she was, to bring her back, and it was as if she'd been transported out of her body, her mind flying off to cling to some hidden perch and her muscles working all on their own. The lamp was of brass. It clanged and clanged till it was a bell tolling for the dead, *Bring out your dead! Bring out your dead!* She remembered Leora throwing her arms around her—restraining her—and Leora's emollient voice pouring like syrup into her ear. And then they were on the couch together, the Chinese hurrying off to mix a shaker of martinis because this was an emergency, that much was clear—the lamp destroyed, the wall rutted and gouged and blood spattered there too and Miriam with her skinned knuckles and the straps of her swimming costume slipped down her shoulders and the wrap come loose so that her breasts swung free—but Miriam was sobbing so convulsively she couldn't tell her friend what had happened. And when she tried, when she fought to get the words out, the shame of it overwhelmed her. Frank—the man she loved, her *husband*—was casting her aside. For a long while Leora just held her, murmuring, "Hush, hush now," and finally the martinis were there—the beaded shaker, the delicate stem of the glass, the olive skewered on a toothpick—and Miriam felt the calm descend like the curtain falling at the end of a play.

She took the cocktail and downed it in two gulps. Tears clouded her eyes. "Frank," she began, "Frank, he—"

"You've got to be strong," Leora said, and who could blame her if her first thought was morbid? "At his age, well these things have to be expected . . . Lord knows, I should know. And Dwight lingered, that was the worst of it."

"No, no, you don't understand—Frank's *divorcing* me."

Five minutes later, the Chinese was out in the flowerbed, recovering the fragments of the summons. Which, after a second martini, they painstakingly reconstructed as if it were a jigsaw puzzle. The first thing, they both agreed, even before calling Frank, was to write the judge in the case and insist, or rather plead, that she wanted a reconciliation, that she loved her husband still, that their separation was temporary—for her health, just till she recovered her health—and she'd never even dreamed of divorce. Leora helped her with the letter, which ran to three pages, typed, and immediately she felt better. She thought she might like to put something on her stomach—veal chops, mashed potatoes, *haricots verts* (the Chinese really was a marvelous cook)—and then she went to the telephone. Or no, she took up the telephone as if it were a weapon, a sword she could wield with a single hand and still manage to draw blood at a distance of two thousand miles, eight o'clock in California—ten there, just when he'd be in the studio, lost to the world over his drawings, unless he was having one of his musical nights amidst the foreign toadies and kiss-ups he'd surrounded himself with.

The operator got her the number and her heart began to race as she waited for the connection to be made. There was a sound of static, a soft mechanical buzz, and then a voice she didn't recognize—a man's voice—came at her out of the ether: "Hello?"

"I want Frank," she said and she wished now she'd taken a shot to calm her nerves. She was wrought up all over again, the tension tearing at her till she felt as if she were reliving the shock of that first moment at the door when that little man, that fleck of human detritus, had handed her the summons—

"Yes?" the voice said. "Who is this?"

"Miriam. His wife. And who the hell are you?"

"Uh . . . sorry." The phone was muffled; someone was whispering. "One moment, please."

Frank came on the line then and his voice was bluff and businesslike. "Yes, Miriam, hello. What can I do for you?"

She couldn't contain herself, the air ratcheting up out of her lungs and tearing at her throat as if she'd swallowed a pneumatic pump: "Criminal!" she shrieked. "Weasel! You, you *fucking* vermin! How dare you treat me like this? Really, how dare you!?"

"Miriam," he said. And he might have said something to calm her, something in the soft priestly tones he used when he was being holier-than-thou, which was about eighty percent of the time, but she didn't hear him, didn't want to hear him.

"Shit!" she shouted. "Shit! You think you can cast me off like some whore, some, some bitch you've used for your pleasure and got enough of, is that what you think? Because if you do—"

There was more, a whole lot more, and tears too—she couldn't help it, she was only human and this was the lowest, dirtiest thing that anybody had ever done to her—and he tried to be meliorative and soft but the sound of him, the smugness, the finality in his voice, just turned all her jets on high till he began to harden and the connection was suddenly, violently, broken.

In the morning, once she'd bathed and done her hair and used her pravaz to spread its creeping warmth even to her toes and fingertips and numb her to whatever the day might bring (and yes, she'd hidden her kit from Frank as much as possible and from Leora too, not that she was ashamed or in danger of becoming a *morphinomane* or anything of that nature, but because her medicines were private, her own affair and no one else's, no matter how close they were—*or had been*), she sat down with Leora over breakfast and they both agreed that she needed a lawyer of her own. Frank had a lawyer. Why shouldn't she have one? How many women had they both known who'd been tossed out in the street like so much baggage and without a dime to their names? Or a nickel? Not even a nickel.

After breakfast she went back out to the bungalow

and used the telephone to make an appointment for that afternoon with William Siddons Barker III, an attorney who specialized in divorce cases and came highly recommended by any number of people Leora knew. She spent a long while on her face and clothes—the better part of the morning—finally selecting a spring suit of her own design, an all-wool Poiret twill in navy with a silk peau de cygne lining, and her blue velvet cape and turban to match. She completed the outfit with her pearls and lorgnette along with two strings of jet beads and a diamond brooch her mother had bequeathed her. "Oh, my, my," Leora said when she had a look at her, "you *are* a marvel."

"You think the brooch is too much?" she said, surveying herself in the full-length mirror in the front hall.

Leora had taken some care with her dress too and she did have style, no doubt about it. She wasn't nearly as dramatic as Miriam herself was, but then Miriam could carry it off in a way Leora never could—and yet still she had to admit her friend looked terrific in mauve crepe de chine and a bob hat with a spray of pheasant feathers that trailed prettily over one shoulder. "No, no," Leora murmured, her lips pursed and her eyes fixed on her. "You want to make an impression."

"You like it? You do? Really?" Miriam felt a flood of satisfaction and for a moment forgot the underlying purpose of all this. They were going to lunch at the Beverly Hills Hotel, yes, but that was just a diversion from the real meat of the day—the interview with the attorney and just what that meant. "You know, this brooch—and the cameo, see the cameo? It's meant to be the Three Graces, Aglaia, Euphrosyne and Thalia—isn't that darling? Brilliance, Joy and Bloom. This was all my mother's and her mother's before her. My jewelry"—she caught a glimpse of herself in the mirror and saw a tall regal woman staring back at her, the sort of woman who could fend for herself, fetch attorneys, fight Frank Wright till he was sorry he'd ever been born—"is my one real hedge against the worst. If I have to go begging, at least I've got something to fall back on."

"And the ring? Is that the Cleopatra ring?"

"So legend has it. I don't know the whole story, nobody does, I suppose, but it had been in my husband's family—his grandfather had it from a jeweler who'd dealt in all sorts of antiquities, especially Egyptian. It's supposed to be a scarab, you see? They say Cleopatra wore it as a talisman to keep her lovers faithful." She laughed. "As if anything could control a man when the urge comes over him. But did you know I almost sold it in Paris when the war broke out? There was a man from the museum there, very charming, very persuasive, but I just couldn't part with it. And I'm so glad. It's my most important piece." A smile now, rueful, a delicate delicious infusion of the lips with blood—and she could see Leora was skeptical, or maybe jealous, maybe that was it. Jealous, but doing her best to hide it. "It's my ring of vengeance, darling. And don't you think Frank doesn't know it."

As it turned out, William Siddons Barker III was very happy to see her, though he sympathized with what she was going through, of course, and it was a shame, a real shame (she broke down in his office, she couldn't help herself, even with Leora at her side), and he assured her that he would do everything he could for her. He was true to his word. Through his Chicago associate, Frederick S. Fake,* he was able to get Frank to drop the suit by threatening to counter-sue on the grounds of physical cruelty—yes, and how would that look in the papers, WORLD FAMOUS ARCHITECT BEATS WIFE—and they moved

* Actual name. No need really to comment on these absurd juxtapositions of function and fate, but I did once consult a dentist in New Haven by the name of Dr. Hertz.

on from there, very slowly, step by faltering step, toward the inevitable.

It hurt her. Every day it hurt. Who was he to throw her over? She was the prize here, not he. And she wrote him to that effect, letter after letter, alternately damning him and reminding him of the passion they once shared, a passion that towered above the petty loves and conventions of the masses—nine years his mistress* and never a complaint out of her, or barely, barely a whisper—and she called long distance whenever the rage boiled up in her, just to hear the iron in his voice and listen to his pathetic rationalizations, to berate him and scream and sob and curse over the wire till all the operators' ears from Los Angeles to Spring Green must have sizzled like fat in a pan.

He was adamant—there could be no reconciliation. There was no question of it. On that he wouldn't give an inch. Still—and this puzzled her—he went out of his way to be reasonable when it ultimately came down to reaching a compromise. More than reasonable: generous. Him, of all people. Frank, who considered an invoice a kind of memorial only and who wouldn't pay up even if he had the money right in his pocket and the sheriff was at the door. And when they did finally agree some four

* From 1914 to 1923. Wrieto-San took her up after the death of his previous mistress and first moved her into Taliesin in 1915, though he was still married to his first wife, Catherine, who refused to grant him a divorce. As indicated above, the people of the community—simple types, holding fast to their rustic mores and easily manipulated by tub-thumping editorial writers and backwoods preachers—were scandalized, treating Wrieto-San as a pariah. This animus may well have precipitated Wrieto-San's decision to take on the commission for the Imperial Hotel and move—with his mistress—to Japan, a far more compliant and civilized country.

months later on a divorce settlement—$10,000 in cash, $250 a month maintenance and a half-interest in Taliesin—he even threw in a bone. She'd always claimed she wanted to go back to Paris, his lawyer told hers—that was his understanding—and he wanted her to know he was amenable to that. So much so that if she would leave for Paris within six weeks of signing the settlement, he would give her an additional one thousand dollars on top and exclusive of everything else, just to help ease her transition.

She thought about that—Paris—the rooms she'd taken over an antiquities dealer on the rue des Saints-Pères, the artists she'd counted among her closest intimates, the bistros, the cafés, the gay life she'd led after Emil had passed on, and she very nearly relented. Paris in winter. Paris for Christmas. The smell of roasting *marrons* hanging over the streets, the blue-gray light of the afternoon, real life, real food, *bouillabaisse, foie gras, les fromages.* But there was something going on here she didn't like, something he was hiding from her. She knew him. She knew the way his mind worked.

What she didn't know about—not yet—was Olgivanna.

CHAPTER 3: THE WAY THINGS BURN

Frank took to Svetlana as if she were his own, and during the first month of the new year it seemed to Olgivanna as if he were going out of his way to spoil the child—endless trips to the zoo, concerts, ice-skating parties on Lake Michigan, frankfurters, popcorn balls, candied apples on a stick—but that was just part of his charm. He never did anything by half measures. He was an enthusiast for life, in love with her and her daughter too, genuine and unself-conscious, though when they were seen on the street together people naturally mistook Svetlana for his granddaughter and that seemed to throw him off his stride. He was no grandfather, he would protest (though he was—his son John had a daughter of three or four, that much Olgivanna knew), but if he was living an illusion, strutting at her side like a young lover and reveling in it, why deny him? Svetlana could have been his daughter—she should have been, an exquisite long-limbed beauty of seven with much more of her mother than Vlademar in her, and she loved the attention, loved the treats and the piggy-back rides and climbing up beside him on the piano bench to pound the keys and sing "Shine On, Harvest Moon" and "Sweeter Than Sugar" along with him, her voice piping and probing even as his own mellow tenor held fast to the melody.

Olgivanna was aware that he was auditioning for the role—*Daddy Frank,* that was what her daughter called him, just let him step into the room and she'd jump up and spring for his arms, shouting out "Daddy Frank, Daddy Frank!"—and she gave him credit for it, for the headlong rush of his desire and commitment. He was a force of nature, that was what he was, an avalanche of need and emotion that swept all before it. And she was in love too, mad for him, for the pleasure he took in her and the pleasure he gave her in return (Vlademar was nothing compared to him, nothing, as appealing as a dishrag, a milksop, and for the rest of her life she would say that she didn't know what love was—the physical act, the uniting of two bodies above and beyond the intertwining of their spirits—until she met Frank). And more than that, she was in search of something to hold on to—a cause, a modus vivendi, yes, but security and protection too—and he was there to provide a pair of broad shoulders* when she most needed them—her savings were dwindling, her husband wasn't doing much to help and it was awkward living at someone else's pleasure, a guest in that overcrowded apartment in Chicago with people she'd never really liked to begin with. So when he asked her to come to Taliesin again, with her daughter, and not just for a weekend, but to move in and be part of the life of the place, of his life—she never hesitated.

This time the route was familiar to her. And if the countryside seemed bleaker than it had at Christmas when even the most dismal farmhouse was enlivened by a wreath at the door or a candle in the window, at least now she had Svetlana with her to keep her company.

* Metaphorically speaking, that is. At this stage of his life, in late middle age, Wrieto-San was growing stocky, devolving into the Welsh farmer he was born to be. By my reckoning, his shoulders were no wider than average.

They had their sandwiches, milk for her daughter, coffee for her, Svetlana alternately chattering to her new teddy bear ("Eat your sandwich, Teddy; Pack your things; We're going on a trip!") and bent in concentration over a tracing book and a box of colored pencils Frank had bought her. Everything they had in the world was packed into a single steamer trunk in the luggage car somewhere behind them (and it wasn't much—a few changes of clothes, books, letters, two porcelain dolls Svetlana couldn't seem to exist without—because all this time they'd been living under Georgei's regime and Georgei preached asceticism).*

"What's it like, Mama?" Svetlana would ask every few minutes and she would try to summon the place—it wasn't the château at Fontainebleau, outside of Paris; it was a rambling tawny stone bungalow of the Prairie Style on the outskirts of Spring Green, Wisconsin, and it would necessarily have to be self-sufficient in terms of its culture and amusements. "You'll like it," she said. "You will. It is—I don't know—like a castle, only without the turrets."

The pencils flew over the page, good high-quality tracing paper that wouldn't tear through. Svetlana took a moment to finish what she was doing—red for the chimney of the house she was tracing, black for the

* To say the least. Typically his acolytes were allowed no more than four hours sleep a night and they spent the remaining twenty in the Master's service, putting themselves through a routine of hard physical labor, dance movements and spiritual and psychological exercises designed to awaken them from the death-in-life of the closed consciousness. Some would call it slave labor, but in the end it wasn't much different from what Wrieto-San would expect from his apprentices, though we did sleep, on average, an hour or two longer. And we didn't dance. Not if we didn't want to.

smoke—and then she lifted her face. "What are turrets?"

"You know, towers—like in 'Rapunzel, let down your hair.'"

"Like in France."

"Yes, that is right. Like in France. Only this place—Daddy Frank's place—doesn't have any of them."

"What does it have?"

She wanted to say it had beauty, it had genius, soul, spirit, that it was the kind of house that made you feel good simply to be inside it looking out, but instead she said, "It has a lake."

"For ice-skating?"

"Mm-hmm. And in summer"—she tried to picture it, the fields come to life, the barn doors flung open and the cattle grazing, fireflies in the night, constellations hanging overhead in the rafters of the universe—"we can swim. And take the boat out. And fish too."

"Are there ducks?"

"Sure there are. Geese too." She was guessing now, running ahead of herself as the train rolled through the deep freeze of the countryside, twenty below zero, thirty below, the rivers like stone, the trees in shock, not a living thing moving anywhere in all that loveless expanse. "And swans. Swans that come right up to you and take the corn out of your hand. Remember those swans in Fontainebleau—the black ones?"

Svetlana stopped drawing now, two pencils—the green and brown—bristling from the knuckles of her left hand, the red one arrested over the chimney even as the roof spread wide to enclose the stick figures she'd drawn beneath it: two of them, just two, mother and daughter in matching triangular skirts. Her eyes went distant a moment and maybe she was seeing the swans, Lionel and Lisette—that's what they'd named them, wasn't it?—or maybe she was just tired. What she said was: "Are we almost there yet?"

* * *

Frank and Kameki were waiting on the platform to greet them, their breath streaming, hats cocked low, collars pulled up high. They leaned into the wind, their eyes searching the windows of the train as it slowed with a seizure of the brakes, and then Kameki turned aside and cupped his hands to light a cigarette and Frank started forward, the skirts of his heavy twill cape fanning and fluttering round the tight clamp of his riding breeches and the sheen of his boots. He was right there, so close she could have reached out and touched him, but somehow he didn't see her, and the train slid past him before it jerked to a halt just up the line. Svetlana couldn't contain herself. She sprang up on the seat and pounded at the window, calling out his name over and over until finally he looked up and saw them and his face changed. Olgivanna waved then, her heart lifting.

But there was something wrong, she could see that the minute she stepped off the train. Frank was as brisk and energetic as ever and he was wearing his broad welcoming smile as he helped first her and then Svetlana down from the train, and yet he seemed distant. He didn't look at her, not right away, and that was strange. He bent instead to Svetlana, gave her something, a sucker, and asked if she'd had a pleasant trip, but Svetlana, the drawing book clamped under one arm and Teddy under the other, was shy suddenly and could manage only a whispered "Yes."

A savage wind swept the platform, crushed leaves and bits of refuse skittering before it, the sky roiling overhead, and Olgivanna had a moment to take in the deserted streets and battened-down buildings of the town—village, hamlet—where she'd be spending the immediate future and maybe longer, much longer, before he did look at her. The engine exhaled with a long shuddering hiss of steam. Kameki hustled off after the baggage. And Frank finally did acknowledge her, but he didn't take her in his arms, didn't kiss her—instead he held out his hand for a firm handshake, his glove to hers, as if she were a business acquaintance or a distant relative . . . and still he hadn't said a word, not a word, not *hello* or *welcome* or *I'm glad to see you*.

He dropped her hand then and leaned forward with a quick dip of his shoulders. "I'll tell you about it later," he said in a low voice, his breath caught up in the wind and gone. "It's the neighbors. The papers. We can't have a fuss."

"Daddy Frank," Svetlana cried, tugging at his scarf—and she'd recovered herself now, oriented to the cold and the moment of arrival and the town that wasn't worth a second glance—"can we go see the swans?"

He seemed to wince at the sobriquet—Daddy Frank, *Daddy*—his eyes jumping from Svetlana to her and back. The smoke of the engine twisted in the wind and drove at them, harsh and poisonous. Something caught in her eye and she blinked. "Swans?" he repeated. "What swans?"

"I have told Svetlana"—and she was dabbing at her eye with her handkerchief—"that we would see the swans on the lake—and the ducks too."

"Oh, yes, yes, the swans. Of course, honey, of course we will. But not now, not till summer. Now we have ice. You like ice, don't you?"

"Can we go skating? Today? Right now?"

But Frank was distracted—two men in overcoats were disembarking now and behind them a beanpole of a boy who immediately snatched at his hat to stabilize it—and he didn't answer. His eyes kept darting from Olgivanna to the far end of the platform where Kameki was in receipt of the trunk, the porter sliding shut the door and the conductor giving two admonitory toots of his whistle, and then, even as he said, "Yes, yes, certainly,

Svet, once we get settled," he suggested they wait in the car, out of the wind.

The car*—long and sleek, with a canvas top, and was it new, was this the car that had picked her up in December?—stood at the curb, engine running, Billy Weston behind the wheel. It wasn't till they were inside it, the door shut firmly behind them and Billy hurrying off to lend a hand with the trunk, that he gave her the embrace she'd been waiting for—and a kiss from his cold, cold lips. "God, it's great to see you and to have you here—and you, Svet, you too, you're going to love it—but you've got to understand, well, you know how this community is, all the hens clucking and the newspapermen warming up the road for us . . . you know what I've been through—"

She didn't say anything. And she couldn't imagine what this was all about. Had she misread him, was that it? Was he rescinding the invitation? Was all the talk of love just another fantasy? She ducked his gaze to dab at her eye—soot there, a speck of coal dust.

"So we've concocted a fiction, and it's nothing to me, really, you know how I feel about these biddies meddling and gossiping and trying to control people's lives—what I mean is, I'm telling people you're the new housekeeper."

She couldn't keep the bitterness out of her voice. "A Serb. Another impoverished immigrant, is that what you say? A cleaning lady?"

"Just till you get your divorce—and I, well, till I can quit Miriam officially."

Svetlana was sitting beside her, feigning deafness.

* The Packard? I know Wrieto-San had one of these automobiles in 1929, a touring car he took with him to Arizona, but I'm not certain of the provenance of this one. Perhaps it was the Cadillac in which he fled to Minnesota in 1926 to escape prosecution on Mann Act charges. In any case, Wrieto-San changed cars the way most men change socks.

She kicked her legs rhythmically against the seat, out and in, out and in, and then began tracing a pattern in the scrim of ice on the window.

"Then," he said, "then we marry and they can all go to hell."

If anyone believed the imposture, Olgivanna couldn't say. There were always people from the village around—from the countryside and surrounding towns, from Helena, Spring Green, Dodgeville, Arena, workmen, farmers, women to do chores—and while most of them wouldn't speak two words to her face she was sure they had plenty to say out of earshot. But she was the housekeeper, that was the story, and if anyone wanted to check up on her they'd see her out there in the foulest weather, splitting wood for stove and fireplace alike, slopping the pigs and pacing off the frozen fields where the vegetable garden would go come the first hint of spring, getting the lay of the land, settling in. By the end of the first week she'd pretty well taken charge of the place, apportioning out the jobs to the household help and even involving herself in the kitchen whenever she could maneuver around Mrs. Taggertz, who fiercely resisted any encroachment on her domain—especially from a woman whose status was a matter of speculation no matter what story the head of the household might choose to circulate.

"And the father of your child"—Mrs. Taggertz would throw over her shoulder while she pounded meat on the cutting board, rolled out dough for piecrust, sent up a rolling thunder with her pots and pans for the simple authoritative pleasure of it, "what was his name again?" A pause. "He's still in Chicago as I understand it?" "Yes," she'd reply, hoping to leave it at that. But Mrs. Taggertz wouldn't leave it at that. Mrs. Taggertz was on the offensive. "Any hope of reconciliation? Because, what I mean is, a child needs her father around—a girl especially and especially when she gets to that certain age, if you know what I mean?" "No," she would say, and suddenly she remembered something that needed doing outside or down the hall, "no hope, none at all." And then, almost apologetically, "I'm afraid."

But Frank loved the dishes she concocted from the old recipes—nothing too extreme, of course, but something different for a change, something with flavor, he'd say, pointedly—Serbian specialties like *pasulj* and *prebanac* (with homemade sausage substituting for kielbasa) and the yeast nut-bread *(povotica)* everyone exclaimed over, and Mrs. Taggertz had to give way, at least occasionally. Plus there were cookies practically every night, molasses cookies, chocolate chip, raisin and plum, Pfeffernuesse from a recipe Dione's mother had taught her and Nobu Tsuchiura's bean cakes.* It was a beautiful thing, welcoming and wonderful, to go into that kitchen after Mrs. Taggertz had left for the night with Dione, Sylvia Moser, Nobu and her daughter, sororal, an adventure, like being back with her sisters again.

And if Frank was gone most of the week in Chicago overseeing his new offices or climbing aboard the Santa Fe California Limited to Los Angeles to make adjust-

* *Amanatto*, made from adzuki (red beans). My personal favorite are *chitose*, sweet-bean dumplings covered with pink and white sugar representing the glow of sunrise and snow on Mount Fuji. Each year for Setsubun my mother would make tray after tray of them, even when we were living in Washington, and allow my brothers and me to gorge on as many as we could hold. Which was fewer than you might think—bean paste is surprisingly filling, especially when it's been sweetened to perfection.

ments to the houses he'd built there,* she didn't notice his absence as much as she thought she would. She was busy. Furiously busy. If she wasn't actually the housekeeper, if she was something more—mistress of the house, Mrs. Wright-in-waiting, major domo of the Taliesin enterprise—she might as well have been, and within the month Frank had let go of Mrs. Dunleavy, the square-shouldered farmwife who'd performed that function (without remuneration, as it turned out, or rather with an initial payment and the transient promise of more to come) for the past year. There was always work to be done, and of course everyone pitched in, even Svetlana, because no one was a guest here and Frank had a hundred improvement projects going simultaneously, winter and summer, everything in flux.

Her divorce was granted during the second month—March—and she hardly noticed because she was devoted to a new regime now and Vlademar was nothing more than a memory in any case, a stooped too-thin little man crying out in the morning for his socks, where were his socks, and Get me coffee, Olgivanna, before I die. He was an architect. He was in Chicago. And she would deliver Svetlana to him for his visitation rights according to the terms set out in the divorce papers. That was it. That was all. But Frank was delighted by the news—"Miriam's next," he said, "one more swing of the pendulum and we'll be free, both of us"—and they made an evening of it, gathering everyone round the

* La Miniatura, constructed in a ravine in Pasadena, was especially problematic. As were the flat roofs of all four of these unique, Mayan-inflected concrete-block houses, architectural treasures all. Leakage was to be expected—it was the fault of the climate, Wrieto-San would insist, nine months of desiccating sun, three months of monsoon rains—but he did personally see to the flashing for Mrs. Alice Millard, chatelaine of La Miniatura.

fire while the wind cried in the treetops and they all had hot chocolate and coffee and cookies, singing the old songs round the piano till the night wound down and she found herself in bed with him, nestled in the recess of his shoulder beneath the goose-down comforter and with the coals glowing red in the grate.

Spring blew up early out of the south that year, a succession of progressively warmer rainstorms scouring the snow from the ground and delivering up rhubarb sooner than he could ever remember—rhubarb pie, nothing better—and before long the flowerbeds were rife with color and the fruit trees in bloom and the barley sprouting in the long naked furrows of the fields. Every minute of every day he felt supercharged with energy, out of bed before dawn and sitting at his desk before breakfast, working over the drawings for the National Life Insurance Company skyscraper and the Nakoma Country Club, writing an article a month for the *Architectural Record* and still finding time to oversee construction around the place and get out into the fields and the garden and dig with his pitchfork till the ideas began to take hold and he'd have to scuttle back to his desk even as his apprentices looked up from their drafting tables in alarm until he sang out a joke and then another and another. He was so full of spirit—Olgivanna, bless her, was the foundation and impetus of it—that he just had to bounce up from his chair and show the boys what he'd done and look over their drawings and maybe pontificate a little here and there. Dinner was a treasure, the conversation and joy of it, and the Sunday evenings when they all dressed in their finest and sat round the living room or on the balmy nights under the big twin oaks in the courtyard making music or reading aloud from Whitman, Thoreau, Emerson, *Whoso would be a man must be a nonconformist* . . .

For years now—longer than he could remember—he'd been rolling a stone up a hill, a boulder that picked up weight on each revolution like a ball of snow, and Miriam's face was imprinted on the side of it—or no, hammered into the rock—so that every time he rolled it over there she'd be again. Miriam. Miriam of the cramps and headaches and rages, coming at him with her fists and her gaudy ring flashing like a weapon, everything in motion, the beads lashing round her throat even as she screamed and showed him her teeth as if she meant to swallow him whole. The psychiatrist—what was his name, Dr. Hixon—had diagnosed defective affectivity, whatever that meant, but the man had assured him there was violence on the horizon. All was quiet now, but wherever she was, Los Angeles, San Diego, Hollywood, he could feel the heat of her percolating up out of the ground beneath his feet like magma, white-hot and ready to incinerate everything, and every time the phone rang he felt his stomach sink. It had been months since he'd heard from her—six or seven months and counting. And Olgivanna was here now—and Svet and Richard and Dione and Kameki—and his life was moving forward. There were whole days when he never gave Miriam a thought, but she was there all the same, down deep, waiting.

And then there was an evening toward the end of April when the phone did ring—once, an awkward discontinuous sort of buzzing rather than a ring per se—and he put it down to a fault in the wiring he'd rigged up to connect the bedroom phone with a buzzer in the kitchen, a simple device to communicate simple wants, as in a hotel.* They'd just finished dinner, he and Olgi-

* While he may have been the world's greatest architect, Wrieto-San lacked expertise when it came to electrical devices. Half the wiring at Taliesin was jury-rigged and we were forever watching a lightbulb sizzle in the socket or plugging in a lamp or radio to the sound of an explosive pop and the odor of scorched wires.

vanna and Svet—the rest had all gone off to town, but for Kameki and Mel,* the new driver—and they'd eaten in the little detached dining room on the hilltop because there was a storm building and he thought it would be something to watch it come across the hills. The cook had gone home. Olgivanna had served the meal herself and it was as if they were an ordinary family, husband, wife, daughter, gathered round the table for an ordinary meal. The wind came up while they were eating, branches beating against the windows, and there was a feeling of security, of shelter—let the storm do its worst: they were snug enough. "You see, Svet," he'd said, pausing over a forkful of Montenegrin beans, "this is what organic architecture gives you—you're indoors and you're out at the same time, all this continuity of line, the views all around. You wouldn't get that in one of your gingerbread houses in Chicago. You wouldn't even know a storm was coming."

"Will there be lightning? I'm scared of lightning."

"Sure," he said, "there'll be lightning. But there's no reason to be scared. It won't hit here. And it won't hit you as long as you stay inside."

The clouds were elongating, running with the wind in threads and stripes, and on the horizon the first shock of the lightning. They all three turned their heads to watch it tug at the sky.

"And away from the lake," Olgivanna put in. She was dressed in blue, a belted jacquette blouse and skirt ensemble he'd designed for her himself, simple and elegant at the same time. And stylish too. He'd seen something like it in a catalogue—and on any number of women in Chicago—and so he'd surprised her, delivering the pattern to the dressmaker himself and then bringing back

* No surname available. No one seemed to recall anything about him, except that he was called Mel.

the package on the train. There was color in her face—she'd been out of doors all afternoon, turning over the kitchen garden for planting because there would be no more frosts this year, he'd promised her, solemnly, he swore it, no more frosts—and he saw that her nails were faintly rimmed in black and her hands hardened with the work of the place. She looked healthy. Looked contented. And pregnant. Two months' pregnant.* She'd told him just that morning—in bed, before Svetlana was awake—and he was alive with the news. Tomorrow, he'd told her, tomorrow we celebrate, when everyone's here.

He'd just gone to the bedroom for something—the book he'd been reading, his glasses—when the phone began to buzz. He picked up the receiver and the line went dead. Mystified, already irritated, he went down to the kitchen, only to find that the buzzer there wouldn't switch off no matter how many times he depressed the button. And where was the screwdriver? He was going to need a screwdriver to take the thing off the wall—and a pair of pliers too. For a minute he just stood there, the buzzer rasping in his ears, looking round him vaguely for a tool—anything, a butter knife, the thin edge of a dime—and he rifled the drawer and actually had the knife in his hand when a gust thumped at the windowpane and he glanced up to see smoke leaking out of the bedroom windows.

Smoke. Dark tongues of it, torn by the wind and flung down into the courtyard. It was as if the steam locomotive had left the station, sailed out over the countryside and lodged itself there, in his bedroom, the stoker all the while feeding coal to the glowing mouth of the fur-

* One wonders if Wrieto-San ever stopped to think what he was doing. To create the fiction of Olgivanna as his housekeeper and almost immediately impregnate her begs the question.

nace. But that was impossible, that was absurd, the delirium of a disconnected mind—the fireplace, it must have been the fireplace, sure it was, the flue flipped shut by a gust of wind, that was what he was thinking, and yet even as he heaved himself down the corridor, he knew there'd been no fire laid because it had been warm all day, too warm for the season, the air heavy with the coming of the storm and no reason to waste good oak that had to be sawed, split and stacked.*

By the time he got to the bedroom the wall behind the bed was riotous with flame, the curtains there come to life in red snapping ribbons and the bedclothes leaping up to join fire to fire. Two seconds, that was all it took, and then he was back down the corridor shouting "Fire!" and here was Olgivanna with her shocked eyes and blanched face and Kameki running mad in the wrong direction and would the hose in the courtyard stretch that far?—no, no, not even close. There were buckets in the stables and now Mel was involved, a bucket brigade, up the corridor to fling water at the wall to the *shush* of steam and the stink of incineration and then the next bucket and the next and no time for the taps or the hose bib, just plunging into the garden pool again and again and up the corridor and down the corridor to the long alliterative *shush* of steam . . .

No thought for anything in those first minutes, no thought of the art treasures below or the specter of the first fire, the one that had raked the heart right out of his chest and baked it hard, no thought for Olgivanna or Svet—and here she was, straining under the weight, *Daddy Frank*, another bucket—or of his own safety or anything in this world but the flames on the wall and the bed and the curtains. After the first bucket flew from his hands he leapt to the casement windows and pulled

* By apprentices.

them tight and latched them even as the wind beat at the roof and the lightning flashed over the hills and the flames climbed the wall. "The flue!" he shouted to Olgivanna, and she was right there, slamming it shut with a sharp grating of the hinges, starving the fire of air till the twentieth bucket, the thirtieth, he'd lost count, began to sizzle in a different way, the soft dying hiss of a snuffed campfire, and the flames fell back on themselves and collapsed.

"There," he shouted, his lungs heaving, his hair wild, his shirtsleeves blackened and his hands burned red where he'd folded the flames into the bedclothes and flung them to the floor beneath his stamping feet, "there, it's done." Olgivanna came surging through the door then, a bucket in each hand, and she barely glanced at him before heaving first one, then the other, at the dead black wall and the charred bedstead, two more buckets for good measure. He put a hand out to restrain her even as the water ran down the wall and into the cracks between the floorboards. "We got it, Olya, we got it," he said. "I think we—"

It was then that he became aware of a new sound, a ticking or scratching in the ceiling above the bed, as if the slats there had developed an itch or a squirrel had gnawed its way in and now wanted out, Svet and Mel and Kameki crowding into the room behind him with superfluous buckets and looping eyes and the wind skreeling over the roof and beating at the panes. Kameki, in shirtsleeves and galluses, breathing hard, let out a low exclamation: "What in God's name?—" The scratching grew louder. No one moved. And then there was a long trailing *whoosh*, as of the gas in an oven reacting to the stimulus of the match, and he knew that the worst had come: the fire was in the dead space between the ceiling and the roof and the wind was feeding it through every crack and sliver. "The roof!" was all he could say before he was down the hall and out the door, shouting for a ladder, more water, the fire department, somebody call the fire department!

The wind was like a hurricane and it tore the door from his hands and hurled grit in his face as he flung himself across the courtyard for the ladder in the garage, Mel and Kameki at his heels. "No," he roared, "no—*water!* Fetch the water!" And he had the ladder in both hands, running again, running still, and now the ladder was against the roof and he was scrambling up it, the roofing breached in half a dozen places, cedar shake going up like tinder—and it was tinder, shaved thin as bark and ten years dry. And this was the nightmare: leaping atop the shingles from one emergency to the next, the soles of his shoes seared with the fury of the heat, the water buckets coming up and down the ladder—pitiful, nothing at all, he might as well have been flinging teardrops into a volcano—and within minutes the roof over the bedroom collapsed with a roar onto the doomed bed and the condemned floor.

Overhead, the sky darkened toward night, the storm running on the wind, squeezing closer, the lightning playing over the trees. He fought the flames, driving them back here as the wind seized them there, and his eyebrows were gone, his socks smoldering, shoes scorched, and though people were coming now, neighbors, coming at a run to help and gossip and gawk, he had to retreat, backing away from the living part of the house to the rear, where the working part was—his studio and the rooms for the apprentices and guests—and that was going to go too, he could see that now, no hope, none at all. The flames were gaining. He couldn't breathe. The smoke thickened and the fire surged, hotter than any Fourth of July bonfire and fed on everything he held precious. "Get away, Frank!" somebody was shouting. "It's no use! Get away!"

Was it a judgment? Was it the God of Isaiah, the fateful, vengeful God, striking at him yet again for his hubris, his too-perfect creation, the spark that made him godlike himself? He couldn't have helped wondering, if he'd had time to reflect, but he didn't have time, not then, not till it was over, and by then he'd let it pass and accounted himself lucky. Because at that moment, twenty minutes into the ordeal, with the house an inferno and temperatures so intense the windows were reduced to puddles of molten silica and all his furnishings and peerless art destroyed, a blast of thunder sounded overhead, the wind suddenly shifted and the rain came like forgiveness.

For days the ruins smoldered, a thin stench of incineration hanging on the air, a sour smell, as if it were a thousand barrels of vinegar that had gone up and not the heart and soul of the place she'd come to love as if she'd built it herself. That smell would haunt her as she lay beside Frank in the too-narrow bed in the guest quarters, everything shifted now to accommodate the new life, the building life, the night fast with the density of darkness absolute and the blankets binding like tourniquets, and she would drift off to the sourness and awaken to it in the first light of dawn. Even the smell of the morning's bacon rising out of the confines of the temporary kitchen was overwhelmed by it, the sweetness of the turned earth spoiled, the flowers driven down. She felt sick in the mornings now, sicker than she'd been with Svetlana, but she forced herself out of bed and into the kitchen to negotiate the space with Mrs. Taggertz and make good and certain that Frank's breakfast was delivered to him in the studio because now more than ever he had to keep up his strength.

She worried over him—she couldn't help herself. She'd awakened at dawn that first day, the day after the fire, and he was already gone. Had he slept at all? And what of his burns?—they had to be re-bandaged, washed, new salve had to be applied. She wrapped herself in her robe and went out the door to the ashes and the stink and the birds singing obliviously, riotously, the sun perched like a golden wafer on the hill to the south and the cows standing in the green, green fields, and there he was in the ruins with the garden rake, stooped and saddened, everything hot to the touch still, and she asked him if he needed help, comfort, anything, but he waved her off. Later, she looked out the window and saw Billy Weston there with him, recovering fragments of pottery, bronze, shards of marble that had crumbled to a friable white dust, calcined by the fierceness of the heat. They were putting things in a bucket, useless things—it was all destroyed, couldn't they see that?—and she wanted to say something, wanted to interfere, but she held back.

Heat shimmers rose from the ruins. They stooped and dug. They didn't speak, not a word, the silence between them like shared thought, and they were back now in the past, she was sure of it, gone back to the first fire, the one that had taken everything. She barely knew the story—Frank went quiet at the mention of it—but she knew his mistress had died that day, his first mistress, the one he'd built Taliesin for.* And there was Billy's loss, Billy's too.

The worst of it, though, even worse than the crowds that had gathered round to fold their arms and gossip and chew as if the tragedy were their entertainment for the evening ("Hyenas," Frank called them), was the press. The reporters were there at first light, clamoring for a statement. They didn't care that Frank was exhausted, mentally and physically, that he'd just suffered a loss greater no doubt than any of them had ever experienced

* Martha (Mamah) Borthwick Cheney, 1869–1914.

or that he might need time to recover himself—all they cared about was when and where and how and didn't this happen before and can you tell us how you feel? At this juncture, that is? Mr. Wright, Mr. Wright! Can you give us a statement? He turned a heavy face to them, alive only in his eyes, and gave them what they wanted because he was a public figure, because he was famous, because he had to. He told them he was relieved in that no lives had been lost, that he regretted having been so poor a trustee for the great works of art that had been inadvertently destroyed—valued at half a million, that's right, half a million at least*—and that yes, he intended to rebuild. And then Billy Weston and some of the other workmen escorted them off the property so that they could race one another to town to wire the stories already taking shape in the scrawled-over pages of their notepads: WRIGHT BUNGALOW GONE; FIRE AT TALIESIN; BLAZE DESTROYS LOVE COTTAGE OF FRANK L. WRIGHT.

A lesser man would have been defeated, or at least bowed, but not Frank. Before the ashes had cooled he was drawing, working through the day and into the night, measuring, coloring, erasing, Taliesin III† beginning to take shape under the impress of his pencil while the blackened stone of the walls stood silhouetted against the hills like the ruins of a Roman villa. He'd sit down to dinner and gaze up at her out of his naked face, looking

* A considerably inflated figure, it seems to me. But then Wrieto-San was always over-valuing his collections—his Japanese woodblock prints (*ukiyo-e*) especially—in order to raise money against them as a sop to the vast armies of his creditors.

† Three mistresses, three Taliesins. One can only imagine how Olgivanna must have felt with regard to the line of succession. Given her private education, certainly she must have been acquainted with Henry VIII.

like a Chinese sage with his eyebrows gone and his naturally springy hair slicked back to hide the places where she'd cut out the worst of the burned spots, and there'd be a joke on his lips. Always a joke. He'd clown for Svetlana, sing "O, Susanna" a cappella and wish aloud for a piano to replace the one turned to ash. "Or a banjo, at least. How about a banjo, Svet? Is that one I see on your knee there?"

And he was good with her too on the subject of the fire. Wonderful, really. Far better than Vlademar would have been. Svetlana was a sensitive child, very adult, always concerned with security and order and the underlying causes of things, and the fire had been especially hard on her, the violence of it, the dislocation—and just when she'd begun to settle in and find herself. First she'd been uprooted from Fontainebleau, then from her uncle's house in New York and from Chicago and Vlademar, and now there was this, her dresses and her books and the indispensable porcelain dolls gone forever.

Frank had come in whistling at lunch one afternoon not a week after the fire, the day gloomy and oppressive, the sky like iron, thunder rumbling, stanchions of lightning propping up the clouds all around them. And that smell, that smell on the air still. "I see you're in a good mood," Olgivanna said, pulling out a chair for Svetlana as the cook fussed round the table.

"Oh, sure," he said, "sure," lifting his eyebrows, where spikes of white hair had begun to sprout, "is there any other kind of mood worth being in? Huh, Svet? What do you say?"

"There's lightning," she said in a very small voice. "Again."

"Well, it's a fact of life. Electricity. Without it we'd have no lights at night. You wouldn't want that, would you?"

She didn't respond, Mrs. Taggertz setting down

bowls of soup and a loaf of fresh-baked bread, just the three of them at lunch, the workmen dining separately on the wall beneath the oak trees, the Neutras, Mosers and Tsuchiuras displaced now and gone. A long roll of thunder drummed at the hills.

"Now, listen, Svet," Frank said, setting his spoon down to reach for the bread knife and saw at the loaf with both hands, "you know perfectly well it wasn't lightning that caused the fire, but bad wiring. And bad luck, I guess." He handed her a roughly hewn slice of bread. "But if it wasn't for the rain, we wouldn't be sitting here all snug and happy because the whole place would have gone up."

"I know that. But if it wasn't for the wind—" She made a vague gesture with her spoon.

"Sure," he said. "Sure. I know what you're driving at, honey, and there's no good answer for it. You take the good with the bad. The main thing is not to let it get you down." He paused to address the soup, but he wasn't done yet. "You know, I've told your mother this, but I have to say I'm humbled by it too. It does seem sometimes as if some higher power is up there throwing the dice against us—and by that I mean God, the God of the Bible with his manna in one hand and his hellfire in the other. Take Maple, for instance."

"Who's Maple?"

"She was a pedigree Holstein Maplecroft worth more than a hundred ordinary cows—we bought her to breed her and start our own line. And one day, during a storm just like this, she was out in the field with two ordinary old milk cows worth not much more than their hides and bones. I was sitting on the stone terrace with a cup of tea, watching the storm come in, when there was a powerful jolt—Boom! Just like that"—he snapped his fingers—"lightning striking right there in the field." He lifted a finger to point beyond the windows. "Sure enough, ten minutes later a worker came to me breathless to say that one of the cows had been killed—can you guess which one?"

"Maple?"

"That's right, honey: Maple. And I tell you, you can draw your own conclusions, but what I say is you've got to put your head down and work, work till you add tired to tired, and never look back. Never."*

It was amazing to see how quickly the ribs of Taliesin III went up, a whole crew of carpenters, stonemasons and laborers from the surrounding villages going at it from dawn till dusk through the cumulative outpouring of each lengthening day, and Frank right there in the middle of it. He was inexhaustible, utterly absorbed, and if he wasn't climbing the frame with his carpenter's level or snapping a plumb line from one corner to the next, he was at his desk, refining the plans, firing off letters to prospective clients and old friends, using all his charm and persuasion to secure commissions (retainer urgently requested) and outright loans. Insurance would cover some of the cost of rebuilding, he assured her, though unfortunately—tragically—the art hadn't been included in the coverage, and the structure he envisioned was far grander than either Taliesin I or II—here was a chance to consolidate things, eliminate the design flaws of a place that had grown by necessity and accretion. Where the money would come from, he couldn't say, but he never let money stop him, not mere money. Oh, no.

* I don't know how far this homily would go in assuaging the fears of a young girl morbidly afraid of lightning, but I had it from a reliable source—Svetlana herself. And she was a perfectly well-adjusted (and quite fetching) girl in her teens when I knew her at Taliesin. Of course, she did run off at seventeen to elope with Wes Peters, incensing Wrieto-San.

May turned to June, June to July. She hadn't really put on any weight—or not that anyone could see, except Frank when they were in bed together and he ran his hands over the bulge of her abdomen as if this were another of his projects to be gauged and measured against a set of blueprints—but soon her condition would be evident to anyone with a pair of eyes. Like the cook. Or any of the workmen—or their busy wives. They had a talk about it one night, the two of them naked and sweating and Frank examining her under the lamplight, his face shining, the taste of him on her lips still. "We've got to do something before people start talking," he murmured.

She traced a single finger down his nose to his lips, his chin, his chest. "What," she said, feeling playful, "exactly, do you propose?"

"Miriam," he said, and waved a hand in extenuation.

For a long moment she said nothing. The name itself—*Miriam*—was enough to break the mood, sour the sweetness of the moment, and there was that smell again, the faintest whiff of burning. She watched the shadow of his hand move against the wall. Beetles hurled themselves at the window screen like bullets. He'd lain here in bed with Miriam just as he was lying with her, opened himself to her, told her he loved her, swore it, swore it a hundred times. And what was she now? A stranger. An irritant. A name, just a name. "What was she like?" she asked, and her voice seemed to stick in her throat. "Was she beautiful?"

"No," he said. "Not compared to you. Nobody is."

"But she *was* beautiful."

He shrugged. "Listen, Olya, that's not the point. I don't want our child born out of wedlock, that's all. We need to be married as soon as possible, you see that, don't you? Before word gets out. You've got your divorce, now I've got to get mine. I'm going to the lawyer tomorrow, first thing in the morning, all right? And we'll see what happens. Maybe—as long as she doesn't know about you, about us—she'll take the bait and we can be done with her." He paused, looked to the window, the beetles there—and what were they doing? Mating she supposed, like any other creatures. "She'll need money, I know her. Maybe, just maybe, she'll come to terms."

"Do you love her still?"

"Love her? She's been dead to me for years. She's a disturbed woman, violent. Especially if she doesn't get her way. If she even suspected . . . I mean, that you were here—"

She remembered how he'd fumed over the newspaper accounts of the fire—"So much trash and sensationalism, as if I live my life for the amusement of Mr. and Mrs. Schmutzkopf over breakfast in the Loop, 'Love Cottage,' and all the rest"—but was exultant that none of them had mentioned her. They didn't know. No one knew. It was their secret, *Architect Living in Sin with Pregnant Montenegrin*, and if they could guard that secret just a while longer, all would be well, he promised her. She hadn't really thought about it, not until the fire and the clamor of the newspapermen. Everything had seemed so natural to her, so involved with the earth and the change of the seasons, so distant from the city and society and all the dull decorum that went with it. She thought of Georgei then. It was no more than what—eighteen months ago?—that she'd first come to New York with his troupe. She'd been enclosed within him then, all her life a function of her master and his Work, her spirit ascending, the drums and flutes speaking a secret language that fed her limbs as she danced across the stage, danced in private, danced to a music no one else could hear, present only in her mind and her heart—and Georgei's. How distant it all seemed now.

Georgei. The force of him, the way he could mesmerize an audience. He would sweep out of the wings like a prophet, urging the rapt crowd to lift the veil and see the universe for what it was, and he would astonish them with his music and feats of hypnotism, but the true *coup de foudre* was the moment the dancers broke the plane of the stage and hurled themselves into the audience. It was a leap of faith. They all spun to the accelerating beat of the music and then they rushed the lip of the stage and leapt blindly into space—and it was faith alone that kept them intact even as they landed in the orchestra pit or the boxes in front, sprawled amongst the gentlemen in their fancy dress and the ladies in their gowns. That was the leap she'd made now. For Frank.

"We'll lie low," he said, "just as we've been doing. And you're hardly showing." He touched a hand to her cheek. "You know what I'll do? I'll sketch some dresses for you, lots of material, ruffles maybe—I know, I know—but something to hide your condition. As long as possible. Because if word gets out . . ."

But word does get out. Word travels fast, it seeps and bubbles and runs in the ditches like heavy rain in a wet country, and when she began to show, when there was no hiding it anymore and the leaves turned and dropped from the trees and the clouds moved in low to scatter sleet across the new windows and new roofs of Taliesin III, the phone rang again. They were sitting by the fire, she and Svetlana and Frank, reading aloud, and the instrument gave a long trailing bleat and then another. She looked up at him and she saw his eyes retract, his jaw harden: he was thinking the same thing she was. The phone hadn't rung, not at this hour, in a very long time—not since summer, when he'd filed the divorce papers. Then it rang daily, continually, and the letters came in a deluge—she'd seen those letters, the envelopes addressed in a finishing school hand lost to the fierce accounting of haste and desperation, and inside the chilling avowals of love couched in the iconography of sex and death. *Oh, my gallant knight*—struck out—*once gallant*—struck out again—*never gallant knight who took me to his bed and made of that bed an ancient bark plying the stormy seas of Eros, hard by the Isle of Thanatos and the Peninsula of Despair, how could you betray me? My trust, my heat, my blood, my heart? How could you? How could you?*

On the third ring he set down the book and rose to answer the phone. She watched him pad across the carpet as if in slow motion, watched him lift the receiver from the hook. Even though she was on the far side of the room and there was a record on the phonograph and the fire was making a noise with a log of too-green wood, she could hear the shrill insinuation of the voice on the other end of the line. "Miriam," Frank was saying. "No, Miriam, you're wrong," and he had to pull the receiver away from his ear.

"Liar! Fraud!" The voice rose in an ecstasy of hate and accusation. "Housekeeper!? *Housekeeper!?* You expect anyone to believe that, Frank, you, you"—and it wavered, all the sorrow and jealousy and rage wadded up in the expletive that followed. And then a shriek, so raw and explosive it was as if the woman on the other end of the line were being stabbed in the throat: "You used that lie up already. On me. I was the housekeeper, Frank, *I* was!"*

* True enough. Wrieto-San employed the same subterfuge with regard to Miriam's role in the household when he moved her in ten years earlier, even going so far as to draw up a contract putting her wages at $60 a month, but it proved transparent. Within days, the papers were decrying the architect's continued flaunting of convention, denouncing Taliesin as a "Sin Nest" and "Love Bungalow" and the like.

CHAPTER 4: IOVANNA

I tell you, missus, if you want to bring this matter around in your favor you'd be well advised to come out here to Chicago—" There was a pause, phonograph music in the background, the sound of a match being struck. Miriam could hear the man—the detective, *her* detective*—breathing into the mouthpiece, a hoarse ratcheting insuck and outlay of breath as if his lungs were blistered. "Because your party is conducting himself in a scandalous manner, not to mention being in violation of the laws and statues." That was what he'd said, *statues*, but Miriam knew what he meant, and it shot an electric jolt right through her.

"You've got him dead to rights, missus."

She didn't want to hear what he had to say, couldn't stand it, couldn't tolerate another word. She should have broken the connection right then and there, but she didn't—she held on, her whole frame gone rigid with the dread of what was coming, the certainty she'd contracted for, proof positive. "And I'm sorry to have to say it"—he insinuated his voice into the speaker, parceling out the

* Jasper J. Jesperson, 3720 Figueroa, Los Angeles, California. Private Investigations of a Discreet Nature.

words as if she were paying extra for each one—"but what I mean is in flagrante delicto."

Leora was watching her from the sofa. She knew her face had gone white, drained of color as surely as if she were the heroine of a Saturday afternoon melodrama, the news they'd both foreseen come home to them, to *her,* long distance from Chicago. She wasn't kidding herself—she wasn't born yesterday. She knew Frank. She knew what he was capable of. But to hear it now, from the lips of a man every bit as odious as the one who'd slithered up the front walk and handed her the summons on that concussive day in July, shook her nonetheless. Frank didn't love her anymore. There was no going back. "No," she said, "no," not knowing what else to say.

"What I mean is he's at the Garfield Arms, right now—with her and the child—and you can catch him with his pants down, that's the beauty of it. You'd a thought he'd have the savvy to hide the whole business, but I guess not. He's even registered under his own name. And her too."

Leora mouthed something to her from across the room. Was it "guilty" or "got him"?

"Missus?"

All the blood was boiling up in her brain. You didn't register housekeepers at your hotel. Housekeepers stayed home and kept house. She felt dizzy suddenly—betrayed, betrayed yet again—and she could barely manage a response. "Yes?" she whispered.

"I'll tell you something else too—his consort or mistress or whatever you want to call her?"

"Yes?"

"She's big as a house. Out to here, if you know what I mean."

She was on the next train for Chicago, staring out the window of her sleeper at the naked mountains and the bleak dead midsection of the country, everything in shades of tan, no color anywhere, no life, no hope. She'd practically begged Leora to come with her, for support—she just didn't know if she could go through with this on her own—but Leora had been planning her Thanksgiving party for the past two months now, a fête for forty, black tie, the sort of thing that would make her neighbors stand up and take notice, and she couldn't just go and cancel at this late date, could she?

No. No, of course not.

And so Miriam was traveling alone, the pravaz her only companion. She didn't knit, didn't sketch. Cards bored her to tears. She had the latest Zona Gale with her and Lewis' *Arrowsmith*, an excellent book really, about a fine and noble man—an idealist like herself—but she was too anxious to concentrate and wound up spending hour after hour staring out the window on the rolling vacancy of America. A colored porter stuck his head in the door every once in a while and people nattered at her in the dining car and she tried to respond, if only for the sake of civility, but the conversation (the quality of the food, the ease and speed of rail travel, something that had happened to somebody's sister in Omaha) held nothing for her. Thanksgiving fell on the last day of the trip and though the chef went out of his way and the waiters did their best to make the turkey with mashed potatoes, gravy, chestnut stuffing and peas with pearled onions look and taste like something prepared at home with the family gathered round, it was a sad imposture and everyone in the dining car knew it. The laughter was brittle, the attempts at witticism as stale as the pie à la mode. She left the dessert untouched and retreated to her compartment.

That night she barely slept, her mind racing along with the incessant pounding of the wheels on the track, Frank's face rising up before her like a cork in a gutter, Frank grinning at her, mocking her, Frank superimposed over the very attractive single gentleman in the next compartment who'd trained a long look of wonder and sympathy on her every time she squeezed past him in the corridor because she was a desirable woman still, supremely desirable, with taste and class and education, worth any hundred dancers, a thousand, whole troupes of them . . . Frank, Frank, Frank . . . Frank strutting along the sidewalks of Chicago in his arrogant cock-of-the-walk way, Frank, his eyes shut tight in rapture, working his bare white buttocks atop some other woman. Some dancer. Some foreigner.

Olgivanna Milanoff, that was the name the detective had supplied her. *Olgivanna Milanoff.* She said the name aloud in the dark, just to taste the bitterness of it on her tongue. The coach rocked and steadied itself and rocked again. Anonymous stations slipped past in the night, each one an outpost guarded by a single naked light, even as the wheels hammered out the tempo beneath her, Milanoff, Milanoff, and the sadness that gripped her then was like nothing she'd ever felt, not even when Emil came back to her in the hush of the alienist's parlor and laid a hand of ice on her shoulder. It was as if a cautery had been run through her heart. This woman—this *dancer*—was pregnant by him, pregnant. Carrying his seed, his child. Was that what he'd wanted—another child?

It was news to her. Because there'd never been any question of children between Frank and her—they were in their forties when they met, with grown children of their own, and from the beginning their union had existed on a higher plane. They were companions, soul mates. Not mere breeders like all the rest. Anybody could be a breeder—look at the peasants and their strings of ragged dirty children with their mouths hanging open and their hands outstretched in the undying expectation of a coin or a crust, the world already too small a place for so many mouths, so many hands. And

Frank had agreed with her. Or was it just a matter of expedience?

But Jesus God he worked fast, glad to be rid of her, to cast her aside and find someone new, someone younger, someone pretty and naïve and unformed to pour himself into, to mold and hammer and shape the way he never could have shaped her. Well, she pitied the woman. And she could have him, this Olgivanna, this Russian or whatever she was, have her Frank Lloyd Wright, the great man bestriding the world like a colossus for all to see when in actuality he was the most venal dirty insufferable little coward she'd ever known—and a lecher, a lecher to boot . . .

Chicago was cold and clear, the sun as pale as suet and hanging low over the houses and factories and the shadowy monoliths of the skyscrapers. The cab took her through quiet streets, cars drifting past like untethered boats, people gazing numbly from behind their curtains or trudging past one another as if speech hadn't been invented yet. She checked into her hotel, freshened up in her room and immediately went back down to the lobby to order a car (though in truth she was so worn-out and exhausted she could have slept for a week). Standing there at the curb, waiting for the doorman to assist her, she nearly lost her resolve. But the thought of the divorce settlement—how Frank had manipulated her, hiding everything from her, his deceit, his adultery, his Russian paramour *(Paris, Paris indeed, and how convenient for him)*—steeled her. There'd be no settlement now. She'd never sign—she'd tear the papers up and throw them in his face. The bastard. The son of a bitch. He would see—she would make him see—because the balance had turned and it was all in her favor now.

She had the car drop her off a block from the Garfield Arms*—it wouldn't do to get too close. She was on her way to the museum, that was the story she and the detective had concocted in concert with her Chicago lawyers, when she just happened to see her husband's car pulled up in front of the hotel where she'd stayed with him on occasion. She called out a greeting to his chauffeur. Exchanged pleasantries with him. And, curious, she'd gone into the lobby to inquire after her husband, only to discover, to her horror, et cetera.

The wind was in her face—and if she'd thought she was in California still, she was disabused of that notion, the cold a force of its own, bits of paper and refuse driven before her like drift, the manholes steaming, businessmen buckling under the weight of their scarves and greatcoats. She was wrapped in fur, her hair pulled back in a bun and imprisoned beneath her turban, her heels beating a martial tattoo on the pavement. Up the street she came, determined, her shoulders thrown back, her head held high. And it was just as they'd planned—there was the car sitting idle at the curb, and there was Billy, hunched over a cigarette and giving her a sheepish woebegone look. "Billy," she cried, bending to peer in the

* An indication that Wrieto-San was attempting to be discreet, if not deceptive. In recent years, he'd come to prefer the Congress, on Michigan Avenue (an undistinguished edifice, really, built in 1893 as an annex to Louis Sullivan's Auditorium Building across the street), perhaps because it was *the* place to be seen, its Pompeian Ballroom attracting the smart set as well as Chicago's social elite. I never stayed there myself, even in later years when I could easily have afforded it—the only time I spent a night in Chicago during my apprenticeship was when Daisy Hartnett and I were able to get away on the pretext of her mother's illness. The hotel we chose was inconspicuous, to say the least. And a whole lot cheaper than the Congress.

window of the car, "what a surprise. What are you doing here? Is Mr. Wright staying over?"

"Yes, ma'am."

She watched him wriggle a bit, and it was clear whose side he was on. "Down from Taliesin on business?"

"Yes, ma'am."

"Well, I've just come back, you know. California was lovely, but my place is here with my husband. I'd thought he was in Wisconsin still—but how convenient that he's here in Chicago. Perhaps I'll just stop in and say hello—"

He had nothing to say to this, but oh, he was wriggling now. Good. Good. Let him suffer, the apostate, with his false face and bugged-out eyes.

"—and then maybe we can all go up together, just like old times. Right, Billy?"

Still nothing. His face was set, one hand held fast to the wheel, the other working the cigarette at his lips. Finally, because the conversation was over—that much was evident, even to him—he raised a finger to his cap in salute.

Inside, the lobby was busier than she would have expected, and she had to wait a moment behind a couple checking in (with enough baggage to mount an expedition to Timbuktu) before she could catch the desk clerk's attention. The clerk was a man in his thirties with a toothbrush mustache and blue-black hair greased to a seal-like phosphorescence, no one she recognized, but then staff turnover was scandalous these days, not at all like it used to be when you could count on seeing the same faces down through the years. He showed his teeth. "May I help you, madam?"

"Yes, I'm Mrs. Frank Lloyd Wright. It's my understanding that my husband is currently in residence here."

There was a flurry of activity at the door behind her,

bellhops, baggage, people sweeping in from the cold. A great fat man in a beautifully tailored wool suit sank into an armchair on the far side of the room and then immediately rose again with a roar of laughter to greet a smart young woman in a fox coat. There was a sound of music drifting in from somewhere, two bars of a popular tune, and someone out on the street was impatiently honking an automobile horn. The clerk gave her a blank look. "Mrs. Wright, did you say?"

"Mrs. Frank Lloyd Wright," she repeated, and the man checking in beside her at the long marble-topped counter gave her a covert glance, "and I have reason to believe that my husband is here under suspicious circumstances. Now, I'd like to have a look at the register, please."

"I'm afraid I can't allow that, madam. It's against our regulations."

"That is his automobile pulled up to the curb out there. That is *our* chauffeur at the wheel. Again, I ask you: let me see the register."

The man beside her—she had a vague impression of whiskers, starched collar, the flush of the alcoholic—was staring openly at her now. Had she raised her voice? She hadn't meant to. She'd told herself to stay calm at all costs, to avoid making a scene—or too big a scene at any rate—and here she was, losing control of herself. The clerk's eyes were locked on hers, dismissive eyes, eyes that reduced her to an aggrieved nonentity, a nuisance and nothing more, and she felt a wave of emotion rising in her throat as if it would choke her—she hadn't thought it would be this hard, this disorienting and tragic, but the fact of the matter was undeniable: Frank was upstairs with his paramour and she was left stranded at the desk like a beggar.

"I'm sorry," the clerk said, and all at once the wave broke in a flash of anger that consumed her like white phosphorous. She made a snatch for the register, his hands there, the cuffs of his shirt shooting back, and they were actually tugging on it like two children fighting over a bauble on the playground and somebody—was it she?—was shouting, "Call the manager! Call the manager!"

Yes, it was a scene—she'd created a scene and she wasn't sorry about it at all. She heard the clerk let out a yelp—a squeak, the sort of sound you'd expect from a rodent in a cage—and the register slipped from her grasp. People stared. All the ice of the place melted and then refroze again. And here was the manager coming up the corridor in a stiff-kneed jog, coattails flapping, eyes wild, a pale sprinkle of cake crumbs lodged in the corners of his mouth. "What is it?" he gasped, throwing the clerk an exasperated look. "What's all this, this"—he seemed to take her in then, his eyes making a quick revolution from her shoes to her skirts to her furs and jewelry and the rigid furious compression of her face—"confusion? Is there anything amiss, madam? May I be of assistance?"

Oh, they were watching now, everyone in the place, though the more discreet tried to cover themselves by making a pretense of consulting watches or newspapers or counterfeiting a conversation, but they weren't fooling her. She might just as well have been perched on the proscenium of the Apollo Theater, the curtain poised to come down, the revelatory words on her lips. "Yes," she said, teasing out the sibilance of that sematic little *s* till the room hissed and crepitated with it, "yes, you may." She paused to draw in a breath. "You can start by ringing up the police."

His eyes jumped round the room. He was terrified, whipped already, she could see that, his only desire to soften, placate, give in. There was the hotel's reputation to consider. The other guests. His own scrawny worthless neck. "The police?"

The fury came over her again, a surge of the blood and its secret hormones that had her trembling as she snatched off her glove and pointed a single accusatory finger at the clerk. "I want this man arrested."

"Please," the manager was saying, "let's just step into my office and I'm sure—"

"For aiding and abetting a crime in progress, a crime of venality, vice—and I'll have you arrested too—"

"Madam, please"—and was he going to touch her, was he going to dare reach for her arm?—"be reasonable. Whatever it is, we can rectify it, I'm sure, if you'll just give us the opportunity. In my office. Wouldn't you feel more comfortable in my office?"

She stepped back from him, jerked her arm free. "Don't you touch me," she hissed, and she was glowing, glowing. "My husband is up there, don't you understand?" She lifted her chin, forced her eyes to sweep the room, people turning away now, murmuring, embarrassed, caught in the act of eavesdropping, gaping, staring. "He's up there," she said, fighting to steady her voice even as the tears—real tears, true and spontaneous and blood-hot—erupted to sting her eyes and stain her cheeks, "up there . . . with his . . . with his *whore*."

By the time she swept down the stairs to the lobby of her own hotel an hour and a half later, she was as composed as could be expected under the circumstances. She'd had an opportunity to put something on her stomach—the oysters Rockefeller and a handful of crackers, and that was about all she could tolerate given the state of her nervous system—and she'd changed into something a bit more demure than she'd worn to the fray (a low-waisted calf-length dress in violet with emerald satin collar, cuffs and hem and a bow of the same color at her hips, set off by a broad-brimmed felt hat in a lovely pale green to bring out her eyes. And her scarab ring, of course. And her beads and lorgnette).* Her lawyer had restricted her to two champagne cocktails, as a calmative, and she'd

* Miriam was noted for the originality of her dress.

strictly avoided the pravaz—at least for the time being—because the point of this, the first press conference she'd given in years, was to produce an effect of fashionable languor combined with the wilting distress of the abandoned wife, and she understood that an excess of languor—or wilt—just might play against her.

For all that—and for all her experience of photographers during her years with Frank—the flash powder startled her so that for a moment she lost consciousness of where she was, the speech she'd mentally prepared vanishing along with the drift of white smoke.* She must have put out a hand to steady herself—blinded, absolutely blinded—because her lawyer, Mr. Jackson, an associate of Mr. Fake, took her by the elbow and whispered encouragement to her even as the next flash went off. "It's all right," he was saying, "this is fine, fine. Look aggrieved. That's right. Good."

When she came to herself she registered the faces ranged round her in a rough semicircle—eight or ten men, with their pencils poised—and she caught the reflected dazzle of the chandelier overhead and the pure gleaming expanse of the marble floors, the plush weave of the Oriental carpets and the exotic herbage of the potted palms, and felt a thrill run through her. She was the

* Magnesium oxide. Remember magnesium oxide? The famous photograph of myself and three other apprentices leaning over Wrieto-San's shoulder as he plied the tools of his trade was taken during the flashbulb era, of course, but I still have the photograph my father insisted I pose for in commemoration of my return to the United States some four years earlier. The picture shows an earnest, slim (I wish it were so now) young man in jacket and tie and formally lubricated hair who is about to experience a coughing fit as the cloud of magnesium dust engulfs him on a wayward gust off the San Francisco Bay. I believe I spat up white phlegm for a week.

focus here—the star, the cynosure—not Frank. These men were waiting for her, to hear what she had to say, to record and broadcast her words to the nation.

"I want to remark," she began, drawing in a breath so moist and deep it was as if she'd been underwater all this time and was only now coming to the surface, "how sad an occasion this is for me and how much I appreciate your coming here today." She paused, let her eyes rest on each face in succession. They were staring at her, rapt. No one moved. No one said a word. "And I'd like to make it clear no matter what my husband might say in contradiction, or how skillfully he might manage to twist the truth, that I never left him. He is my husband. My legally wedded and lawful husband in the eyes of God and man—and the true and shining love of my life."

One of the newspapermen, a boor in a cheap suit and an asymmetrical haircut, interrupted her: "I'm sorry to have to ask this, but we didn't know that you *were* married—weren't you both advocates for free love?"

She waved a hand in dismissal. "We were married in the most romantic moonlight ceremony anyone could imagine, even the greatest poets of the ages—at midnight, on the bridge at Taliesin. It was the crowning moment of my life."*

There was a pause while they scribbled, heads bent, pencils scraping.

* This was a private ceremony, in November of 1923. The reporter's confusion may allude to Miriam's comments to the press in 1915, shortly after it was discovered that she had moved into Taliesin as Wrieto-San's mistress. At that time she quite forcefully expressed her contempt for the institution of marriage ("Frank Wright and I care nothing for what the world may think. We are as capable of making laws for ourselves as were the dead men who made the laws by which they hoped to rule the generations after them").

“Still”—and she was in command now, absolutely, the thrill of vindication running through her like a new kind of drug—“there are some things a woman simply cannot abide no matter how faithful she may be.”

And now the room fell silent. Here was the real meat of the story, the scandal they were all waiting for. Very softly, in her steadiest voice, she explained that he had left her no recourse but to sue for divorce, in spite of all the love she held for him. He’d been cruel to her, had physically abused her—and here she began to falter, she couldn’t help herself, all her sorrow, all the humiliation of her position and the raw hurt of it pressing down on her like the weight of some medieval torture. “I went west,” she continued, and she had to pause again to gather herself, “for my health. On doctor’s orders. The pure dry air of . . . of Los Angeles . . . and then I come back to my husband only to find that he, that he—”

Mr. Jackson held an arm out to her—and what was he doing, patting her on the back, was that it?—and her voice thickened in her throat till she didn’t think she could go on, all those eyes locked on her, the man with the flash saying *All right, boys, ready, one more,* and there was that coruscating explosion of light all over again. “All I want,” she managed to say, “is what is . . . what is . . . rightfully mine.” Her chest began to heave, no holding back, not now, and suddenly she was sobbing, sobbing so hard she had to turn away and let Mr. Jackson help her to the nearest chair, a glass of water—“Will someone get her a glass of water!”—but she still had the strength to turn her face to them once more.

Her eyes were brimming, her lashes gone to paste. She couldn’t see their faces—they were just a blur to her—but something else rose up in her field of vision, some transient imagined presence, a figure out of a dream, gravid, round of abdomen, full of breast, smiling with the soft satisfaction of the Madonna, a false Madonna, a Russian Madonna, unwed and fucked, fucked, fucked, and she heard her voice lash out in a tinny yelp: "I want him back. I just want my husband back!"

That night, late, she sat up in her room and tried to filter out the sounds of the street below. She was too exhausted to read, too alive in her thoughts to sleep. Someone kept pacing the floor of the room above her. There were odd thumps in the walls, a mélange of voices murmuring somewhere, the drawn-out mechanical torment of the elevator down the hall—and was the operator playing on the cables with a horsehair bow just to drive her to distraction? Was it a plot? She didn't smoke—or hardly at all, not anymore, because Frank didn't approve, or hadn't approved—but she smoked now, one cigarette after another. She rose from the bed and went to the window, thinking a little fresh air might help.

For a long while she stood there at the open window, oblivious to the cold, the automobiles and delivery trucks tapping out a secret code below her, a language of squeals and rattles and the rising pitch of engines straining against the gear, and then there was the deluge of the trolley washing down the avenue like a tidal wave. A clanking, a banging, an assault. She turned to the comfort of her pravaz then—just left the window open behind her and drifted into the bathroom, where she kept her kit—for the second time that night. Over the past few days she'd gradually increased her usual dosage, and there was a danger in that, she knew it, but she was so fraught and torn and run-down she just couldn't help herself.

She sat on the edge of the bed and fanned back her robe to inject herself high up on the right thigh where the blemish—*la tache*—wouldn't show. And she was careful there too, because she'd known too many women in Paris who'd developed ulcers as a result of carelessness, repeatedly injecting themselves in a favorite spot, creatures of habit, their needles gone dull from use, their flesh ripe as rotten fruit. But tonight she needed comfort. Tonight was terrible. When she'd cried out to those hard men with their dog-eared pads and quivering pencils that she wanted him back, her husband, Frank, her man, her love, she hadn't known what she was saying, but in some part of her she knew it was true. He was her husband. They'd been in love—all those years they'd been in love, burning up with it, clinging to each other through the sweat-soaked nights in Tokyo, the sere clarity of Los Angeles, the icehouse of Wisconsin. He'd been gentle with her, he understood her, their temperaments equally matched—they were artists, artists together in defiance of the world and its conventions.

She lay back and closed her eyes and tried to think only those thoughts that brought her closer to him, but it was no use. There was that thumping, that clamor, footsteps in the hall, and the other Frank came back to her, the hateful one, the beast, the mocker and belittler, the cheat and fraud and womanizer. At some point she tried to get up to shut the window, shut out the noise, but the potion the bald little Mexican had mixed for her was just too potent to overcome and she slept on and on in a dreamless void till the sun was pushing through the curtains and all the noise was focused in a sharp peremptory banging at the door.

It was Mr. Fake's associate, Mr. Jackson—"Harold, call me Harold"—and he'd been worried about her. It was getting late. Could she come to the door?

Her voice was weak in her own ears, the voice of an invalid, an old woman croaking out her days in a rocker: "No, I'm afraid I can't. I . . . I'm just bathing and I won't be—what time did you say it was?"

"Twelve-thirty."

She pushed herself up from the bed, feeling cored-out, ashen, as if there were nothing left of her but a husk. And where were her slippers? Her robe? "I must have overslept, what with the journey, and the, the—"

He projected his voice, leaning into the crack where the door met the frame. "Have you seen the papers?"

She hadn't.

"Well, you've made a sensation. The press is on our side in this, no doubt about it—and you look magnificent in the photographs. Very proper and attractive, very put-upon. And they've printed just about everything you've said. Verbatim." There was a pause and she could hear him shuffling his feet, shifting something from one hand to the other—the papers, he had the papers with him. "You must see this," he was saying—or no, he was crowing, his voice ringing with triumph. "Won't you open up?"

She didn't respond. She'd begun to cramp again and she was thinking she had to eat something, a soft-boiled egg, toast, a cup of coffee, anything, because she wasn't feeling right, not at all, and the distance from the bed to the door might just as well have been a mile for all she was capable of. He shuffled his feet. Rattled the doorknob. "Mrs. Wright? Miriam—are you still there?"

"Yes, I'm here." *The papers. She was in the papers.*

He was saying something about meeting with her—soon, as soon as she was able, because time was of the essence, strike while the iron is hot, that sort of thing, but she wasn't listening. There was more, his voice pinched with the strain of talking through the crack of the door, and she didn't catch much of it, not that it mattered. *She was in the papers.* And then he came clear again, his parting words, stirring, redemptive, vengeful: "Because we're going to go after separate maintenance and full payment of legal fees and there isn't a doubt in my mind that we'll win. Not after this. Not after the show you've put on."

When he'd gone—footsteps fading down the hallway like the tread of an angel taking flight, her angel, Mr. Harold Jackson, Attorney at Law—she pushed herself up and went to the door. She looked through the peephole, listened a moment to be sure no one was present, then unlatched the door and bent to snatch up the newspapers. And it was all there, just as he'd said. She read through each of the articles twice and for a long while stared at her photograph—she did look charming and sad and *trés chic* too, and she'd have to clip it out and send it to Leora—and then she ordered up breakfast and began to think about what she might wear for her next press conference.

Five days later the newspapers ran another sort of article altogether, a simple birth announcement that had somehow been transmuted into the stuff of headlines, and she didn't even know about it, didn't even see it till late in the afternoon and then only because Leora called her long distance from Los Angeles. And then her daughter Norma called. And then Mr. Jackson. And then a man from the press, wanting her reaction, but by that time she'd got hold of the *Tribune* and the *Daily News* both and she cut the connection and left the phone off the hook.

She'd been eating a late lunch or early dinner or whatever you wanted to call it when Leora phoned and she'd been out earlier for a walk in the frozen air hoping the exercise would clear her head, but as it happened she'd felt utterly drained when she got back to the hotel and laid her cheek down on the pillow for a nap that must have stretched on for hours. She was exhausted, run-down, miserable. Because she wasn't sleeping well at night. Wasn't eating well either. And so she was in her rooms, staring numbly at a plate of *suprême de volaille* and stewed carrots when Leora's call came through.

"Oh, hon," Leora blurted without waiting for any of

the usual blandishments, and it was as if she were right there in the room with her. "I'm so sorry."

"Sorry? For what? What's happened?"

A pause, just to let her heart skip a beat. "Haven't you seen the newspapers?"

"No. Not today. Not yet. I was out walking and then I, well, I—why, what did they say?"

What they'd said was burned into her brain now, in eighteen-point type: DANCER GIVES BIRTH TO WRIGHT'S LOVE CHILD.* *Gives birth. Love child. Frank's love child.* Six pounds, seven ounces. A girl. They'd named her Iovanna. And what kind of name was that? Iovanna, Olgivanna, Russian names, names with treacly little foreign suffixes as if this were some suburb of Moscow—but this wasn't Moscow, not the last time she'd looked. This was Chicago, in the U.S.A. There was no Volga here, no windblown steppes and Bolshevik revolutions—and what was he thinking? What was Frank thinking?

Oh, she'd known it was coming—she'd been bracing for it since that weasel of a detective called to annihilate her afternoon, her holiday, her autumn, her winter, her year—and yet she'd never dreamed it would come to this, cheap headlines, cheap sensation, a mockery of everything she was in her deepest self. Everyone she knew would be laughing at her now, Maude Miriam Noel, wife of the adulterer, the woman who couldn't satisfy the great architect or even appease him, who couldn't give him a child because she was too old, because she was broken down, over the hill, cast out and abandoned. She was dirt. Lower than dirt. She was nothing.

Even as she flung the papers across the room and

* As will be seen below, the yellow press of the day came to refer to Wrieto-San and his "affinities" in a kind of shorthand nomenclature, so notorious were their affairs and so public the airing of their laundry, as the saying goes.

took up the first thing to hand—a vase, a hotel vase with an arrangement of dried flowers that infuriated her, that made her feel as if she were dried up and dead too—just for the satisfaction of seeing it explode against the near wall, she knew that the pravaz would give her no release, not today, not the way she was feeling. It took her no more than five minutes to see to her face in the mirror and wrap herself in her furs, and then she was downstairs and out on the street in the air that hit her like a dose of smelling salts. The whole world opened up then. The doorman. The cabbie. Streets, pigeons, a crust of snow. And where to? The hospital. The one named in the paper, where mother and child were reported to be doing well. And resting. Resting comfortably.

She'd show them rest, oh, yes, she would, and already she could picture it, another scene like the one in the hotel lobby, and let them come, let the reporters come. *I want to see the baby!*, she would scream until there was no one in all that towering edifice with its gleaming corridors and sheltered rooms who couldn't hear her loud and clear, *I want to see my husband's baby!*

CHAPTER 5: THE RICHARDSONS

There was a taint of antiseptic—of carbolic acid or rubbing alcohol or whatever it was—emanating from every corner of the room, suffusing the air, choking her till she felt she could barely breathe. The shades were drawn. There was a dull hum of electricity, lights flickering and brightening and flickering again. Infants mewled, trays rattled, someone somewhere was stewing tomatoes, beets, cabbage. And meat. Meat that stank of the pan and the icebox and the slaughterhouse. She kept asking the nurse to open the window and the nurse kept telling her to lie back and rest and not to worry herself—rest, that was what she needed. "Just close your eyes now," the nurse whispered in her liminal tones. "You want to regain your strength, don't you? For the sake of your baby? And your husband?"

Olgivanna couldn't help smiling. Her husband was the last person she wanted to see, but how would the nurse know that? Unless she read the papers. But of course she did read the papers. They all did and they all knew that Iovanna—Pussy, her Pussy*—the most perfect and exquisite infant in the world, in the history of the world, was born out of wedlock, an illegitimate child, a bastard, a bastard for

* Precise derivation of the nickname unknown. A Montenegrin endearment?

people to sneer at and revile. Olgivanna didn't read the papers. And she didn't want her husband. Her *ex*-husband. She wanted Frank, but Frank was working in his studio and he'd promised to be back to see her in the evening, yet wasn't it evening now? And why was it so stifling in here and why, why, why couldn't anyone throw open the window or even raise it an inch, half an inch, anything—anything to dissipate the staleness of the air? "Nurse!" she called out, and she tried to sit up but felt nauseous, felt weak, and let her head sink back into the pillow.

Later—how much later she couldn't say, but it seemed to be darker now, didn't it?—the nurse appeared at the door with Iovanna. Her daughter. Her newborn. The light of her life, the reason for all of this, for this room with the flowers Frank had sent over, a private room with a window and a reek of carbolic acid, and the weakness she felt too. She could barely lift her arms to accept the baby, the bundle of her, light as a thought and yet heavy suddenly, impossibly heavy, miniature hands clenching and flying open again, and then the feel of the suction at her breast, a long sweet release that brought her up out of the bed and the room and out into the ambient night, soaring.

In her dream she flew high over the embracing roofs of Taliesin, the baby clutched in her arms, and there was Frank, dwindling below her, and he was shouting to her, his hands cupped to his mouth, *Look out, watch out, be careful* . . . And then there was a noise, a sudden sharp thump and rattle, something clattering in the hall, a woman's voice rising up out of a confusion of voices, and what was it? "I'm sorry, ma'am"—her nurse, Alice, straining against a whisper—"but visiting hours are over."

"Don't be ridiculous. Get out of my way!"

"I'm sorry, but— Dinah, Dinah, would you come here, please?"

"Which room? I insist you tell me which room—"

"Please, please, ma'am, won't you hold your voice down? The infants are— Dinah, will you please tell this lady that we just cannot accept—"

Pussy began to stir, kicking out her legs in a spasm even as her eyes flashed open, two pinpoints of light in the muted darkness of the room. She wasn't fussing, not yet, just lying there orienting herself, awakening to the world once again. Olgivanna's eyes went to the door. Which stood ajar—or half-open, actually, because the nurses liked to be within earshot in the event of an emergency, but this wasn't an emergency, was it?

The voices rose, tangled, fell back again. There was a brief tap dance of heels on the linoleum flooring, renewed protests, and then the sounds receded down the hall in the opposite direction. Though she wasn't feeling particularly alert—it was as if she'd been drugged, and why couldn't she regain her strength, what was wrong with her?—she had a moment of clarity that allowed a single pulse of alarm to flash through her. What if it was Miriam? Frank's wife. Miriam. The madwoman. He'd warned her about how irrational Miriam could be, how violent and unpredictable.* And she could still hear the tortured cry that had come at her over the telephone wire, that choked mad searing expostulation that was like no human sound she'd ever heard. She drew Iovanna to her and held her breath.

Suddenly there was a clatter of footsteps, bold and rapid, hurrying down the hall toward her. She heard

* She'd allegedly been jailed for a brief period in Paris after attacking her ex-lover with a knife, and from the beginning she made it known to Wrieto-San that she was not to be trifled with. She kept a pistol. And she firmly believed that her scarab ring was invested with the power to reconcile her accounts in the supernatural sphere, almost in the way of the Voodooists of Haiti and New Orleans.

Alice cry out "Stop!" in a breathless gasp and then there were more footsteps and a man's voice was repeating the injunction even as the door of the room across from hers was flung open and a woman entered her line of vision, all skirts and hat and angry flailing shoulders. A thought darted in and out of her head—should she try to hide the baby, tuck her in under the bedclothes, the pillows, slip her down on the floor beneath the bed?—and then the door flew back and there she was, Miriam, her face bloated and red, her eyes set close as an animal's, Miriam in the flesh, her mouth twisting round the only word she could summon: "You!" she shouted. "You!"

By the time Frank arrived—out of breath, his hair windblown, his face drained—the danger had passed, or the immediate danger, at any rate. The orderly had seen to that. Miriam was gone now, long gone, ushered out the door in a whirlwind of threats and insults, and the corridors were hushed as in the aftermath of some natural disaster, but Olgivanna could see her still. Feel her. Feel her hate and envy and fear radiating out of the very atmosphere itself. There'd been a moment of suspended time as the door struck the wall and rebounded in slow motion, this woman, Frank's *wife*, poised on the threshold of the room, her features working through the shadings of her emotions, a moment in which Olgivanna, as weak as she was, as terrified and humiliated, could see into her, the abandoned wife come face-to-face with her successor, her bugbear, the succubus that had stolen her husband away. She felt something move inside her. Not aggression or the will to defend herself—though there was that if it came to it—but something akin to pity.

It was short-lived.

Because even as the orderly vaulted into the frame, even as he seized Miriam by the arm and Miriam turned on him like a cat tossed in a bag, the vile words began to spew out. "Slut!" she shrieked, jerking away from him and thrusting her face back into the room. "Vampire! Whore! You leave my husband alone!" But then Alice was there, slipping past them to secure the door and press her weight against the impervious slab of oak while Iovanna, compromised on the third day of her inchoate life, began to cry with a sharp sudden intake of breath, her face suffused with blood and her hands grasping at the air as if she could possess it.

"I know you're weak," Frank was saying. He was pacing the room, five steps to the right and pivot, five steps to the left and pivot again. "It was a difficult birth. You need your rest. But I can't let this sort of thing go on—it's just too risky. And the newspapers—"

"She has frightened me. And the baby. The baby has started crying."

"Damn her. Damn that woman."

The bedclothes pressed down on her like the lid of a tomb. She'd never felt wearier in her life. "She is your wife, Frank. But how could she be? How could you have *loved* her?"

He didn't come to her, didn't take her hand or put his arm around her or smooth her hair away from her face—he just kept pacing, and the question, the question of love, then and now, went unanswered. All at once the room seemed to shrink, dwindling before her eyes. She felt as if she were in a prison cell, and who was the jailer? He was. Frank was. "She's vengeful," he said, "that's all. A spurned woman—and she was the one who left me, let me remind you . . . But we've got to get you out of here, which is why I telephoned to your brother."

"My brother?"

"It's all arranged. First thing in the morning, hours before Miriam or her spies are even out of bed, we're taking you to the train—on a stretcher, if need be. I've reserved a compartment for us, and Vlada* will meet us at the other end, in New York."

And so, like thieves, like refugees, like cowards, they stole away in the dark.

At some unfathomable hour a pair of orderlies appeared with a stretcher, as promised, along with the nurse Frank had engaged to look after the baby. Olgivanna remembered waking to the shuffling of feet and the sudden glare of the lamp at her bedside. And to Frank. He was leaning over her, rumpled and worn from a night spent dozing in the straight-backed chair in the corner, and Svetlana was there too, standing awkwardly in the doorway with her suitcase and a new toy, looking somber. Or frightened, she looked frightened, the poor thing, uprooted yet again. Olgivanna held out her arms. "Darling, come here," she whispered, her own voice sounding strange in her ears. Svetlana hesitated. She was going to be difficult, Olgivanna could see that. She patted the bed beside her. "Come on. It's all right."

"Olya, it's getting late," Frank said.

"Come on, Svet—it's only me. I'm fine. I'm going to be fine. Don't worry." Still nothing. "Do you not want to see your baby sister?"

"No."

And somehow, there she was—Pussy—enfolded in the nurse's arms, and who was this woman, this girl, thin-lipped and slouching, to whom Frank had entrusted their daughter? "Give her to me," she demanded, and the girl looked to Frank and Frank nodded, and her daughter, already setting up a thin wail of distress, was handed over like a parcel from the grocery. "You see?" she said, holding up the baby for Svetlana. "You see how tiny she

* Vladimir Lazovich, a shipping agent living in Queens, New York. Olgivanna's brother. Not to be confused with Vlademar, her former husband.

is? Her little fingers and toes? She is going to need her big sister to look after her—do you not want to look after her?"

"No."

From Frank: "Olya."

"We are going to Uncle Vlada, honey, for Christmas. Christmas in New York—will that not be charming?"

She knew her daughter. Knew her moods. The answer to this and all other questions posed at this hour in this place would be exclusively negative. The child didn't even bother to respond. She just clamped her lips and looked away. Frank stepped in then and began giving orders—he was good at that—and the nurse took Iovanna back from her and the men helped her onto the stretcher and the corridor yawned and narrowed before her. There was the elevator, the night rearing over her, a breath of air that was like a taste of heaven compared to the medicated aridity of the hospital, and then they were at the station and in their compartment and Svetlana came to her to lay her head on her shoulder for a good cry and at some point the car lurched and they were moving, moving again.

For Frank's part, there was no turning back. Olya wasn't well—you didn't have to be a medical man to see that. She was a young woman, younger than either of his daughters, and yet as she lay there in the shifting compartment, the baby and Svetlana asleep beside her, he had a glimpse of the way she would look as the years fragmented and fell away, and it startled him. The softness had gone out of her face, replaced by the rigidity you saw in the very old, the faintest lines tracing the hard angles of her face, her color faded, her hair thin and lusterless. She was anemic. She was exhausted. Frightened. Upset. He'd been talking to her in a low voice over the rattle of the rails, trying to keep her spirits up as the baby fidgeted and Svetlana cried herself to sleep, but finally he realized she'd drifted off, her breathing harsh and catarrhal, a single globe of moisture caught like a jewel in her right nostril.

He felt a stab of guilt.* This was a mess and no two ways about it. He should never have moved her into Taliesin—not till Miriam's hash was settled. He knew better. Knew from hard experience, and yet what had experience taught him? Nothing. He saw what he wanted and he took it. That was his nature. That was his right. And here she was, the object of his desire, pale and wasted and with a thin stripe of saliva painted across her cheek, wedged into a narrow railway berth with two needy children—a child herself—and no place to call home.

There was a sudden flurry of conversation in the passage outside the door—a man's voice, a woman's, fraught with venereal undertones and the giddiness of travel—and when they'd passed, he glanced back at Olgivanna and felt a kind of impatience rising in him. What was the matter with her? Was she somehow frailer than he'd imagined? He didn't remember Kitty's birthings as being as hard as this—and she bore him six children.†

But he was exhausted himself. The wheels clattered

* For Wrieto-San an uncharacteristic emotion.

† Catherine "Kitty" Tobin Wright (1871–1959), Wrieto-San's first wife. They married, against all sense and advice, when he was twenty-one and she just out of high school. The children—Lloyd, John, Catherine, David, Frances and Llewellyn—came in rapid succession, like plums dropping from a tree. By all accounts, Wrieto-San seemed bewildered by them. It is unlikely that he would have given much thought or consideration to Catherine's pregnancies, beyond the obvious financial and architectural exigencies to which they gave rise.

on the tracks and he felt his stomach sink. He realized he hadn't eaten since the night before. He checked his watch. It was quarter past nine in the morning, the train rolling through open countryside now, and though things were desperate, things were terrible and getting worse, the sight of the neat farmhouses and the solid red barns with their quilts of hay and the firewood stacked outside the kitchen door cheered him. He thought he would get up and fetch the nurse to come look after the baby and then make his way to the dining car to put something on his stomach, eggs and flapjacks, a slice of ham, gravy, fried potatoes, but he lingered, watching over Olgivanna and the children as they drew in air and expelled it, one breath after another, in the soft descending rhythms of sleep.

What he hadn't told her, not yet, was that they couldn't go home to Taliesin, even after their exile at her brother's, because Miriam was on the attack like some sort of turbaned and bejeweled Harpy flapping through the air with her claws drawn and her jaws flung open in an otherworldly shriek of outrage, no quarter given or expected. Each day it was something new. She wasn't content to harass a sick woman from her hospital bed. Oh, no, not Miriam. She went straight to the immigration authorities and compounded the mischief by filing a complaint to have Olgivanna deported as an undesirable alien. The affidavit named Olga as a foreign national who had come to Taliesin—to *her* home, Miriam's home—under false pretexts, masquerading as a servant when in fact she was her husband's "sweetheart." His inamorata. His whore.

He felt his heart clench with hate. All he could think of was Miriam, how he'd let her come into his life when his guard was down, how foolish he'd been, how weak and deluded. His mood soured. The farms began to look uglier, less tidy, in need of paint and upkeep. For a long while he watched them loom and vanish amidst the barren skeletons of the trees and the frozen bogs and the shrubs dead to their roots. And he didn't get up for breakfast or for coffee or the nurse or anything else, but just sat there till the fields ran continuous and everything beyond the windows became a blur.

If the journey was a trial, arriving was worse. Queens was grim, a regular horror of a place, and Vlada's apartment grimmer. But no official came knocking at the door, no agent from Immigration or newspaperman or spy of Miriam's, and after the first few days Frank began to relax his guard. His lawyers had instructed him to lie low for a period, to travel, keep out of sight until matters could be arranged with the immigration authorities and the divorce negotiations concluded, and here he was, in exile in Queens, New York, frustrated and angry—and what was worse, Olgivanna showed no sign of improvement. She wasn't eating. Her brow seemed warm to the touch. The baby clung to her, colicky and restive, draining her of what little vitality she had, and Svetlana threw one tantrum after another. And her skin—it was so pale it frightened him. All he could think of was the hide of a dogfish he'd once seen preserved in a jar of formalin, bleached round its folds and grinning its grin of death.

And talk of boxes within boxes: the rooms were close, stifling. They stank of whatever Vlada's wife was continually boiling up in a battered pot in the kitchen, borscht or *bozbash* or whatever it was, and it maddened him. Just to get away, to get out of the hermetic box of the apartment and do something—breathe, walk, think—he found himself taking the train into Manhattan each day with Vlada and wandering the streets, sketching, or slipping into the public library to write up his impressions of the city, all the while shielding his face with his scarf and wide-brimmed hat, striving for anonymity.*

It was Vlada who suggested Puerto Rico. Olgivanna needed warmth, sun, the clean white sand and endless horizon—and Florida wouldn't do. They could still track her down in Florida, but in Puerto Rico no one would know them, no one would care. Even better: Puerto Rico was an American protectorate and you didn't need a passport to travel there. Vlada made the arrangements. Passage for two adults and two children—Mr. and Mrs. Frank Richardson and family—out of New York bound for San Juan. They were moving again—and he'd never acquired his sea legs, sick in his stomach all the way down, sicker than Olya—but each hour of each day the winter fell away behind them and the sun rose higher in the sky.

They put up at the Coamo Inn,† which featured hot-sulfur springs and endless plates of beans and rice and *platanos* graced with a skewer of marinated goat or pork, they bathed in the mornings and took long drives in the afternoons, and each day he joked and paraded up and down the patio in his bathing costume, keeping up the pretense that this was just what Olgivanna needed. Was she improving? Not visibly. Not that he could see. He hired a woman to look after the baby, had their meals brought to them in their rooms, read aloud

* This must have been especially trying. Wrieto-San was the world's greatest self-promoter (with the possible exception of P.T. Barnum), and to walk down a street or step into a room without broadcasting the news was pure poison to him.

† One can't help wondering where Wrieto-San came up with the funds for this expedition, given that he was in debt for the rebuilding of Taliesin and Miriam's upkeep at the Southmoor Hotel, not to mention legal fees. In all of 1926, he built only two very minor commissions.

to her and Svetlana at night. It was restful, almost like a vacation. But it wasn't a vacation, it was exile, and they both knew it.

Beneath the shimmering surface, beneath the glaze of the banana plants, the primavera aflame with blood-red blooms and the nocturnal perfume of the jasmine, the place was corrupt in the way of the tropics, deeply wanting, a reverse image of Wisconsin. At night the mosquitoes descended like a black rain. There were open sewers. Emaciated dogs skulked in the shadows and roaches the size of field mice clung to the ceilings and clattered beneath the bed. "We are living like the Gypsies, Frank," Olgivanna kept telling him, something harsh in her tone he'd never registered before, the tan on her cheeks like rouge on a corpse, her limbs thin as the stalks of sugarcane greening in the fields, "and I cannot have one degree of peace until I am home where I belong. And Svetlana—what of Svetlana? She must have a proper life. She must have schooling—you can see that. And this is no country for her. It is a poor place. It saddens me to have to be here and see these degraded people in their rags."

"This is their home," he countered, though he privately agreed with her. If only Puerto Rico could exist, like a kind of paradise, without the people. "This is the only thing they know."

Her voice was thick, a lashing of blunted consonants. "Yes, but I do not want to know it."

They lasted a month. On the final day, the day before they booked passage to New York and from there to Chicago, Madison and Spring Green, come what may, he was on his way back from the plaza when he was startled to see a man on horseback leaning forward to shout something unintelligible into the low casement windows of the hotel kitchen. He was very dark-skinned, this man—almost black—and for one crashing irremediable moment the image of Carleton* came into his mind, Carleton as he would have been in middle age, and he pulled up short. There was a rising fecal odor. A pair of electric-green dragonflies settled in a puddle and chased away again. The man's horse rocked in place, so twisted and starved it was like the ghost of a horse, its eyes vacant and its coat dulled with the dust of travel, and he saw now that the man had something cradled in one arm—a chicken bound up in a scrap of torn red cloth. "*Gallina,*" the man was shouting, "*se vende una gallina. Muy barata.*"

There was the sound of clattering pans from the kitchen. No one responded.

If it hadn't been for the light, the way it etched the geometry of the near wall and sliced into the angles of the outbuilding as if to create something new altogether, something fluid and independent of concrete block and stucco, something created entirely by the sun in that moment, he would have moved on—he was in a hurry, arrangements to be made, suitcases to be packed, lawyers to be consulted and retained by wire and some sort of lunch served up for Olya and Svet—but he stayed, fascinated by the play of movement and shadow and the strangeness of the scene. It was then that one of the waiters from the hotel came hurtling out the door and began berating the man in a high strained voice. The man immediately slumped over in the saddle as if he'd been punched in the stomach. "*Barata,*" he pleaded. "*Barata.*"

"What is it?" Frank said, addressing the waiter. "What does he want?"

The waiter was a round-faced man in a white jacket, sweating titanically round his soiled collar, and he'd been sweating since they arrived and would go on sweating after

* Julian Carleton, 1888(?)–1914. Manservant, Barbadian, murderer. See below.

they'd left. "It's nothing, Don Frank," he said, giving an elaborate shrug. "He comes down from the mountains, that is all"—and he pointed a finger over the red-tiled roof to the hazy crags of the central cordillera, at least ten miles distant. Another shrug. He gave the man on horseback an embittered look. "To sell this chicken that has less meat on its bones than a pigeon, a sparrow even."

"But why? Why would he come all this way just to sell one chicken?"

Both men fixed their eyes on him now.

"Because he has nothing. Because he needs the money."

Suddenly he felt very dense. He stood there in the glare of the sun, picturing the one-room shack thrown together without benefit of blueprints, without nails or hammers or any tool but a worn machete, the porous roof, the rude furniture, no electricity, no water, no glass for the solitary window and not a single object of beauty anywhere in sight. "Tell him I will buy his chicken," he said.

"You? What do you want with it?"

"Just tell him."

The money was exchanged, a few coins, the man's hand fluttering delicately against his own. And then he had the thing in his grasp, the rag over its eyes, the feel of the withered reptilian feet against his knuckles—a pitiful thing, a runt, half the size of one of Taliesin's birds—and immediately he tried to give it back, thrusting the warm bundle up across the sweated neck of the horse, but the man wouldn't take it. He just held up his spanned fingers and open palm, then nodded and turned the horse back down the road.

Early the next morning, before the sun had climbed up out of the sea to cut away the shadows and illuminate the shanties in the hills, Frank took Olgivanna and the children and caught the boat for home.

* * *

So she had to endure another trip, reverse logic, running to instead of from, the sea mutating from a fragile turquoise to verdigris to a deep metallic gray as they steamed back into winter, Svetlana pestering her with her interminable questions—"Where're we going, Mama? Uncle Vlada's? Where're we now, do you think? Can I have a sweet?"—and then the thundering headache of the steel wheels pounding over the icebound rails all the way to Spring Green, Wisconsin, the Richardsons peregrinating as if it were their profession. Or fate. There was the car at the station. The familiar road. The river, the bridge, the lake. The long penstroke of the walls and the flourish of the roofs. Were they home? Were they really home?*

At first she felt relief, the interior opening up to her with its familiar smells—brass polish, the wax Frank used on the woodwork, linseed oil, the sourness of the ash spread cold across the stones of the hearth all this time and a lingering hint of the charred remains beneath the floors—her bed, her things, the kitchen and its promise of homemade meals and bread and cakes and cookies, cookies like the ones she'd baked with Dione, Sylvia and Nobu, but by the time she rose the next morning, she could feel nothing but the heaviness of the place. Mrs. Taggertz reappeared to do the cooking; a skeleton staff moped round the corridors. They were burning green wood. Everything was out of place. She wanted to get up and take charge, but she was weak and ill and all the

* Of course, Wrieto-San was the apostle of home, his revolutionary Prairie houses built round a central hearth and the rooms open to one another so as to provide an integrated familial space. "A true home is the finest ideal of man," he famously pronounced in *An Autobiography* (but concluded the maxim, rather schizophrenically, I'm afraid, with this: "and yet—well to gain freedom I asked for a divorce").

color seemed to have gone out of the world. And Frank—he wasn't himself either, stealing around like a burglar in his own house, peering out the windows as if he expected a cordon of sheriffs, marshals and federal agents to come marching up the drive at any moment. What good were the windows, what good were the views, when all they did was make you feel naked?

"You can't be seen," Frank told her the day after they'd arrived, "not till this is settled," and immediately went off to consult with his lawyers.

Then there came a morning in April when the sun edged up over the southern flank of the house to warm the stones of the courtyard and she moved a chair outside to sit beneath the awakening oaks and read to Svetlana. If her daughter couldn't go to school—if *she* had to be kept out of sight too—then at least Olgivanna was determined to educate her in her own way. Each day there would be dance, art, music, readings from the great books in Frank's library—the American poets, *Wilhelm Meister, The Man Without a Country,* Victor Hugo's *Notre-Dame de Paris*—both of them improving their command of the spoken and written language. And Svetlana was very good about it, an angel—she really did seem to want to learn. Or maybe she was just bored, and who could blame her? She felt the tension too—they were all waiting for something indefinable, a point of release that seemed as if it would never come.

The housekeeper had just brought them each a cup of hot chocolate. The grass was greening on the hill behind them and there were birds everywhere, their chirrups and catcalls dampening the eternal thump of construction from the far end of the house. Frank was down there somewhere, his shirtsleeves rolled up, banging away with Billy Weston and the others. She handed the book to Svetlana. "Now you read—here—the last stanza."

"'This is the poem of the air,'" Svetlana began in a

soft aspirated voice, "'Slowly in silent syllables recorded; / This is the secret of despair. / Long in its—'"

"Yes," she said. "Go on."

But Svetlana was no longer looking at the page. She was staring over her mother's shoulder, her tongue caught in the corner of her mouth. Olgivanna turned to see a stranger with an oversized satchel striding up the drive as if he'd been invited, as if he belonged here, and her first thought was that he must be one of Frank's lawyers, but what lawyer would wear a pair of trousers as tight as a high school sophomore's? Or a polka-dot vest? Or go without a hat?

"Olga," he called out in a voice meant to be hearty and winning, a booster's voice, his lips giving shape to an automatic smile, his right hand flapping over one shoulder in a simulacrum of greeting. Before she could rise from the chair, he was on them. "No need to get up"—he winked, shrugged, tugged at his sleeves—"I won't be a minute."

She set down the teacup. Her hands went to her hair. And what was he—a salesman? A curiosity seeker? And how did he know her name?

It all became clear in the next moment. He was digging into his satchel like some sort of deranged postman and she could see that he was trembling, his hands shaking, a twitch settling into his shoulders, until finally he produced a bundle of newspapers and laid them in her lap.

"Name's Wallace, from the *Trib.* You've seen these?"

She looked to her daughter, but Svetlana gave her nothing. She could feel the color rise to her face, hot blood burning there with her shame, because that was what it was—shame. The newspapers bore dates from November through December—DEPORT OLGA? IT CANNOT BE DONE, WRIGHT ASSERTS—and then there was a more recent one, from February, the leaf turned down to a quarter-page photograph of herself, in a silk gown and her platinum filigree earrings and looking away from the lens as if she had something to hide, and under it the legend: ACCUSED. And, in smaller type: *Olga Milanoff, to Whom Mrs. Frank Wright Charges Husband Fled.*

Frank had kept the papers from her. They would only upset her, he said. It was nothing, he said. It would blow over. It was nothing. When there she was, for all the world to see. And gloat over. Like some freak in a sideshow.

"What we want," the man was saying, "is your side of the story."

WRIGHT FLEES TO DODGE U.S. LAW, SAYS WIFE. *Claims Architect Is with Russian Danseuse.*

He was chewing gum, his teeth working round the remnants of his smile. "Do you have anything to say? For the record?"

CHAPTER 6: MIRIAM AT THE GATES

The windows were flung open wide to the sun, the curtains bowing with the sweet breeze coming in off the lake, and Miriam felt very settled, very content, as she sat at the escritoire the hotel had provided for her, writing. In the past week she'd gone through nearly a hundred sheets of fine mouldmade kid-finish paper, with deckled edges and matching envelopes, and had just that morning called down to the stationer's to place her order for another hundred, these to be embossed with her initials: MMNW, Maude Miriam Noel Wright. Twice now she'd had to get up to rub hand cream over the second joint of her middle finger, where a callus had begun to develop as if she were some sort of grind, a nail-bitten secretary or bloodless law clerk who never saw the light of day, but she felt strong and her hand barely trembled over the paper. She'd had breakfast sent up to the room—coffee and a bun, nothing more—and then allowed the pravaz to take the tension out of her shoulders and free her hands for the day's work.

She was writing letters—angry, slanderous, denunciatory letters—and addressing them to anyone she could think of who might take an interest in her situation. She wrote to her husband's creditors, to the Bank of Wisconsin and all his clients—past, present and prospective—to the newspapers, her lawyers, and to him, most of all to him.

He was a scoundrel, a fraud, that was what she wanted the world to know, and she would be damned if she would live out of a suitcase like a—a *carpetbagger*—while he paraded around in luxury with his *danseuse.* Her bill had been owing now for more than two months and the people at the desk had begun to give her insolent looks—and that she should have to endure such looks, she, his lawful wife, was unconscionable. Especially in light of the fact that the Dane County Superior Court had ordered him to pay her attorneys' fees and per diem expenses while the divorce was being contested and he most emphatically was not living up to his end of the bargain. What's more, she wrote, she was being threatened with eviction if the account wasn't settled, and where would she go then?

She was in the middle of an urgent plea to the governor of Wisconsin, weighing a question of diction (should she use the term "blackguard" to describe her husband or did it sound too antiquated?; she wanted to call him a "heel," because that was what he was, a heel and a son of a bitch, but then women of her class didn't stoop to such language, not in letters to the governor, at any rate) when the telephone rang.

Her attorney, Mr. Fake, was on the other end of the line. "Mrs. Wright, is that you?" He had a low, considered voice, deeply intimate, as if he'd been born to collusion.

"Yes," she returned, "I'm here," and she couldn't help adding a note of asperity. "And I'm doing as well as can be expected under the circumstances. The looks I'm getting—"

"Well, that's why I'm calling. There's been no movement on their side, none at all, we're just simply deadlocked, and I think I may have a solution for you—"

She held her breath. This was what she wanted to hear—tactics, movement, action, her forces gathering for the assault. "Yes?" she said.

"There is simply no reason I can think of for you to have to continue living hand to mouth in some hotel when Taliesin remains community property. Taliesin is your rightful and legal home and I really do believe that if you were to move back in—"

"Move *back*?" She was incensed at the thought of it, all those pastures reeking of dung, the dreary vistas opening up to yet more pastures mounded with dung, the yokels, the insects.

"What I'm trying to say is that it might just force the issue."

"But he's there. With *her*."

"Precisely."

All at once the image of Taliesin rose before her in such immediacy she might have been staring at a photograph. That yellow place on the hill—or *of* the hill, as Frank would say with all the pomposity of his ladies-of-the-club tones—that palace, that monument to himself. Oh, the idea warmed her. Taliesin wasn't his to do with as he pleased—it belonged to both of them. Equally. That was what community property meant, the very definition of it. And if she'd been willing to allow him the use of it till the fair value of the estate was ascertained and they could make an equitable division of property, now she saw what a fool she'd been. How dare he try to exclude her when his prize breeding bitch was installed there, living in all the luxury he could afford her, sleeping in *their* bed, in *their* bedroom, commanding the place like some sort of upstart queen out of a Shakespeare play, Lady Macbeth herself?

"All right," she said, crossing her legs and leaning forward to reach for a cigarette, "and how do you propose I go about it?"

A pause. Then the soft creeping tones, as smooth as kid leather: "Well, I've been thinking that you just might want to consider announcing a press conference."

They all gathered in the lobby like dogs early the next morning, dutiful dogs with their teeth sharpened and a smell of the meat wagon on the air, and she held herself erect, struggled briefly with her face—with her mouth and chin and the emotion welling up like a geyser there because this was her life, her very life she was fighting for—and let them all know how Frank Lloyd Wright had betrayed and abused her and how he was living in defiance of a court order with his foreign concubine in the house that was as much hers as his and how she was facing eviction from her modest rooms even as she stood there before them. "If my husband continues to defraud me, and I'm sorry to put it in such strong terms, but that's what it amounts to"—she'd meant to pause here for dramatic effect, but now, in the heat of the moment, she rushed on instead—"I'm afraid I'll have no resort but to sell off my jewelry, the prints we collected together in Japan, the jade necklace and earrings given to me as a keepsake by Baron Ōkura* himself, my screens and shawls and the little inlaid rosewood tables that are practically the only things I have left of my home—just to pay my bills, my own meager upkeep, while he spares himself nothing."

Her eyes were luminous, moist. She couldn't seem to feel her feet, though she must have been standing on them. She had a sudden vivid recollection of her school days, Mrs. Thompson's elocution class, the air sleepy

* Baron Kishichirō Ōkura, 1882–1963. Playboy, hotelier, motorcar enthusiast. As president of the Imperial Hotel and son of the head of the investment group formed to fund its construction (Baron Kishichirō Ōkura, the elder, 1837–1928), he was instrumental in awarding the commission to Wrieto-San. I met him twice, at receptions my father gave in Tokyo. He was a sleek, chillingly handsome man who favored Western dress and was interested in two subjects only, as far as I could ascertain: single-malt scotch whiskey and very fast automobiles.

with the scent of magnolia and she driving home her point about Tennyson's use of the heroic simile with such force that the entire class came back to life and Margaret Holloway, the most popular girl in the school, gave her a look of such undisguised admiration from the second row left that the glow of the moment had stayed with her all these years. "I don't know," she said finally, steadying herself, "that I won't be thrown out into the street." But was this the moment for the photograph? Yes, and she posed for the flash before delivering the kicker:* that she was left with no choice but to return to her rightful home—and that she intended to do so that very day.

"Mrs. Wright!" a reporter sang out, and she turned her eyes to him, a thin man in a gray suit with liverish eyes and hair that faded away from his brow in a pale blond crescent. "Can you give us some idea of your itinerary?"

They watched her, these hounds of the press, ravenous, while she put a hand to her bosom and let a little Southern molasses accumulate in the lower reaches of her voice, on familiar ground now, the lady in distress—and she was in distress, she was, and they ought to recognize it, the self-serving sons of bitches. "Oh, I just don't know. I really am all but indigent, I'm afraid." And then the little dig she couldn't suppress: "My husband may be able to afford a fine motor or the price of a first-class rail ticket, but I really am just as poor as a church mouse."

Five minutes later, as Mr. Jackson led her to the ele-

* I can't speak for the authenticity of this usage. I have my doubts that the term was commonly employed in the 1920s, except perhaps among votaries of the game of poker—I certainly don't remember having heard or used it in conversation myself—but O'Flaherty-San assures me of its accuracy. Of course, he wasn't born until 1941. In a place called Tootler's Falls, Virginia.

vator (Mr. Fake had had to excuse himself—he was in court that morning), the reporter caught up with her. "Pardon me, ma'am," he said, nodding to Mr. Jackson, and she was thinking only of her pravaz, her nerves thoroughly jangled by the strain of the whole business, "but I was struck by what you had to say back there—you've had a pretty punk deal and no two ways about it—and I wondered if I might be able to help?"

She paused to take a good look at him, his jacket open now to reveal a fawn vest stippled with polka dots, the tight trousers hiked up over his glaring tan boots, and how old was he—twenty-five, thirty? Mr. Jackson didn't say a word. Mr. Jackson was a friend of the press, a very good friend. She decided to be bemused. "And how do you propose to do that?"

"Well, listen—I'm Wallace, of the *Trib*? Mr. Jackson can vouch for me"—another nod for Jackson, which Jackson accepted and returned with an almost imperceptible dip of his chin—"and it just happens that me and my wife were planning on driving up to Baraboo this morning because her mother's been having trouble with her feet and we'd be pleased if you'd—"

"Sure," Jackson said. "I don't see why not." He was staring at her now, calculating, and she didn't especially like the look he was giving her. "What do you think, Mrs. Wright? It might be interesting if this fellow and his wife were able to help you out here, don't you think?"

"That's right," the reporter said. "Myra and I'd be more than happy to do anything we could. And Mr. Jackson can vouch for me, right, Harold?"

At least it was a sedan. At least there was that. The reporter drove, and his wife—pregnant with twins, it seemed, or maybe it was triplets—sat beside Miriam in the backseat while another man from the newspaper, whose name flew in and out of her head three or four times in the course of the morning and well into the afternoon, sat up front. He was the photographer, or so she gathered, and that was the only thing of significance about him. The roads, of course, were execrable, and the motorcar's coils or springs or whatever they were didn't seem to function in any capacity whatever so that for the entire drive she was thrown from one end of the seat to the other like a rag doll, and the wife—Myra—had to cling to her to keep from being flung out the window herself. Conversation was glacial. They passed through two thunderstorms, stopped twice at filling stations, once for sandwiches in Madison and once in the godforsaken precincts of Mazomanie, where she felt an urgent need to visit the washroom.

All four of them got out of the car there—the pretense of Baraboo, if that was what it was, had long since been abandoned: they'd gone west out of Madison on a road she knew all too well and no one had a said a word about the presumptive mother and her podiatric crisis—and the two men had a good stretch and made a show of examining the tires while she and Myra used the facilities at the railroad depot. A brass plaque on the wall inside the door of the depot informed her that the village had been named for an Indian chief whose name, when translated into English, meant "Iron That Walks." There were three people in the waiting room, one of whom—a farmwife in a kerchief—seemed to have some sort of animal partially concealed in a wicker basket at her feet.

Miriam insisted that Myra use the facilities first—what a nightmare it must have been to be pregnant in that place, in that heat, in that car—and she stood there staring at the wall for what seemed an eternity while she listened to the trickle of water behind the closed door. It was June. Hot. Muggy. The season of bugs. And they were everywhere, crawling up the walls, clinging to the ceiling, beating round the ticket window as if it were the only place in the world they could breathe and exude their fluids and scramble atop one another so they could produce yet more bugs. In the distance—and maybe it was over Taliesin itself—there was a peal of thunder.

When it was Miriam's turn, she locked the door behind her, lit a cigarette and immediately extracted her kit from her purse. She needed something—but not too much, not her usual dose, just a modicum—to quiet her nerves. They were close now, no more than fifteen miles or so, and the thought of confronting Frank made her stomach sink. In one corner of her mind she saw him falling on his knees to beg her forgiveness, wooing her all over again, just the way it was in the beginning when he would have died for the touch of her, the lamps and candles lit and everything aglow with the presence of fine art and fine minds too, the little Russian sent packing, booted out the back door with her bags and her babies while the lord and lady of the house made tempestuous love to the keening of violins on the Victrola—or to jazz, the jazz she adored and he was indifferent to. But in another corner—a corner that grew disproportionately till it filled all the rapidly expanding space inside her skull with pulsing clouds of color, the red of hate, the green of envy—she knew she would fly at him the minute she stepped through the door. *She would . . . she would . . .* She looked down and saw that her hands were clenched and the pravaz still lodged in her thigh, the skin uplifted round a single bright spot of blood.

The remainder of the journey was something of a fog. There was a side trip to Dodgeville, the county seat, to file the writs Mr. Jackson had arranged for in advance—a peace warrant for Frank, and just so she wouldn't feel left out, one for his little Russian on a morals complaint. She might have called the justice of the peace by the wrong name and she seemed to recall something about a dog, but it was all inconsequential: she'd filed the complaints and the sheriff had been summoned to see them acted upon. The road curved and dipped and curved again. There seemed to be geese, ducks and chickens everywhere. Things flapped at the windows. The engine droned.

The conversation picked up as they got closer to Taliesin, that much she remembered, both men trying to get a rise out of her with questions about what she meant to do once they arrived and how she felt about her husband and about this dancer usurping her place, and one of them—the photographer, she thought it was—producing a flask of what he called "good Canadian whiskey"* to take the edge off. "Here's to Dutch courage," somebody said, and the flask went round the car, the alcohol lodging like sand in her throat, and why was

* More likely it was some combination of grain spirits colored with caramel—or worse. It was possible to obtain *la chose authentique* from the French Canadian bootleggers who smuggled it across the Great Lakes or the gangsters who employed them, but that was only in theory. Most people—and I was among them—had to settle for the degraded product of amateur distillers, which was often laced with rubbing alcohol or antifreeze and occasionally resulted in blindness, paralysis and even fatalities. In my student days, I once obtained—for twelve dollars a quart—two bottles of what was reputed to be bonded Kentucky bourbon but which, on closer inspection, turned out to be a lethal combination of molasses and turpentine. If you knew where to look, however, *sake* was always available. Out of the stone jug, with the *kanji* lovingly inscribed on the round protuberance of its cool little belly.

she so dry all of a sudden when everything around her was silvered and shimmering with the wet of the storm that blew over them in a burst and released the skies to a shattering sunstruck explosion of grace and eternal light? Why was that? And why did everything seem so much denser and richer than she'd ever imagined so that when the river flashed beneath them and the long low golden walls suddenly appeared as if they'd created themselves in that moment, just by her imagining them, she felt nothing but loss?

"Here," she said, "here, turn left. Now right. There, that's the gate there."

What was odd—and it struck her immediately—was the confluence of automobiles collected at the gate, three, four, five of them, and a group of men in shabby suits stationed beside them. To a man, they wore their hats cocked back on their heads and to a man they were watching the progress of the sedan out of narrowed reptilian eyes, unmoving, unflinching, and she would have thought they were statues but for the faint blue traces of smoke rising from their cigarettes and cigars. It came to her then that these were newspapermen, gathered there to document her grand entrance—and that Mr. Jackson must have put them up to it. Publicity, that was his byword. And Mr. Fake's too. *Let the press do the work for us and you'll see your husband come around smart enough.* Her hands went to her hair, tucking the loose strands of it up under her green velvet turban, and as the car slowed to pull in at the gate she was busy with her compact and a fresh application of powder and lipstick.

Only then did she look up. The gate, which normally stood open, had been pulled shut and barred with a conspicuous padlock she'd never seen before. Standing there in front of it was Billy Weston and two of the other smirking inbred local morons who would have starved to death a generation ago if Frank hadn't paid them to hang about the place and look busy. She saw the trouble in Billy's eyes when she stepped out of the car and the reporters all snapped to attention as if they'd been reanimated, flinging down their cigarettes and converging on her in unison.

The shoulder of the road was a morass of dirty brown puddles—country life, how she hated it, and what had she been thinking?—and immediately her right heel sank into the soft earth so that she staggered momentarily before bracing herself against the fender. The reporters watched her with flat eyes, but none of them offered her a hand. The sun was in her face. She felt a finger of sweat trace the ridge of her spine. She took a moment to freeze them all with a sweeping look, then marched up to the gate.

"You, Billy Weston," she snapped, "open this gate at once." She'd been debating whether or not to cry out *What is the meaning of this?* in tones of high dudgeon, but there was no point: the meaning was clear. Frank—and his henchmen, these village idiots with their open collars, battered hats and filthy trousers—intended to keep her out.

From Billy Weston (a thin gawky man, so gray and pedestrian he was barely there at all, his eyes blunted and his mouth set): "I'm sorry, Mrs. Noel, but Mr. Wright says to admit no one."

"The name is Mrs. Wright, as you know perfectly well—Mrs. Frank Lloyd Wright—and I live here. This is my house, not yours. Or his. Now you open this gate and be quick about it."

No reaction. He exchanged a glance with the other two, but that was the extent of it.

"Have you gone deaf? I said, open this gate. At once!"

Suddenly she seemed to have her hands on the cool iron panels and she was jerking the gate back and forth to the grinding accompaniment of its hinges and to hell with her gloves, to hell with everything. "Frank!" she screamed, focusing all her attention on the inert face of the house rising up out of the hill above the dark sheen of the lake. "I know you're in there! Frank! Frank!"

It was useless. She was over-exerting herself. She could feel her heart going and the sweat starting up on her brow beneath the tight grip of her turban. This was what he'd wanted, the scheming bastard—he'd planned it this way, to humiliate her. Well, two could play at that game.

She let loose of the gate as suddenly as she'd taken hold of it, wheeled round on the reporters and saw the look of awe flickering from face to face as the puddles reproduced miniature portraits of the sky, and the moths and bees and grasshoppers sailed across the field in bright streamers of color. "Boys," she said, addressing them all even as she threw her shoulders back and stalked to the sedan, "where I come from we like to say there's more than one way to skin a cat. If he thinks he can keep us out of here, he's sorely mistaken." She brushed by Wallace, who was just standing there watching her with his mouth agape, as if he were at a baseball game or a hypnotist's ball, and threw back the door of the car herself. "Come on now, what are you waiting for!" she cried, and if she was flailing her arm like some soapbox preacher, well, so what? These were her troops, she saw that now, her men-at-arms, ready to storm the place at her command, and the thought exhilarated her. "Get in your cars, everybody. We're going up the back road—and see if they can stop us!"

There was a burst of excitement, men squaring their hats and running for their cars, Wallace sliding into the front seat with the photographer and Myra lifting herself ponderously up across the running board and into the back, doors slamming, dust rising, a man's voice echoing behind them—*Hey, wait for me!*—and they were off.

Miriam held fast to the door handle, barking directions at the back of Wallace's head. The green fields rushed past the window. The air was in her face. She was filled with a fierce joy, the joy of combat, of movement and action, her only thought to seize the initiative, catch Frank unawares, bring him to his knees. But when they arrived at the back entrance five minutes later, she had her second surprise: Frank had blocked the road with one of the farm trucks and there were three more men, men she didn't recognize, standing before it with their caps pulled low and their arms crossed in a display of pugnacity. And obtuseness. And hatefulness. And, and—"Move this truck!" she commanded. "I insist that you move this truck right this minute!"

No one budged, not even so much as to shift weight from one foot to the other.

Wallace was there now (and what was his given name? Rudyard? Yes, Rudyard, after the English writer, or so he claimed), his jacket thrown casually over one shoulder, leaning into the fence as if he belonged there, as if he were a rube and hayseed himself. "Say, fellas, can't you see your way to letting us up the road here for just a minute? We won't be a bit of trouble—just want to take a picture maybe for the Saturday edition—and you know Mrs. Wright here, don't you? Come on, be white about it."

They might as well have been posts, stones, piles of dung stacked up and molded into the shape and form of men. "Bah!" she spat. "Don't waste your time. Forget them. Lowlifes, lackeys, country morons." She swung round, furious, even as both her heels sank into the muck. "Back to the front gate, boys—we'll let the sheriff handle this!"

The evening shadows were deepening when they pulled back up to the gate, and where had the time gone? As soon as she flung open the car door she could hear the bullfrogs starting up in the lake, *eh-lunk, eh-lunk,* a sound so dismal she wanted to cry,* wanted to tear her hair out and fall down on her knees and beat the earth with her fists—to be locked out, locked out of her own house, and in the evening no less, at suppertime, when she'd stood behind those commanding windows in her best clothes more times than she could count, entertaining brilliant and celebrated people while the whole countryside could do nothing more than whip up their buggies and shovel their manure and gape and wonder—but she told herself she had to be strong. And she was strong, stronger than he was, Frank, the milksop, the little man, and of course he was nowhere to be seen. Billy Weston was still there with the other two, though, looking tense. And the gate was still locked. She looked up at the windows of the house glazed with the declining sun till they were like blind eyes and even if she'd had binoculars she couldn't have seen inside—not from here, not from the road—and the thought of that made her furious all over again.

But who was this? A beery calabash-headed man in some sort of uniform that was distended like sausage casings round the midsection and down the tubes of the legs, and he was coming forward now, separating himself from the crowd—and it was a crowd, the yokels gathering for the show with their chew and their cigars and their big-knuckled pasty faded women as if they'd been summoned by the fire whistle, Frank Lloyd Wright and his locked-out wife the best entertainment in town—and suddenly it dawned on her that this was the sheriff himself. "Ma'am," he said, touching the brim of his hat.

She should have been pleased to see him, should

* I vividly recall hearing this batrachian vocalizing myself, during my first summer at Taliesin. It is, indeed, a dismal sound, depressing in the extreme, as if the earth were vomiting up its dead.

have thanked him for turning out at such an hour to do his duty and succor her in her time of distress, but the very look of him infuriated her even more. *This* was her hero? Her knight? Her paladin? His shoulders sagged. He wouldn't look her in the eye. "They've locked me out of my own house," she said. "And he's up there right now, gloating. Him and his, his"—she wouldn't say "whore," not here, not in front of these people, though that was what she was—"his slattern."

He smacked his lips, dug with one delicate finger at something lodged between his teeth. "Who would that be, ma'am?"

"Who? What do you mean 'who'? Frank Lloyd Wright, the man named on the peace warrant. Are you going to go up there and arrest him?" She let her eyes rove over the crowd, then gestured angrily at Billy Weston. "And these men? They're, they're . . . *obstructing*, that's what they're doing. Obstructing justice. Arrest them. Arrest them right this minute."

Someone let out a laugh and then the laughter became general, rising abruptly and then dying out when she swung round on them, furious. "Laugh," she snarled. "Laugh, you idiots. And you"—pointing a finger at Billy Weston—"I'll have you fired, the whole lot of you, the minute I get control of Taliesin."

"Well, ma'am, I don't, uh"—the sheriff was fumbling in his breast pocket for the warrants, two thumbed-over slips of paper that could have been used as wadding at this juncture—"well, these men say he ain't up there. And her, neither."

She was astonished: Wasn't he going to do anything? Had he been bought off, was that it? Had Frank somehow got to him?

"You mean to tell me you're just going to take their word for it?" she said, fighting to control her voice. She was glaring at him now, and he was a small man too, for all the puffed-up flesh of him, a conniver, a fool, a coward. "Well?" she demanded. "Aren't you going to look for yourself? Aren't you going to do your duty? Your sworn duty? Isn't that what you're here for?"

He snatched a look at her, then dropped his eyes and began working at the dirt with the toe of one worn boot. "I suppose I"—he glanced up at Billy Weston—"well, I guess I could, maybe, well, just take a look around the place, considering these warrants and all."

They all watched him gather himself up and shuffle to the gate, watched Billy Weston produce a key to release the padlock and swing back the bars to admit him, and they all watched as he trudged along the road and on up the hill to the house, the weariest man in the world. A feeling of anticlimax settled in—they'd wanted action, a raw burn of emotion, the seigneur on the hill exposed and humiliated, handcuffs, protestations, the puff of flash powder—but there was only this, this heavy-haunched, slope-shouldered figure receding in the distance and the frogs *eh-lunking* and the sun stuck fast in the treetops. People began to stir. One woman produced a sandwich. The newspapermen convened over cigarettes, and the farmers, trained to patience, squatted in the dirt and began to talk in soft voices. Before long the birds would go to roost, bats would flicker over the water and the whole countryside would become comatose as if a switch had been thrown.

Miriam was having none of it. Her shoes were ruined. Mosquitoes had bitten her—were biting her even now. She'd come all this way, produced the warrants, summoned the sheriff, endured more abuse and humiliation than any woman could be expected to take for even a single minute of a single day in an entire lifetime, and *still she was locked out*! Before she could think she was at the gate, a sign there—NO VISITORS ALLOWED—and she was jerking at it till the screws gave and she flung the thing down in the dirt and stamped on it with both feet as if it were the effigy of Frank himself. And now they were roused, all right, everybody on their feet—this was what they'd come for and she was going to give it to them. "You see!" she cried. "You see how it is? The sheriff can pass through these damned stinking gates and I can't? I, the legal owner of the property, of the gates themselves? Is that right? Is that what this country has come to?"

She could feel it all boiling up in her, a stew of rage and hate and despair, and she fed on it till there was no coming back. The sign was there at her feet and she kicked it till it skittered away from her and suddenly she was whirling around on them all, shouting now, the veins rigid in her throat. "You!" she cried, focusing on the nearest man, a farmer in overalls. "Aren't you ashamed? All of you, all of you should be ashamed of yourselves. Isn't there a man among you? Nobody to aid a lady in distress against these, these—" but another sign caught her eye, the Taliesin sign itself, set in glass, and she was snatching up the first thing that came to hand, a stone the size of her fist, and here she was battering the glass till it shattered in a rain of bright hard nuggets and she flung the stone away from her in a single savage gesture.

"Miriam!" somebody called. "Here, Miriam, pose for a picture!"

She wanted to wreck it all, tear the place down, see it in ashes. The dirt leapt at her, the sky collapsed. And what was this? A stick. She had a stick in her hand—*Miriam, a picture!*—and the photographer was setting up his tripod for the flash, Wallace scurrying to help him, the farmwives gaping, Myra swelling and swelling till she was ready to burst like a soap bubble, and at the very moment, the moment she was posed there with the stick held high, vengeful, heroic, imbued with the power of Diana the Huntress and Queen Elizabeth and every other woman who'd stood up for herself against the tyranny of men, Billy Weston and his minions sprang in front of her with a canvas tarp and the flash flashed on nothing.

"Yes," she was saying, "yes, I'm sure he was in there all the while, laughing up his sleeve. That's what insults me more than anything else—to think of him thinking he's got the best of me, and truly, Leora, I've never been so mortified in my life—"

There were flowers on the table, two dozen long-stemmed roses in a shade of red that edged toward violet, a color that reminded her of the sacred heart of Jesus glaring from the statue outside St. Mary's Church in Memphis. Frank had paid for the flowers—indirectly, at any rate—because Mr. Fake and Mr. Jackson had got him to cough up some of what he owed her, and given the mood she was in she felt she needed flowers. Just to cheer her. And she needed a glass of champagne too, and strawberries in cream and a piece of smoked sturgeon to pick over till her fingertips smelled of the smokehouse and the sweet imbricate slabs of flesh.

Leora made a sympathetic noise on the other end of the line, a noise so faint and vague you would have thought she was in California still and not just across town, on Lakeshore Drive, visiting her sister.

"And the newspaper account was disappointing too. Didn't you think so? Really, 'Miriam Storms Taliesin; Repulsed,' and that sort of thing. Or what was the other one? 'Miriam Lifts Taliesin Siege; Returns Home.' Makes me out to be—oh, I don't know. Pitiful."

"Or sympathetic," Leora said. "People can't help but sympathize—"

"And the photograph. They blocked the one that would have done me justice—I told you that, didn't I? And this one they printed . . ." She was staring down at the newspaper, open to the picture of her posed against an anonymous backdrop of twigs and shrubs instead of the gate itself, her cape flaring, her face distorted under the burden of her hat. You couldn't even make out her features—and was her face really that wide? There seemed to be a glowing white ball descending from the turban and nothing more than two poked holes for eyes and a slash for the mouth as if in some child's drawing. "I don't know, do you like it?"

"Honestly? No. It doesn't quite . . . but what do you expect from the newspapers?"

Very slowly, as if it represented all the wealth of the world, Miriam poured herself a second glass of the wine, for which she'd had to bribe two bellhops and the man at the desk—the real stuff, they told her, the finest, when in fact it was no better than the rotgut they served in the speakeasies. But it bubbled and frothed and it reminded her of better times. "I did like this," she said, "in the second column? *'You are nothing but a bunch of blackguards,' she shouted to the defenders grouped in front of the locked gate.* There's a certain courageousness to that, don't you think?"*

"Do you know what I think? I think you should consider a suit—"

"I am. We are. Mr. Fake said just this morning—"

"No, no—I mean against *her.* For alienation of affection. Margery McCaffery sued her husband's secretary that time I was telling you about . . ." Leora lowered her voice to a whisper. "The secretary disappeared the very next day—probably ran to her mother in Barstow or some

* I've seen the newspaper clippings. What Miriam is overlooking here—or perhaps "suppressing" is a better way of putting it—is Wrieto-San's counterattack under the headline WRIGHT HINTS AT SANITY HEARING FOR OUSTED WIFE.

such place. And when he came crawling back, Margery just laughed."

The odor of the fish rose to her nostrils, vital and strong, blunting the perfume of the roses. She lifted her forefinger to her lips and idly licked it. Alienation of affection. She hardly knew what it meant beyond the literal meaning of the phrase, but the idea of it appealed to her. She closed her eyes and saw the blanched naked face of that woman in the hospital, childlike and afraid, little Olga, put-upon and harassed. And how did *she* rate Frank? She didn't. Nobody did. Nobody.

"Don't you see? That's the way to flush them out."

She filed the suit at the end of August in the amount of $100,000, Mr. Fake arguing that Mrs. Olga Milanoff, the Montenegrin dancer, had deprived her of her husband's society for the past eighteen months, a society she valued, after careful consideration, at some $5,500 a month. The only response from Frank was through the press. He dismissed the suit out of hand, claiming it was just one more attempt on his wife's part to annoy and harass him, and he refused to divulge the whereabouts of Olgivanna—it was no business of his wife or her lawyers either, he informed a reporter from the *Chicago Tribune* by long-distance telephone from Taliesin. Which only confirmed what Miriam had known all along—that he was hiding her there. He might have managed to pull his strings and get the warrants dismissed, both of them, but if he thought she was going to give in, he was as deluded as the fools who thought the Great War would last no more than six months. Oh, his little dancer was there, all right—of that Miriam had no doubt. She could picture her cowering someplace in that labyrinth of moldy rooms and reeking outbuildings, afraid of the light of day, confined to the kitchen and the pantry with the servants and the mice, jumping at every sound, and not just the reporters after her now but the process server too.

Yet the fact remained that the summons hadn't been served and you couldn't very well sue an apparition. Miriam brooded over that as August gave way to September, her resources dwindling even as Frank reneged on the hotel bill and Messrs. Fake and Jackson began to press her with statements for services rendered and the walls of her rooms seemed to close in on her as if she were the one caught in a snare and not Olgivanna. It rained for two days and she did nothing but sit at the window and watch the patterns the water made in the street. The black cars streamed by like hearses. People huddled beneath umbrellas—but at least they were going somewhere, doing something, anything, even if it was hateful. She was not one for stasis. She needed movement, action, excitement, and who didn't but the dead or the soon-to-be-dead? She called Mr. Fake. Repeatedly. He had no news for her. Mr. Jackson would take the phone. He had no news for her either. And then they were both out and the secretary was very sorry.

Just when she'd begun to give up hope, when she found herself going down to dinner with her face discomposed from sobbing into her two cupped hands for what seemed hours at a time, when the pravaz went dull and she thought the rain would never let up, Mr. Jackson telephoned to report that Taliesin was hers. He'd arranged for a court order granting her admittance—those workmen had no right to keep her off her own property, no right in the world, and the court had come down firmly on her side—and he offered to drive her all the way up to Wisconsin himself. She could take possession of the place, move things in, do anything she liked with the artwork, the furnishings, the livestock. She could cut down the trees, drain the lake, sell off the corn, fire the staff wholesale and let the dust and cobwebs accumulate till the place looked like the catacombs under one of those old churches in Italy. If it struck her fancy, she could board up the windows, order a dozen Victorian loveseats, hang doilies from the famous cantilevered eaves. And Frank could do nothing to stop her.

This time when she stepped out of the car, there was only Billy Weston at the gate. She stood there glaring at him under the hellish sun, enduring the mud and the insects and the assault of rural odors while Mr. Jackson handed over the papers and the two conferred. Even then, Billy stalled. He had to go up and telephone to Mr. Wright's lawyer, he said, and, infuriatingly, made her wait there at the locked gate while he ambled up the hill, disappeared into the house for a good ten minutes, and then ambled down again. "Only her," he said, addressing Mr. Jackson as he turned the key in the padlock and grudgingly pulled back the gate. "That's what the papers say, only her. Not you."

She felt strange coming up the drive, everything so familiar—the crunch of the gravel under her feet, the shadows, the angles of the buildings, the way the courtyard opened up like a pair of welcoming arms—and yet different too. How long had it been? Two years—better than two years. But Frank never stood still, that was for sure. He'd been busy since the fire, she could see that, new roofs sprouting over the living quarters, the back buildings more elaborate, more fully integrated into the whole. And the house was beautiful, she had to admit it. There was an aura of peace about the place, everything so still and ageless, and she had a thrill of recognition that took her all the way back to her years in Europe and the first time she stepped into the arching recesses of the Pantheon or St. Peter's Basilica. She was wrought up, of course she was, but the simple transparent beauty of the place had a calming effect beyond all thought of confrontation and loss, and the memories came back to her in a rush.

There may have been a lock on the gate, but there were no locks on the doors—Frank didn't believe in keys*—and she passed through the courtyard and slipped in the main entrance. It was like plunging into a pool, cool and mysterious, the stone pillars burnished with an aqueous light, the wood glowing as if it were wet, and everything silent as a dream. He wasn't there. She wasn't there. Nobody was. All those rooms, all that empty space, and not a soul around, not even the servants. For a long while, Miriam hesitated at the door, breathing in the scent of the place, orienting herself—Frank was gone, vanished, and he'd ducked out on her again, the coward, the bastard, the little man—and then, gradually, it came to her that it was better this way, and her heart decelerated and her breathing slowed, and step by step, she entered deeper into the house and began to explore.

Every detail, every change, leapt out at her,† and it was almost as if the flesh of a new house had been stretched over the bones of the old—and it had, because all this had been burned, but for the stone itself, hadn't it? She ran her hand over the rough pillars to feel the grit

* House keys, that is. He never carried them, considered them a nuisance, and as for the keys to his various automobiles, the chauffeur of the moment could always be counted on to produce them when Wrieto-San felt like taking a spin.

† She would have seen for the first time—and, I might add, the last—the garden room and decorative pool, for instance, off of Wrieto-San's bedroom, as well as the new balcony and second-floor guest room above the living room and the six-panel screen by Yasunobu (pine, birds, cherry blossoms) he'd installed on the wall beneath it.

there, sat in the chairs, took in the views out the living room windows like an interloper, a thief of views. The more she explored—or was she snooping, was that what it was?—the more agitated she became. She saw the new carpets, the furniture, new artwork to replace the old. He'd been extravagant here, sparing nothing, and all the while pleading poverty to the court. But then he was just a two-bit schemer, wasn't he? A liar and a skinflint. He took from the rich and gave to himself and he didn't give a damn about anybody so long as he got what he wanted.

She moved through the house like a detective in a dime novel, examining everything, the canned food in the cupboard, the table set for an uneaten meal, the dirty plates in the sink, the unmade beds—he'd decamped in a hurry, she saw that, but it gave her little satisfaction. There were the sheets in the master bedroom, sheets that smelled of him—yes, she raised them to her face—and something else too, another presence, her, Olgivanna, the usurper in her husband's bed. For a long while she sat there on the edge of the bed, her mind ranging so far that she forgot all about Mr. Jackson waiting for her at the gate and Billy Weston, whom she was going to sack the minute she had the opportunity, and all the rest of the toadies and ingrates too, and she might have stayed there till night came down but for the two very sympathetic gentlemen from the Bank of Wisconsin, Madison, who knocked meekly at the door to inform her that her husband was in arrears on his mortgage, which, sadly, had been inflated by the rebuilding loan, and that they were foreclosing on the property forthwith.

Unless, of course, she, as co-owner, could come up with the sum owing.

And how much was it?

Twenty-five thousand on the mortgage, plus a further chattel mortgage of $1,500 and liens for unpaid bills of $17,000, totaling, in all, $43,500.

She invited them in, apologizing because she was unable to offer them anything under the circumstances, and she sat there in Frank's grand living room with its gleaming treasures and baronial views, staring numbly at them, thinking first of her pravaz and then of Frank—he'd outmaneuvered her again, that was what he was thinking. Wherever he was. Out of the country, no doubt. Living in a cheap hotel where no one asks any questions. Maybe he was wearing a false beard—that would be funny, Frank in a false beard like some baggy-pants comedian on the vaudeville circuit. He thought he'd put one over on her. Thought he was having the last laugh. But he'd lost Taliesin and Taliesin was his life. And he stood to lose a whole lot more any day now. Because what he didn't know was that Mr. Jackson was also representing the little Russian's husband—Hinzenberg—and that the husband had brought adultery charges against him. And more: he was suing Frank for $250,000 for alienating the affections of his wife and daughter, filing a writ of habeas corpus for return of the child and offering a five-hundred-dollar reward for capture of the fugitives. Even then, even as she sat across from the lip-licking bankers and let her gaze rest on one of Frank's precious Chinese Buddhas, the sheriff of Sauk County, Wisconsin, was circulating photographs of him. And of her. And of the child.

Yes. And who was having the last laugh now?

CHAPTER 7: NOT A DANCER

Olgivanna hadn't spoken with the reporter, hadn't admitted he was alive and breathing and standing there before her, his hands in constant motion and his face rearranging itself around every plea and provocation. She blocked her ears too, rising swiftly from the chair, taking Svetlana by the hand and marching straight into the house to close the door firmly behind her and instruct Mrs. Taggertz to send word down to Frank so that Billy Weston and the others could escort the man from the property with whatever degree of physical persuasion they deemed necessary. But the incident had its effect. For weeks she was afraid to leave the house, even to sit in the courtyard, though Frank tried to reassure her—he'd instructed the men to keep a lookout and he swore he'd have any and all trespassers prosecuted, "whether they're newspapermen or gypsies or Bible salesmen"—and she found herself growing paler and weaker by the day. Just to get out, just to free herself of all the little irritations of the household, the baby's colic, Svetlana's moods, Frank's all-encompassing presence, she found herself roaming the fields at night, in the fastness of the dark, and when the mosquitoes came to suck her blood it was almost a relief.

Very gradually, as spring deepened toward summer, she began to regain her strength. She felt it in her legs first, her calves hardening ever so perceptibly and the long muscles of her thighs and groin stretching to accommodate the pace of her nightly rambles. In the mornings, even before the sky began to shade to gray beyond the windows, she forced herself from bed and out into the garden, though she was weakest then, coughing with a persistency that alarmed her—and cold, cold all the way through, as if she'd never warm up again. But the garden needed tending, that was what she told herself. The peas and green beans were drowning in weeds, the tomato and pepper seedlings were delicate still and the sweet corn was at its most vulnerable, and while she slept a whole army of rabbits, gophers, beetles and caterpillars crept out to the feast. She didn't eat, didn't brew a pot of coffee or a cup of tea or even rinse her mouth with water from the pitcher on the stand beside the bed—she dressed in the dark in an old skirt and sweater and went straight out into the silent breath of the morning while the children were asleep still and there was nobody to see her.

Once the sun was up, she came in for breakfast, Frank already at work in his studio, Mrs. Taggertz feeding the children, the workmen hammering and measuring and sawing away at the perpetual revivification of Taliesin. She ate then—a soft-boiled egg, a slice of toast, coffee with cream and sugar—and afterward, if she had the energy, she sat with the baby and put Svetlana through her paces, an hour of dance, an hour at the piano, readings from the poets, drawing, painting, calligraphy.* In the afternoons, she slept.

* Svetlana's education was sketchy, a consequence not only of her constant uprooting, but of her mother's artistic inclinations and Wrieto-San's antipathy for formal instruction. Iovanna's case was even worse. She was functionally illiterate when I met her in 1932 and she did not attend school until two years later, at the age of nine, when she had to be held back from the fourth grade in Spring Green because she hadn't yet learned her alphabet.

And in the evenings, after Mrs. Taggertz had served dinner and the baby had been put to bed and she'd sat reading in the living room with Svetlana and Frank, she went back out to the garden, furtively, rising from her chair as if she were going to the kitchen or the bathroom and slipping out the door into the gathering dark. Moonlit nights were a blessing, the hoe an extension of her hands, her arms, her shoulders, one task leading to another until it was eleven, it was midnight, and still she was at it, the work consecrating her in routine. She spread the soil, paid out the hose, bent and clipped and dug, and the world of the reporters receded like a ship leaving the dock in a very dense fog.

By June, she'd begun to relax. The telephone rang still, rang continually, but she learned to ignore it. She put on weight—a pound or two, at any rate. Her complexion improved. Frank complimented her on her looks. She even began, tentatively, to sit out in the courtyard again without feeling as if she were being spied upon and twice she took Svetlana down to the lake to feed the ducks in broad daylight. And then one evening, as she played with the baby in the living room while Svetlana skipped rope outside the door with a rhythmic slap as regular as a heartbeat and the smell of fried ham and potatoes and onions rode a current of air from the kitchen, she happened to glance out the window to see a number of motorcars pulled up at the front gate. Absently, she rose to her feet and crossed the room to get a better look. There was a gleam of glass and metal, the roofs of the cars mirroring the sun in neat oblong sheets, movement there, people—men in hats—gathered in groups of two and three, as if they were looking for work.

Or a story. A newspaper story.

Her first reaction was to shrink back from the windows, though they couldn't possibly see her at this distance, could they? She went to the bedroom next, not to hide herself like a scared child—she was angry suddenly, and she'd never hated any class of people in her life the way she hated these professional snoops and meddlers and why couldn't they just leave them alone?—but to fetch the binoculars from the table beside the bed. She wanted to be sure. Wanted to know her enemy. And then she would call to Frank and Frank would send the men down to confront them and everything would go on as before.

She came back into the room in a crouch, gave a glance to the baby, who was preoccupied with a stuffed toy in the middle of the carpet, sensing nothing, knowing nothing, then went down on all fours and crawled to the window. The scene jumped at her in magnification, the lake a slap of color, the lawn crying out till every blade of grass came starkly visible, the gate trembling and then sliding into focus. She saw Billy Weston there, his back to her, and two of the other men with him. And then the newspapermen, their hats creased, ties askew in the heat. There was a shout, muffled by the distance and the interposition of the glass, the noise startling a flight of ducks up off the water to wheel over the house and throw a pulse of shadow across the room, and it was then that she saw there was someone else there too, a figure in motion—a woman—bending, rising in violent pantomime, bending again.

It was Miriam. It had to be. She was certain of it even as she shifted the binoculars to focus on the woman's face, but then the figure ducked out of view, erased momentarily by the torsos of the converging men before coming up triumphant to fling something down in the dirt in a dull blur of color. Another shout. The men smirking. Easing forward. A photographer there, setting up his tripod, the sun exploding against the windows of the cars and the woman whirling away from them all to stamp furiously at that thing in the dirt as if she were killing it. Only then did she stand still long enough to reveal herself.

Olgivanna had seen Miriam in the flesh just once—in the corridor of the hospital—but she must have studied the photographs of her a hundred times, fixated on her, fascinated, every line of her rival's face as familiar to her as her own, and now here she was, unmistakable, Miriam in all her belligerent glory, come to claim her own. She recognized the pug nose, the set of the jaw, the clamped insatiable mouth and the outsized hat slipped down over the eyebrows—and the eyes themselves, so startled and wide it was as if she'd been pricked with a pin every minute of her waking life. It gave Olgivanna a strange thrill to see her this way, reduced at the end of a long optical tunnel, flattened and derealized, but it was short-lived. Any minute now—she was sure of it—Billy Weston would stand back and Miriam would pass through the gates and sally up the drive with her horde of reporters, and what then? Would they have to run out into the fields and hide? Crawl under the beds? And where was Frank?

Svetlana's rope beat and beat and beat again, echoing through the open door that gave onto the courtyard. There was a dull ringing from the direction of the kitchen, the cook rapping a spoon against the lip of a pot. And Olgivanna, absorbed in the spectacle of Miriam, forgot all about Pussy until something came crashing down behind her and she spun round to see the baby tangled up in the cord of one of Frank's lamps, the glass shattered, the frame bent*—Frank would be furious, that was her first thought—and Pussy expelling the first startled shriek of breath. Panic swept over her then—the electricity, the shards of glass—and she dropped the binoculars, sprang to her feet and snatched up her daughter

* Yes, and how much would that lamp be worth today?

and she didn't care who was watching. In the next moment she was in the corridor, Pussy raggedly wailing—startled, but no blood, and the lamp hadn't hit her, had it?—and calling for Frank in a voice that was a bitter distillate of rage and fear and impatience. "Frank! Frank! Where in God's name are you?"

He was in his studio, drawing, always drawing, no matter what the crisis, and he looked up sharply when she burst in on him—the children, especially bawling, red-faced infants, were strictly interdicted from distracting him while he was working because how could she expect him to earn a living if he was to be forever interrupted every time Svetlana skinned her knee or the baby passed gas?* "What is it now?" he demanded.

"What is it?" she threw back at him, even as Pussy's screams climbed up the register and then stalled while she spat up a pale sour wad of pabulum on her mother's shoulder. "Have you looked out the window? It is that woman. Your wife. Miriam. She is here"—she felt the warm seep of the baby's fluids through the fabric of her dress, and it would have to be washed now, and Pussy's dress too—"right outside at the gate. With, with, I don't know—*reporters*! They look like reporters."

* Wrieto-San's complaints over the chaos fomented by his six children with Catherine are legendary. For all his talk of the sanctity of family—and the conceit was central to his philosophy, along with a firm belief in independence of spirit, pioneer gumption and a don't-tread-on-me mentality—he seems to have been the sort of man who preferred family life in the abstract to the actuality. But then what man hasn't, at least on occasion, found himself deeply disillusioned with the distracted wife, the night alarums and the diaper pail, not to mention the expressive howls and systematic material destruction of the growing child?

He didn't get up from the desk, didn't offer to take the baby, didn't even bother to turn his head and look out the window to the sloping lawn that gave onto the lake and the meadow and the gate crowded with cars. "I'm aware of the situation," he said in a quiet voice.

Aware of the situation? She was stunned. And though she was a linguist, though she had French and Russian at her command in addition to her native language, as well as her English, which, if heavily accented, was nonetheless perfectly fluid and intelligible, she didn't know what to say. He was *aware*—and he was just sitting there?

His face was composed, his eyes locked on hers even as the baby kicked and struggled and let out a thin mewl of protest, and she could see that he was willing himself to stay seated, to project an air of coolness and indifference—for her sake. So as not to alarm her. He let out a sigh. "It seems Miriam has been up to her mischief. She claims to have some sort of court order—I've been on the phone to Levi* over it—but I can guarantee you that she'll never set foot on this property again, no matter what it takes. I've got both roads blocked. And Billy's in charge. You know Billy. He would die before he'd give us up."

* Judge Levi H. Bancroft, who, along with Wrieto-San's old friend Judge James Hill, was representing Wrieto-San's interests in the divorce suit. Both he and Judge Hill were eminently capable men—as capable, some would say, as Clarence Darrow, who'd defended Wrieto-San against an earlier charge of violating the Mann Act (in transporting Miriam across state lines in 1915 for allegedly immoral purposes, if sexual congress between consenting adults on any side of any artificial boundary can be seen as immoral). But then, Wrieto-San always surrounded himself with the best of everything, including people.

"Court orders? What sort of court orders? What do they say?"

"It's nothing. Legal wrangling, that's all."

"Yes, and that is what you are telling me with the reporters too, till that horrid man from the newspaper came here, and—I don't like it. I hate this, Frank. I hate it."

"Now listen," and he was out from behind the desk now, moving across the carpet to her, to take her and the baby in his grip that was like the grip of a Titan, a hero who could hold the whole world up in his two arms, "there's nothing to worry over, nothing, nothing at all."

But he was wrong.

Within the hour they were both of them cowering like criminals in the hilltop garden, crouching over wooden stools in the dirt and whispering stories to Svetlana and the baby as if nothing in the world were the matter, while the sheriff, armed with his warrants, poked through the living room, the Blue Loggia, the kitchen, the bedroom and the studio. Within a day Miriam would be back on the attack. And within two months' time they would have to run yet again, packing up so hastily the beds had to be left unmade and the clothes strewn across the floor, breakfast abandoned on the dining room table to draw flies and the garden left to the crows, the gophers and the pulsating hordes of insects with their clacking mandibles and infinite mouths.

Frank tried to make it seem like an adventure, just as he had when they'd gone to Puerto Rico, but it was no more an adventure than fleeing the hospital when she could barely lift her head from the pillow or enduring the ragged have-nots of Coamo with their splayed dirty feet and toothless smiles and their emaciated goats and pustular dogs and the fried bananas that tasted like cardboard soaked in grease when she wanted only to be home at Taliesin with the baby beside her and the smell of fresh bread rising from the oven. He steered the vast gleaming hulk of the Cadillac across the countryside, heading west, terrifying her at every turn because he was always going too fast, as if the whole purpose of driving wasn't to get someplace in comfort and safety but to defy every law of the road, and he kept up a running monologue the whole time. For Svetlana—to keep her spirits up—but for her too. That was one thing about Frank—you never had to worry about a lull in the conversation.

"You're going to love it, Svet," he kept saying, "our own little cottage in the woods. On a lake. Lake Minnetonka. Can you say Minnetonka? Come on. You can say it. And I'll tell you, this isn't just a little puddle like the pond at Taliesin, but a true and veritable lake, full of fish, pike perch and suchlike. You like pike perch, don't you? And bears in the woods, wolves, and what else?—moose. You'll see moose too. Probably hundreds of them. And you know what? They've got a miniature canoe there, just the right size for a little girl—what do you think of that?"

Trees arched over the road, denser here, the woods alternately thickening and thinning as they drove west through Montfort, Mount Hope and Prairie du Chien and then north along the Mississippi to La Crosse and on into Minnesota, one hamlet after another falling away behind them and the farms losing themselves in palisades of timber. Svetlana played along—"Moose? How big are they? Bigger than an elephant?"—and if she was upset she didn't show it. But how could she fail to be upset? How could anyone, let alone a child? Perhaps Frank had seen all this coming—the lawsuits,* Miriam's

* Miriam, in a fugue of litigious ecstasy, had filed an additional suit against Wrieto-San for involuntary bankruptcy and pressed for his arrest on Mann Act charges, an irony that certainly wouldn't have eluded her.

seizure of Taliesin, the foreclosure and pending eviction, the sheriffs and the lawyers—perhaps he'd kept his own counsel and planned ahead, finding them this refuge that lay somewhere up the road, but here was the vagabond life all over again, everything they'd need for a month—two months, three, who could say?—packed into the trunk of the car in an early-morning panic when every squeak of the hinges, every thump and rattle, was the furtive annunciation of the police come for them. And not just to serve writs or argue fine points of the law, but to arrest them both and take them to prison, lock them up behind bars like anarchists or bank robbers, and what then? More newspapers? More humiliation?

She tried to put the best face on it she could, tried to control herself for Frank's sake and the children's, but all she could think of was her garden, the flowers, the horses and chickens and cows—was everything to be sold off at auction? Would the tomatoes rot on the vine and the hydrangeas go brown for lack of water? It didn't improve her outlook when they stopped for dinner in La Crosse and Svetlana developed one of her moods, refusing to eat because she didn't like steak and didn't want pork and she hated fish and hamburger too, and no, she didn't want wieners or even ice cream or anything—and then the baby had diarrhea and it was one diaper after another and would they run out before they got to where they were going? And Frank, all the while the gayest, most carefree man in the world, chanting, "Minnesota, Minnesota, where the fish 're bigger 'n Dakota!"

If she was abrupt with the Thayers, who'd arranged the rental for them, well, she was sorry, she never meant to be rude with anyone, not the woman who owned the place or the cook cum housemaid she'd left behind, but her nerves were strung tight and the first few days in the new house were a trial. There were the usual tribulations associated with moving in—getting the children settled, stocking the larder, dealing with a new servant, going through the charade of making a home out of some stranger's house filled with a stranger's things—and the whole affair was complicated by the imposture of their new identities. She couldn't be Olga anymore and Svetlana couldn't be Svetlana. They were the Richardsons* all over again, Frank and his wife, Anna (a good ethnic name to account for her accent), their daughter Mary and the infant who wasn't Iovanna or even Pussy any longer but simply the baby.

What to say? She'd been in a state of perpetual dislocation since she was a girl of eleven when she was sent to live with her sister on the Black Sea in Russia, learning a new culture and a new language, and then having to abandon it all at nineteen when the revolution broke out. She'd barely had time to make a home in Tiflis with Vlademar and her infant daughter when they had to flee in advance of the White Army, Georgei courageously leading them and a small band of his followers through Constantinople to safety, and then she'd found a home at Fontainebleau until Georgei's accident, and then at Taliesin, and was it too much to ask to have some peace, to sleep in the same bed two nights in a row? To be part of something? To live a normal life like anyone else?

* I've often wondered if Wrieto-San chose this pseudonym in honor of Henry Hobhouse Richardson, one of the luminaries of the Arts and Crafts movement, whose bold primitive stonework prefigures not only Taliesin but the Imperial Hotel and the Los Angeles houses as well. Unfortunately, I was never able to ask him, because, as you might imagine, it would have been awkward in the extreme even to make casual reference to this period of Wrieto-San's life, when he was a plaything of the press, bankrupt and bereft of commissions, the "fugitive architect" fleeing the authorities in all the fullness of his white-haired glory.

Perhaps so. But she was nothing if not adaptable and the house did have its charms, Tonka Bay struck with light from early morning till late in the afternoon, loons calling across the water, the weather holding through September in a long lazy spell of Indian summer, and when it did turn in the first week of October the frost came at night to fire the trees in a display of color as rich as she'd ever seen. And they were together, just the four of them, with no battery of workmen hammering away, no clients to mollify, the outside world forbidden to them and their inner world all the richer for it. She adjusted to the cuisine of the new cook (a Miss Viola Meyerhaus, thick-legged and spinsterish, of indeterminate age, with her blond hair worn in an inflexible braid looped atop her head, whose dishes were invariably heavy with gravy, *Kartoffeln,* kraut and sausage, though she did make a wonderful *Himmel und Erde*, a mixture of mashed potatoes, apple sauce, onions, diced bacon and roast pork even Svetlana seemed to like), and on the cook's day off Olgivanna took the time to prepare soups and stews and bake confections till the house smelled the way a house ought to smell. Every day they went sailing on the lake, and in the evenings there were rambles in the countryside and then hours spent by the fire. Frank, ever restless, hit on the idea of writing his autobiography—if he was denied architecture, he could at least use his time fruitfully, couldn't he?—and she loved to sit and listen as he dictated the book aloud to the stenographer he hired on the strictest confidence.

All went well, aside from the occasional slipup—neither of them could seem to remember to call Svetlana "Mary" when there were people about, and the Cadillac, with its Victoria top and Wisconsin tags, had to have been fairly conspicuous, especially as the newspapers were running photographs of both Frank and her and trumpeting the not-inconsiderable reward for information leading to their arrest and prosecution—and if she were to look back on this period in the years to come, she would have seen it as being as close to a pure idyll as anything she'd ever experienced. Given the circumstances, that is. She was happy, genuinely happy, and again, just as she had at Taliesin that spring, she began, despite herself, to relax.

She was in the kitchen brewing a pot of tea one morning, Frank at work in his makeshift study on the pages he would dictate that evening to Mrs. Devine, the stenographer, the baby asleep, Svetlana playing some sort of game in the canoe (which was firmly tethered to the dock and under no circumstances to be untethered—or paddled—without an adult present) and Viola busy at the stove, when a man in his thirties with a high vegetal crown of yellowish hair came up the back steps and entered the house without knocking. Before she had a chance to protest or even open her mouth, he was holding out his hand to her, simultaneously apologizing for the intrusion and introducing himself. "I'm Mrs. Simpson's son?"* he said, making a question of it. "And I'm so sorry to bother you, but I happened to be out from Minneapolis for the day—I'm an attorney, I don't know if my mother told you?—and I was just, uh, well, I mislaid my fishing pole and I had an appointment to go fishing this afternoon with one of my clients. I wonder if you wouldn't mind? I'm sure it's in the attic."

He had an eager look to him, as if he were a boy still—tall enough to graze the doorframe but without the

* Wrieto-San, in his ineffably charming and charismatic way, had persuaded the owner of the cottage (a Mrs. Simpson; we don't have a given name for her) that she needed a vacation for a three-month period so that she might rent him her house, fully furnished, and rent him her housekeeper too. How he paid for this—or rather if he paid for it—remains a mystery.

excess flesh so many men put on as they drift into middle age, his face as bland as a fried egg and his eyes unwavering and clear—so that the request carried with it an automatic stamp of plausibility. He'd lived here, grown up in the house. His fishing apparatus was in the attic. What could be more reasonable?

"Oh, I'm sorry, hello, Viola," he said, addressing the cook before Olgivanna could muster a reply. "I didn't see you there. Are you well?"

"Yes, Jimmy. Very well, thank you. And your mother?"

A glance for Olgivanna, just to see how far he could go. "She's enjoying her vacation—thanks to you, Mrs. Richardson. She went up Duluth way to visit with my aunt, but you know Mama, Viola, she's back with me and my wife now—and just loving looking after Buddy and Katrina."

Frank must have heard the male voice echoing round the kitchen because he came out of his study then, looking neutral—not alarmed, not yet—and said, "Well, well, who do we have here? Is it Mrs. Simpson's son, is that what I hear?"

The man gave a visible start before he recovered himself, his voice rising to a kind of yelp as he moved forward to take Frank's hand, "Yes sir," he said. "Jim Simpson, at your service." And then he explained his errand. "You wouldn't mind if I just dashed up the stairs—it won't be a minute. Of course, I didn't mean to . . . well, I guess I've already put you out—"

Frank didn't demur. He stood there a moment, looking up into the man's face, trying hard to read him. "You do much fishing, Mr. Simpson?" he asked finally.

"Oh, yah—but not as much I'd like. You know how it is, busy, busy, busy all the time."

"And what are you after—pike perch?"

"Yah, mostly."

"Panfish, I suppose?"

"Yah."

"Any whitefish in the lake? That's the fish I prefer"—and he turned to her then—"isn't it, Anna? Best-eating fish around."

"Well, you know, Mr.—Richardson, right?—I'm not sure on that. Don't know if I've ever—well, listen, I've taken up enough of your time already."

"Go on ahead," Frank said, "go get your fishing rod. And I'll say goodbye to you now, sir." They shook hands again, as if sealing a bargain. "I'm right in the middle of something," Frank added, by way of explanation. He winked. Grinned. "Work, you know. No rest for the weary."

"Or the wicked either. But if you don't mind my asking, what is it you do?"

"Philately."

"Stamps?"

Frank nodded. "That's right."

"Well, that must be—interesting, I suppose. Is there a living in it?"

"Oh, you'd be surprised."

The man shot a glance round the room, showing his teeth in a quick smile. "Well, all right, then, as I say, I don't want to keep you—"

There was a murmured thank you and then the pounding of feet on the stairs, the slamming of a door, the squeak of hinges—one of those pull-down things, she imagined, with the ladder attached—and then the odd rattle and thump from above. Frank went back into his study without a word. She listened briefly for the baby, glanced out the window to see Svetlana sitting on the dock now, rocking the canoe with her feet, then she poured herself a cup of tea, sat down at the table with the book she'd been reading, and forgot all about Jimmy Simpson until the hinges squeaked again, the door slammed and the footsteps thundered on the stairs. Then he was in the kitchen, his face riding high across the room as if he were carrying it on a platter right on out the door with a holler of "Thank you, Mrs. Richardson" and "See you later, Viola."

The footsteps retreated across the porch and fell off into a well of silence. "Nice boy," Olgivanna said, just to say something, but she didn't feel the truth of it. Just the opposite, in fact. There was something, well, *fishy** about him. And if she wasn't mistaken—she couldn't be sure, he'd gone by so fast—he wasn't carrying a fishing pole either.

"Oh, yah," Viola returned, "salt of the earth."

There was a chill in the air that evening—it was the third week of October now, the trees dropping their leaves, geese crying out overhead like lost souls in the ether—and she'd come back from a long walk round the bay to the rich astringent odor of Viola's sauerbraten and a fire of oak and sweet-scented apple from a windfall tree Frank had cut and stacked earlier in the day. Outside, beyond the windows, the sky was tied up end to end with pink ribbons of cloud under a cold red sunset. Svetlana was busy over a drawing, the baby asleep, Frank in his study. Olgivanna helped Viola with the table, setting out

* Another of those felicitous American expressions, deriving, I presume, from the odor of suspect fish. Of course, we Japanese, as an island people, have a great respect for the utility of all the creatures of the sea, and we would never dream of preparing a fish for sashimi, sushi or even stock for ramen without either seeing it caught personally or giving it a good, long and thorough sniff. And while this isn't the place for animadversions, I can't help saying that what passes for "fresh fish" in America wouldn't serve as offal for the cats in Japan—and our cats don't really eat all that well.

the plates and cutlery, tucking a red-flecked leaf into the fold of each napkin and taking her time over an arrangement of dried flowers and pinecones she'd collected on her walk, a simple thing, but Frank would like it. He was a great one for bringing nature into the house—they'd already made an expedition in the Cadillac to a local farmer for their Halloween pumpkins and the cornstalks to frame them, and practically everything in the place that could serve as a vase sprouted a sprig of cattails or yarrow or Queen Anne's lace.

As they ate, they watched the lake transmuted from copper to silver to lead, and then the windows began to give back the light of the room and Frank went round the house, turning on the lamps one after the other. Afterward, Mrs. Devine came in to take Frank's dictation while the cook washed and stacked the dishes and Olgivanna put the children to bed, the baby in the master bedroom and Svetlana on the glassed-in porch. Then she sat by the fire with her knitting—she was making matching caps and scarves for the children in a snowflake pattern she'd devised herself—and listened to Frank's voice as it rose and dipped through its modulations. She loved listening to him, even when he backtracked to correct himself or when he lost his patience and began wisecracking or broke into song, because he was telling a story, his own story, the narrative of his boyhood when he was sent to his Uncle James' farm each summer to labor from dawn to dusk. " 'Whosoever would sow must hoe,' " he dictated in his strong clear tones, then paused to glance over his spectacles. "Paragraph break. And continue: 'And if he who hoes would reap—he must weed.' "

It was ten o'clock, Mrs. Devine stifling a series of yawns, Frank as indefatigable as ever, the wind up in the trees and the clock on the mantelpiece announcing the hour in a sleepy repetitive drone, when there was a knock at the kitchen door. The first thing that came into Olgivanna's head was Mrs. Simpson's son—was he returning the fishing pole? Still looking for it? But then she glanced at Frank and went cold. He'd come up out of his chair so fast the pages of his notes looped away from him to spill at his feet and he stood poised there, every fiber of him straining toward the kitchen, where Viola, in carpet slippers and a gray cardigan buttoned up over the glossy floral print of her dress, rose heavily to answer the door.

A man's voice carried in out of the night—"Is Mr. Richardson at home?"—and Viola, innocent of everything, murmured, "Yes, I believe he is."

In the next instant half a dozen men in hats and overcoats shouldered their way into the room even as Frank took a step back as if he were uncertain on his feet, and Olgivanna saw the fear in his eyes, real fear, for the first time since she'd known him. The room filled. There were more men in the kitchen, on the porch. Their faces were tight and waxen as they blinked against the light and they brought a smell with them, a harsh odor of the night, the primeval mud on their shoes, cigar smoke. Mrs. Devine, the stenographer, let out a gasp so sharp and sudden it was as if someone had punctured a tire. And all Olgivanna could think was *We're the Richardsons, that's all, just the Richardsons. We're nobody. We're harmless. They can't touch us.*

"You're all under arrest!" one of them shouted, the one in the middle, with the massive jaw and the brutal shining oversized boots and the eyes that chewed up and spat out everything in the room, and she saw that he was brandishing a badge. There was another one beside her, crowding her, breathing his beer or whiskey or whatever it was right in her face—and somehow she seemed to have gotten up out of her chair without being aware of it, the baby's cap dangling by a thread from one hand, the other at the collar of her dress, the sudden assault scrambling her senses, strangers, hateful strangers right there in her house as if she were under the whip of the Cheka, as if she were in Russia still and all the rest had been a dream.

"Don't be ridiculous," Frank snapped, trying to brave it out. "On what charges? And what do you mean bursting in here like this?"

It was then that another man shoved his way into the room, a jowly tall looming presence in a tan overcoat that fanned out behind him like an Indian blanket. "Well, here they are," he bellowed, "—at last. Now, where's the kid?" And then, before anyone could stop him, he jerked open the bedroom door and burst in on Iovanna with a shout. "Yeah, here it is, in here, the baby!"

That was when Frank made a move for him and the big one, the sheriff, took hold of him—"No violence now," he said, "and you come quietly"—and Frank said, "Get that man out of there or I'll—"

And suddenly she was moving, forcing her way into the bedroom even as the man in the tan overcoat snatched the blankets off Pussy and Pussy's eyes flashed open on the ugly brutal slab of his face and she let out the first startled cry—he was the lawyer, Miriam's lawyer, that was who he was, and for Olgivanna the realization was incendiary. She shoved him aside, actually shoved him, and in the next instant she had the baby pressed to her and she was the one who was shouting now. "You get out of here! You have no right! You stop this, this persecution!"

But he wasn't listening because he was already reeling back through the door, drunk with the imprimatur of authority, crying out in a towering voice, "Now, where's the other one, where's Hinzenberg's kid?"

The rest was chaos, Svetlana dragged in off the porch by some flat-faced goon, shocked out of her sleep and crying aloud in a series of ascending whoops, Pussy shrieking in counterpoint with all the shearing power of her developing lungs and Frank wrestling with the men at the door while the stenographer and cook looked on in horror and bewilderment. And worse: distaste. In all the confusion and the wrestling back and forth, the look Viola gave her came closest to breaking her down—and she wasn't going to give way to tears, not now and not ever, because she was stronger than that. But here was this mild unremarkable woman who'd shared the house with them for six weeks now, day in and day out, their intimate, trusted and trusting, and her eyes showed nothing but contempt. It was as if she'd stepped on a snake while mopping the kitchen floor, taken hold of the broom and had it sprout teeth and bite her, and Olgivanna wanted to explain it all to her, tell her that they'd been forced to live like this, to lie and assume fictive personalities, to cower and hide like criminals when they were innocent, innocent of everything but persecution. Miriam, she wanted to shout, Miriam's the criminal.

But a man was there at her side and he was telling her that she had to come along—"No!" Frank roared. "Just me, just take me. Let them stay here, under guard if need be, but let them stay!"—and Svetlana broke free then and ran to her, screaming, and Olgivanna lost all control. Suddenly it was her voice and her voice alone that every person in that room was hearing. "Enough!" she shouted. "You men should be ashamed. Can you not see that you are terrifying this child—both these children?"

The flat-faced one took a step back. The sheriff loosened his grip on Frank's arm and Frank jerked it away, indignant, outraged. Both the children gasped for breath and the fire hissed and every man in the room looked down at his shoes.

"Now," she snapped as if she were shaking out a rug,

"we will cooperate, but I want every one of you here to tell this child"—she swung Svetlana around to face them—"that everything is going to be all right. Well? Do you hear me? Is there a man in this room who does not have a little boy or girl at home right now? A niece? A nephew?" She glared at them. "Are you beasts?"

There was a murmur, the rough voices muted, and then it was all right. The sheriff crossed the room to her, removed his hat to reveal a compressed tangle of sweat-soaked hair, and told her he was sorry and that if it was up to him he'd let her stay. "But you have to understand, ma'am, it's my duty to serve the law and these warrants must be answered to." His voice was soft, almost sweet, and for a moment she thought he was going to reach out and pat Svetlana's head. "Now, we'll give you time to gather your things and put aside some clothes for the kids, but they're going to have to go into protective custody, you understand, at least till the morning."

Frank started back in then, his voice high and querulous—"Protective custody? Are you mad? Can't you see these children need their mother?"—and she saw the sheriff's face harden. It was no use. The mood of the room shifted back to animosity and they took Frank by the arm and then she and the children were in their coats and hats and the door opened on the night and the cold steps of the porch and the hot hard flash of the photographers' cameras.*

* Wrieto-San is not at his best in these photos, less master of the situation than mastered by it. He seems befuddled, as if he's just realized that he's put on some stranger's coat and hat and taken up an ersatz cane. And I mean no disrespect, but in studying these pictures, I have to say that he looks woefully ordinary, like a podgy shoe salesman wandering the aisles or the owner of a delicatessen who can't seem to remember what he's done with the sliced bologna.

* * *

There was the night in prison, locked behind bars, a night without the children, without Frank—and they'd planned it this way, Miriam's lawyer and the police and their accomplices in the press, to make the most of Frank's suffering and humiliation, to bring him low—and then there was court and bail and a fresh assault of the cameras as they came down the steps of the courthouse in Minneapolis. She hadn't slept. Hadn't combed her hair or pressed her clothes or used a tube of lipstick or even brushed her teeth. The jail stank of the animal functions, of the communal toilet and the disinfectant they tried to cover it up with. The other inmates—drunks and prostitutes and morphine addicts, low people, uneducated, unwashed, ragtag and bobtail—moaned and gibbered through the night in a low hopeless drone and all she could think about was the children. Svetlana had been mortally frightened, clinging to her as the matron separated them, and the baby, alive to her sister's distress, never stopped crying all the way down the long corridor and out of sight.

"They'll be all right," the woman kept telling her, "I'll be with them myself all night and I'm sure you'll be out by tomorrow, all of you," but they wouldn't be all right, they'd never be all right, never again. How could they be? They'd been terrorized, brutalized, torn out of bed by strangers and locked away by strangers beyond any reason or justification that even an adult could begin to comprehend. "Mama, what's happening?" Svetlana kept asking her as they wound along the dark roads in the police car, Frank reduced to a shadow in the vehicle ahead of them. "Mama, did Daddy Frank do something bad? Did you? Where are we going? What's happening?"

She had no answer for her—she could only hold her as the car lurched and the baby squirmed and sputtered and the headlights pulled them toward some final climactic panorama of debasement and disgrace—and she had no answer for the mob of reporters the next morning either. The arraignment was a public humiliation, no different in kind from what the Puritans had inflicted with their stocks and ducking stools, the whole procedure, from standing before the judge to the release on bail, a shame so deep she could barely breathe. When she passed through the courthouse doors and out into the daylight, she was disoriented. The flash blinded her. Her feet were unsteady. "Olga," they shouted as if they knew her, as if they were her friends and intimates, as if they only wanted to help, crowding in on her en masse like some perverse scrummage. "Olga! Olga!" It was drizzling. The pavement shone. Frank had her by the arm and his lawyers were there, one on either side, trying to shield them both. "Olga! Olga! Will you give us a statement? Frank? Mr. Wright?"

All she wanted was to hide herself away—she, the granddaughter of Marco Milanoff, Montenegro's greatest general and patriot, daughter of Ivan Lazovich, chief justice of Montenegro, and Militza Milanoff, herself a general in the Montenegrin army, transformed into an outcast, a criminal, an adulteress—but Frank paused there on the steps in the rain to tell anyone who wanted to hear how abused he'd been and how contrived these charges were. She shrank. She died. And he talked on while the drizzle thickened and the pencils slipped across the page. She stared at the ground—"Olga! Olga!"—and he held tight to her even as he gestured with one arm and let his voice ride up and down the ladder, and then they were moving again, the reporters and a hundred or more hyenas with nothing better to do sweeping along in a train behind them.

And where were they going? To a place with four walls and a friendly face, clean sheets, a bed with blankets to pull up over their heads for the duration? Some lightless cave a mile down in the earth where no one could get at them ever again? No. They were crossing the street to the municipal courthouse to answer the federal charges under the Mann Act because unbeknownst to them they'd been observed driving across the state line at La Crosse—by spies—which action indicated, to the dimness of the law, that Frank had coerced her to his will and that she was an accomplice in his depravity. When she realized what was happening—the spectacle, another flight of steps, another courtroom with another set of pale reproving faces—she felt her legs go weak. She couldn't go on. She couldn't endure it. The shame, the shame. Olga, Olga! But Frank held her up, the doors opened wide, the mob parted and she found herself in the temple of justice once again, heroic statuary rising up before her, fluted columns, marble floors, people turning to stare. Her footsteps echoed off the tiles. Boomed. Shouted out her guilt.

Two men in dark suits intervened then, showing her into a side room off the main corridor despite Levi Bancroft's puffing and hand-wringing—she saw a flag, a desk, half a dozen wooden chairs, but no judge, no spectators, no press—even as two others materialized to lead Frank off in the opposite direction. "Bear up," he called over his shoulder, and he might have told her he loved her, but he was already gone. She clutched her bag to her. Shot a look at the windows and the dark varnished stain of the door at the far end of the room, and the sight of it, of that door, terrified her—it led to another cell, she was sure of it. "We're federal agents, ma'am, and we have a few questions for you," one of the men said, pulling out a chair for her. She held herself rigid while they sat heavily across from her. The one who'd spoken produced a cigarette case and offered it to her, but she wouldn't look at it, wouldn't move. There was the sound of a match striking, then the odor of tobacco, harsh and raw.

For a long moment, none of them spoke. The room was dim, sterile, cold as an icebox. Here were these men, these strangers, who held her by force of compulsion, and they hadn't even thought to turn on the lights or the radiator, and the idea of it, of their indifference, depressed her even further. She wanted her children. She wanted release. But the ritual must play itself out: they were federal agents and she was a fugitive, an undesirable alien, caught in a tangle of lies.

The second man cleared his throat and said, "Let's begin with your name. You are Olga Lazovich?"

"Yes," she said, "yes." And then she bowed her head and in a very soft voice found herself telling them everything, telling them the truth and too much of the truth—"Puerto Rico? Do you mean to say you fled to Puerto Rico and then reentered the country without a visa?"—until it seemed as if she were bound up in her own chains and that nothing, no force of law or mercy or public opinion, could save her.

Another night in the lockup. In the hoosegow. Isn't that what they called it?

*Hoosegow**—she chanted it softly to herself through another sleepless night, frantic with worry and chewing over this absurd little degraded excuse of a two-syllable word as if it were a prayer. *Hoosegow, hoosegow.* It was

* When I first acquired this term, I kept pronouncing it with an extra syllable, voicing the intercalary *e*, all but certain it must have been of Norwegian derivation. It is, in fact, a corruption of the Spanish: *juzgado,* sentenced, from the verb *juzgar,* to judge. In attempting to make light of what must have been among the most painful periods of his life, Wrieto-San had this to say of his decline and fall: he had gone "From Who's Who to the Hoosegow."

cold. The single blanket was thin. She began to think she hated Frank—not Miriam, but Frank. Frank was the one who'd got her into this, Frank and Frank alone. Frank had destroyed her. Annihilated her. Brought her to the lowest level of the lowest seep of humanity. She pictured him in his cell somewhere in the other wing of the building, boasting, strutting, keeping up a face for his fellow convicts, the great man, the Master, even in his downfall. And then she began to think she hated herself. Because if she'd been stronger, if she'd resisted him—and Taliesin, the peace and beauty of it, the promise it held out of home, sanctuary, permanence—if she hadn't gone to him on the recoil from Georgei, if she'd only waited, none of this would have happened.

They woke her at dawn with a hard roll and a cup of coffee in a tin cup.

They took her back to the courthouse.

The cameras flashed.

Flashed again.

And then, to her amazement, though she expected the worst—prison, deportation, the loss of the children and Frank too—they set her and Frank free on surety of $15,000 each, supplied by Frank's friends, who had rallied to him. Vlademar, after meeting at length with Frank and his attorneys,* came to his senses and dropped the adultery complaint and the lawsuit as well. The sheriff of Sauk County was reportedly moving to release them from the charge of being fugitives from justice and the Mann Act charges were being reconsidered in light of the fact that Vlademar, who had furnished only sixty dollars that year toward child support, had stepped down, and it could be seen clearly that she and Frank were living as husband and wife and that Frank was providing for

* For five hours, according to the *Chicago Tribune*. One would like to have been privy to that meeting.

the children. This time there was a car waiting when they came down the courthouse steps. The children were in the backseat. The chauffeur slammed the door on the reporters and they were gone.

One thing remained. And Frank started in on it the minute the car left the curb and wouldn't let it go through the reunion with the children, through lunch and dinner and on into the night, his attorneys chiming in like parrots whenever they had the opportunity. "We're not out of the woods yet," Frank kept saying till the sound of the phrase on his lips made her flinch as if she were being battered with a cudgel carved out of the worn remnants of the language, of English, the English language and all its laws and proprieties, and what was wrong with the woods, anyway? At least it was dark there. And deserted. "And"—with a look to whichever of the lawyers happened to be present—"while public sympathy has definitely swung in our favor, we do need to press our advantage. If Miriam can use the newspapers, so can we. Don't you agree? Isn't it time to tell our side of the story?"

It was the day following their release. She was staying at the home of one of Frank's friends, enjoined from leaving the state of Minnesota until all charges had been cleared. Her head ached, her stomach revolted. When she looked across the room, the intermediate distance seemed to blur and shift shape until nothing was recognizable. She thought of her mother, who'd been so fierce and uncompromising in battle that the Turks swore to bind her between two horses and tear the limbs from her body if they ever got hold of her. That was what she wanted now, two horses to tear her apart. It would be a joy compared to facing the press.

"It won't be a press conference, but just an interview. Right here. Right in this room. And with a single reporter. A female. What do you say?"

She glanced past him to the depths of the room, palm fronds cut like the fingers of a monstrous grasping hand against the glow of the lamplight, the pattern of the Persian rug alternately dilating and shrinking away. She was so exhausted she could hardly form the reply in her head, let alone her throat. The lawyers—barely kempt and battle weary—leaned in. Frank went silent. "No," she breathed.

Frank had been seated beside her, solicitous, gently smoothing a hand over her forearm and wrist, but now he jumped up and began pacing the length of the rug. The light of the overhead lamp saturated his brow and seeped into his eyes so that they seemed like lights themselves, radiant, blistering. He was adamant. He was angry. And she knew what was coming, knew he was going to try to twist her to his point of view. "But all the filth, the lies Miriam's spread—"

Firmer now: "No."

"Yes," Frank said. "You must."

"No."

"Yes," he repeated. "Yes, absolutely yes."

And so she spent her third sleepless night in a row, this one in a bed the size of a tennis lawn, with a parade of pillows, a smell of lilac and a view down a tranquil moonlit avenue, all the while rehearsing what she would say, how she would explain herself, her family history, her nobility of purpose and the sanctity of her love for Frank and her children and Taliesin too. How she'd been wronged. Misrepresented at every turn by a vindictive and perhaps even mentally unstable woman. How everything that was pure had been willfully controverted so that good appeared evil and love was demeaned and envy elevated and all the rest. She made unarticulated speeches all night long, the words throbbing in her head till they wouldn't stop and her eyes wouldn't close and the light came hammering through the windows and she was still murmuring to herself through the breakfast she took alone in her room and her toilet and the long lingering sequence of combing out her hair, selecting a single strand of jet beads and dressing herself in an almost austere gown and shoes that were solid and respectable, last year's shoes, shoes that would verify and underpin everything she had to say. She would right the record. She would defend herself. Make use of every high-flown phrase and stirring sentiment she could muster. She was nothing low. She was high, higher than any of them.

Still, when she walked into the room to see the solitary woman rising from the chair with her clenched face and painted nails and the pencil and pad she brandished like plated armor, all she could say was: "Please, can you—will you say that I am not a dancer?"

CHAPTER 8: VALE, MIRIAM

Money was the problem. Cash. Spondulics. The means to pay for the necessities of life so that you didn't have to live like some half-naked beggar in a loincloth on the streets of Calcutta. That was what she tried to impress upon Mr. Fake, because her husband—and he *was* still her husband—was most emphatically evading his obligations to her. He was vituperative. Mean. Petty. And he hadn't paid out so much as a nickel for her upkeep since she'd filed the alienation of affection suit and what did he, Mr. Fake, expect her to subsist on? Wasn't he her attorney? Wasn't he being paid to look after her interests, to protect her from the vultures her husband employed? Did he realize that she'd been forced to move in with her daughter because the Southmoor had all but thrown her out in the street? And that the situation was intolerable? That she was ill, fatigued, depressed? That her son-in-law looked at her across the dining table as if she'd come to steal the bread from his mouth and that the room she'd been given was a repository of unwanted furniture and a broken bicycle and that it smelled of some deceased thing trapped in the walls?

And what did Mr. Fake tell her? Settle. Settle now and get out while you can because public opinion had turned against her, and her husband's friends* were pulling strings to have all charges against him dismissed and the suit thrown out of court.

"What do you mean, 'public opinion'?" she spat back at him. She was seated across the desk from him in his offices on a damp ironclad day in early December, feeling out of sorts, and not simply because of the painfulness of the situation or because he'd kept her waiting in the anteroom a good half hour, but in a deeper way, a way of malaise and physical depletion. It was the flu. It was her heart. Her liver. She wasn't well, wasn't well at all.

"You've seen the newspapers," he said in his soft conspiratorial tone. He'd made a cradle of his interlocked fingers and he was resting his chin on it and giving her a look that was meant to be Solomonic. A framed oil painting—a bucolic lacustrine scene in atrocious taste and worse execution—hung on the wall behind him. His wife must have been the artist—it was the only explanation Miriam could think of, because no one in his right mind would actually seek out and purchase something as offensive to the sensibilities as that. Or perhaps an adolescent daughter. Did he even have children? She realized she didn't know a thing about him, whether he was married, divorced, a widower, bachelor or monk—but then what difference did

* Carl Sandburg prominent among them. But perhaps the "kicker" with regard to public sympathy was his first wife's unflagging defense of him—astonishingly, Kitty announced to the press that she was prepared to come up to Minneapolis and stand by him in his time of need. Now, I never met her and cannot speak either to her motives or her mental state at this juncture, but one has to marvel at Wrieto-San's magnetism and his ability to have such a lasting effect on a woman he'd turned his back on. Twice.

it make? He could have been Joseph Smith himself with half a hundred wives so long as he put the screws to Frank.

"Mrs. Wright? Miriam? Are you listening to me?"

She was, of course she was. She gave a little wave of her hand. *Public opinion.* The fools, the idiots. To favor some little adventuress, some adulteress, a husband-stealer, over her . . . She could still see the headlines: WRIGHT'S OLGA BARES LIFE STORY; *Public Misled; Begs Merciful Heart for Baby;* and then, down the page: *Not a Dancer; Toils Without Luxuries.* Oh, it was all there, the whole sob story—how the little Russian had cooked and scrubbed and chopped wood at Taliesin till her fingers had practically fallen off, how she'd only come to Frank after Miriam had deserted him, and how she wasn't a dancer any more than Frank was a piano player because he liked sometimes to sit at the keyboard to play an air for the family and that the press had stuck her with the sobriquet only as a means of cheapening her as if she were some cabaret performer or cigarette girl when in fact she came from the most distinguished family in all of Montenegro—but it didn't matter a whit. The pretty pictures, the downcast look, the naked cry for sympathy. Anybody could see she was a whore and whores qualified for nothing, not mercy or sympathy or credibility or even notice.

"You can't go on expecting the impossible," he was saying, leveling that look on her. "Now—and let me remind you once again—his most recent offer, totaling twenty-three thousand dollars, including five thousand in cash and an additional three thousand for expenses and attorneys' fees to be paid out immediately as a means of discharging your obligations, including the one thousand and some odd dollars owing to the Southmoor, seemed perfectly reasonable to me, as you well know—"

"Seemed *reasonable* to you? I suppose it would, because at this point I can only imagine you're more concerned with your own welfare than with mine. You want your fee—that's the long and short of it, isn't it? But this is my life we're considering here. I'm the one who's been dragged through the mud. I'm the one who has no means of support and no hope of it."

"Even your children . . ." he began, taking another tack. And was he debating her now? Was that what she was paying him for? Debates?

"What have my children to do with it?"

"They're in agreement with me. Settle, that's what they say. You can't expect them to—well, I know this is a delicate matter and perhaps none of my business beyond anticipating the timely remuneration of your legal fees to this firm—but you can't expect them to continue taking on your debt in the hope of . . . I don't know what." He paused to remove his spectacles so that his eyes floated up at her like two faintly greenish fish in a yellowed aquarium. "What is it that you want exactly, Mrs. Wright—Miriam? Vengeance? Do you want to see him destroyed, is that it?"

It came to her then that he was a small man too, self-serving, narrow-minded, a coward like all the rest. She was so angry all of a sudden, so inflamed and eruptive and just plain irritated she had to bite her lip to keep from screaming. "I won't settle," she said finally, her voice as dry as two husks rattling in the wind. "Never," she said. "Not till I die."

He looked away, shifted in his seat, impatiently clamped the spectacles back over the bridge of his nose. "You don't want an attorney," he said, and he was the one struggling to control his voice now, "you want an avenging angel."

She rose abruptly from the seat, all the listlessness scorched right out of her. Her hands were trembling as she reached down to snatch up her bag and for a fraction of a second everything seemed to blur as if she'd been punched in the face. She was halfway to the door before she swung round on him. "That's right," she said. "That's exactly right."

The days began to flicker at her like a motion-picture film on a screen she couldn't reach—somehow she was stuck in the back row, in the cheap seats, watching her own life transpire with a foreign logic until, inevitably, it sank into melodrama. And sorrow. A sorrow so deep she couldn't bear to get out of bed half the time. There was that smell in the walls, the stench of fatality, of rot. The wallpaper was hideous—where was Norma's taste? The broken bicycle. A table with three legs, propped up on an overturned wastebasket and a volume of Dickens—*Bleak House*, and how bleakly appropriate. Most mornings she was sick in her stomach, the cramping there, sick in her bowels, as if nothing would ever pass through her again. She found herself sweating, even outside in the arctic blast that reanimated the dead limbs of the trees and scoured the gutters. Her son-in-law irritated her. Norma irritated her. The idea of Christmas drove her into a frenzy of loathing, the spangles and the balls and the phony good cheer dispensed by every grinning hostess and street-corner drunk. *Merry Christmas.* It was like a war cry to her. Chicago: she hated it. Winter: she hated it. And here she was, forced to spend half her time out in the full fury of the season tramping from her lawyer to the doctor and then on to the next doctor and the next, the only thing that gave her comfort in the shortest supply.

And where was Frank while she was stuck here living hand to mouth? He was in California, released finally from Minnesota pending a grand jury investigation into the Mann Act charges, living off his friends, his bounteous friends, no doubt sitting at that very moment beneath a tangerine tree with the sun on his face. And her beside him. The bitch. The breeder. She couldn't recall which day it was—one dead ice-bracketed eternal afternoon of that week between Christmas and New Year's—when she decided to go to Leora, who was back now in Santa Monica as any sensible person would be. She'd just made use of the pravaz, the elixir seeping through her veins while the radiator belched and Norma's husband tramped by in the hall as if his feet were encased in lead, when she had a sudden incandescent vision of the red bougainvillea climbing the bleached white stucco wall of Leora's guesthouse while hummingbirds hovered and the Chinese tiptoed out of the house holding his tray aloft in a pillar of sunlight. The next day she was on the train.

She hadn't followed Frank to California, that was what she told herself—and Leora agreed with her. She'd come for her health. For the air. The sun. And if Jesperson had tracked down Frank's address for her (and he wanted to be paid too, the four-flusher, because in his profession that was all that mattered, money), there was no reason she shouldn't use it to see him prosecuted. At the first opportunity, as soon as she was rested from her trip, she went downtown to the police and filed a charge of desertion against him, then made another foray to Tijuana and the very accommodating little brown man in the *farmacia* there. That was good, that was fine. But just then Frank wasn't in Los Angeles—she got wind of the fact that he'd gone to New York to oversee the sale at auction of his precious prints as a stopgap to save Taliesin from the bank. Immediately she wired her new attorney* and her new attorney wired a colleague in New York to appear on the scene with a warrant of attachment for the

* Miss Tillie Cecille Levin. Presumably, at this juncture, Miss Levin was more attentive to her needs, both real and imagined, than Mr. Fake.

prints, which were, after all, community property. For two days she sat with Leora at the dining room table, in the living room, in the twin chaise longues on the back lawn, smoking cigarettes and calculating her share and how it would clear her debts in a single stroke, and for those two days she was happy, genuinely happy for the first time in months, till the news came back that the collection had sold for a fraction of what it was worth—less than $40,000*—and that even worse, the auction house had put in a legal claim on the entire proceeds to cover past loans against the worth of the collection. Once again, and she couldn't help feeling the hand of fate in this, Frank had outmaneuvered her, even if he'd managed to outmaneuver himself in the bargain.

"I don't know, Leora, I just don't know," she said after the news had sunk in. "Sometimes it seems as if the whole world is against me." She was sipping a cocktail and the sun was bleeding through the windows, brightening the carpet in a long narrow strip and picking individual flowers out of the pattern on the chintz sofa. "He'll lose Taliesin now, that's for certain"—she paused, drew in a sigh, because she was feeling something, truly feeling it, though she'd have been hard-pressed to put it in

* Wrieto-San valued the collection at $100,000, and though, as I say, he continually over-valued practically everything he owned, he was perhaps at least somewhat accurate here, as the government of my country, alarmed at the way in which foreign collectors were depleting the stock of indigenous art, had strictly limited the export of these prints, thus driving up the price of those already in private collections. Hiroshige's masterwork, *Monkey Bridge in Kai Province* (*Kōyō Saruhashi no zu*), an exquisite double vertical *ōban*, was among the rare pieces up for auction, but Wrieto-San, because this was in effect a fire sale, actually received less for it than he'd paid some years earlier.

words, something to do with Frank and the way he was when she first met him, his enthusiasm for the place and for her and her in it—"but it just doesn't give me much satisfaction to think about it. Or not as much as I thought it would." She traced her finger round the rim of the glass and watched the sun slice Leora's face as she leaned forward, her lips compressed in a moue of sympathy, and then she let out a bitter little laugh. "I suppose it's the shock of having gone from fifty thousand dollars in the clear to zero—zero dollars and zero cents—don't you think?"

Leora's eyes—and strange she'd never noticed this before—were as pinched and slanted as the Chinese servant's, but maybe that was only the effect of the light. And her powder. Leora had got to an age where she really couldn't seem to exercise any judgment when it came to combating the erosion round her eyes and mouth, canyons there, craters, whole deltas of tributaries. And her nose—it looked as if it had been dredged in flour. Miriam had always congratulated herself on having inherited her mother's complexion, but now she strained to catch a glimpse of her face in the reflection of the curio cabinet—all of this turmoil must certainly have begun to show round her eyes, and what if she should end up looking like Leora?

Oblivious, Leora took a sip of her cocktail, removed the olive and sucked at it meditatively. "You're not getting soft on him, are you?"

"Me? Soft?" She considered the accusation a moment, observing the way Leora was watching her in that satirical posture that was so much a feature of her, perhaps the defining feature, the arched eyebrows, the southward slant of the mouth. Another sip of the shaken gin, fragrant as heaven, cold as hell. "Never. Believe you me, Mr. Frank Lloyd Wright—Mr. Philandering No-Good Wright—hasn't seen anything yet."

"Good for you," Leora said. "I was beginning to worry."

Still, as the days wore on and Leora began dropping hints—Charles was coming to dinner, Charles Schumocker, the producer, the widower, just fifty-eight years old and without doubt the wittiest man she'd ever met and really, Miriam, you should have heard what he said the other night at the Derby, Charles this, Charles that, Charles ad nauseam—and the local judge, another little man, a pygmy, a dwarf, threw out the desertion charge on the grounds that the infraction hadn't occurred in California, Miriam felt herself losing control, very gradually, gradient by gradient, in the way of the slippage the geologists said was causing the earthquakes that made the guesthouse a veritable percussion section once a week or so. Deep down—and Charles tried to explain this one night at dinner, making use of the china to illustrate his point—the rock plates were grinding against one another like saucers, if only saucers weren't smooth-edged but rough. That was what was happening to her, slippage, and everything that was smooth was abrading under the placid sun until it was too much for her to bear.

The negotiations went on through the spring and into the summer of 1927, Miss Levin wiring her periodically with offers and counter-offers, Norma dunning her by post and long-distance telephone, Charles, with his high forehead and emperor's (usually dripping) nose practically installed in the house now and Leora chattering on like a girl about the inexpressible romance of second marriages. Miriam felt—well, *depleted*. She was at loose ends. She needed money. There was no place for her at Leora's, at least not during the reign of Charles, and she couldn't afford a hotel. Finally, though it was like driving spikes right through the palms of both hands, like self-crucifixion, she gave in.

She instructed Miss Levin, by wire, to accept her husband's latest offer—$5,000 in cash plus payment of all legal fees, a trust fund of $30,000 and a $250 monthly allowance for life*—on one condition: that he renounce Olga for a period of five years. Word came back a day later. He refused. Categorically. Oh, she could see right through him, the coldhearted bastard. He had the upper hand now and he knew it. He was going to wait her out, that was what he was going to do—starve her, if need be, see her turned out in the streets like a beggar. And the minute the divorce was finalized he would start counting off the days till he could marry his little Russian, just as he'd done with her as soon as he'd got free of Catherine.† But she wouldn't give in, she wouldn't. Not yet, anyway.

She took the train to San Francisco because she couldn't think of anything else to do and Alvy Oates, an old friend from her Chicago days with Emil, had offered her a place to stay just as long as she wanted. All the way up the coast, as the train beat along the tracks, she cursed Frank and cursed him again. And when she got there and saw the way Alvy's face had aged—all those pouches and wrinkles, the dewlaps of an old woman who sits in a corner all day sopping up gravy with a crust of bread—

* And how, one asks, did Wrieto-San expect to pay out this amount in cash? Ingeniously, and with the cunning that characterized his financial dealings throughout his life, he persuaded a group of friends to incorporate him—as Frank Lloyd Wright, Inc.—against future earnings, at a cost to each of $7,500. Which, needless to say, none of them ever saw again.

† Wisconsin law at the time prescribed a one-year waiting period before remarrying.

she took a good hard look at herself and went directly into a clinic there where a truly wonderful doctor who understood her every need and assured her that she had the most beautiful skin he'd ever seen on a woman of her age gave her a face-lift that would make her look ten years younger than the ten years younger she already looked. Which her husband would pay for. Soon. Very soon.

She sipped liquids through a straw while her face healed and never changed out of her dressing gown. None of her children would return her wires. Alvy went off to club meetings, bridge parties, events at the museum, the symphony, the yacht club, and she stayed behind, working crossword puzzles and reading detective novels. It was a time of excruciating and limitless boredom. One afternoon, after spending what must have been a full hour watching a lizard creep along the wall beneath the trellis on Alvy's patio, she wired her attorney to accept terms without proviso and on August 27 she was granted a divorce from Frank Lloyd Wright on grounds of desertion, Miss Levin submitting her testimony by deposition. It hurt her as nothing had ever hurt her before, but the money was paid out and she immediately booked a one-way fare to Chicago, where she planned to stop in to bid farewell to Norma on her way to New York and then Paris. Yes, Paris. Where she could forget all about Frank Lloyd Wright and his machinations, where she could focus on her own art for a change and grow and develop and spread her wings and maybe, once she was settled and moving in the circles she was accustomed to—or had been accustomed to before the war—she'd even remarry.

All well and good. But things bog down, things muddle. At the end of September, unaccountably, she found herself in a hotel room in Madison, Wisconsin, of all places, writing to Frank to tell him just what she thought of him and if her language was harsh so much the worse because he was the one in violation of the divorce order, not her, he was the one sneaking back up the hill to his "love nest"* so he could *stick his prick into the little Russian's cunt and fuck her and fuck her just as if they were goats, two fucking goats,* and she knew what was going on and it wasn't right. A week later she hired a car and drove out to Dodgeville with Tillie Levin and went right on up the steps of the rinky-dink town hall and demanded to see the district attorney, another weasel by the name of Knutson. "Do you have any idea what kind of filth is going on in this county?" she shouted the moment he came through the door of his office. He looked startled. Looked as if he'd had his hide exchanged for something that didn't fit quite right, and he was a man too, with a belly and braces and a tie stained with whatever he'd had for lunch, and no, he said, he didn't have any idea. "Frank Lloyd Wright!" she shouted. "Frank Lloyd Wright! Does that ring a bell?"

And what was Tillie saying—"No, no, stay calm, Mrs. Wright"—and why in Christ's name was this moron just standing there gaping at her?

"Listen, ma'am," he was saying, trying to back into his office with the firmest intent of shutting the door on her, and he wasn't going to get away with that, he

* Actually, at this point the bank still owned Taliesin, though Wrieto-San's friends were negotiating for a grace period with regard to the outstanding debt. He was living with his sister Jennie in her house (Tan-y-deri) on the Taliesin grounds, however, and doing his best to repair damage from yet another fire that had occurred in his absence. (And what is it with this man and fire?)

wasn't—"I've told you over the telephone that this office will not revive those charges and that those charges are dead—"

"He's fornicating!" she screamed. "Immoral purposes, the Mann Act, in violation . . . everywhere. Of, of—of everything!"

There was breakage, and she couldn't help that, because the coward ducked back into his office and shut the door on her and he wouldn't do his duty, wouldn't serve the writ, wouldn't stop the fucking—and things spun out of control after that no matter how Tillie tried to mollify her. And what next? What next? At dinner that very night, as she tried to summon the desire even to lift the fork to her mouth over the miserable excuse for a meal the Lorain Hotel of Backwardsville, Wisconsin, put before her, a man with a face like boiled meat and two little pig's eyes identified himself as a federal agent and put her under arrest on a charge of sending obscene material through the mails on account of the letter she'd sent Frank to just tell him off because who did he think he was, and they put her in her room and guarded the door as if it were a prison cell. She beat on that door till her hands were raw and she screamed, oh, she screamed. Five hundred dollars, the judge said. And she fired Tillie. And Paris was a dream. And she went right to the governor of Wisconsin himself, Fred R. Zimmerman, over the way she'd been treated and he wouldn't see her and she went back to Chicago and that room with the broken bicycle and found the governor there for some sort of convention and she marched directly through the dining room of his hotel crying out that she demanded to see him on urgent business and he was the littlest of little men because he actually got up from the table when she was still twenty feet from him and scuttled sideways through the kitchen and out the service entrance into the street and he was probably still scuttling. And Frank went to Arizona* to get away from her and she just had no choice in the matter but to follow him there and demand that somebody put a stop to this *fucking*.

Where next? Well, she was beaten down and exhausted and she had her money in hand, but she took out a warrant in Arizona charging him with whatever she could think of and when he went off to California she went there too. It was fall now, Leora married to Charles, the palms up and down Sunset Boulevard whipping in the winds that tore like cellophane over the dun mountains, sere days, chilly nights, a smell of smoke on the air. She called Jesperson, a man happy in the knowledge that he'd been paid for services past and would be paid again and paid well, and Jesperson gave her an address down south near San Diego, in La Jolla, where he said he'd found her husband holed up with his little dolly. In a cottage. On a quiet street. With a prospect of the ocean.

She wasn't reasoning. Reasoning was for little people, lawyers, architects, district attorneys. In the train on the way down from Los Angeles she went into the washroom and injected herself. Everything was very bright. She watched the ocean solidify outside the window till it might have been verdstone, shingled all the way to the horizon. People got on and off. She smiled at them all.

* This would have been at the instigation of Albert Chase McArthur, who hired Wrieto-San as consulting architect for the Biltmore Hotel in Phoenix for the sum of $1,000 a month, which monies Wrieto-San must sorely have needed at this juncture. It should be said in this connection that while McArthur is officially credited for the design, which makes use of the textile-block construction Wrieto-San pioneered in the Los Angeles houses, anyone with the least sensitivity to architecture can see that this is quite clearly one of Wrieto-San's buildings in all but name.

When they arrived at the station, the conductor had to help her off the train because she didn't recognize a thing—palm trees, the ocean glare, it was all the same to her—and there was nothing the porter could assist her with, thank you, as all she had with her was her purse and in the purse nothing but her pravaz, half a sandwich and a scrap of paper with the address on it.

The man in the cab—and why did he look so familiar?—said he knew the place, and after they lurched up and down a farrago of streets that were indistinguishable one from the other, various dogs darting out to yap at the wheels, skinny boys in undershirts and baseball gloves flitting past on the parched lawns and all the stumpy tile-topped haciendas rushing at her with their fangs bared, they were there. She saw an open lot, a scattering of trees, sand, the bright spank of the water. "Wait here," she said to the cabbie, and she crossed the lot unsteadily, struggling for balance in her heels. She had no plan. She just knew that he was there and she was there and that it had to end. The ocean smelled of decay. A gull sailed in out of nowhere and settled on the roof in a disclosure of feathers so marmoreal and bright it hurt her eyes. Sand leaked into her shoes. There were clumps of dune grass and they brushed her legs and the feel of them took her all the way back to the beach at Tokyo* and she remembered how she and Frank would picnic on the cool wet sand just beyond the breakers to escape the mugginess of the city, everything fresh in the golden light on the other side of the world. He adored picnics, Frank. Adored adventure and spontaneity like the boy he was and would always be. Frank. Frank. How she'd loved him. She had. She truly had.

But here was the house. His house. *Their* house. No one answered her knock. The front door—she tried it—

* Niijima, possibly, popular these days with surfers.

was locked, and that wasn't like Frank at all. Was this the right house? Across the lot, out on the street, the cabbie sat watching her from behind the windscreen of his car. She thought of going back to him, to make certain he'd got the address right, but perhaps if she just . . . peered through the window to see . . . if she might happen to recognize—

One of his prints was staring back at her. The actor. The one with the sword and the bold pattern of squares within squares on the front fold of his robe, the Shunshō, and what was it called? *Ichikawa. The Actor Ichikawa-Something.* Yes. She'd know it anywhere. And there was one of his screens on the wall behind the sofa. And that table—that table wasn't his. She'd gone to the shop to buy it herself, haggling with the shopkeeper like some fishwife in rudimentary Japanese—*"Tēburu, tēburu,"* she kept saying, *Kore-wa ikura desu-ka?* and he kept pretending he didn't understand her—and now Frank had it, now *she* had it.

The back door was open. And where was Frank, the criminal, the lecher? Out and about, no doubt, eating lobster somewhere with his whore, telling jokes, making demands. The thought of it made her seethe. She went through the house, room by room, everything strange and familiar to her at once. The little Russian's petti coats, her perfumes. Children's toys. The bric-a-brac Frank loved to surround himself with, as if he were the lady of the house. But it was all too much and before she knew what she was doing she was at the cupboard—a cup of tea, that was what she wanted—and she couldn't help it if all those jars and bottles were in the way and the merest touch of her hand sent them hurtling to the floor in an explosion of sound and color and texture. She couldn't help it. She couldn't. In fact, it was so satisfying, that simple act, that primal clatter, that she ran her hand over the next shelf and the next, till everything there was splayed out across the floor, flour, sugar, catsup, oats and vinegar, all the crude farmer's fare Frank glutted himself with like the rube he was. Her hands were trembling when she put the kettle on to boil and they trembled when she brewed the tea and sat at the table and lifted the cup to her lips.

At first all she'd meant to do was reclaim her property—her table and that fan and the enamel box—but once she was there, once she was inside, sitting in his kitchen with the teacup in her hand, the old feeling came over her, a rising counterweight of violence and hate. The teacup flew at the wall. And then she was up and jerking violently round the room, slamming at things as if each and every one of them—each plate and saucer and cruet—were the face of Frank himself, of his mistress, of their pinch-faced pig-tailed little bastard. She paused, barely winded, the wreckage of the kitchen lying at her feet. Then she went into the living room.

She picked up the table first—an end table of rosewood, intricately carved—and the sound it made when it tore the screen from the wall was like the overture to a symphony. Cloth gave. Wood. Plaster. Glass rang and chimed and hit all the high notes ascending the scale. She found an axe propped up against the fireplace and brought it down on the dining room table, the bookshelf, the chairs, the divans, the desk, Frank's desk. There was the whoosh of a ceramic vase grasping at the air, the shriek of splintering wood, the basso profundo of the andirons slamming to the floor. And who was it who alerted the police—a neighbor? The cabbie? The guardian angel of philanderers? Of fornicators?

Oh, but she fought those apes in uniform, with their locked-up faces and blistering eyes, giving as good as she got, and if there was blood—and flesh, flesh too—caught beneath her fingernails, well so much the worse for them. She was at the window with the axe when the first of them came through the back door, a boy, a puny shoulderless wisp of a boy in a uniform two sizes too big for him. "Ma'am," he said, "ma'am," as if that were her name. "Now calm down, ma'am, please."

She swung round on him in her rage, and who could blame her? And it was a good thing for him that he ducked out of the way when she flung the axe because that axe was nothing more than an extension of herself, of her will, and if she had a thousand axes it would only be a beginning. "What right have you to accost me here!" she demanded. "This is my house, mine, and I'll do with it as I please. Now, get out of here. Out!"

There was another one now, older, settled into his flesh and the dog pouches round his eyes, shanty Irish, and low, lower than low, she could see that at a glance. He shouted out a whole blathering garble of threats and admonitions as if he were under the misapprehension that she was hard of hearing, but she ignored him because at that moment her eyes lighted on the most intriguing little Chinese vase . . .

The judge lectured her and he couldn't see how ill she was, didn't care, because men stuck together and he was a man and Frank was a man and so was the policeman who'd taken hold of her arm as she flung the vase out onto the lawn through the shattered window and the Shunshō on its heels. Thirty days, the judge intoned, and then suspended the sentence on condition that she stay away from her ex-husband and from La Jolla and refrain from any and all criminal malfeasance whatsoever. She held herself erect. Never so much as blinked her eyes. And though it took all her strength to keep from throwing it back at him—criminal malfeasance indeed, and who was the real criminal here?—she never offered a word but for a murmur of acquiescence. Yes, she understood. Yes, she agreed to the conditions. And no, she had no intention of returning to La Jolla. Afterward, at her press conference, she looked into the faces of the reporters and felt as serene as she'd ever felt in her life. Something had shifted deep inside her, the plates slipping and grinding until now, finally, they were interlocked, and the pravaz—the pravaz would fix them there with a new kind of permanence. Frank—and all that life as Mrs. Frank Lloyd Wright—was behind her now, and that was what she told them. "I'm moving forward with my life," she said, her voice breathing in her own ears like a second voice, an ingenue's voice, a coquette's. "I've had another offer of marriage."

The room went quiet.

"Who is it, Miriam?" a voice rang out. "Who's the lucky man?"

"Oh, I can't reveal that," she said, and she was Maude Miriam Noel all over again, the Belle of Memphis, each word sweetening on her lips till it had the intensity of pure cane sugar, "but I will say he's a European gentleman of conspicuously high pedigree—heir to a throne, in fact—and that I've recently borne him a daughter who is now in her father's care. In Europe."* She faltered, lost her train of thought—or very nearly, and where was she, where was she?—but the *morfina* whispered in her ear and it came back to her. "Across the sea."

"Can you give us her name? The child's name?"

"Miriam," another called, "Miriam—"

"There's one more thing," she began, and they all fell silent. She fed on that silence and took a long slow look round her, feeling supreme, joyous, on top of the world. A smile for them, for each and every one of them, and for the cameras too. "I just wanted to announce," she went on, and here that unfortunate little tickle began to play at the base of her neck and she brought a hand to

* She was fifty-nine at the time.

her hair as if to smooth it back and held it there a moment till the tremor subsided. And yes, there was the flash, there it was. She laughed, actually laughed aloud, with the surprise of it.

"Yes, Miriam? Madame Noel? You said you were going to make an announcement?"

"Oh, yes, yes. I wanted to announce that I've taken a bungalow in Hollywood"—another pause, another slow pan of the room—"and at the suggestion of a number of prominent men in the motion-picture industry, I will be sitting for a screen test in the very near future."

There was a murmur of voices, the shuffling of feet. Somewhere off to her left someone was laughing or maybe crying, and outside, beyond the walls, she could hear the metallic clank of the streetcar and the dull fading rumble of the wheels carrying down the avenue. She didn't know what else to say and so she smiled again and thanked them all for coming.

CHAPTER 9: TALIESIN REDUX

It was like a haunting, like a slow, steady descent into the lair of the demon-lover, no peace, no respite, a fresh horror at every turning, chaos without end. Each time she and Frank set up a household, whether at Taliesin, in Minneapolis or Phoenix or on the very farthest verge of the continent where the land gave out and the waves pounded the shore, Miriam was there to wreck it. Each time they left the house—to go for a walk, to the grocer's, an exhibition, a restaurant—Olgivanna never knew if it would be there when they got back. Ash, that was what she'd come to expect. Scorched earth. Ruins. The sheriff would be at the door with yet another warrant. Immigration men would pop up out of nowhere. Bankers. Lawyers. The windows would be shattered and the furniture smashed and a policeman stationed on the porch with the Shunshō print propped against the rail like a bit of refuse flung up out of the maw of a hurricane. And what if this madwoman came at them with a knife? What if she tried to harm the children? What then?

She tried to ask Frank about it, but he just waved her off. "Miriam's a very disturbed woman," he'd say, as if the pronouncement itself would diminish her, neutralize her, take the edge off the blade, jam the bullet in the chamber.

"But you have said yourself that she has attacked people with a weapon, have you not?"

"There's nothing to worry about," he would tell her, but she could see that he didn't believe it. She found him checking the windows at night. He even began locking the doors.

Her cough worsened. She developed hives, allergies, a fungal infection. The sound of her own daughters' voices began to grate on her—their squabbling, their needs, *Mama, Mama!*—and the incessant suck and draw of the surf made her feel as if all the vitality were draining out of her in a pale rinse of foam. She couldn't walk into a room of that cottage without seizing with dread and fear and hate, the tables gouged, the mark of the axe on the mantel, the walls, the baseboard. And though Frank was tender, responsive, unfailingly cheerful, whistling over a drawing or the pages of his manuscript, singing in the shower, doing a little dance round the icebox with a glass of milk in one hand and a sandwich in the other, there were times when she wanted to get up and batter him with her fists, scream till she was breathless. She wasn't yet thirty years old and she felt as if she were sixty. She began to hate the way the sun came out of the east each morning. Everything tasted like nothing, like sand. Grit. Dirt in her mouth.

And then, just when things looked darkest, came a sea change. Miriam was charged with breaking and entering, in addition to vandalism and violating a prior restraining order. She was the one before the court now. She was the one with her photograph in the paper, the one shamed and publicly humiliated. And finally, at long last, the newspapers began to see her for what she was—an imbalanced and vindictive woman who would go to any lengths to destroy her ex-husband's happiness—and they turned against her, just as Frank had said they would. "I'm not a dancer," Olgivanna had told them, and that had carried weight, certainly it had, but it was the revelation that Miriam had hounded her out of the hospital with her newborn child that truly aroused public sentiment. That portrait of the young mother hustled out the door on a stretcher while her infant clung to her breast and the sleet drove down out of the sky was all but biblical—she might have been Mary hiding the Christ child from Herod, and where, in the public eye, did that leave Miriam? And then their year of probation was up and Frank married her* and gave her the present of Taliesin, rescued, at least for the time being, from the bankers.† "We're going home," he told her, "back to Taliesin. To stay."‡

All the way across country, married now, legitimated, holding her happiness inside her like a rare and shining thing, in love with her husband and her children all over again, she could think of nothing but Taliesin. Her garden was two years dead, the livestock sold off at auction by the Bank of Wisconsin, the flowerbeds given up to weed. The house would be a mess, she knew that, damaged by the weather and neglect, perhaps even vandalized, but it was home and they would soon be there and that was all that mattered. Home. Taliesin. The house of the hill. She saw it when she closed her eyes at night, one scene after another shuffling in her head like cards in a deck, and it was there in the daytime too, solid, impreg-

* ARCHITECT WRIGHT MARRIES DANCER, the headlines read.

† By the corporation, which was soon to go bankrupt.

‡ Within three months of their arrival in the fall of 1928, they were off to Arizona (with a party of fifteen, including draftsmen, the cook and Billy Weston and the pie-in-the-sky prospect of a hotel, San Marcos in the Desert, which would, alas, never be built).

nable, while the countryside rolled by and all the towns and villages and farmhouses in the world vanished behind them in a swirl of fading specks. When the car finally turned into the drive and they came up the rise to the courtyard, she was so overcome she sprang out the door before it had rolled to a stop, running on ahead while Frank and Billy Weston fumbled with the luggage and the children shouted out, and here were the flagstones beneath her feet and there the overgrown garden and the sentinel oaks and the Chinese bell she'd longed to ring again—and she did ring it, jerking hard at the clapper to let the sound carry out over the countryside in all its annunciative fervor.

Inside, it was different, and she wasn't prepared for it. She pushed open the door and the first thing she saw was a heap of rubble hastily swept against the wall—broken crockery, the shards of a vase, the spark of glass—and a rug rolled up in the corner and soaked through because of a leak in the wall above that was even now dripping, dripping. It was cold. Late October, the day lying soft as a glove over the hills, but in here, where no fire had been lit in a year and more, it was winter. And where was the wood for fuel? Unfelled, unchopped, unsawed, unsplit, unstacked. She wandered into the bedroom next, the girls' voices echoing behind her—"Mama, where are you? Oh, no, look at this! Mama, Mama!"—and saw that there were no bedclothes, no blankets, no pillows even. They'd stolen everything, the neighbors, the farmers, their upstanding, decent and God-fearing countrymen who could hardly wait till Frank's back was turned to descend on the place. Thieves, that was what they were. Thieves and hypocrites.

She drifted through the rooms in a daze, shivering, defeated, and even Frank couldn't warm her, though he sent Billy for wood and had him light the fires in the living room and bedroom and the boiler in the cellar.

Things were smashed everywhere. They'd stolen the crockery, the silverware, tools, towels, the kitchen implements, Frank's drafting set, his bow compasses and protractors and calipers and even the collection of colored pencils he'd been building for twenty years—and what one of them, what smirking farm boy or his whiskery hog-stinking father, could have any use for those pencils except spite? Except to show what they thought of Mr. Frank Lloyd Wright and his fancy dress and his manners and his mansion on the hill? It sickened her. There was the smell of urine in the corners, as if they'd marked their territory like animals. That was what their neighbors thought of them. That was what they were worth.

She might have let it conquer her—wreckage, everything wreckage, strewn from one end of the country to the other, as if they were living under an evil spell and condemned to act out their futility over and over again—but she didn't. There had been a revolution, the worst had been done, and it hardened her.* And hardened Frank too. Within the month the house was transformed, essential furnishings in place, the larder stocked, fresh-split oak accumulating, a pair of milk cows lowing in the barn and new faces appearing each day. Projects were coming in—a house for Frank's cousin to be built in Oklahoma, a massive twenty-three-story skyscraper in New York and a grand luxury hotel in the Arizona desert that would cost as much as three-quarters of a million dollars—and he needed draftsmen, architects, carpenters, clerical help. By Thanksgiving, Taliesin was alive again, all of them—

* I wouldn't want to indulge in amateur Freudianism, but perhaps the trials of these years were what molded her into the unsmiling and unyielding taskmaster of Taliesin, known universally among the apprentices as the Dragon Lady.

even Svetlana—working so furiously there was hardly a moment for reflection.

They fell into a routine. While Frank spent his time in the studio or out amongst the men, giving orders, as exacting as the demiurge himself, all the rest was left to her, and that was a good thing, a vital thing, because it was work and work was what she'd done for Georgei and now she was doing it for Frank, for her husband. And herself. For herself too. And the children. And Taliesin, let it rise again. This was the time of seventeen-hour days. Up in the dark, to bed at nine in a numb, tumbling descent to the pillow. The smell of sawdust on the air, of linseed oil, paint. The strength coming back into her hands, her forearms, her wrists and shoulders. She scrubbed, plastered, painted, washed, kneaded, peeled and chopped. Ordered the supplies, oversaw the cook, drew up a rotating schedule of household chores for the draftsmen, prototypes of the apprentices to come, who had no choice but to pitch in lest the whole enterprise collapse around them. They might have worked in an office in Chicago or Milwaukee, might have lived with their parents or in an apartment with a whole world outside their door, might have taken their meals at a boardinghouse or cafeteria, but now they were here and it was one for all and all for one.

Winter settled in. The lake froze and Frank insisted on taking time out for a skating party. And then it snowed and they all went tobogganing. There was hot cocoa. A wienie roast. Porridge in the mornings and great cauldrons of soups and stews, heavy with cabbage, beans, rice and potatoes because meat was scarce on a farm that hadn't been farmed, six, seven, eight loaves of bread a day, cookies, cakes, hot cider and pot after pot of coffee, so much coffee Olgivanna began to think they were floating the foundation on it. Butter, cheese, eggs, flapjacks. Apples two years in the barrel. Cane syrup. Molasses. Sugar. They needed fuel for the body. They needed heat—above all, heat. Because for all its rare beauty, Taliesin was as frigid, drafty and ice-bound as a medieval mead hall. Innocent of central heating, reliant on individual fireplaces that half the time burned down to embers,* its rooms open one onto the other and banks of single-pane windows wrapped round the entire structure, it was practical only as a dream made concrete and why, she kept wondering, couldn't Frank and his ancestors have settled in the tropics? Bermuda or some such place. Florida. The Gulf Coast.

One afternoon she was in the kitchen with the cook and one of the draftsmen—a boy of twenty-three who'd come up from Chicago for the chance to work with Frank Lloyd Wright, a good boy with a ready smile and a croaking octave-splitting voice Frank liked to imitate when he took on the persona of Eeyore the donkey for Pussy's benefit. His name was Herbert Mohl. He had eyes the color of rainwater, hair so fair it was nearly translucent. He was peeling potatoes—had been peeling potatoes since he'd washed and dried the breakfast dishes—and the job got away from him, a dull job, a job no boy would choose or want. Every time she glanced up he was sitting there motionless, the peeler in one hand, an unscathed potato in the other. "Herbert," she said finally, glancing to the two tubs of potatoes—a bellying white mound in the one, a dirt-brown mountain in the other—"you know we're going to need those potatoes for tonight, and then you're on the wood detail and cleanup after that."

He gave her a long look, the potato clutched like a grenade in his hand. The light was dim, the windows

* Woe betide the apprentice who let even one of them go dead on his shift.

gray. "You know what? I don't care. I just don't care anymore."

She was at the counter, on her feet, kneading the dough for tomorrow's bread. Her feet ached. Her shoulders ached. Her nose was running and all morning she'd been surreptitiously wiping it on the sleeve of her sweater. She wanted to say something soft, mollifying, she wanted to cajole, but she wasn't very good at cajolery and she was in no mood for argument or even, at this point, conversation. "You'd better care," she said, "if you want to eat."

He rose from the stool so swiftly it startled her. "I'm an architect, not a scullery maid," he said, his face flushed. "I didn't come here to peel potatoes and tend your precious fires and scrub pots and pans till my fingers go stiff. And what about pay? I've yet to see a single cent out of this place." He was verging on insolence and insolence she wouldn't tolerate. Mrs. Taggertz, busy at the stove, stiffened. Money was a sore point with her too, and what was this, the Bolshevik revolution all over again? "Didn't you ever think I might have needs—*we* might have needs, all of us, George, Cy, Henry?"

"Only just peel."

Predictably, he flung down the potato and the peeler with it. Then it was the apron and then he was at the door. "I'm sorry," he said, "but I didn't sign on to be anybody's slave. I'm going back to Chicago if I have to walk."

She looked to Mrs. Taggertz, but Mrs. Taggertz wouldn't return her gaze. The woman had never been particularly forthcoming—she didn't seem to have much to say to anyone, but then she hadn't been hired for her ebullience but rather for her ability to stretch one pot of soup into two—and when she did make conversation it was almost always couched in the form of gossip critical of someone or something. She was of the neighborhood and the neighborhood didn't approve of Frank Lloyd

Wright. Or of Olgivanna either. Even if they *were* married now. "I cannot believe my ears," Olgivanna said, just to hear her own voice. She was furious, seething. How could this boy dare to speak to her like that? "Did you hear? Did you hear what he said to me?"

Only then, only because she was directly addressed, did Mrs. Taggertz look up. Her hands were busy—she was chopping onions with an easy effortless stroke, as if her arm worked on a hinge—and she paused to scrape the residue from the knife. "He never washes the dishes right, that one," she said, scraping. "And the silverware," she added, shaking her head. "Disgusting."

Olgivanna thought of going to Frank, but she couldn't bring herself to bother him when he was working. It was up to her to manage affairs around the house, just as she'd done at Fontainebleau with Georgei, and she was determined to do it. Without thinking, she set the dough aside to rise and took up the potato peeler.

For the next hour, she kept replaying the confrontation in her head, thinking of what she should have said, how she should have been firm and yet yielding at the same time. Frank had particularly liked Herbert—he was a precise and unerring draftsman and an accomplished flautist who'd enlivened their musical evenings—and she'd liked him too, and now they would be a man short when there was so much work to be done. It was a shame and she could only blame herself. She'd been in a mood, but that was no excuse—she was in charge here and she should have demonstrated more self-control, more reserve, dignity. Never let anyone see what you're thinking, that was what her mother had told her. And her mother was as fierce and commanding as any woman on this earth. Finally, when she'd finished with the potatoes, she went looking for him.

By then, it had begun to snow. She'd smelled the change on the air early that morning, a premonitory scent of moisture riding high overhead in the steadily unfolding clouds, and she felt it too as an expectant softness that seemed to envelop her as she threw feed to the chickens and loaded lengths of split oak into a wheelbarrow and hauled it across the yard to the house, her breath streaming before her. Now the snow was beading down, swift and tightly wound, with a hiss you could hear the minute you opened the door. Herbert wasn't in his room and the fire there had burned out. The bed was made, but his clothes, his suitcase and the flute were gone. She felt a pulse of alarm: Had he really meant it? Was he that headstrong? That foolish? She slipped into her coat and went out to the courtyard to find his tracks there, a draftsman's unerring line heading off down the drive and into the gauzy curtain of the storm. Already, they were filling in.

In her haste—she had to get him back before Frank found out, and that was all there was to it—she'd neglected hat and mittens both. She found a cotton scarf in the pocket of her coat and wrapped it round her head to protect her hair, which was wet already, wet the moment she darted out the door, and she knew she should have gone back for the mittens, but she was in too much of a hurry to bother. Twice she slipped and fell going down the drive, her bare hands stinging in the cold. The wind picked up and threw pellets of ice in her face. Herbert's tracks grew fainter. No matter: she knew where he was going.

It was three and a half miles to the station at Spring Green. In optimal conditions, with her long purposive stride, it would have taken her just over an hour to reach it, but the snow was already ankle-deep and slick beneath with a thin transparent layer of ice and she had to pick her way carefully. The road was deserted before her. The hills swept round and plunged to the river, the faded image of the bridge plumbing a line to the far shore.

Nothing was moving, nothing animate, but for the birds exploding from the bristled crowns of the trees that rocked in the wind with a frictive moan like the keening of the dead. Halfway there her cough came up on her and she had to lean against a fencepost to catch her breath, the snow sifting down around her, granulating in the folds of her coat, whitening the ends of the scarf and the frozen hem of her dress. Her nose was tender where she kept wiping it with the back of her hand. Both hands had gone numb. She couldn't feel her feet.

Still, she pressed on, telling herself she was just out for a stroll, thinking of the girls—they were with the housekeeper, ostensibly entertaining themselves, and by now they would have begged to go out of doors to sled down the drive, and perhaps they would have come looking for her, for their mother, for permission and assurances, and begun to wonder where she was. (*Has anyone seen Mama?* Svet would ask and she'd poke desultorily through the rooms, the kitchen, the living room, the loggia, the bedrooms, but she wouldn't dare burst in on Frank—that was verboten—and in that moment she'd shrug it off and pull on her boots and mittens and go out to the stall where the sleds were kept.) She held that picture in her mind as the snow climbed across the fields and the landscape lost its features and everything strove for a cold white uniformity. She wasn't lost. There was no chance she could be lost because she knew this road as well as any road in the world and that stand of trees ahead would have marked the edge of the Perry property and soon she'd see their farmhouse and smell the smoke of their chimney and then she'd be past it and the buildings of Spring Green would begin to define themselves against the burden of the snow. She kept on, feeling light-headed, feverish—was she catching cold, was that it?—and when she coughed she brought up a sputum the color of tapioca.

She found Herbert at the station, sitting huddled on

a bench under the eaves of the depot. He was hugging his shoulders, the suitcase at his feet, the narrow leather tube of the flute case set atop it, gathering snow. She came up the street, trudging through the drifts, and kicked her way up the steps to him. "Herbert, what are you doing?" she demanded, impatient despite herself. "You're not serious about this, are you?" She had a whole speech prepared about the essential contribution and integral value of each member of the Taliesin community and how much Mr. Wright depended on him and she too, she too depended on him, but the cough clawed at her throat and stole the air from her lungs.

"The station's closed," he said, his voice a doleful drone against the wind. "There's nobody here, no fire in the stove, nothing. I don't know how they expect . . ." he trailed off. His eyes were liquid with emotion.

"I have come here all this way," she said, her own voice toneless and weak, drawn down the funnel of her cough. "In the snow," she added redundantly, waving an arm to encompass the dead street, the buried rails, the soft shifting backdrop of the storm. She was thinking of Georgei in that last winter when he broke up the coterie at Fontainebleau, of the way he'd thrown them all over with an indifferent shrug and how it had hurt her more than anything in her life. Under him they'd experienced something collectively no one of them could have experienced alone, a bond that transcended the physical and the knowable, a reason for being and waking and worshipping. Without him, they had nothing. She knew that. She felt the loss of it even now. And when she looked down at the boy shivering there on the bench, she knew she would never let go of it again. "I have come here," she repeated, and she was coughing into her fist, the refrigerated poison of the air scouring her lungs and the brittle pellets beating at her face, "to take you back."

* * *

There was Christmas at Taliesin that year, Frank as entranced with the season as the children, caroling and snowballing and tobogganing and even donning a false beard to impersonate Father Christmas, and then he packed up everything and everybody—including Herbert and Mrs. Taggertz and Billy Weston and his family*—and drove them out of winter and into the perennial summer of Chandler, Arizona, where the sun blasted the splintered rock and the agave plants sent up their centennial spires. "We have no choice," he'd told her, "if we're going to have money to eat on," and the promise of San Marcos in the Desert, a hotel that would dwarf the Biltmore and bring in a commission of some $75,000 and maybe more, glowed on the horizon like a mirage, just beyond the windshield of the open Packard Frank piloted out front of their little caravan.† At first they put up in a Phoenix hotel—more dislocation, more confusion, clothes in a suitcase and Svet and Pussy looking as dazed as the parched and delirious Spaniards who first laid eyes on the place—but that experiment ended almost as quickly as it began. The expense of housing and feeding the whole troupe would have bankrupted them in a week—she told Frank that, told him again and

* Including Billy's son, Marcus, who was born three months after the murder of his elder brother, Ernest, at Taliesin in 1914.

† This adventure, of course, was to provide the seed for Taliesin West. I have concentrated memories of making the pilgrimage to Arizona each winter, Wrieto-San out front of a procession swollen to seven or eight vehicles and some twenty-seven people, his hair flowing like the fur of a pinniped in a heavy sea, going, as the expression has it, hellbent for leather. He always seemed genuinely surprised, if not shocked, by the presence of other drivers, as if the national matrix of lanes, cart-paths, thoroughfares, boulevards and interstate highways had been created for his use and pleasure alone.

again—and so Frank, never at a loss, hit on the idea of building a working camp on the job site. Ocatillo Camp was the result, a small miracle of timber and canvas, replete with kitchen, living areas, studio and bedrooms and the grand piano Frank insisted on installing no matter where he was. Electricity was brought in. Telephone lines. Water. Navajo rugs brightened the place and kept the dirt down. The girls browned in the sun. Herbert Mohl went back to the drafting table and Frank kept his whole team working through the day and into the night on the plans and models for the hotel and the New York City skyscraper.

They stayed through May, and then—because the heat was infernal, like an invisible wall you walked into every time you stepped out the door, and because the funding for the hotel hadn't come through yet and because she was nagging Frank about Taliesin and the neglect it was falling into yet again—they decamped and drove back across the country to the verdant hills of Wisconsin. "Mama, it's so green," Pussy cried out, and it was, Taliesin, as green as life. There were the old smells, old faces, the animals and the fields and the daily reward of being alive to Frank's creation. For his part, Frank kept working. Kept pushing. And the funding for both projects kept floating just out of reach, $19,000 added to their debt now as the cost of Ocatillo Camp, a place already vandalized, already tumbling to ruin, money run like water through their hands, but who could have guessed what was coming in October of that year?* No one. Least of all Frank.

The commissions evaporated. The leaves blazed and fell. No one was building anything. And here came the holidays again and the cold and the compulsion to live with less, to do without, to pinch and scrape and hoard even as Frank, mercurial as always, denied himself noth-

* 1929, that is.

ing and the debts mounted. The draftsmen drifted away, all but for Herbert, who stayed on—as did Billy Weston and a handful of the workmen—for the promise of sustenance alone. Christmas was narrow, New Year's narrower yet.

There came a day just after the New Year when Olgivanna was helping the housemaid with the wash, stringing wet clothing on a line in one of the back rooms (the girls' things, always filthy, half a dozen of Frank's shirts, his underwear and socks), feeling vaguely irritated because the housemaid claimed she had a touch of the flu and wasn't feeling well if you please, ma'am, and there was so much to be done. The previous day's thaw that took the temperatures up into the thirties had been nothing more than a tease—a high-pressure system had settled in overnight and when she woke that morning the thermometer in the courtyard had registered ten below zero. Which was part of the problem she was now having—the clothes had stiffened on the line because the fireplace wasn't drawing properly and no matter how much wood she stacked up she got nothing but the palest feeble lick of flame. And Mrs. Dunleavy (rehired because there was no one else) was all but useless, shifting about as if her feet had been nailed to the floor, her eyes rheumy and her face the color and consistency of the ball of dough Olgivanna had set aside to rise in the kitchen.

Exasperated, her fingers stiff and the breath hanging like a shroud at the tip of her nose—she might as well have been outside for all the good the fire did her—she dropped the garment in her hands, crossed the room and bent impatiently to the fireplace. She poked at the fire a moment without effect, then snatched up the tongs and began extracting the logs, one by one, laying them on the stone apron though they were half-burnt and smoking still. "It could be the flue, ma'am," Mrs. Dunleavy opined, even as the room filled with smoke. Olgivanna squinted up the chimney. The flue was open, as far as she could determine, but she beat at it with the poker in any case, leaning deep into the aperture and running the iron rod as far up the chimney as she could, hoping to dislodge some of the soot and resin there. She tried to keep her eyes closed, working the poker by touch, running it round and round, beating at the stone till she could feel the blackened particles sifting down into her hair and settling on the back of her neck. Then the larger chunks began to fall, and more yet, soot everywhere and the room choked with smoke.

When she was satisfied, she sent Mrs. Dunleavy to the pantry for newspaper and then she meticulously restacked the logs atop a crosshatch of kindling, and this time, when she held a match to it, the fire took. Almost immediately the smoke began to clear and both women edged closer to the fire to warm themselves. "You're all dirt, ma'am," Mrs. Dunleavy said, but Olgivanna didn't hear her. She stood there, feeding the flames and warming her hands, her hair come loose from the frugal bun into which she'd twisted it that morning, her face smudged and hands blackened. They would be eating chicken for dinner that night, roasted, and chicken in a ragout for the next week, because something had got into the henhouse, a sleek killer of the night that killed for the pleasure of it, for the love of chaos, and left the corpses behind. The pipes had frozen in the main bathroom. The generator had given out and she'd sent Billy Weston to see about it, and so they'd be dining by candlelight. And what else? A tree was down across the back road and she didn't know what they would do for eggs in the morning. But it was nothing, nothing to her, and she took it all in stride. She was in charge now, just as she'd been at Fontainebleau with Georgei, but there she was just one of Georgei's disciples, one of his women. Here she was a wife.

Frank needn't bother with any of it, and that was her pride. Increasingly, in any case, he was away from home, lecturing to make ends meet. He'd been in Chicago all week, delivering a lecture at the Art Institute and doing his best to attract commissions along the way, and he was due home any minute now—she could picture the car winding up the hill and pulling into the driveway, the wheels glittering in the weak winter light, the headlamps radiant—and she told herself she should clean up, put on a fresh dress, comb out her hair, but there was the laundry still and then the bread and dinner after that and a thousand other things. As it turned out, she was so busy she never even heard the car. She was in the kitchen, seeing to the bread while Mrs. Taggertz basted the chicken and the girls played in the bedroom. Everything was still, dusk coming down, the only sounds the rhythmic swish of Mrs. Taggertz's basting brush and the steady purr of the fire in the stove.

Then Frank was there, striding into the kitchen in his hat, coat and scarf, bringing the scent of the outdoors with him and all the fierce joy of his uncontainable energy—Frank, Frank Lloyd Wright, the genius of her life—and he stooped to brush her cheek with a kiss though there was a smudge of soot on the flange of her nose and another on her chin like the beginnings of a beard, and he was talking, already talking, bursting with the immeasurable tale of his drive up and the people at the lecture in Chicago and how he was certain, one hundred percent certain, that he had a commission for a new building there and that he'd heard from Darwin Martin and his cousin Richard and both of them were committed to the designs he'd presented them and the money would be there soon, soon, soon. His arms were laden with packages. A gift for her, gifts for the girls and for himself, a statue he couldn't resist, for the Blue Loggia. "And this," he said, handing it to her quickly because the girls had heard the car and here they were hurtling into the room to leap round him and sing out his name, and what was it, a newspaper? "There's something here for you," he said, and in the next moment he was gone, the girls spinning in his wake.

She took her time, setting the gift-wrapped box and the newspaper aside till she was finished with the task at hand—the bread had to be timed to Mrs. Taggertz's schedule and she had to get Herbert in to set the table for eleven, or no, twelve tonight. The windows darkened. Steam rose from the pot of potatoes on the stove. She could smell the chicken browning as she shaped and braided the loaves and set the pan in the oven. Then she sat at the kitchen table to unwrap the gift he'd given her—it was a piece of jewelry, very simple, a single opal teardrop on a gold chain. She reached up to fasten it around her neck and felt the grit there from the chimney, thinking she'd have to draw a bath after dinner, and that would involve stoking the steam boiler in the cellar and yet more wood for fuel. Finally, she took up the newspaper, expecting another article about Frank, a review of one of his lectures or the announcement of an honor bestowed on him. He'd folded back the page and marked it with an asterisk. She moved the candle closer.

It wasn't what she'd thought. What she was reading—and she had to catch her breath with the sudden shock of it—was an obituary. Maude Miriam Noel had passed away in Milwaukee two days earlier after slipping into a coma following an intestinal operation. She was sixty-one. *Fifteen years ago*, the article read, *when she first figured on the front pages of American newspapers, she was a striking beauty with russet hair and hazel eyes—a talented sculptress cherishing honors won in the art circles of Paris.* And now? Now she was dead. Her estate, consisting of her personal effects and a $7,000 judgment against her ex-husband, Frank Lloyd Wright, was bequeathed to a friend of her youth, Mrs. Leora Caruthers of Santa Monica, California. Miriam's three children, with whom she'd fallen out, were left one dollar each. Services were to be held in Milwaukee.

For a long moment, Olgivanna stared down at the newspaper before her, smoothing it over and over again while the candle guttered and Mrs. Taggertz moved vaguely on the periphery, shifting things atop the stove. She told herself she felt nothing. Or almost nothing. Relief, she supposed, but not triumph and certainly not regret or even sympathy. A strangeness, just that, as if the world had gone away a moment and then come rushing back in all its immediacy. She was just about to rise from the chair and see to the bread—she could smell it suddenly, the hot layered scent of it expanding through the room till it overwhelmed everything, even the chicken—when all at once the lights flickered and came on again. Without thinking, she leaned forward and blew out the candle, then got up to take the loaves out of the oven.

PART II MIRIAM

INTRODUCTION TO PART II

In the second year of the Fellowship, tuition rose from $675 to $1,100—a sixty-three percent increase—and I wrote my father for additional funds and my father indulged me. By this time, I was so thoroughly committed to the Fellowship, to Taliesin and to Wrieto-San himself I couldn't have imagined any other way of life—if my father hadn't come through I think I would have gone out and robbed a bank in order to stay on. Truly. I do. It's difficult to explain, but the fact of the matter is that in all eras, whether prosperous or constrained, people—especially young people, and I *was* young then, young and unfinished—want desperately to find their niche, believe in a vision, belong to something greater than themselves. I was no different. I lived and breathed Taliesin. The sun rose in the east and lingered overhead for no other reason than to illumine those golden walls. Winter, spring, summer, the year rushed by so precipitately it was as if the days were fanned by a breeze in one of those filmic sequences that play havoc with the calendar. Was it October again? I couldn't believe it. None of us could.

Though I'd been slim to begin with, I wound up losing eight pounds that first year. All the flaccidity of my student days was sweated out of me, sinew and muscle tautening in its place. My fingers were nicked and scarred, my thumbnail blackened with the errant thump of the hammer. I was tanned till my skin shone like a red Indian's and I was as familiar with the teats of a cow and the grunts and odors of the pig wallow as if I'd been born with a stalk of grass between my front teeth and hayseed in my hair. And I could drive a nail, saw a board, split wood and plaster a wall as well as any man in the glorious state of Wisconsin. All this thanks to Wrieto-San's hands-on approach and his ongoing impecuniosity that forced him to put his apprentices to work as a means of survival. Was it slave labor, as some have claimed? Perhaps. But there was a spirit of camaraderie, of all for one and one for all, that elevated our labors into the realm of the sublime, far above the reach of the carpers and critics, with their dwindling souls and limited imaginations. We were the acolytes, Wrieto-San was the Master. We lived to serve him.

My father wrote me a six-page letter adducing his objections to Wrieto-San's regime—which, when distilled, amounted to a single rhetorical question: What was I doing milking cows and pitch-forking hay like a peasant in a hempen *kosode* and shit-caked *geta* when I should be designing buildings back home in Japan? He concluded with a proverb: *Kappa mo kawa nagare* (even a *kappa*—a water sprite—can get carried away by the river; i.e., anyone can make a mistake). With all respect to his paternal wisdom, not to mention the check he'd enclosed, I countered with *Sumeba miyako* (roughly: wherever you live, you come to love it). And I did love Taliesin as I'd never loved anything in my life, though I had to concede that I would have preferred a bit more time in the drafting room and a whole lot less at hard labor.

At first, Wrieto-San had paid carpenters, stonemasons and farmhands from the surrounding villages at the rate of two dollars a day, plus meals, to carry forward the work on the Hillside School, which was then being converted to residences for the apprentices, as well as a theater and a new studio removed from the main house, but in this fourth year of the Depression, he'd had to let them go because he was, as always, flirting with bankruptcy. In fact, the only viable project on the boards at the time was the Willey house, and so, when we weren't out in the fields or hammering away at Hillside, there was precious little to do in the drafting room but copy out Wrieto-San's old designs by way of exercise and instruction.

Typically, our days would begin with the six-thirty bell followed by breakfast at seven. We ate communally, but for Wrieto-San and Mrs. Wright, who took their meals in a private dining room attached to the larger one reserved for the apprentices, and though we sometimes lacked for meat there were eggs, flapjacks and enough oatmeal to ballast a ship of the line (Wrieto-San believed firmly in the virtues of oatmeal, both as the body's fuel and its scouring pad). In later years, once Svetlana graduated from musical prodigy to impresario, breakfast would be followed by half an hour's choral practice under her direction, but in the fall of 1933, we went straight to work. There was an afternoon break from twelve to one-thirty, then work till five and dinner at six. On Saturday evenings we were all required to dress for dinner, after which those amongst us with musical abilities—I was not one of them—would perform for the assembled apprentices, Wrieto-San and his family and any prospective clients or other guests who happened to be in attendance. Sunday-morning breakfast was the reward after a long six-day week, and here there would be preserves, bacon, ham, eggs, biscuits and pie, and then there was the formal Sunday dinner in the incomparable living room, and we were all able to bask in the fully realized expression of organic architecture at its apex. Ten o'clock was lights out, enforced by the shutting down of the hydroelectric plant.

Of course, the rigors and isolation of country living weren't for everyone, and a number of apprentices left after the first year, including four of the five women. The one who stayed, Esther Grunstein, an almost supernaturally homely girl of twenty-two or -three who favored sacklike dresses and who had oversized hands and a frizz of hair that made it seem as if she was wearing a bonnet even when she wasn't, was rumored to be available to any of the men for a price arranged on a sliding scale according to her whim. She wouldn't—and I had this from Herbert Mohl—"go all the way," but she would perform what were called hand-jobs, and if she was in the mood and an apprentice had the money, fellatio. My relations with her were strictly collegial, I should say, though our isolation, combined with the fresh air and exercise, certainly kept the sap rising in us all and eventually, in extremis, even she began to look good to me. But then it was October and a squad of new apprentices made their appearance, suitcases and freshly drawn checks in hand, and we were all relieved to discover that there were four women among them. More significantly, one of those women was Daisy Hartnett.

On the day Daisy arrived I was in the studio in the main house, working with Herbert and Wes and some of the others on the preliminary drawings for a newspaper plant in Oregon that would never be built, when the phone rang in Wrieto-San's office. We could all hear the phone ringing quite plainly, just as we could hear every word Wrieto-San spoke into the mouthpiece as he wooed clients and begged off creditors, since his office was separated from the studio only by means of the high stone vault in which he kept his most precious Japanese prints. There was the click of the phone lifted from its cradle and then Wrieto-San's mellifluous tenor singing over the fractured silence. "Who?" he said. "Apprentices? At the station, did you say?"

In the next moment, Wrieto-San emerged, as he did a hundred times a day to work over our drawings, throw a log on the fire, seize on one or another of us to run an errand, fill a gap in the kitchen or trot out to the fields to refresh the wildflowers in the ranks of vases spread throughout the house. We all stood, as we did every time he entered the studio, no matter how deeply engaged we were in the work at hand. He went straight to my desk. "Tadashi," he said, leaning in close with a fresh pencil in his hand, smelling of graphite and cedar shavings, "I'm going to need you to run down to the station and fetch two of the new apprentices. Just arrived." He paused, looking from me to the drawing and back again. "The Stutz is in good working order, I trust?"

"Yes, Wrieto-San," I said, fumbling out of the chair to give him an abbreviated bow. "We've managed to repair the front fender where it, uh, and the tire too—"

The car—Wrieto-San had never ceased his criticism of it—had been subjected to some fairly rough usage over the course of the past year, degenerating from the sporty road machine I'd plucked off the automobile lot to a harried and dilapidated farm vehicle. The front wheels were out of alignment, the tires patched so many times they were like patches themselves and the body seemed slowly to be taking on a new shape altogether. And the paint scheme was no longer pit-of-hell black and canary yellow, but rather a uniform Cherokee red. Cherokee red was Wrieto-San's totemic color and he insisted that all his vehicles—all the vehicles at Taliesin, whether they were properly his or not—should be graced with this hue. An obliging garage man in Madison had done the trick for me, at my own expense, much to Wrieto-San's satisfaction.

He was already plying his eraser, making wholesale

changes to the drawing I'd spent the entire morning on. He barely glanced up. "Two of them. Greiner and Hartnett, females."

I didn't know what to expect and I didn't want to get my hopes up. I wasn't exactly shy—"reserved" is the word I would have chosen—but there was almost a hundred percent certainty (Greiner, Hartnett, *females*) that these women would be Caucasian, as was virtually everyone else in the lily-white state of Wisconsin. Not that Wrieto-San didn't surround himself with an international set—the paid draftsmen we succeeded were from Japan, Poland, Switzerland and Czechoslovakia, and one of my fellow apprentices, Yen Liang, was Chinese—but the Fellowship was otherwise exclusively American. And these were American girls. And American girls generally observed the taboos against miscegenation. I knew this. We all knew this. What choice did I have but to be reserved?

Unfortunately, it was raining. Hard. I could certainly have made a better impression in the Bearcat with the top down, but now we would be forced to wedge ourselves into the steaming interior, which smelled—again, unfortunately—as if the chickens had been roosting in it, and maybe they had. And then there was the problem of the front drive. Every time it rained its permeable surface was transformed into an Amazonian mire, and so it was now. Twice the rear wheels sank to the frame and I was forced to go back up to the house for a shovel to extricate them. By the time I reached the road my shoes were no longer shoes but slick glistening sculptures of varicolored mud, my jacket was soaked through and the cuffs of my trousers were as limp as the hides of two freshly skinned squirrels. I fought the clutch, rocketed through pit, puddle and chasm and pulled up in front of the station just over an hour after I'd left the drafting room.

Dimly, through the slash of rain and the fogged-over

windshield, I could make out two figures huddled on a bench under the eaves of the depot. Female figures. Blouses, hats, the swell of a feminine calf against the crease of a skirt. They were flanked by shadowy parcels, hatboxes, swollen suitcases—and a single steamer trunk the size of a grand piano. Neither of them moved. I shut down the engine and stepped gingerly into the street, which was awash in braided ripples of dun-colored water. The pounding of the rain flattened the hat to my head even as the outer layer of mud was prised from my shoes and carried on down the street in two black dissolving crescents.

"Hello!" I called, wading through the gutter and springing up the steps, beaming like a department-store greeter in the Ginza. "Welcome to Spring Green!" I was feeling an excess of energy at this point—or nerves, call it nerves. "I wish we could have arranged better weather for you," I added. Lamely.

Both women, their faces vague and bloodless, gazed up at me warily from beneath the brims of their hats. One of them (Daisy, as it turned out) was smoking, hunched forward over the hump of her knees and the trailing wet skirts of her overcoat, brightening the flame at the tip of the cigarette with a long casual inhalation till the glow lit her face, and though she hadn't planned it—she was merely smoking—the effect was theatrical. She wore a cloche hat with a stiff circular brim that masked her eyes and hid her hair, blond wisps of which were visible at the base of her neck as she bent to the cigarette. Her legs, what I could glimpse of them, were sleek and shapely, but sturdy too. I could see in an instant that she had *hara*, a quality that is often translated into English as "spirit" or "heart" (as in "she really has heart"), but in fact refers to the stomach, which we believe to be the true center of one's body and the gateway to the soul. My mother, in her time, was possessed of great *hara*. As was my father, though, sadly, the afflictions of the war seemed to have taken it from him.

The other woman—or girl, I suppose, since she was all of nineteen—was unremarkable, but for the quick seizure and release of her damp bovine eyes. And her freckles, freckles that maculated every visible swath of her skin—her wrists and ankles, the backs of her hands, her cheeks, her brow, her chin. Her name was Gwendolyn Greiner. Her eyes took hold of me. "Who are you?" she demanded.

I bowed deeply and resolutely. "Tadashi Sato," I said. The rain cascaded from the eaves. There was a smell of drenched fields, of mold, hidden rot, rurality. "Wrieto-San sent me."

"*Who?*" Gwendolyn Greiner in that moment exhibited two characteristics that would define her during the coming weeks and months at Taliesin: an assaultive peevishness, nasally inflected, and an interrogatory lifting of her upper lip, exposing the outsized dentition of a horse. Did I like her? No, not at all. And her freckles—her spots—gave me a genuine shudder of revulsion. To think of her forearms beneath the sleeves of her coat and the material of her dress, her upper arms, her chest, her back, her—well, I'm sorry to have to interject a personal prejudice here, but in my view the skin of a young woman should be as smooth and unmarked as the softest chamois, a beginner's skin, a virgin's, a child's.

I bowed again, my eyes on Daisy, who held the cigarette to her lips as insouciantly as if she were already installed in her room, her clothes hung neatly in the closet, books on the shelf, her feet ensconced in embroidered slippers and the fire snapping brightly in the hearth. "My apologies. What I mean to say is Mr. Wright. Mr. Wright has sent me for you. From Taliesin."

Gwendolyn: "You? *You're* from Taliesin?"

"Yes," I said, my greeter's smile beginning to fade.

"I'm one of Wrieto-San's—Mr. Wright's—senior apprentices."

It was then that Daisy spoke for the first time. "Oh, for Pete's sake, Gwen, can't you see he's just trying to help?" She was on her feet now, coming toward me with her hand outstretched, her lips contorted as she expelled a ribbon of smoke over her shoulder. "And what did you say your name was again?" she asked, taking my hand in hers. (Her eyes were the deep venerable blue of Noritake ware, incidentally, and her skin was flawless.)

"Tadashi," I repeated, bowing so deeply my forehead grazed her wrist. "Tadashi Sato."

Gwendolyn Greiner gave me a face, then ducked into the car while I fumbled with the maddening angles of the trunk. To her credit, Daisy braved the rain and did her best to help me secure it in the rumble seat—"No, no, Tadashi, here, this way," she murmured, touching my arm for emphasis as the streets ran and the rain fell and everything in the palpable universe dripped. We managed finally to wedge the thing nose-down on the sopping seat, and since I had no rope with me (I'd been prepared for suitcases, carpetbags and the like, but not an object of this size, and I began to wonder if Daisy and her companion had somehow confused Taliesin with a resort hotel in the Catskills or maybe a transoceanic liner), we had to hope that the force of gravity would keep it there for the run home.

And it might have, but for the rudimentary lesson in physics presented by the final incline of the Taliesin drive. In order to coast clear of the mud I had no choice but to open up the engine and hit the drive at speed, the rear wheels fishtailing (wonderful expression, incidentally) and the Bearcat straining against the grade. At some point, the steering wheel seemed to develop a life of its own, as if animated by a hidden spirit pulling in opposition to my conscious efforts to keep the wheels beneath us and the chassis right side up while making forward progress at such a speed as to render the mud impotent. We were perhaps three-quarters of the way to the top, the crest of the hill and the welcoming arms of the courtyard in sight, when there was a sudden lurch, Gwendolyn Greiner spitting out air as if she were drowning and both girls bracing themselves against the dash as the trunk sprang free and catapulted into the muck behind us even as the Bearcat skated to the right and came to rest against one of the half-grown trees we'd planted the previous spring to enliven the prospect of the drive.

Daisy was closest to me. I could smell her perfume, lilac and lavender. Her eyes were wide. I was embarrassed to a certain degree—I'd hoped for a better outcome, but as Wrieto-San was always saying when one of us broke a leg or stuck a pitchfork through his hand, "Something always happens in the country."

"Jesus," Gwendolyn Greiner hissed, leaning past Daisy to give me a mottled glare, "where did you learn to drive?"

The trunk had come to rest a hundred feet behind us. The tree was still in place, though it was canted ever so slightly away from us and the front fender of the Bearcat was showing a drepanoid scar of pit-of-hell black beneath the Cherokee red. I gave her the only answer I could think of—"Chicago"—and Daisy, bless her, burst into laughter. Her laugh was contagious, dimpled, sweet, musical, and in the next moment Gwendolyn and I were laughing too, laughing so hard the car rocked with the force of it even as the rain began to slake and the mud firmed beneath the wheels.

Ultimately, though I labored mightily to free the thing, we were forced to abandon the car where it was, slosh down the drive to recover the trunk (or at least I sloshed down the drive to recover the trunk, forever dutiful, and yes, *proper*) and make our ponderous way up the grade, through the courtyard and on up to the kitchen door. The girls had a sodden suitcase in each hand and a pair of dripping carpetbags flung over their shoulders, while I dragged the trunk along its own widening furrow in the mud. Our shoes were basted black, my trousers were ready for the scrap heap, and the girls' skirts clung wetly—and intriguingly—to their thighs. We stood there a moment, shivering beneath the eaves, before I thought to kick off my shoes and crack the kitchen door.

Immediately I was struck by a gland-clenching whiff of cabbage soup à la Montenegro and the shrill rising tones of Mrs. Wright, who was stationed at the counter with Emma, Mabel and an onion-chopping apprentice. "Out!" she shouted. "Get out now—you're all mud!"

"But, Mrs. Wrieto-San," I began, instinctively narrowing the aperture to a crack, "I've got the new apprentices with me, Greiner and Hartnett. Women. Two women."

In the next moment, Mrs. Wright was at the door, thrusting her long mournful face at us. Gwendolyn put on a smile. Daisy was trying to light a cigarette. "There is no smoking to be allowed on the premises," Mrs. Wright said in a flat voice, no offense meant, none taken. "Mr. Wright is opposed. And I also."

She held the door half-open. The apprentice—he'd arrived the previous day and I didn't yet know his name—gave me a look of bewilderment, as if he couldn't imagine how he'd wound up swapping his drafting tools for an apron and a paring knife. Out of the corner of my eye I saw one of the hens emerge from the garage, pick at something in the mud and vanish into the shadows. Rain drooled from the eaves. "And I am afraid," Mrs. Wright went on in her thumping orotund tones, "—Well, you're all mud and you will have to change before we can . . .

Tadashi, you will show them to their rooms, won't you?" She made a sweep of her chin for emphasis and revolved her eyes round the sockets like an actor signaling to the wings. "Outside, down the courtyard behind you—in your old quarters?"

She made a question of it, as if I might somehow mistake her and bring the girls tramping through the Blue Loggia or the living room, which were off-limits to apprentices save for those glorious few hours each Sunday at dinner, but there was no misconstruing her intentions. Now that I was settled into Hillside with a number of the other male apprentices, she intended to segregate the females here at the main house. Where she could, presumably, keep an eye on them.

I gave a short bow. "Yes, of course, Mrs. Wrieto-San."

She focused on Gwendolyn and Daisy then, her mouth struggling toward a parting of the lips in what was meant to be a gracious smile. "And welcome, girls. Welcome to Taliesin. We will have a good deal of time to make our introductions once you have dried yourselves." She paused. The smile closed down, replaced by an interrogatory moue. "You do cook, don't you?"

The more I consider it now, what with the passage of time and the reflection on certain painful matters my grandson-in-law's collaboration in these pages has afforded me, the more I come to realize that Mrs. Wright was as culpable in suppressing my relationship with Daisy—"throwing a wet blanket over it," as the expression goes—as her husband. Certainly they were in league in this. I don't mean to suggest that Wrieto-San himself harbored any racial bias—certainly all the evidence, both public and private, shows unequivocally that he revered my people and my culture—but undeniably he exhibited what I can only call hypocrisy in his attitude not only toward my love affair but the personal affairs of all the apprentices. What am I trying to say? He was a dictator—*Daddy Frank*—and she, Mrs. Wright, Olga Lazovich Milanoff Hinzenberg Wright, was his accomplice and henchman. Or henchwoman. It was as simple as this: because of their own scandalous conduct during what scholars call "the lost years" and the way in which it had adversely affected relations with the community and, more materially, Wrieto-San's ability to earn a living as a working architect, they were both determined to stifle any odor of impropriety in the Fellowship. If that meant manipulating the lives and emotions of the young people under their guidance, then so be it, without regret or further review: realpolitik.

Right from the beginning, Daisy and I were attracted to each other, all cultural and racial differences aside. There was the look she'd given me at the station, the natural grace with which she accepted my assistance, and, after I'd delivered the trunk to the room she was sharing with Gwendolyn (and wrestled it through the narrow doorway, skinning an elbow and barking both shins in the process), the lingering handshake she'd offered up as a reward. And why not? Despite my demurrals, I was more than simply presentable—my mother wrote repeatedly to tell me how handsome and elegant I appeared in the photos I sent her, and my previous lover, the one who'd left me for the trombone player and will remain nameless here, avowed that I was all the talk of the girls' dormitory and more than once assured me I put the other men to shame, in bed and out. (Which begs the question, rather puzzlingly, as to why she broke off with me.) Further, as I've mentioned, the outdoor life had transformed me into a rugged, perhaps even dashing figure. I had a ready wit, my English was adequate, my talent for architectural design as great or greater than that of any of my fellow apprentices, and I was descended from one of the oldest and most venerated families in Japan. Was it any wonder Daisy fell for me?

That very first night, after an excruciating dinner during which all the men fumbled round trying to make conversation with the new arrivals and Herbert Mohl goggled at Daisy as if she'd been served up on the half shell for him and him alone, I took her aside and asked her to join me—or rather us, a mixed group of us—for a nightcap at the local tavern. We were standing in the corner of the dining room, Gwendolyn distracted by the attentions of four or five male apprentices who apparently didn't share my prejudice with regard to epidermal blemishes, the rain descending from the gutterless eaves with a Niagara roar, the electric lights flickering, the air steamy, fecund, everything held in abeyance as we each privately weighed the option of turning in early or indulging our youthful high spirits. I was obliged to raise my voice in order to be heard over the tumult of the rain. "Would you like to go for a drink?" I practically shouted at the very moment that Wrieto-San and Mrs. Wright, accompanied by Svetlana and Iovanna, sallied into the room.

I don't know if my face blanched or if the final fatal noun stuck in my throat, but I was taken by surprise. We all were. The fact was that the Wrights rarely joined us after dining, but rather went round outside, down the hill and across the courtyard and into their quarters. On this particular night, however, they apparently chose the expedient of remaining indoors as long as possible, passing through our dining room and kitchen before braving the rain. In any case, Wrieto-San was his usual self, gesturing and broadcasting, making quips about the weather and Yen's new haircut, but Mrs. Wright looked up sharply, as if she'd heard me. I smiled. Bowed. Waved. But she was already passing by and I dropped my voice to finish the invitation: "At Stuffy's."

Daisy—I'd already complimented her on how much better she looked in a dry blouse and mudless skirt—leaned in complicitly. "Stuffy's?" She let out a low laugh—or more of a giggle, actually. "Sounds like a mattress factory. Or pillows. Feather pillows."

Stuffy's, as I informed her, was a tavern built, owned and operated by one of the local dairymen, Stuffy Vale, who had sold his cheese factory in the face of competition from Carnation and other large-scale concerns and used the proceeds to erect a drinking establishment, much to the consternation of Wrieto-San and the delight of the apprentices. It was located on "our" side of the Wisconsin River, halfway to the town of Helena. That is, an easy walk. Even in the rain.

"You'll see," I said. "It's not far."

"We're walking?"

"Yes," I said, lowering my voice still further as Mrs. Wright and her daughters passed out of the room. "Because, well, you see if we start up one of the cars at this hour, Wrieto-San will be sure to hear it—"

"And he would disapprove." She was watching me closely, her lips drawn back in an expectant smile. She was wearing a floral skirt and a white cardigan that gripped her in just the right places. Her hair, released from the prison of the hat, was combed out in a rolling tide of crimped curls after the style of the actress who'd humbled the ape in that year's big Hollywood extravaganza.

"Yes," I admitted, and I couldn't help glancing up nervously to where Wrieto-San had lingered over a table of apprentices—Herbert, Wes, Yen, Edgar Tafel—holding forth on one of his myriad subjects. *His boys* he called us collectively, conveniently eliding the existence of the females amongst us.

"You sound as if you're scared of him."

To my credit, as I recall, I didn't attempt any of the usual bluster or bravado males usually summon in response to such a question, which at root amounted to nothing less than a challenge to one's masculinity. I simply looked away from her eyes and told the truth. "Yes," I said.

And to Daisy's credit—she was a free spirit and no doubt about it—she took hold of my arm and whispered, "Well, what are we waiting for then? To Stuffy's!"

The specifics of that night escape me after all these years, and, of course, the occasion blends memorably with so many others, but we would certainly have been convivial, quaffing beer and something stronger too, dropping coins in the jukebox, chattering, dancing, feeling as if the roof had lifted right off the place and given us the heavens just for the asking. I do, however, remember the aftermath. There was the slog back in the rain, ten or twelve of us spread out across the road that was a black vein dropped down out of a blacker sky, male hijinks, the terrorizing of the innocent cattle of the fields and an inebriate obliviousness to the dangers of vehicular traffic (of which there was none), and yet more male hijinks. We were young men. There were women to impress. Some one of us—I believe this was the night—made his mark by micturating into the radiator of Wrieto-San's Cord Phaeton. There was, in addition, very likely to have been a degree of noise in the courtyard as we gallantly saw the women to their rooms.

The next morning, while I was bent over a section I was doing for a wing of the prospective newspaper plant, my brain swelling behind my eyes and my alimentary tract on the verge of a fatal dehiscence, one of my fellow apprentices—Herbert Mohl, he of the colorless hair and transparent eyes, looking sheepish—came to me to say that I was wanted in the living room. My eyes leapt to his. Wanted? "Yes," he said, his voice hovering like an executioner's. "By Mrs. Wright."

I tried to keep my emotions in check as I made my

way across the drafting room and through the loggia to the living room. Mrs. Wright didn't summon people casually, we all knew that, and she did seem to have an almost clairvoyant hypersensitivity to what went on in the house, so that even when she wasn't present you could feel her sending out tentacles all the same. She could be disappointed with the way I'd decorated my room or she might have noticed something I'd done while we were out in the field harvesting the potatoes or perhaps she had some complaint about my driving or my dress—it could be anything. But of course—and I will admit my blood pressure was up—the most likely occasion was what had happened the previous night. Mrs. Wright didn't like Stuffy or his tavern. She didn't like drinking. And she most especially didn't like the apprentices drinking in public—and in mixed company no less.

It was still raining, the view beyond the windows obscured in cloud, the rooms damp and cold and smelling as organic as ever. For once, I took no notice of the statuary, the furniture, the bold geometry of the carpet or the way the various surfaces of the room seemed to grow out of the stacked stone pillars as if out of an infinitely branching tree. I just went on mechanically and then hesitated at the entrance to the living room long enough to clear my throat.

"Enter," Mrs. Wright called. She was enthroned in the window seat across from the fireplace, wrapped in a shawl. Her hair had been pulled back severely so that it seemed clamped to her head. She didn't smile. She didn't offer me a seat. She simply waited till I was standing there before her on the edge of the carpet and then, in a low voice, observed that I had disappointed her. "Or not just me," she went on, "but Mr. Wright and all he stands for—truth in the face of the world, the cause of organic architecture, the struggle against the tastelessness and vapidity of the International Style—not to mention letting down your colleagues, letting down Taliesin itself."

"Is this about last night?" I ventured.

"It is."

"Well, I—once in a while, or just this once, I felt, well, that it would be fitting to welcome some of the new people in a collegial way, let our hair down, that sort of thing—"

"Drinking."

I held my silence and watched her eyes, dark eyes, as dark and impenetrable as the bricks of baker's chocolate in the pantry.

"Alcohol," she said, her lips drawn down in distaste. "Beer, whiskey, gin. And at a low place—how do you call it, a dive?—a dive like Stuffy's Tavern. What sort of impression do you think this gives to the people who would see Taliesin destroyed? The people of the community, of the press? The gossipmongers?"

I hung my head. Murmured something nonsensical. I was so distraught at this juncture I might even have slipped into Japanese for all I knew.

"And relations between the sexes," she went on, interlocking her fingers and dropping her hands to her lap. The cold killing light of the rinsed-out afternoon clung like a wrapper to the right side of her face. "We cannot be seen to encourage such a thing, not among the unmarried apprentices, like yourself." She paused long enough for the dismal sound of the rain to swell up like the background music in a celluloid melodrama. "And this new girl, Daisy. Daisy cannot be compromised. *We* cannot be compromised. As I am quite certain you are aware, Tadashi."

There was nothing to say, either in apology or extenuation. "Yes," I answered.

Another pause, the rain swelling, the fire eating at the log the apprentice on house duty had laid across the andirons. She unclenched her hands and began to rub them, one against the other, as if all the source of her discontent were concentrated in the rough callus of her palms. "Have I made myself understood?"

I bowed as deeply as I could—bowed my shame, my contrition, my capitulation—and then I bowed my way out of the room, turned on one slow muffled heel and crept back to the drafting table like the penitent I was.

Later in the day, just after we quit work at five, Wrieto-San asked to have a word with me. He was in his office, dictating correspondence to his new secretary, Eugene Masselink, and he barely glanced up as I hovered in the entranceway. Had there been a door I would have knocked, but absent that option I just stood there, trying to look at ease, as he orated and Gene Masselink's pencil flew across the page. "'My Dear Mr. and Mrs. Willey,'" he intoned, "'I suppose you are by this time anxious about your architect, more or less convinced that he has not the Willeys much in mind?' Paragraph. 'But he is very much on the job notwithstanding delays which are only helpful, let us hope, and with the new home for you very much in heart.'"

I stood there through the remainder, which proved to be a combination pep talk, sermon and bill of goods, in equal proportions, before Wrieto-San recognized me. "Tadashi, just a word," he said, nodding toward me from where he sat at his desk. Gene—he was young, younger than I, lean and loose-jointed, with a prey bird's beak and a stiff sheaf of hair rising up off the crown of his head like a mold of feathers—looked up in alarm, his glasses catching the light.

"Yes, Wrieto-San," I said, bowing.

"These women," he said. He fixed his eyes on me, his architect's eyes, the eyes that missed no detail, that shone always, even when he was exhausted, as if lit with an internal wattage that never peaked or flagged or brooked an interruption of service. He was Frank Lloyd Wright, the greatest architect of his or any other period, and he was assaying me. Critically. I felt myself shrivel.

"And this consumption of alcoholic beverages." He paused and felt for his cane without taking his gaze from me. "Alcoholism—and believe me I've seen my share of it in the building trades—is a deadly disease, a sickness, a vice. It destroys men, Tadashi"—he'd begun to tap the cane on the cypress floorboards, as if to underscore his point—"without regard to status or race or anything else that distinguishes one man from another. Or woman. Though the vice is of course stronger in the male."

I began to protest. "But, Wrieto-San, you've known me for over a year now. You've seen me work. Certainly you, of all people, must know that I am no alcoholic—"

"Denial is the first sign of it. Drink has you in its hold, Tadashi, and Mrs. Wright tells me you're leading others astray—this business last night—and we just can't have this sort of behavior at Taliesin. It sullies us. Makes us look like imposters out here in the country where good hard exercise and plain food should be all we need to sustain us."

"But—"

"And women, Tadashi. Marriage is a serious undertaking and I really do feel that you're too young and immature at this juncture even to consider an attachment that carries so much—well, essence—not to mention the young woman involved, whose cultural leanings and aspirations may be quite the opposite of what you expect. What is it your people say? 'A woman should obey her father in youth, her husband in maturity and her son in old age.'"

He paused to level a glance on Gene, as if to warn him off too. The cane never stopped tapping. "You are aware, aren't you, that Miss Harnett is a student of the fine arts, invited here to study sculpture, textiles and painting in addition to absorbing the benefits of living architecture? That she is an independent spirit, hot-headed even—perhaps a bit wild—and that her father, a medical man, has agreed to pay her tuition in part because in his estimation she needed a change of scene? Am I getting through to you?"

I said nothing. My face had colored. I wanted to laugh aloud, spin my head round on my shoulders and bellow "Daisy Hartnett? But that's crazy!" I'd just met her—I'd known of her existence just over twenty-four hours at this point—and here Wrieto-San was talking of marriage?

He was sober now, his face drawn down round the focal point of his thinly pursed lips. "Sexual matters," he said. "Intimacy. The sort of thing that belongs properly only to matrimony—this is why she's here, Tadashi, this is her burden. And we won't make it heavier for her."

"I just—Wrieto-San, with all respect, I've just met her. And I don't mean anything, I didn't know, I just—what about collegiality? One for all and—"

"Tadashi, and I'm very sorry to say this, to *have* to say this"—he turned away from me, snatched up a draft of the letter and made as if to examine it—"but you're fired. You'll have to pack up and go." And then, softening the blow: "I'm afraid that's all there is to it."

There are times in life when you feel as empty as a reed, your inner self obliterated in a thunderclap, all you've gained and loved and hoped for gone in a single stroke. I felt it in December of 1941 when the reports came through the radio that Pearl Harbor had been attacked and again in the 1950s when I was living in Paris and a wheezing man in mustache and cap climbed three flights of stairs to hand me the wire notifying me of my father's death. And I felt it then, felt it as a single savage deracination of the *hara*, as when Tojo's militarists turned their swords on themselves in defeat. Fired? Cast out of Taliesin? I'd seen others leave in disgrace for one infraction or another and I couldn't imagine it for myself. Not yet. Not now.

I bowed. Bowed so deeply I might have touched the floor. And then I heard my own voice emerging in a choked whisper: "Wrieto-San, I accept your judgment as one unworthy of the high ideals of Taliesin." I paused, my breathing damp and tumultuous. "But before I go, may I ask you one thing about the design for the Robie house? I've always, and my countrymen too, we've always admired this design as the pinnacle of your Prairie architecture, and I was just wondering how you came up with the solution of situating it to the road on such a narrow lot?"

I remember Wrieto-San setting down the letter and twisting round in his seat to stare at me. It took him a moment, shifting gears, calibrating, a slow flush of anticipatory pleasure infusing his features. "Well, you see," he began, entirely forgetting himself, "as you point out there was the problem of the site to begin with, a relationship to the street, you understand, and the existing structures on the block," and he talked straight through, hardly drawing a breath, till the dinner bell rang. The rain had let up. It was dark beyond the windows. He stood slowly and stretched himself, as if he were just waking from a nap, looked to Gene, who'd risen too, and then to me, seeing me—really seeing me—for the first time in the course of the hour. "Well, Sato-San," he said at last, "no harm done really, I suppose. You'll stay on, then. But no more of this"—he waved his hand as if to signify everything, every possible behavior, every error and slipup and falling away from the path of organic architecture—"this, this . . . anyway, your work has been satisfactory. And if I'm not mistaken, the dinner bell has rung."

*   *   *

I should point out that in the course of my tenure at Taliesin, I was called on the carpet half a dozen times and thrice fired, each time managing to distract Wrieto-San long enough for his umbrage to dissipate—the fact was that he loved to talk, loved to reminisce, make pronouncements, level judgments and animadversions, never happier than when delivering a sermon on any subject that came to mind, all the while striding back and forth across the floor, twirling his cane and gesticulating, and we apprentices learned to take advantage of it. And I should say too, as will be apparent to attentive readers of the text above, that Daisy and I carried on an exhaustive love affair under the noses of both the Wrights, finding access to various rooms late at night, making use of the fields as the weather warmed, and even, on one memorable occasion, the celebrated windmill tower he'd built as a young man for his aunts and named (appropriately enough for our purposes, as it turned out) Romeo and Juliet. And that the very evening he'd warned me off, not ten minutes after I left him, I walked into the dining room and felt my blood sing in a key that knew no restraint or regulation when I saw Daisy sitting there amongst the others like an empress among the commoners. I meant no disrespect to the Master or to Mrs. Wright either, but I believed then and believe now that no one has the right to proscribe relations between young people who feel a strong mutual attraction. Lovers, that is. We were lovers, Daisy and I, and through all these years I've never gone through a single day without thinking of her.

At any rate, it was at about this time that I had an opportunity to prove my worth to Wrieto-San in a more direct way than plying T-square and triangle (or pledging allegiance to some absurd monastic regime, for that matter). It was a brisk day toward the end of October, the sun casting a pale cold eye over the fields, the season in decline, the trees lifeless, even the shadows bleached out and enervated. I was in the orchard picking apples with a crew of apprentices when Wrieto-San came striding over the rise in his jodhpurs and long trailing coat. As he drew closer, we could see that he was wearing a new tweed jacket and the high stiff collar and artiste's tie he favored on formal occasions. Herbert, who was standing on the seat of the tractor and using a rake to dislodge the fruit from the upper branches, paused a moment. "Looks like he's getting ready to drive into town," he observed in his hollow fractured tones. "Wonder which of us is going to be the lucky man?"

Wrieto-San tried not to show favoritism, selecting one or the other of us at whim to accompany him to a potential job site, run an errand or simply pick up a hoe and listen to him expatiate on whatever subject he was revolving at the time. On this particular day, he strode right up to our little group—Esther and Gwendolyn were working with us, as I recall—and sang out, "Tadashi, how about joining me in a little excursion to Madison. To pick up those tools for the Hillside project, I mean, and a few other little necessaries?"

He drove with the top down, though, as I say, the day was brisk and made brisker by the winds generated by the Cord as he accelerated at will past farm vehicles, looming trucks and the creeping shapes of less powerful automobiles. He kept up a discourse the whole way, talking of his lectures and the money and recognition they were bringing Taliesin and how within the coming months we were sure to have a plethora of commissions piling up, enough to keep us all busy in the drafting room six days a week. I wrapped a muffler round my throat, patted at my flying hair and listened. As we came into the outskirts of the city, I couldn't help feeling a sudden swell of pride—Wrieto-San had selected me as his companion and all the world could see it. There I was, seated at his right hand, trying to look worthy and oblivious at the same time, and failing, I'm afraid, to suppress a smile of the purest bliss. The superlative automobile growled as he shifted gears, the hood shimmering under a fresh coat of apprentice-applied wax, the wheels chopping at the light, and we glided through those depleted streets with their spindly Fords and down-at-the-mouth Chevrolets in an aura of grace and privilege. Everywhere we went, heads turned.

We stopped to eat at the sort of establishment Wrieto-San preferred—a drugstore lunch counter given to excesses of gravy, chopped meat and great mounds of potatoes and succotash—and then went into the hardware store, the Cord stationed at the curb out front and attracting an army of small boys and gaping men in overalls and winnowed hats. Wrieto-San focused all his charm on the man at the counter, paid something on account—he was in arrears for several hundred dollars—and we collected the tools and made our way out the door, Wrieto-San strutting ahead of me while I brought up the rear, burdened with packages.

Just as I stepped out onto the sidewalk, one elbow bracing the door as I stood aside for a stout farmwife in a patched cloth coat who managed to look fleetingly familiar, I was seized from behind. Two arms looped round me, tight as cables, and I was drawn back into a kind of shuffling dance as I lost my grip on the packages and a pair of crowbars and a shingling hatchet rang on the pavement at my feet and wood screws exploded from a brown paper bag. I fought back, twisting my head to get a glimpse of my antagonist, but he'd burrowed his forehead into the crook of my neck for leverage and all I knew of him was his furious reeking breath that came in hard bursts and grunts of labor. "Let go of me!" I shouted, and people were stopping on the street to gaze up in alarm. "Are you mad? Let go!" I jerked furiously. He held tight. We danced across the sidewalk, rebounding from the display window of the hardware store not once but twice, the glass shuddering with the impact. I didn't know what was happening. I fought to work my right arm free and rake at my attacker's throat.

And then I saw Wrieto-San and understood. He'd been arrested at the door of the Cord by a farmer in overalls and a sweater torn at the elbows. All the blood was in the farmer's face. His eyes were squeezed almost shut and there was a single deep trench of animosity dug between them. "You son of a bitch," he said, and he wasn't shouting, wasn't making it a curse or an accusation, merely a statement of fact. "You think you can cheat my wife out of her wages and then ride around in your fancy machine like some sort of king? You think you're so high and mighty?"

Wrieto-San was puffed up like a rooster, the cane raised in a defensive posture. He backed up against the car, shouting "Stay away from me! Stay away!"

But the farmer wouldn't stay away and he had no more words. He took a step back to brace himself and then suddenly lashed out, the oversized wedge of his fist jumping out of the sleeve of his sweater to make audible contact with the bone and cartilage of Wrieto-San's unresisting nose. It was a shattering blow. Wrieto-San—he was in his mid-sixties, remember—floundered, sliding across the polished fender of the Cord like a seal slipping into an incarnadine sea, the cane clattering to the pavement, his hat glancing away all on its own and only his overcoat to break his fall.

"Wrieto-San!" I cried out—bellowed, bleated—and everyone froze in place for the smallest fraction of an instant. And then the arms broke their grip and I whirled round on my attacker—the same slab of a butter-stinking Irish face as the farmer himself, the same eyes, only wider and younger—and there was a swift exchange of meaningless blows even as Wrieto-San, as he described in his account of the incident in the revised edition of *An Autobiography*, sprang up off the pavement and locked arms with his adversary (only to be flattened again), the two rolling off the curb and into the mud and refuse of the gutter. For a moment, Wrieto-San was on top, the unremitting flow from his mashed-in nose washing over his assailant in such volume and with such force I thought he was bleeding to death, but then the two were tangled again and the farmer was on top, his fist rising and falling in swift violent thrusts. "Take him off!" Wrieto-San was crying. "Take the man off me, for Christ's sake! He's killing me!"

I grabbed the farmer by the shoulder and there were others there now too, a big-bottomed shopkeeper in shirtsleeves and galluses wading into the fray while a man in some sort of regimental regalia commanded, "Get out of that now!" in a voice of iron. The farmer whirled round—his neck inflamed, his face the size and color of a prize ham—gave me a violent shove and darted off into the crowd that had materialized out of nowhere.

Several of us helped Wrieto-San to his feet, where he stood woozily against the fender of the Cord, his hair disarranged, one cheek scraped and muddy, a dripping red handkerchief pressed to his nose. "Get that man," he ordered in an unsteady voice. "I want him arrested. Do you see what he did to me?" He let his gaze wander over the crowd of storekeepers, farmwives, urchins. "Lawlessness is what it is. Lawlessness right here in the streets of Madison."

No one moved. The farmer had vanished, along with his son and wife (Mrs. Dunleavy, if you haven't guessed). It was up to me to help Wrieto-San into the passenger's seat and tame the violent mechanism of the Cord long enough to get us to the nearest medical facility, where I waited while a stooped old country doctor set and bandaged his nose in a spidery arrangement of gauze and antiseptic tape. And it was up to me to drive us home to Taliesin in the chill of the declining day, with the wind up and Wrieto-San in pugilistic mode. I don't recall if Boris Karloff had made his dramatic appearance in *The Mummy* by then, but this was what Wrieto-San looked like, his face lost to its bandages, the cane poking at the darkening sky, his voice rising in wrath and fulmination all the long way home.

As it developed, that wasn't the end of it.

We'd no sooner come up the drive and rolled into the courtyard than a handful of apprentices, curious over our late arrival and eager for any sort of diversion from the routine, streamed out of the studio at the sound of the Cord's mighty engine in its dying fall. Wes was in the vanguard. "My God," he boomed, bursting through the outer door. "What happened? Was it an accident?" In the next moment everyone had crowded round, goggling at Wrieto-San's bandages and taking in the spectacle of me sitting behind the wheel in the privileged position, my color high and a shining stippled contusion painting my right cheekbone.

"Mr. Wright, are you okay?" a voice cried out.

"Mr. Wright—do you need help?"

"Mr. Wright?"

"Tadashi, what is it, what happened?"

Wrieto-San threw back the door of the Cord, waved away a dozen eager arms with a bellicose flick of his cane, and climbed out of the car to stand there erect in the drive, his shoulders thrown back and his eyes on fire, apparently none the worse for the loss of blood and the blast of icy wind. There were dull brown stains on the lapels of his overcoat and I noticed them now for the first time. His shirt—as crisply white and freshly starched as an apprentice could make it just that morning—was torn and bloodied and the crown of his hat was crushed. He said nothing. Just glared round him as if every man and woman present were responsible for what had befallen him, then turned on his heel and marched to the house. Only when he'd flung open the door and stepped into the shadows of his private quarters where none of us could follow, did he appear to break down. "Olgivanna!" we heard him bray in the voice of a schoolboy who'd skinned his knee on the playground. "Olgivanna, where in hell are you?"

As soon as the door slammed shut, everyone turned to me. I was still seated behind the wheel of the Cord, my hair an unholy mess, my teeth rattling with the cold, reluctant to let go of the moment. Daisy was the one who brought me out of it. She was right there, leaning into me, her face suspended in the light of the windows as if it were floating free. She was unguardedly beautiful. She was talking to me. "Tadashi, come on now, we're dying to know what happened. And you must come in out of the cold—and have something to eat. I asked Emma to put a plate aside for you—"

And then her fingers were entwined in mine and we were heading for the kitchen, three-quarters of the apprenticeship at our heels even as I tried to reconstruct the story amidst a storm of shouts and expostulations. I was standing at the counter—pinned to it actually by the crush of bodies—an oven-warmed plate of plain wholesome gravy-drenched food in front of me, and everyone was talking at once. Wes, the giant, whose head and torso and massive shoulders rose above us as if he were standing on stilts, cried out in a high strained voice: "It was Dunleavy, then—is that who it was? Dunleavy?"

"Yes," I told him and for the sixth time in as many minutes described the scene outside the hardware store and my part in it, all the while rubbing the side of my face (which hardly stung at all) to bring attention to the badge of honor I would wear for the next week and a half.

I didn't eat. Couldn't. The Fellowship—my companions and bunkmates, mild men and women who honored ideas and the aesthetics of design above any physical expression of emotion—had been transformed into vigilantes, a lynch mob in the making. It was decided, by whom I no longer remember, that we would pile into a car—into my car, the Stutz—and drive to the Dunleavy farm and have it out. "We'll horsewhip him!" Wes roared as we charged out into the courtyard and he, Herbert, Edgar and I catapulted into the seats while the others shook their fists and hooted like Comanches. I fired up the engine and tore down the dark hill and into the night, their calls echoing in my ears.

It was Mrs. Dunleavy who came to the door in answer to our thunderous knock. She was in a housedress, wearing an apron. Her hair had fallen loose in a sloppy scatter of pins and loose ends. It was, I noticed now, the color of barnyard ordure. Her mouth began to work but she was too startled to speak.

"We want your husband," Wes said, and there was an ugly edge to his voice.

"And your son. Your son too," Herbert put in. He was just behind me, as wispy and pale as a child, and Edgar stood behind him, slapping a braided leather whip against one thigh. We were four. We were caught up in the moment. We thought only of vengeance.

I saw comprehension seep into Mrs. Dunleavy's eyes and along with it, fear and hate. Behind her, appearing on the scene like extras, were the two boys I'd seen that day just over a year ago when I was a young man of urban inclinations, lost in the wilds of the Wisconsin farm country, and their dog, bewhiskered and alert, a low warning growl caught in its throat. At that juncture I was going at full throttle, far beyond the pale of normalcy or civilized behavior. I actually spat on the floor between her two slippered feet. "He attacked the Master," I snarled, and it was as if I were reading the lines of a play, "—and now he's going to pay."

I don't know if Farmer Dunleavy or his rubicund son were at home that night (though there's no reason to imagine they weren't—it wasn't as if rural Wisconsin abounded in cultural divertissements or that these ignorant half-civilized bumpkins would have made use of them if there were) because Mrs. Dunleavy, with a suddenness and swiftness of movement that startled us all, slammed the door in our faces and drove the bolt to with a resounding clap. After which she apparently went directly to the telephone and called the sheriff. We stood on the porch in the faint yellowish glow of the porch light (until it was abruptly extinguished from inside the house), privately questioning our rashness and wondering what to do next, if only to save face with one another. Wes looked at me. I looked at Herbert. Herbert looked at Edgar. Then Wes turned back to the door and began hammering its cracked pine panels with the anvil of his fist. "I know you're in there, you coward!" he shouted, amidst a host of threats and accusations. "Come on out now! Take it like a man!" I began to feel embarrassed.

A good deal of time went by—fifteen minutes or more—while we shuffled around on the porch, muttering imprecations and giving out with muffled yelps of outrage for each other's benefit. There was no sound at all from inside the house, but for the occasional distant quarrel of the dog. I don't know which of us picked up the stone and shattered the front window, but the sound of the fragmenting glass operated on us like an alarm and we all broke simultaneously for the car.

Unfortunately, the sheriff was waiting for us just off State Highway 23 when we made the turnoff for Taliesin. All four of us were placed under arrest on a charge of assault and escorted, in handcuffs, to the county jail. The Bearcat was impounded. And we spent two days there, locked up like common criminals, before we came to trial, where we were allowed to plead guilty and absorb fines of fifty dollars each.

My father, rest his soul, never learned of it. But Wrieto-San did, of course. And he, in his turn, took Farmer Dunleavy to court, where he arrived in all his pomp and glory, swaggering behind his cane and surrounded by a formidable group of male apprentices (I am second from his right in the celebrated photograph that appeared in the Spring Green, Madison and Chicago papers). The farmer was found guilty of assaulting Wrieto-San, lectured by the judge, sentenced to a week in jail and fined, after which he and his threadbare family found they could no longer sweat a living from the local soil and joined the impoverished hordes heading west for the promise of California. Needless to say, I'm not particularly proud of the role I played in all of this, nor of the fact that in the view of the officials of Iowa County, Wisconsin, I remain to this day a petty criminal, if not the very mark and model of the undesirable alien. In Wrieto-San's eyes, however, I was elevated into the select company of the very first rank of "his boys," so that in the months and years to come I would hear him wax sentimentally—and boastfully too—of how his boys had stood up for him when the chips were down. He would pause in the middle of one of his perorations, his eyes growing distant. "Yes sir," he'd say, "if there's one thing I can count on, it's my boys."

I see that perhaps I've gone on at too great a length concerning this period of Wrieto-San's life, in what is meant to serve, after all, merely as an introduction, but I do think these recollections should help to illuminate the character of the man whose greatness has touched us all.

In closing, I should mention that my distinguished collaborator, Seamus O'Flaherty, is, in addition to the aforementioned translations, the author of two novels, *The Ladies' Heat* (not what you might think—its subject is women's track and field) and *Kit and Caboodle* (also a surprise—this work deals with a fictional detective agency established in Okinawa by two Englishmen, Jonas Kit and Malcolm Caboodle, in the years immediately following the conclusion of the second war). At this point, sadly, neither has found a publisher. And yet, as I'm sure you'll agree, O'Flaherty-San brings a unique artistic perspective to the text here as it unravels backward in time to attempt to define the true essence of Mr. Frank Lloyd Wright, *Wrieto-San, Wrieto-San, banzai!*—the guiding light and enduring genius of all working architects, past, present and future.

CHAPTER 1: DIES IRAE

August 1914. There was a war on in Europe, the Archduke Ferdinand assassinated, the old alignments breaking down, trenches dug, want and terror and ruin spreading outward like ripples on the surface of a pond, but the rumor of it barely touched him. Nothing touched him. A week ago he'd been as secure and genuinely happy as he'd ever been in his life, Mamah blossoming along with Taliesin, working on a book of her own and winning over the neighbor women with her God-given grace and charm and the long trailing diminuendo of her laugh, the scandals behind them and the hounds of the press onto other shames and miseries, his own work on Midway Gardens coming to fruition in a last-minute frenzy of alterations, substitutions, delays and shortages and the mad concentrated efforts of a cadre of men working against deadline, just the way he liked it. But now he was alone. Taliesin was in ashes. And Mamah was dead.

Past midnight on a day he couldn't name—Monday, Tuesday, what difference did it make?—he was sitting on the hill above the ruins of the house, crickets alive around him, roaring as if their lives would never end and the frost never come, fireflies aping the stars overhead, the grass lush, the trees burdened with fruit and the bitter reek of ash hanging over everything. Five hundred copies of the Wasmuth portfolio, printed on the finest German stock, were still smoldering in the basement—even now he could segregate the smell of them, a thin persistent chemical stink of colored plates, elaborated plans and burned-out ideas—and when he turned his head he could see the deeper darkness, black smoke against the black sky and the dense textured shadows of the freestanding chimneys that were like the remains of a civilization gone down. Everything was still. And then, suddenly, a noise came at him, abrasive and harsh, the grind of boot heels amongst the cinders, and he caught his breath. There, a quick flare of light—a match lit and snuffed. *Joseph,* he thought, *it's only Joseph,* the farmer's son he'd hired to walk the property with a rifle to keep out the looters and anyone else who might want to do him harm.

Further harm. Fatal harm. The Barbadian was in the Dodgeville jail, but who knew if he had collaborators, a whole army of disaffected Negroes in white service jackets hunkered in the bushes over their hatchets and knives? He almost wished it were so. At least then he could do something to release the grief and rage boiling up in him. Literally boiling up. His back, from tailbone on up into the hair at the nape of his neck, was a plague of boils, inflamed suppurating sores, and he'd never in his life suffered so much as a pimple or blemish. It was as if what the gossipmongers were saying was true and verifiable, that divine justice had come down on his head for violating the laws of God and man in taking Mamah outside of marriage and then compounding the sin by establishing her in Taliesin as if to rub all their noses in it. Mamah had paid the ultimate price, yet he'd been spared by a fluke of fate, away in Chicago and so pressed and harried he'd taken to sleeping right there on the job site in a pile of shavings.

Spared, as the editorialists had it, so he could twist and suffer for the rest of his life. Arson, murder, desolation, boils. What next—frogs dropping down from the heavens? Locusts?

They called it sin, the preachers denouncing him from their pulpits, crowing, gloating, and the newspapermen right there alongside them, but was there any such thing? He didn't believe in it any more than Mamah or Ellen Key did, not when it came to honest and loving relations between women and men, but how else could you explain what had happened? It was the God of Isaiah come down to lay his hand over the hillside, the God before whom Ein Tad* had made him tremble when he was a boy. The words were on his lips now, involuntary and poisonous, but he could no more stop them than he could go back in time to stay the murderer's hand: "'The grass withereth,'" he said aloud, the sound of his voice an assault on the solitude of the night, "'the flower fadeth, because the breath of the Lord blows upon it; surely the people are grass.'"

He'd buried her himself. In a plain pine box fashioned by Billy Weston with his two burned hands and gashed scalp and it was no trouble for Billy, the smallest thing, because Billy was making a box of his own, child-size, for his son Ernest, murdered alongside Mamah and the others and laid out on the stones like a burnt offering. The box stood there in the courtyard, smelling of sap and shavings, isolate and actual, a thing he could touch and feel and run his hands over. White pine. The planed

* Welsh for father. Richard Lloyd Jones, Wrieto-San's maternal grandfather—father, that is, of the clan—took the fortieth chapter of Isaiah as his personal testament and had Wrieto-San and his sisters memorize it. Its view of human life and endeavor is, I think, especially bleak. There is nothing like it in the Shinto tradition.

edges. But it was too small, wasn't it? Too reduced and confined for a spirit like hers, and his first thought was that Billy must have miscalculated. He kept stalking round it, unable to grasp the problem, to discover the solution in the conjoined boards and the light, shifting grain of the wood—architecture, it was only architecture—till his son John found him there. "Too small, too small," he kept muttering, closer then to breaking down than at any time since he'd stepped off the train. "No, Papa," John told him, "it's just right," and it was, he understood that finally. It was.

There were sickles hanging on hooks in the barn and he'd gone out there and fitted one to the grip of his hand, then took down the whetstone and sharpened the blade till it shone in the dense shifting August light. When he was satisfied he strode out to her flower garden and cut it to the ground in a fury of wide slashing strokes till his hands were wet with the ichor of the stems, a whole field of cut flowers lying there in sheaves, enough to fill a casket and a raw hole in the ground too. He chased off the undertaker. Chased them all off, the newspapermen, the farmers and their wives, the gawkers and gapers and bloodsuckers, the ones who never knew her and never would. He was the one who knew her, the only one, and he was the one who bent to bathe her in blooms, her own blooms, the ones she'd toiled over herself, petals opening to the sun and closed now forever.* Then he hitched up the sorrel team and led the funeral procession down the drive from the scorched ruins, along the county road to the Lloyd Jones family chapel and the churchyard behind it.

* One of the local women had prepared the body, wrapping it head-to-toe in a pair of linen sheets in order to mask the outrages inflicted on it, the skull cloven, brains loosed, limbs and torso blackened by fire.

The service was brief because there was nothing to say, not as far as he was concerned, the blow so heavy, the weight of the pain, the punishment, and then he sent them all away—his sister Jennie, his son John, his brother-in-law Andrew Porter and the handful of others—and took up the shovel himself. Her husband—her former husband, a decent man, decent enough—wasn't there. Nor had he wanted to be. He was on the Chicago train, the train that stopped at every town and crossing, with two caskets of his own, caskets smaller even than the one Billy Weston had made for his son. There was the soft swish of the dirt sifting down into the hole, stones rattling against the planed corners of the box, the thump of a clod, a dangle of severed roots. Rain coming. The dirt smell. And then finally there was the raised mound and he was tamping it with the butt of the shovel, dusk closing down against a sky roiled with clouds. The heat—the August heat—settled in till it was like another kind of fire burning up out of the ground. When the rain did come sometime past midnight, he was still there and though it soaked him through to the skin, it never cooled him.

But now, as he sat in the wet grass of the hillside and watched the moving point of light that was Joseph Williams' cigarette bisecting the planes of the night, a new feeling came over him, as if the ligature round his heart had been loosened by a single coil. She was dead and he wasn't and no amount of brooding or sorrow could amend that. It was as if she'd never existed or existed in another sphere altogether, a kind of permanent limbo to which he had no access. She was gone, in spirit and flesh, but here was the concrete evidence of her—Taliesin. What was left of it, anyway, the studio and back rooms, the garages and stables standing forlorn and abandoned, the place of the hill no arsonist or murderer could ever eradicate. He'd built it for her, as a refuge from the loose tongues and prying eyes of the biddies and gossips and Sunday saints who'd made her life a hell, and in that moment he understood that he would build it again, all over again, as a monument to her.

It was the least he could do—or no, the only thing he could do, the right thing, the *moral* thing—and as he stared into the darkness where the main rooms had stood he was already devising plans against the backdrop of the night, seeing a new way to configure what had been razed to coordinate with the portion of the structure the fire had spared. And this was ordained too, else why had the conflagration stopped short of consuming the whole of the place if he hadn't been meant to rebuild?

When it came to it—and he was being honest with himself now—he'd never really been satisfied with the command of the rooms nor with the limited space for guests and workers, and here was an opportunity to expand on the original, make the grand rooms grander, improve the sweep of the views and build out to the southwest, elongating the foot of the reversed L that gave the house its shape within the structure of the hill, strengthening the lines, improving the flow* . . . He'd add a new wing for guests and servants' quarters and another for his aunts and his mother, just there, to the west. Enlarge the studio, redefine the courtyard. Make the space more intimate and expansive at the same time. He could see it all as if it were standing there before him, graced with light.

* For Wrieto-San, every building at Taliesin was in a state of flux. When he accidentally set fire to the theater at Hillside one windy afternoon in the thirties (brush, kerosene, poor judgment), he took me aside with a wink and a nod and told me he'd been looking for an excuse to renovate the shoddy old thing for years.

He was so caught up in the concept he couldn't keep still and before he knew it he was rushing headlong in the dark, through the sodden grass and the clinging fabric of the night, down the slope and through the door to the studio, calling out to his watchman that it was all right, everything was all right. He had a rationale. He had a plan. *Mamah*, he would do it for Mamah. Spare nothing. Let the details dictate themselves, Taliesin II rising unshakably out of the ashes of Taliesin I as if Isaiah's Lord were the mildest and gentlest of shepherds leading the way.

He lingered there a week, eating little, sleeping less. The sores burst and his shirt stuck to his skin. He paced round the ruins, raked through the ashes for the charred fragments of his pottery, rode horseback over the hills, hair streaming and cape flying till he could have been a figure summoned by the Brontës, grieving all the while and yet planning too, the images coming to him in a flood he couldn't stop. But plans meant nothing sans the wherewithal to realize them, and at the end of the week he left orders with Billy Weston for the cleanup and went back to Chicago. And work.

At the time he was living in a rented house at 25 East Cedar Street, and when he returned he resolutely kept his mother at arm's length (he was grieving; he needed to be alone), and resisted overtures from his daughter Catherine (couldn't he use her help with the housekeeping?) even as he fought Kitty over his monthly payments to her and the disposition of the house in Oak Park where they'd raised the children together. There were projects on the board.* People were making demands on him.

* Notable among them, the preliminary designs for the Imperial Hotel. Wrieto-San was then negotiating with a representative of the Emperor, using all his charm and persuasion in the hope of landing the commission.

The flow of funds at Midway Gardens had fallen off to a trickle, the finish work stalled even as audiences gathered every evening in an arena that cried out for completion. From the press he absorbed the sort of abuse to which he thought he'd become inured—LOVE BUNGALOW KILLINGS; WILD NEGRO CHEF SLAYS 7; WRIGHT AFFINITY SLAIN—but he felt he had no choice but to issue a statement to controvert the assaults on Mamah's character, a woman who was better and stronger and more willing to live her ideals than any woman he'd ever known.*

In the midst of all this, he made the smallest of decisions—a staffing matter, nothing really, the sort of thing he'd dealt with a thousand times over the years—and another woman came into his life. He'd asked around about a housekeeper, someone efficient, quiet, reliable, who could see to his needs in Chicago and then in Spring Green when the renovation started—he was adrift without Mamah there to look after him. The dishes were a nuisance, piled up around the house with unrecognizable crusts of food fused to their surfaces, the rugs were filthy, the linens needed changing, he was running short of shirts and underwear—socks—and he was tired of having to send someone out to the laundry every other day. The smallest thing. That was all he needed. Someone to look after him.

The morning after he'd put out his inquiries—very early, before he'd even shaved or had a chance to think about eggs, frying pans and maple-cured bacon from the butcher down the street—there was a knock at the door. He was half inclined to ignore it. Who could it be at this hour—a newspaperman hoping to provoke him into pro-

* Combative as ever, Wrieto-San's statement to the *Weekly Home News* reads, in part: "You wives with your certificates for loving—pray that you may love as much and be loved as well as was Mamah Borthwick."

viding copy for the evening edition? A creditor demanding payment? Fresh bad news? "Just a minute!" he shouted down the hall from the bathroom. And then, his voice rising in irritation, "Who is it?"

There was no answer, but the banging at the door continued, grew in volume even. He came out into the hall, beginning to feel alarmed—his nerves were on edge, of course they were—and he called out again. He glanced at his watch. It was quarter past six. Continued banging, peremptory, outraged. He went to the door and jerked it open.

A tiny wizened woman was standing there on the stoop, her shoulders rounded, her pale blue eyes rising up to him like gas bubbles in a bottle of seltzer water. She was dressed entirely in black, with button-up shoes and a bonnet out of the last century.

"Yes?" he said, utterly bewildered. Was she lost? Anile? A charity case?

"I'm here to work," she said, her voice booming out at him as if she were shouting from across the street. She already had a hand on the door, was already pushing her way past him and into the house.

"But what are you doing?" he demanded. "Who are you?"

She stood there a moment, scanning the room, muttering under her breath. Then she set down her bag—and now he saw it, an ear trumpet—and started gathering up the plates in a way that was almost comical. But it wasn't comical. It was an intrusion. An irritation. He took her by the arm, the flesh there surprisingly firm, and wheeled her around. "Listen, ma'am, madam, you can't just—"

She gave him a look and he let go of her arm. "Mrs. Nellie Breen," she boomed, "but you can call me Mother. It was your assistant at Midway, Mr. Mueller, sent me. You have my deepest condolences and all the redemptive love of the Saints and the Virgin Mary and the Lord Jesus Himself for the terrible afflictions that came down upon your head, which I saw in the newspapers . . . Which way did you say the kitchen was? And I'll need to see my room, of course."

At first he thought she was too frail for housework, but he was wrong there—she worked throughout the day without stint, in a kind of quiet outrage that took itself out on dirt and disorder. And if he thought the ear trumpet laughable, the resort of whiskered nonagenarians, a prop for the vaudeville stage, he quickly came to appreciate its value. He wanted efficiency. He wanted quiet. And there really wasn't much need to communicate with Mother Breen, not after they'd got through the initial civilities and the dishes were soaking in a pan of hot water in the sink.

The weeks began to topple forward, a series of unanchored pillars thundering to earth one after another. He barely slept. And when he did sleep he was plagued with nightmares, the face of Carleton, a scrim of blood, the children's hacked limbs and the creeping damp inadmissible blotches that infested the sheets under which they lay splayed like roots torn from the earth. Rigor mortis. He'd never known what the term meant, never wanted to know, the miniature bodies laid out in a grotesque parody of rest and surcease. When he closed his eyes, even for a minute, he saw the dead children, saw Mamah, and then the naked pillars and the ghostly chimneys rose up as in a separate reality, skewed, out of plumb, irremediably wrong. No design. There was no design. Just chaos.

He turned to work, buried himself in it—and it might have sustained him if it weren't for the eternal vagaries of finance. Though Midway Gardens had opened to grand success at the end of June—a thousand and more of Chicago's upper crust gathered there in tuxedoes and gowns, the National Symphony Orchestra playing three separate concerts, Pavlova dancing, the hoi polloi mobbing the outdoor beer gardens and everyone enthusiastic in their praise—September came on and still the final details were left unfinished. Waller* was out of money, flat and busted, and that was that. There were gaps everywhere, art glass yet to be installed, sculptures, murals, but no amount of pleading, anger, resentment or even logic could sway the man—the money was gone and Frank would just have to be patient. Patient? He needed a return, needed money of his own to reconstruct Taliesin, and where was his fee? Where was his recompense for the hundreds of hours he'd put in? For Taliesin? For Mamah?

At home, in the evenings, Mother Breen fussed over him and he ate alone—roasts, Irish stew, broiled lamb and Lake Michigan whitefish in cream sauce—then sat working on the plans for Taliesin, the drama of creation taking him out of himself for hours at a time. Mother Breen chattered all the while in her jagged unmodulated tones, inculcating him in the details of her private life as she served the meat, cleared the table, ran a ceaseless broom over the floors, and the sound of her voice, a feminine voice for all its stridulation, was as comforting in his present state as a choir of angels. She was a widow, he learned, née McClanahan, with references from Monsignor O'Reilly and the Howard Turpetts, with whom she'd been in service for thirty-two years till the cholera took them both on a trip to the Orient. Her daughter—she had just one daughter and

* Edward C. Waller Jr., initiator of the project, who'd raised $65,000 against a final reckoning of some $350,000. He was to declare bankruptcy two years later. Since he'd persuaded Wrieto-San to accept stock in the company in lieu of his fee, Wrieto-San was left holding the bag, as they say.

four sons, scattered to the winds—had been a disappointment to her. She went to mass each morning at five to pray for her and for her sons and for him too ("Mr. Wright," she'd say, dropping her voice from the key of fulmination to something like a shout, "I wear my knees out over you, don't you know?") and again after she served the evening meal. She slept under three blankets, even on the hottest nights. "Rheumatism," she explained. "The curse of the old." And she looked at him as if he could commiserate, but he wasn't old, not yet—forty-seven last June and each day feeling his strength and determination returning by increments.

He took her to Wisconsin with him on the train and left her to fight the incursion of ash in the studio, the back bedroom, the kitchen, the pantry and anywhere else a window was left open or a shoe had found its mark, while he walked the site and conferred with Billy Weston and Paul Mueller over what needed to be done. She was a fury and she brought order to the house in a way his own mother never could have, because his own mother, though he loved her more than any other woman in the world and needed her now more than ever, would have nagged and coddled and irritated him in a way this new mother, this artificial mother, never did. Mother Breen. She cooked for the men, she scrubbed and washed and ironed, and she never heard a word you said.

Gradually, through the fading haze of September and on into the rains of October and the early enduring freeze that was November that year, the old rhythms reasserted themselves. He traveled freely between Spring Green and Chicago, cajoling clients, submitting plans and proposals, looking out for materials and browsing shops and galleries for things of beauty to replace what had been destroyed. He manipulated accounts, wrote checks against insufficient funds, placated his daughter when she came round again and again wondering if there was any way she could help—with correspondence, dusting, anything. And his mother. He spent as much time with her as he could, assuring her that he was rebuilding for her, so that she and Aunts Nell and Jane could be with him permanently,* and she seemed mollified, though she kept asking about Mrs. Breen. Who was she? Why was she at his side at a time like this instead of his own mother who'd given birth to him and raised him up to be what he was? Could she cook—was that it? He preferred her cooking to his own mother's? Most of all, though, he worked to rebuild Taliesin, laboring side by side with the men in the bitterest weather, oblivious to the cold and discomfort, watching the patterns emerge day by day from the farrago of wood and stone and stucco.† His muscles ached. He began to recover the weight he'd lost. The nightmares fell away in the face of exhaustion and he slept as he'd always slept, in an unbroken descent into the deepest oblivion.

Throughout it all he continued to receive letters of sympathy from friends and strangers alike, hundreds of letters, an avalanche, so many he couldn't possibly begin to answer them. Each day there was a new sheaf of envelopes on his desk, the newspapers having whipped up an outpouring of unfettered emotion from people all over the world who wanted to share in his grief, wanted to tell

* Wrieto-San, I'm afraid, was something of a mama's boy (*okāsan ko*), and throughout his life, especially in times of duress, he sought the company of women.

† Again, one wonders how Wrieto-San was able to come up with the financing to purchase materials and employ a cohort of some twenty-five masons, carpenters and laborers, many of whom had to be housed and fed on the premises. I can imagine him working his legendary charm, of course, and perhaps even trading off the sympathetic reaction to Mamah's death as a wedge to separate friends, tradesmen and prospective clients alike from their resources, and yet *still* . . .

him of their own losses and bereavements, reassure him, scold him, praise and criticize and offer up their prayers. He couldn't read the letters, not after the first few. They depressed and irritated him. Who were these people to think they could invade his life, whether they meant well or not? Was this notoriety? Was this what notoriety meant? People nosing into your private life like parasites, digging at your soul, insinuating themselves through two thin sheets of paper?

"Burn them," he told his secretary. "All of them. Unless they're from people I know and want to know. Friends, clients, family. Burn the rest. I don't want to see them."

And so it went. But the secretary, a judicious woman, set aside some of the more intriguing and compassionate specimens, thinking they would appeal to his sense of himself in a very specific and therapeutic way. She bound these letters with a strip of ribbon and every few days set them down on his desk. "I thought these might interest you," she would say, quickly adding, "I've burned the rest."

One morning in early December she laid a single letter on his desk. "This one seems very heartfelt," she murmured, and he looked up at the catch in her voice. She gave him a weak smile and excused herself. A cold rain fell beyond the windows. He got up a moment to poke at the fire, then went back to the drawing he was working on, pushing the letter to the corner of his desk. For the next hour, he barely glanced up, trying out one idea after another for the Japanese, envisioning a hotel that would be neither Oriental nor Western, a grand edifice that might combine some of the structural elements of Midway Gardens, layered stone, brick, with a pool out front to bring it down to earth and reflect its lines—preliminary sketches, that was all, because the commission wasn't assured, not yet. Though it would be, he was confident of that, and he couldn't help calculating the commission on a building with a nearly limitless budget, two million, three, maybe more. He'd forgotten all about the letter, but when he next glanced up, there it was, in a cream-colored envelope embossed with the initials MMN.

He took it up idly, his mind in Japan still. A faint scent of perfume rose to him, as if a new presence had entered the room, a woman's presence, sleek and refined and dwelling in abstraction. He put his nose to the envelope—he couldn't help himself, and how long had it been? It was addressed in a bold looping hand that seemed to leap off the page to *Mr. Frank Lloyd Wright, Architect*; the return address gave a street number and arrondissement in Paris, but the postmark was stamped Chicago, Illinois. He unfolded the letter and began to read with an absorption so complete it was as if a spell had come over him:

Dear Mr. Wright,

I am writing to express my deepest sympathy and shock over your tragic loss, knowing how painful such a loss can be, especially at this time of the year, when we all look back upon our sorrows and blessings in the approach of Yuletide as if gazing into a reflection in the vast darkling mere of our lives. Oh, to think of the hand the Fates deal us! Love and death poised in counterpoint, cruelly, cruelly! For I too have borne the terrible tragedy of a loss in love and life and I can tell you that you must think not of what might have been, but of your loved one arisen in the ecstasy of eternal being. We are kindred souls, we two. Battered souls, souls yearning for the shore of lightness and floral display to show its face amongst the battering waves of the dark seas of despair . . .

The confident flowing hand led him on through fifteen closely inscribed pages offering hope and resignation in equal parts and assuring him that new associations, new challenges and joys awaited him as they awaited her and all those whose spirits were undamped and unbowed. *In Sympathy and Affectionate Hope*, the writer concluded and gave a Chicago address beneath the ecstatic looping flourish of her name: *Madame Maude Miriam Noel.*

CHAPTER 2: ENTER MIRIAM

She was sunk into the sofa in Norma's sitting room—or living room, as they called it here—taking a cup of tea and idly shifting the pieces of a jigsaw puzzle round the end table for lack of anything better to do, when Norma came in with the mail. Outside, beyond the gray frame of the window, the weather was dreary, funereal clouds strung from the rooftops like laundry hung out to dry, and so cold even the dirty gray ratlike pigeons were huddled against it, dark motionless lines of frozen feathers and arrested beaks blighting the eaves as far as she could see down both sides of the block. She hadn't been out of the house in two days, hadn't been out of her wrapper, because this cold was like some sort of cosmic joke, a cold beyond anything Paris had seen since the glaciers withdrew in some unfathomable prehistoric epoch when people still went round dwelling in caves. Chicago. How could anyone ever possibly *live* here?

Of course, she reminded herself, she was a refugee now,* and would have to make the best of it. And Norma was sweet, she was, though the apartment was cluttered and overheated, the wallpaper ludicrous, the décor what you might expect of a curio shop, and where was her

* Having left Paris two months earlier in the expatriate exodus following the first Battle of the Marne.

daughter's taste? Had she learned nothing from her mother's example? Inherited nothing? Was it all Emil, then, was that it? Her dead husband's face waxed a moment in her consciousness, and he'd been a good man, really, quiet, considerate, supportive, but with just about as much artistic sensibility in his entire body as she possessed in one little finger. The apartment. Norma's clothes. Her *son-in-law.* She felt the anger come up in her in a buoyant rush, the words already forming on her tongue, wounding words, nagging, but constructive, *reconstructive,* because it was a tragedy to live like this, to, to—when Norma said, "Mama, there's something here for you."

And then it was in her hand, an off-white envelope decorated with a single red square in the lower left-hand corner and above it the initials FLLW. She set down her teacup. It might have been her imagination, but the day seemed to brighten just perceptibly, as if the sun really did exist out there somewhere amidst all that gloom. The anger she'd felt so intensely just a moment earlier dissolved in a sunset glow of warmth and satisfaction. Norma was studying her. "What is it, Mama?" she asked, an anticipatory smile on her lips. "Good news?"

Miriam didn't answer, not right away. She was going to take her time because she didn't have to open the letter, not yet—she already knew what it would say, more or less. He would thank her in an elaborate, courtly way. Express how deeply moved he was to hear of her commiseration and how truly he wished to return the sentiment. He would be intrigued too—he had to know who she was who could know his heart so intimately. There would be all this and more: an invitation. To meet. At his studio. His home. A grand room someplace, one of his shining creations, lit softly with his exquisite lamps, the light of the hearth gathering overhead in the oiled beams, his prints and pottery emerging from the shadows to lend the perfect accents. He would be honored, et cetera, and he didn't mean to be impertinent in any way, but he just had to see her—see this marvel of perception—in the flesh, if only for the briefest few fleeting moments.

Of course, as is often the case, the reality of a given situation doesn't necessarily accord with one's expectations—her years with Emil had brought that home to her, resoundingly—and the architect's response wasn't quite what she'd hoped for. He was intrigued, yes, how could he help but be? And yet he was distant too because he didn't know her, couldn't begin to see her true self through the impress of her pen—he might have thought she was some overheated spinster with a poetic bent, another parlor philosopher, one more petitioner reaching out to cling to his feet as he ascended the Olympus of architecture—and there was no invitation.

Though certainly he was interested. She could sniff that out in the first few lines, anyone could. And she immediately wrote back, her second missive even more effusive than the first (and why not?—she was too great and giving a soul to restrain her feelings) and this time she told him more about herself, about her flight from Paris, her romantic yearnings, her life lived in the service of her art, and she found a dozen ways to praise his genius that had revolutionized the very highest art of them all for an entire generation. In a postscript she begged for a meeting, however brief, because her heart simply wouldn't rest to think of him alone in his torment. She signed herself, *In All Sympathy and Hope, Madame Noel.*

The reply came by return mail. He would be pleased to receive her in his studio at Orchestra Hall* and per-

* Throughout his career, Wrieto-San made a point of arranging meetings in his studio, where he could feel both impregnable and masterful, rather like a tortoise encapsulated in a gilded shell.

haps, if time allowed and she was willing, to show her some recent examples of his own art. Would five o'clock, Thursday, suit her? If not, he'd be happy to arrange another date and time. He awaited her reply and looked forward with great pleasure to meeting her. And he was, just as she'd expected, faithfully hers, Frank Lloyd Wright.

She spent three hours on her clothes and makeup, rejecting one outfit after another until she settled on a clinging gown of chartreuse velvet cut to show her throat, shoulders and arms to best advantage. She powdered her face, did her eyes and lips, brushed out her hair—and her hair was her glory, always had been, as abundant as a debutante's and not a single thread of gray showing through the russet curls that fell en masse at the nape of her neck—and then, after a painstaking inspection in the full-length mirror, she looked to her jewelry. A selection of rings—the scarab, of course—her diamond and seed pearl cross with the rose gold chain to bring his eyes to her throat, the lorgnette trailing languidly from its silk ribbon. She wanted him to see her as she was, *au courant*, cultured, a gifted artist who'd exhibited at the Louvre and was *trés intime* with the salons of Paris, a woman of stature and character, the natural beauty whose presence and refinement made all the rest of the women toiling along the streets of the Windy City seem like so many mutts. "How do I look?" she called out to Norma as she swept into the living room. And Norma, bless her, gazed up at her mother in genuine awe. "Oh, Mama, you look like you just stepped out of the Paris rotogravure!"

She spun round twice, reveling in the fit of the dress and the soft flutter of the skirts at her ankles. "And what do you think of this—for outerwear?" Studying herself in the mirror over the sideboard, she dropped a shoulder to slip into her sealskin cape, then leaned in close to pin the matching cap atop the crest of her curls. A moment to touch up her lips, drawing down her mouth in an irresistible pout—let him resist me, just let him, she was thinking, full of a spiraling ascending joy that threatened to lift her right off her feet—and then she whirled round to give Norma the full effect.

"Well?" she said.

Norma had got up to cross the room to her. She reached out a hand to smooth the fur. "Oh, Mama," she whispered. "It's beautiful."

And Miriam was soaring, soaring, no need for the pravaz, not now, not in the mood she was in because no elixir could hope to match or improve on it—she was beautiful, she was, and she knew it. She bent for a final glance in the mirror, made a minute adjustment to the angle of the cap, patted her hair in place. Then she straightened up and gave her daughter a fervent smile, feeling like an actress waiting in the wings for her cue, the whole dreary apartment suddenly lifted out of its gloom and irradiated with light. She dropped her voice to the register of seduction. "I'll want a taxi," she said.

A brisk anarchic wind seized her as she stepped from the cab, her cape billowing, hat ready to take flight, all the grit and refuse of the filthy avenues and back alleys flung up at her as if in a hurricane, so that her chief concern as she went up the stairs to the lobby was her hair. And her face. Her face, of course. She would be late for their appointment, no question about it—she was already late—and now she was going to have to stop in the ladies' lavatory and make the necessary adjustments. Heart pounding, out of breath, flustered—yes, flustered—she tramped through the lobby looking for the lavatory, and when she found it, when she pushed through the door and into the warm brightly lit sanctuary that was, thankfully, deserted at this hour, she went directly to one of the stalls and locked herself in. What she was thinking was that she couldn't let him see her in this state, her nerves all aflutter as if she were some chorus girl plucked out of the Folies-Bergère, and so to calm herself, to slow things down and give her that air of Parisian languor that was sure to captivate him, she extracted the pravaz from her purse.

Afterward, she saw to her face and hair in the mirror, in full possession of herself once again. She reapplied her lipstick with a hand as steady as a surgeon's, smoothed down the chartreuse velvet and gave a tug at the neckline to make the material lie just so, flared the cape, refreshed her perfume. For a long moment she studied herself in the mirror from various angles, even as two other women—middle-aged drudges* without the faintest inkling of style or carriage—came through the door, chattering over the affairs of some office girl or other. She ignored them—*Let them look, let them appreciate style, real style, for once in their godforsaken lives*—and gave herself one final appraisal. Satisfied, she swept out of the room and across the lobby to the elevator, where two men in beautifully tailored suits stepped aside with fawning awestruck looks as she announced the floor to the elevator man and he tried his best to stare straight ahead.

She was greeted by a young male assistant—the offices lavish with Oriental art, a pair of Ianelli sprites, realized drawings and intricate models, the lighting

* Miriam was forty-five at the time. It may be interesting to note, for contrast, that Olgivanna was then a fifteen-year-old schoolgirl living in Tiflis with her sister, Hinzenberg and Gurdjieff not yet blips on the horizon. I imagine her fast asleep at that hour—it would have been three a.m. in the Russian province of Georgia—her hair splayed out over the pillow, girlish dreams revolving in her head.

exquisite, taste and elevation oozing from the very walls—and then shown into a hallway connecting to the studio, where she caught a glimpse of a short stocky elderly man with an enormous head ducking into a doorway before she was led into the studio proper and seated in a high-backed Craftsman chair. But this was no ordinary chair, and the thought came home to her with the force of revelation—this was a Frank Lloyd Wright chair. *She was sitting in a Frank Lloyd Wright chair, a masterpiece designed by the Master himself!* There was genius here, genius invested in the design that lent verticality to the horizontal lines of the room, in the cut and mold and finish of the wood. In the décor, the walls, the rugs, the hangings. It was as if she'd been ushered into the salon of Des Esseintes himself.

The assistant—he had the face of an acolyte, stooped shoulders, pursed lips, mole-colored hair swept across his brow—had pulled out the chair for her as if performing some holy rite. He'd offered to take her cape, but she'd declined. She wanted Mr. Frank Lloyd Wright to get the full effect of her, *en ensemble*, and now she had a moment to arrange the folds of the cape and settle herself. Her chair, she saw, was one of a group of three—the other two flanked a small inlaid table against the wall—and it had been set here in front of an oversized desk decorated with an enormous vase of cut flowers that gave up their beauty and fragrance in defiance of the weather and the season both; behind the desk an Oriental screen depicted a dark twisting pine with a pair of cranes nesting in the branches. "Mr. Wright will be in directly," the assistant whispered before creeping out of the room. A moment passed, everything as still as a church, and then suddenly he was there, the very man she'd seen in the hallway, catlike, alert and present, immanently present, and could it be? The graying hair, the head of marble? But of course, of course. Those eyes. The lines of grief round his mouth. He was fraught, heroic, and young, much younger than he'd appeared at first glance—

"Madame Noel?" he said, coming round the desk to give a short bow and take her hand in his. "It's a great pleasure—" he began, and then faltered, the customary rituals of greeting failing him because they were inadequate, hopeless, a falsification of everything he was feeling in that moment. She could see it instantly, see her power reflected in his eyes, hunger there, confusion, a gaze of pure astonishment running up and down her body like the touch of his two hands, and something else too, something deeper, primal, naked in its immediacy and need.

She gave him a soft slow smile, the pressure of her fingertips on his, then dropped his hand to lean forward and set her gold cigarette case on one corner of the desk and the little leather-bound volume she'd brought him on the other. "Oh, believe me, the pleasure is all mine," she said, her voice falling down the register till it was a whisper, a purr. "Or no, that's not right at all—the honor. It's an honor simply to be in your presence."

He flushed, fighting to recover himself, his voice too loud all of a sudden: "No, no, I do mean it, the pleasure's all mine. You—your letter. Letters." He'd backed away from her as he might have backed away from a fire flaring up round a length of pitch pine and settled himself behind the desk. "I was deeply moved," he said. "You express yourself exquisitely, tremendous command of the language."

She looked up at him, holding his gaze, then crossed her legs and began removing her gloves, finger by finger, as languidly and delicately as she could manage. All the while, he was watching her, fixated, as if she were performing some miracle of prestidigitation. "Do you mind if I smoke?" she asked, taking up the cigarette case so that he could see it, see her initials engraved there and the ampersand that joined them to the initials of the man who'd given it to her.

"Oh, no, no, not at all." And he leaned forward to light her cigarette, his eyes never leaving her face.

She tilted her head back and exhaled, in her element now, as secure as a porpoise in the deep rocking cradle of the sea. "Well," she said, dropping her chin to focus her gaze on him, "how do you like me?"

It took him a moment—he was, as she was soon to learn, rarely at a loss for words—and then he spoke the truth, the gratifying truth, quite plainly: "I've never seen anyone like you."

She let her smile bloom again and then—had she ever felt so free, so magnetic?—she began quoting Rimbaud in the accent of the transplanted Parisienne she was, and of course he'd never seen anyone like her, how could he have? "'*Mais, vrai, j'ai trop pleuré! Les Aubes sont navrantes. / Toute lune est atroce et tout soleil amer: / L'âcre amour m'a gonflé de torpeurs enivrantes.*'"

He was smiling too, smiling so hard it looked as if his face would rupture, but this was most definitely not a smile of comprehension. Could it be that her hero, this arbiter of taste, this passionate artificer, the Hephaestus to her Aphrodite, did not speak the language of romance? Of civilization?

"*Comprenez vous?*" she tried, leaning forward now.

An awkward moment, the first in this enchanted encounter, passed between them before she switched to English. "It's a poem," she said. "Meant to soothe you in your suffering because you must know that others have experienced desolation too. You're not alone, that's what I'm trying to convey. Not alone." She leaned into the desk. "Listen," she said, dropping her voice lower still, "the poet says: 'But, truly, I have wept too much! The Dawns are heartbreaking. / Every moon is atrocious and every sun bitter.' And now the last line, which applies perhaps more to me in my present state than to you, though I know you've felt deeply and felt the hurt of it: 'Sharp love has swollen me with heady languors.' 'Swollen me!' Isn't that the saddest thing you've ever heard?"

"Oh, I don't know," he said, taking up one of the tools on his desk—a triangle, was that what it was?—and turning it over in his hand. "It's quite beautiful. The French especially. You recite so, so evocatively." He set down the triangle, took up something else now—a T-square. "I'm more of an Emerson man myself. Longfellow. Carl Sandburg—he's a personal friend. Terrific man. Great soul."

And now he was reciting for her, his face lit with the pleasure of it, the music of him, *his eyes*: " 'You will come one day in a waver of love, / Tender as dew, impetuous as rain, / The tan of the sun will be on your skin, / The purr of the breeze in your murmuring speech.' "

She sat perfectly still a moment, letting his words resonate till they were alive inside her, till she felt them like a rhythmic pulse that beat along with her own. "Magnificent," she said. "Bravo! You recite so exquisitely I would have thought you an actor. And your voice—"

His smile showed the perfection of his teeth. He tapped one hand on the glowing surface of the desk as if to keep measure with the lines still flowing in his head. "It's the poet," he said. "Give Carl the credit. Speaking of poets, would you happen to know of Taliesin, by the way? Has he come into your purview over there in Paris?"

He hadn't. She'd never heard of him. She composed her face, all seriousness and a bright eagerness to know. "Is he Italian?"

"No, no, no: I'm talking of the legendary Welsh bard and shape-shifter, the man whose face was so beautiful it was said to radiate light.* Richard Hovey—do you know Richard Hovey? He wrote a masque called 'Taliesin' some years back? No? First-rate. I think you'd appreciate it. Very delicate and deep. Like you." He paused, as if he'd gone too far, his eyes dodging away from hers for just an instant. "Well, anyway, I've named my house after Taliesin—my estate, that is. In Wisconsin. After the poet. And you must see it, absolutely, you must—when, that is . . ." he trailed off.

"I know what you're feeling," she said, with fervor, real fervor. "You poor man. How you've suffered. You have. I know that perhaps better than any soul on this earth, because we're attuned—we're twins, that's what we are, *twins*." She was so excited she very nearly jumped out of the chair to run to him, clutch him to her, heat and heal and solace him with a passion so perfect and deep he'd put all the tragedy and ruin behind him forever. But not yet, not yet: the moment was too delicious. She slid forward till she was perched on the very edge of the chair, her hands in motion, her eyes speaking for her. "But listen," she said, "listen to Gérard de Nerval, just listen: 'I move in darkness—widowed—beyond solace, / The Prince of Acquitaine in a ruined tower. / My star is dead . . .'"

Her eyes were full. She couldn't go on. If she were to look back in that instant on all the heightened moments of her life, all the intensity, the passion, the quarrels and turmoil and transcendent flights of sheer spiritual grace, nothing could have compared to what she was feeling in those precious minutes since she'd walked through his

* See Welsh mythology, the Taliesin chapters of *Pwyll Prince of Dyfed*, beginning with "The Cauldron of Ceridwen." Taliesin is often translated as "shining brow," and Wrieto-San was fond of this designation for *his* Taliesin, the house on (of) the brow of the hill.

door. She couldn't seem to breathe. She felt faint. "I'm sorry," she gasped. "Forgive me. I'm just—it's just that I am so . . . deeply . . . *moved* . . ."

And then he was there at her side, offering his handkerchief, the finest cambric, faintly scented, and she was dabbing at her eyes. "Here," she said, impulsively snatching up the pamphlet she'd brought him, "here, take this as the smallest consolatory gift from me to you in your time of need—and take it to your heart. The scriptures heal—*Jesus* heals. I know. I've been down that road."

He looked puzzled. Son of a preacher, nephew of Jenkin Lloyd Jones, who was one of the great pulpit orators of his time, and he was doubtful? Reluctant?

"Here, take it," she said again, her voice reduced to a kind of sob, and she had to get hold of herself, had to bear down here a moment, or the mood would evaporate, the whole shining room with its glitter of art and hope and beauty dissolved like a vision out of *The Arabian Nights*, and she felt the pressure of his hand in hers and then the book—Mary Baker Eddy's sweet, sweet revelation—passing from her fingertips to his.* "You'll heal," she whispered, her voice steadier now. "Trust me. You'll heal."

Somehow they were both standing. His arm was round her shoulders and his hand—*his hand*—was unconsciously massaging the short thick sturdy hairs the seal had once worn in the polar sea to fight back the chill of the world. It was perfect. It was exquisite. And what was he saying—murmuring—in her ear? "There, there, it's all right. I'll be fine. I will. And you, you kind, beautiful and spiritual woman, you'll be fine

* The book was *Science and Health*. Miriam was a devotee of the author's "curative system of metaphysics" and "spiritual healing." Wrieto-San, as I understood him, was somewhat more pragmatic.

too. I'll read the book. I'll read it because it's from you."

She raised her eyes to him. She was trembling. Her voice was a whisper. "Has anyone ever told you you have the most magnificent head?"

Again he looked puzzled.

But she went on, the words coming in a rush now: "You must sit for me, I won't take no for an answer, and though I prefer hands—hands are my special interest, and feet too, hands and feet, but no matter—I'll mold a bust of you and it'll be magnificent, the grandest thing I've done. But you will sit for me? Won't you? Promise?"

The next two weeks were a *tourbillion* of dinners, dances, museums, art exhibitions and automotive visits to the houses he'd built and of which he was as preening proud as a child with his first assemblage of wooden blocks. He would pull into the drive at one domicile or another without announcing himself, spring out like an acrobat to rush round to her side of the car and wait impatiently while she prepared herself for the blast of the wind, then march her round and round the place, expatiating on every last detail—right down to the origin of the copper in the downspouts—before waltzing into the house as if he owned it and starting all over again with the interior details. All the while, the inhabitants standing patiently by as he criticized the style and placement of the furniture or some element of his conception that didn't seem sufficiently appreciated, he never took his eyes from her. And despite the cold, despite her aching feet and the strain of bursting into the homes of total strangers who looked at her as if she were something between a captive and an invader, his gaze—awestruck, appreciative and undisguisedly carnal—made her glow.

As Christmas approached and Norma began draping random sprigs of holly about the house and trolling carols in the kitchen (flatly and out of tune, because, sadly, she'd also apparently failed to inherit her mother's musical talent, but hadn't she sung "Frère Jacques" so beautifully as a schoolgirl—or was that Corinne?*), Frank's attentions became ever more insistent. There were parties, of course. Parties everywhere. Daily. Nightly. In lavish homes, galleries and theaters, lavishly decorated for Yuletide, colored servants scraping about with trays of drinks and delicacies and all the haut monde of Chicago gathered round in their furs and jewels and fancy dress. Frank became the very avatar of the season, funneling his genius for interior design into a cornucopia of Christmas display and superhuman good cheer, parading her around on his arm as if she were the rarest treasure of all. "You're my jewel," he would say, and kiss her full on the lips, thrusting himself at her till she could feel him hard against her—and she would withdraw as delicately as she could without dampening his ardor entirely, and call him naughty or a billy goat or some such childish designation. And then he was on her again and again till she thought she would split open with the heat of her own desire. He would have her—and she would have him—and soon, soon.

Still, she didn't know quite what to expect when he invited her to his house on Christmas Eve itself. Would his grown children be there? His wife? His mother? The comical little housekeeper with the ear trumpet she'd heard so much about? His friends and associates? The neighbors? Or would it be just the two of them, locked in a passionate embrace as if they had no other attachments in the world?

* Miriam's second daughter. She also had a son, Thomas, who was a traveling man of some sort and didn't seem to have much time for his mother. Or inclination either.

It was past dark when the taxi pulled up in front of the house. This was a small house, modest and neat, the house of his exile from the place in Oak Park he'd given over to his wife and the ruins of his mansion in Wisconsin, and if she'd expected something grander, a structure commensurate with his beauty and wisdom and greatness, she buried her disappointment. This was temporary. She could appreciate that. She was living a temporary life herself, and even as the thought came into her head, she felt a violent upsurge of feeling for him: they were exiles, both of them, and the fates had brought them together for mutual solace. What could be more perfect? More glorious?

Full of hope and love—swollen with it, yes—she came briskly up the walk, watching for patches of ice because it wouldn't do to fall and turn an ankle, though even that would have its rewards, her leg delicately elevated before the fire as he tended to her with a strip of bandage and a glass of champagne, his fingers kneading her flesh, wandering up her calf and back down again, stroking, probing, caressing . . . But here he was, the door flung open on a flood of light, dressed in a black velvet dinner jacket and Chinese trousers, his hair backlit like the nimbus of an angel—"Miriam," he was calling, "my love, my dear, my jewel, here, let me help you—"

The fire leapt up. There were bowls of blood-red roses everywhere. A brazen Buddha. The lamps he'd designed himself with their marvelous geometrical patterns and their soft shimmers of light. Candles aglow. The table set for two. Champagne on ice. And music, delicate, delicious, a string quartet serenading her from the Victrola in the corner. "It's breathtaking," she said, even as he kicked the door shut and took her in his arms. "Everything you touch. Just breathtaking!"

They couldn't stop talking—and kissing, kissing too—ranging the whole world over, from the Greeks to the Romans to the contemporary theater and the joys of Germany, Italy, Japan—she must go to Japan, she absolutely must, he insisted: the cleanest and most perfectly organic society on earth—and, of course, Paris. Which was her province. If she must go to Japan then he must come to Paris—with her as his guide. Oh, and she sang on about Paris as if it were a car ride away, as if they could browse the antiquarian shops and stroll the boulevards before the clock struck midnight. She was intoxicated, absolutely and thoroughly, right to the core of her—and not from any opiate or even the champagne, but from being there with him on the most precious night of the year.

They ate in front of the fire at the table he'd laid there, each dish served up by him on a covered platter, hearty food—cod in cream sauce, salt pork and potatoes, too hearty maybe, too plain and well, Midwestern, but good for all that—and there was no sign of the comical little housekeeper or anyone else. Afterward she smoked before the fire and delicately tipped back a demitasse of coffee and some sort of liqueur she couldn't identify (he abstained) and let her voice sing till she might have been a tropical bird fluttered down out of the grim black sky to brighten this parlor and this house till it shone like the center of the universe—and on Christmas Eve, no less!

"Do you see my ring?" she asked at one point, holding out her hand to him as they sat together on a stiff-backed sofa that might have been a thing of beauty but wasn't sumptuous at all, more like a pew in a monastic chapel, and wouldn't a few pillows or even a quilt go a long way toward improving it—and the comfort of the room too? But all thought flew out of her head because he took her hand in his and kissed it and kissed it again, running his fingers up her wrist to her forearm, the exquisite pressure there, the fire . . . "It was worn by Cleopatra," she went on, but he was bent to her hand still, kissing, kissing, and her breath was coming faster, "to keep her lovers faithful. This . . . very . . . ring . . ."

His hand slid up her arm, along the smooth velvet path, no resistance to the material at all, and he was embracing her throat now and giving her the full weight of his eyes. He murmured something, whether it had to do with Cleopatra and her lovers or the height of the ceiling or the color of her eyes, she couldn't say, but her voice was teasing out the subject, breathy and deep, no going back now—"Beware," she whispered, "to all faithless lovers, but you, you're not . . . faithless . . . are you?"

His hand was on her breast, slipping beneath the material to the naked skin, to the aureole and the nipple which hardened to his touch. And his lips. His lips were on hers. She heard the fire crackle. Heard the record hiss against its label. Wind beyond the windows. The ticking of a clock. She leaned back to accommodate his weight and the slow sweet delirium of his hands and his tongue.

"Are you?" she whispered.

And he, fully aroused, his face gone rubicund and his ears glistening like Christmas ornaments in the quavering light, breathed his answer against the soft heat of her lips. "Me?" he puffed, working, working hard, writhing against her and tugging at the buttons of his trousers as if they were each individually on fire. "Never," he said, sinking into her, "never."

CHAPTER 3: NOW COMES FEAR

Whether Norma or her little toad of a husband approved or not was an utter irrelevance: she was moving in with Frank Lloyd Wright at 25 East Cedar Street and the whole world could choke on its pinched pathetic petit bourgeois notions of propriety for all she cared. She was going to live. Express herself. Roam with the giants. It happened that she was in love with a towering genius, a Wagnerian hero who stood head and shoulders above them all, a Tannhäuser, a Siegfried—and he was in love with her, her and no one else—and if they thought she was going to confine herself to a miserable back room in a hideous flat and live like a Carmelite nun at her son-in-law's sufferance, they were sadly mistaken. She had her bags sent over, the trunks she'd brought with her from France, her clothes, jewelry, objets d'art, and by the middle of January she was established, mistress of her own house once again.

It was a kind of miracle. Like being on a honeymoon all over again and this little house the ship that would take them across the wide ocean into the seas of bliss. The nights were rapturous with lovemaking, the mornings sunstruck (or at least they felt that way), and while he was at his studio spinning out his designs in the company of his scurrying functionaries, she busied herself with making the house just a soupçon more comfortable—or less austere, at any rate. That was the term she used over the telephone to Leora—"He seems so austere, almost Puritanical, as if a plush pillow were a violation of the sumptuary laws or some such thing." She selected curtains for the windows, pillows for the sofa and each of the flat hard-bottomed chairs. She ordered linens and stationery featuring their entwined initials and her familial crest. China, cutlery—carpets, for God's sake. And his taste in cuisine: "I tell you, Leora, I try, I do—and we've been through two cooks already—but the only stuff he seems to like is so bland, so unappealing in every way, I couldn't imagine a single soul in all of France, even the dirtiest peasant speaking some dialect that sounds as if he's invented it on the spot, bothering to feed it to his hogs. No, I mean it. I do. He needs reforming. Needs a good dose of culture, beyond all his drawings and his houses, which really are exquisite, I'm not denying that, not at all—"

By the end of the second week, the punishing gray chill of January folding itself into the unrelenting arctic blast that welcomed February to the bleak canyons of Chicago, they had their first quarrel. The cook, on her instructions—and with her supervision—had prepared a lovely *saumon tartare avec sauce moutarde* for a prelude, followed by a *bisque de homard, salade d'endive* and a spectacular *flambé* of *ris de veau,* and she served a perfectly delicious Sancerre with the salmon and a Margaux with the sweetbreads she'd ordered herself from the wine merchant and had no little trouble finding it, incidentally, in this backwater, and he'd been less than impressed. In fact, at one point he pushed back his plate—shoved it aside as if it were something he'd found in the street—stalked into the kitchen without so much as a word and reappeared a moment later with a glass of water and an apple.

While she watched, astonished, he peeled and divided the apple, feeding it into his mouth slice by slice and washing it down with the water.

"I spent all afternoon on this meal," she said quietly, fighting to keep any hint of severity out of her voice. "And Madeline virtually slaved to bring it off."

He gave her a sharp glance. "Tell Madeline she's fired."

"Fired? Why, I've just hired her. And she's excellent, truly excellent—Montreal bred, perhaps, but—"

"Do I have to repeat myself? She's fired. I'll send to Taliesin for Nellie Breen if this is the best you can do." He stabbed at a slice of the meat with the paring knife and held it, dripping, before him. "This sort of thing may be all the rage in Paris, but it won't do here. We don't eat this tripe—"

"Sweetbreads," she corrected, and she could feel herself going hot all over. The temerity of him, the insult. He was a boor, that was what he was. A barbarian. "You're a boor. That's what the problem is. You need civilizing, are you aware of that?"

"And we don't take alcoholic beverages—wine—with our meals."

She was angry all of a sudden, so infused with rage she couldn't speak. She laughed instead, a bitter cutting sarcastic laugh.

He was standing now, every inch of his five feet six or whatever it was clonic with fury. "Smoking," he snarled. "It's like living in a tobacco warehouse somebody's set afire. It's a disgusting habit. Totally inappropriate for a lady. And I won't have it."

And now the battle was joined, because she was on her feet too, ready to throw it all back at him. "Rube!" she shouted. "Hayseed!"

He gave her a look that chilled her—he was as capable of murder as any cutthroat roaming the alleys of the south side—and he actually took a step toward her, as if he would dare. *Just let him,* she was saying to herself, her feet braced and her body gone rigid. *Just let him.* But he checked himself—she saw the rational part of him take over as if a switch had been thrown, and he was afraid of her, wasn't he? The little man, the coward. "You disgust me," he said finally. And he turned on his heel, jerked round and strode out the door and into the black curtain of the night and he didn't think of his cloak or his hat or the scarf that never once left his throat but when he was sitting at table or asleep in bed.

"Go!" she shrieked, darting to the door with the plate of sweetbreads and the sautéed *champignons de la forêt* and the sherry sauce she'd created from scratch raised in one hand. "Go, you bastard!" And the plate went with him, describing a drooling parabola across the moonlit yard till it crashed to the walk and scattered its contents for the birds and the squirrels and the scavengers of the night.

They made it up, of course—with a furious bout of lovemaking that began almost as if it were a free-fall match between two determined adversaries and ended in the sweetest surrender—but not before he went off to Wisconsin without her. For three entire days. And no word of him. Nothing. It was as if he'd never lived here, as if she'd never known him, and this house, filled with his things, was a memorial only, a tomb of nobody's making. The first night she didn't sleep an instant, replaying the scene over and over again in her head, wishing she'd showed more restraint, less fire and fury, because she did love him as she'd never loved anyone in her life, she was sure of it, absolutely and without question, and she missed him with an ache that echoed inside her like a cry of despair from the cored-out trunk of a withered tree.* The following day was purgatorial, an accumulation of intolerable minutes and torturous hours that made her lash out at Madeline and the various delivery men presenting their wares, and she wouldn't call him at his offices like some castoff baggage who can't keep track of her man, she wouldn't. By the close of the second day, she was certain he was deceiving her with another woman, his secretary, his wife—Kitty, that was her name, *Kitty*, and why not just call her *cunt* and get it over with? She telephoned Leora and sobbed through the thin swaying wires, telephoned Norma to tell her her mother was ruined, and finally, though she fought it, she broke down and telephoned his studio. Where the reedy wisp of an effeminate acolyte came over the line to inform her that the Master—*Mr.* Wright—had gone up to Taliesin to oversee the work there. And when was he expected back? Oh—a long calculated pause—he couldn't say. After that, she had her pravaz, only that. And even then, she cried herself to sleep.

At breakfast the morning after they'd made it up he was tender with her, tender and gentle too, and they sat across the table from each other in a satiate glow, no need for words, their silence broken only by the most solicitous murmurings, *Would you care for another cup of tea, dear? Cream? Can I get you another egg? Darling, if it's not too much trouble, would you please be kind enough to pass the salt?* She clung to him when he got up to leave for work, their kisses so heated he very nearly had her right there on the carpet, and when he came home the first thing she did was lead him into the bedroom. And she let Madeline go, just to please him, and that night she stood over the stove herself, half-dressed, and made him potatoes in the pan with onions and a steak au jus with no flavoring other than a pinch of salt and a dash of pepper. He never stopped talk-

* Miriam, as I understand her, did tend to be self-dramatizing, though perhaps O'Flaherty-San lays it on a bit thick here.

ing, not even to draw breath, and after dinner he sat at the piano and serenaded her till she sank into the new plush pillows like a queen, like Cleopatra herself. He was hers, he was hers, he was hers, and the world was a good and beautiful place once again.

Their second quarrel came at the end of that week and he was the one who set it off—again—because he was in a mood, she could see that the minute he stepped through the door. He didn't like the pillows, that was it. They made the place look like a whorehouse, he said, and she said, "So what does that make me?"

He had no answer for that, and she saw what a little man he was, what a yellowbelly, and no sooner did he divest himself of his cape and hat than he started in on the subject of her stationery and the china she'd ordered. "It's vulgar, Miriam. *Your* coat of arms? What of mine? Don't you think the Lloyd Joneses go back farther than the, the—whoever your people are?"

"My father was a Hicks. And we trace our origins back to the earliest settlement of Virginia. If it weren't for the War Between the States, we'd—"

"The plain red square," he said. "That is how I've marked my stationery all these years and that is how I'll mark it in the future. Do you understand me? I won't discuss it."*

* Wrieto-San adopted the square as his symbol because he understood it to represent probity, solidity, the virtues of the four-square, and, of course, it is testamentary to the rectilinear patterns of his early and middle work. In contradistinction, we Japanese believe the circle to be the ideal form, as it is perfectly harmonious, sans the sharp individual edges of the square. But Wrieto-San was, if anything, a rugged individualist, a one-man, as we say, like the lone cowboy of the Wild West films. Personally, I like to think that it was the Japanese influence that inspired him to employ a circular design for his final major work, the Guggenheim Museum of New York.

She was seething—the way he cut her off, dictated to her. Who did he think he was? "Yes? And what *will* you discuss? Taliesin? Tell me about Taliesin and why I'm not invited there. Is it because of that dead woman? You think I'll sully her memory, is that it?"

He averted his face—a sure sign he was lying—and said, "No, that's not it at all. It's just that we're rebuilding right now and you really wouldn't be comfortable there, what with the dirt and confusion, the limited room, and my attentions of course would be distracted in terms of the work going forward—"

"What about your mother?"

"My mother? What has she got to do with it?" His voice flared. "I suppose you resent her having given birth to me, is that it? Because you weren't there?" He was bent over the lamp in the corner now, jerking at the switch. The light caught his face as he turned to her, everything about him savage and animalistic, like some burrowing thing trapped outside its den, and he was hateful, hateful.

"She's invited, isn't she?"

"Well, I—of course. You know that. I'm building rooms for her and my aunts—and for you, for you too."

"And your children? The children are there, are they not? Catherine, Llewellyn, David, Frances? One big happy family? Where are *they* sleeping? Are *they* so put out by the construction?" He'd turned to her and she came right up to him now, thrusting her face in his. "You're a liar, Frank. A liar. And a ghoul, that's what you are, because you prefer some, some corpse to me! A memory! A dead thing!" She veered away from him, her hand snatching for something, anything she could heft, one of his damned statues, anything—but he caught her by the wrist.

"Don't you say a word against her," he said, tightening his grip.

She twisted away from him, jerked her wrist free, and here was one of his vases and she didn't give two figs what dynasty it hailed from or what precious artisanic soul had fired it in whichever golden Chinese era—and were they *all* golden?—it was in her hand and then it was gone, obliterated against the wall. "Go ahead," she said, "hit me," but she spun out of reach, flung herself across the room and then came at him so swiftly he had to backtrack.

"Cold meat, Frank. But I'm alive, a real live flesh-and-blood woman!" Both her hands were at her collar now and in a single savage jerk she tore the dress to her waist, her breasts falling free even as the cold air of the room assaulted her. "Look at me. Look at my breasts. You've fondled them enough. Suckled them like an infant. They were good enough for you then. And now you prefer a corpse, a corpse over me?"

His face was blanched. He was backing away from her. "Miriam," he pleaded.

"No! No! I'll kill myself first—is that what you want? Is it? Two corpses?"

In the morning—Christ knew where he'd spent the night—two of his assistants appeared at the door, the mole-hair and another tight-mouthed drudge who looked at her as if she were the Gorgon herself. They were there to pack up Mr. Wright's things and remove them to his offices. What things? she demanded, but she already knew. And she didn't attempt to stop them, not by any means. If he wanted to run out on her, desert her, leave her bereft and unprovided for like the cad he was, well, she wasn't about to stop him. She took a cab to Marshall Field's, though she detested the place, and when she returned there was no trace of him at 25 East Cedar Street but for the furniture itself—even his toothbrush was gone. Again she put off telephoning to his offices and again she broke down. Just as she'd suspected, he was at Taliesin and couldn't be reached.

This time he didn't come back. And though it ate at her, through every minute of every day, she stayed on in the empty house. Every time she heard a noise in the street, the scrape of a shoe along the walk or a voice lifted in greeting, she was sure it was him, sure he'd come back to her, but she was disappointed. Over and over again. As the days wore on, she steeled herself—she had resources of her own. And she had her pravaz and a prescription from a very forward-looking physician whose address she'd found in the directory. And this was her house now and she would be damned if she was going to leave it.

Of course, she wrote him—daily, sometimes two or three times a day. She telephoned to him as well and when she did manage to reach him, he seemed distracted—and guilty too—and though he tried to act as if nothing were the matter, as if he was simply preoccupied with the building at Taliesin, she couldn't really be held accountable if her voice did rise above an acceptable level because she was only human, as she reminded him, and not a memory. Or was she? Then his letters, which had been sympathetic, solicitous, kind—but distant, as if he were writing to an aunt or a sister away on a foreign mission—turned more resolute, as if he had finally understood that he and she could never be reconciled again. The one that hurt her most, the one that drove her out of his house and into a first-class compartment on a train headed west for Albuquerque,* addressed

* Why Albuquerque? No one seems to know. But Miriam's pattern, as has been seen, was to go west rather than east, when the east, one would think, would have been a more natural destination. Perhaps—and I'm only speculating—she was imbued with a residuum of that great American pioneering spirit and a personal sense of manifest destiny.

her in tender reminiscent terms, especially as he talked of her charms and the thrill of knowing and loving her and how terrible he felt for having abandoned her. But it was a letter of discharge and no doubt about it. Because he was a little man. Because love—with her, at any rate—led inevitably, through stages, to ruin. "Reason is gone!" he wrote, invigorating the apostrophe with his overwrought punctuation. "Charity is gone—Now comes Fear—Hate—Revenge—Punishment—Then Regret—Shame—Humiliation—Ashes, It is the accepted Road—all ambitious Souls hear me! Sex is the curse of Life!"

She brooded over this ugly proposition all the dreary way across the country—sex the curse of life, indeed; he hadn't felt that way on Christmas Eve when he'd had her twice in succession and then again the following morning, the celebration of Christ's birth and the sacred hymns of the angelic choir notwithstanding. Or in the weeks after when he'd installed her in his house like a houri extracted from his harem and had his way with her whenever the urge struck him, which was any time of the day or night because he was as randy as a goat, the randiest man she'd ever been exposed to, even in France, even in Italy. And now, suddenly, sex was the curse of life. He'd twisted everything, the hypocrite, making her out to be the one at fault, reducing the monumentality of what they'd had together to a vulgar expression of sexual gratification as if they were apes in the jungle or some such rot. Well, she wouldn't have it. And she wrote back to him, page after page, her emotions burning into her fingertips, the fountain pen, the ink that seared the very paper before her.

She blasted him, of course she did, but she expressed the fullness of her love too—and it was no infatuation, she reminded him, but a mature and spiritual love that stood against the petty conventions of a society bound up in its petty rules.* She wouldn't go to Taliesin if he begged her. She couldn't. "Because a spirit walked abroad there whose presence must not be offended by one who truly loved him." She went on in this vein, dredging up every Gothic reference to churchyards, yew trees and demon lovers she could recall, then began to remonstrate with him. Couldn't he, above all people, with his finer sensibilities and conceptual brilliance, appreciate that this pining after a ghost was so false, so cheap, nothing more than two-penny sentimentality, a poor flimsy excuse for real love and loyalty? And she asked him, humbly and sincerely, if he wouldn't accept gratefully a poor loving heart that he had mutilated beyond all thinking. He was the one in the wrong, couldn't he see that? Couldn't he see all she was offering him, in spite of the condemnation of that pitiless and cheaply moralizing society that made her an outcast for the "sin" of loving him? Even as she wrote, absorbed, distracted, resentful and brimming with love all at once, she felt the strength come back to her.

"I SHALL WIN!" she exclaimed. "You'll see! When the smoke of battle clears away I shall be a rainbow again—and, undying name—an altar of fire that you have tried to dash to hell. I shall weave a rose wreath and hang it round your neck. You will call it a yoke of bondage and curse it—no matter. You are afraid of the light I give you. You crouch in darkness. Come, take my hand, I will lead you." And her valediction, intimating in its restraint whole worlds of love and grief and passionate regret, was, simply, *Miriam.*

And then she arrived, shriven, on the high altar of the west, Albuquerque, Santa Fe, Taos. She went barefoot in

* See page 100n.

the mornings. She worshipped the sky. Took *eau naturelle* and unleavened bread. Wrapped herself in diaphanous things and let Jesus and Mary Baker Eddy apply their healing touch to her soul. Time was a mountain. Waters flowed, the wind blew. She watched the eagles rise on the thermals over the Sangre de Cristo Mountains as if they held all the power of the universe in their wings—or perhaps they were vultures, but no matter. She was there. She lived in the moment.

Gradually, his letters softened. Guilt ate at him—he'd seduced and abandoned her when she'd given up everything for him, even to the opprobrium of society, and he understood that now and begged her forgiveness. He sent money. He needed her. Wanted her. Pleaded with her to come back to him—and not just to Chicago, but to Taliesin, to be its mistress. And she? She let him dangle, reveling in her power to reach out to him across all that expanse of raw country and tighten the clamps of her hold on him. So what if it was venereal? He needed her. And he would see what she could give him beyond that, beyond the curse of sex—and yes, she threw the phrase right back in his face. They would walk the world together, she wrote him, hand in hand, stride for stride, and challenge the very gods for their sublimity.

By July, she was back in Chicago. By the end of August, she was at Taliesin.*

* It seems a mystery how two such people could ever willingly come together again. O'Flaherty-San maintains that the adhesive was as much sexual as emotional, but we didn't discuss the matter in any depth, because as you may imagine, certain subjects are strictly off-limits between the white-haired patriarch of an unimpeachable and time-honored clan *(buzoku)* and his grandson-in-law, even if—or perhaps particularly if—that grandson is an American.

CHAPTER 4: FLESH AND BLOOD

He was lonely, that was the long and short of it. Despite the fullness of the days at Taliesin and his utter absorption in the work going forward, despite the company of his children and the ministrations of Mother Breen, despite riding and farming and picnicking and charades and board games and singing round the fire at night till he thought his lungs would burst, he was parched for the touch of a woman. Miriam was right. Mamah was a ghost, dead and gone, and you couldn't lie with a ghost. The thought might have been callous—Mamah hadn't been in the ground a year yet and already she was as faded in his memory as if she'd been gone a century, and perhaps that was a trick of the brain, a defense mechanism, a way of loosening the coils of grief so they didn't choke all the air out of your lungs and drain the blood from your heart—but all he could see in his mind's eye was Miriam. Miriam undressing by candlelight, teasing him, flaunting herself, perching naked on the corner of the bed and pulling him down atop her, Miriam with her breasts exposed over the sweet silken curve of her abdomen, her dress in tatters, crying *Look at me, I'm flesh and blood, flesh and blood!*

Well, so was he. And he found himself burying his face in her letters to catch the faintest scent of her, all the while wondering what she was doing out there in New Mexico—had she taken another lover, was that it? She was a matchless beauty, elegant, brilliant, worldly, and if he'd seen nothing like her in Chicago, what must the hidalgos have thought of her out there under the open sky? He pictured her in the arms of a tall mustachioed figure in a sombrero, some sunburned hybrid of Tom Mix and Teddy Roosevelt, and felt the loss of her like a physical ache. But then it *was* a physical ache when you came right down to it. And he soothed it in a way that was juvenile, unclean and lonely, lonely to the core.

He was there at the station in Chicago when she stepped off the train in a fumarole of porters, bags and scuffling shoes, the engine spewing cinders and ash, steam rising and pigeons settling like an avian snow, people crying out, families reunited, lovers embracing—even a pair of Alsatians wagging their tails and capering for joy—but she didn't seem to recognize him, not at first. Down the platform she came in a magnificent stride that was at once commanding and unabashedly sensual, the Negro porters scurrying to keep up with her and a whole series of men glancing up from newspapers and cigars like dominoes toppling one against the other all the way down the line. He felt the blood drain from his extremities and settle in that one essential place—he knew those eyes, those limbs, those breasts—but didn't she know him? Didn't she recognize him? He started forward, his confidence wilting, wondering if she was still harboring a grudge—or was it her eyesight? She was of an age—and she did employ that lorgnette as something more than a prop . . . "Miriam!" he cried, his voice cracking under the strain even as he lurched out from behind a wall of anonymous men hunched over their cheap suitcases and made himself glaringly visible, his stick raised high and his cape flowing in the liquefaction of its folds. She stopped. Turned toward him. He tore the beret from his head and waved it wildly. And then? Then she was in his arms.

"How was your journey?" he asked, leading her out to the street and the car as the porters brought up the rear and the searing summer air streamed in through the open doors.

"Oh, darling, darling, you don't want to know."

"Was it that bad?" He tried out a smile, ready to make light of it, but his blood was seething, the very touch of her, the scent . . .

"Heat," she said, never missing a stride, and then she was directing the Negroes as they loaded her things into the car. "Like this. Heat like this. Only worse. There was the dust, eternal dust, and people so inconsiderate—and I hate to say it, stupid, stupid and thoughtless—as to leave the windows open wide day and night. Insects. I could write a treatise on the insects of the West and Middle-West. But let's not talk about me, let's talk about you. You look thinner. Or thicker. Definitely thicker about the waist. Have you put on weight? Is the life in the country"—and here she gave him her first smile—"so restful, then? Unclouded days, sap running in the trees, the easeful sway of the hammock? All that?"

He was off then, off on a speech of his own, settling into his rhythms like a jockey feeling the stride of his mount on the stretch run, gabbling on about the structural problems they were encountering, the vagaries of his workforce, the lay of the stone they were quarrying and the quality of the lumber from the mill, not to mention the fluidity of the design and the changes of conception he was making daily, and Paul Mueller, of course, Paul's contributions, and the Japanese, how they were becoming increasingly cordial in their communications and how certain he was that the big project was going to go through. They were halfway across town before she stopped him. "Well," she said, giving him a coy look from beneath the wide floral brim of her hat, "didn't you miss me?"

He had. He did. The blood shot to his groin again. And then the next speech was spinning out of him with all the fluidity and spontaneous grace he'd inherited from his preacher father.* He was indicting himself, begging her forgiveness and forbearance, pledging fealty and love and unraveling a whole spool of excuses, when she stopped him again. "Oh, that's all very gratifying," she said, raising her voice to be heard over the racket of the motor and the yapping of some sort of mongrel or other that had been chasing behind the wheels for the past block and a half, "but where are you taking me?" Another look from beneath the shade of the hat. Her smile was full now, her eyes dancing, lips swollen. And licked. Licked wet with the pink retreating tip of her tongue. "And for what purpose?"

He fumbled a moment, the open wound of Taliesin still lying bloody between them, and the oratorical flow, the sheer dance of words, stuttered short. "I, well, I thought we'd, maybe—if you have no objections, that is, and I know you must be exhausted—"

"The Garfield?" she said, and the way she said it, so casually, so gracefully, so lewdly, made it the most exciting thing he'd ever heard.

"No," he said, grinning, and for the first time since

* William Cary Wright (1825–1904). Said to be one of the most charming and charismatic men of his time, who unfortunately proved to be too unreliable, too footloose and casual about earning a living to suit Wrieto-San's mother. Anna divorced him and wrapped herself instead in the enfolding arms of her family, the Lloyd Joneses of the rich farmlands of Wisconsin's Wyoming Valley. Wrieto-San was seventeen at the time. Shortly thereafter he changed his middle name from "Lincoln" to "Lloyd."

they'd got in the car he reached out a hand to touch her intimately, on the upper thigh, where the material of her dress had pulled tight beneath her when she slid into the seat. "I thought the Congress."

Two days later—and what choice did he have?—he moved her back into the little house at 25 East Cedar Street and did his best to overlook her moods and dietary peculiarities, her florid speeches about art and literature and her continued insistence that he sit for a marble bust. He hadn't time to sit for a bust, he kept protesting (gently, ever so gently). He was a working architect, preoccupied with the business of the world. And busts, in any case, were for dead heroes, for military men and the like. No, she countered, not at all—what of Rodin's bust of Balzac? Of Hugo? Granted, they were in bronze, but marble was for the ages—as he was. He might have told her it was architecture that was for the ages, but he kept the thought to himself. What he wanted, above all, was harmony, and he was determined to establish it this time around, to give as well as take, because he'd suffered the long withering attrition of her absence. If he had to nurture her, if he had to put up with a pillow here or there and eat French food once in a blue moon, what of it? She was his star, his torch, his impetus. Was he in love? He couldn't say. But she was on his arm when he went to the concert hall, when he went out to dine or simply take the air, and she was there in his bed at night, as warm and loving and virtuosic as any man could ever hope to ask or dream.

Inevitably, the question of Taliesin came up again. It emerged one morning out of a perfectly ordinary breakfast conversation. The new cook, a fox-faced girl with a wandering eye and a West Virginia coal miner's accent, an adept at plain things, flapjacks and sidemeat, eggs over easy, grits and hot black coffee, had just served breakfast and taken herself off to hide in the kitchen, and he was commenting on a piece in the paper about the building costs associated with one of the new skyscrapers going up along Michigan Avenue, when Miriam, looking up from her own newspaper, said, "Isn't it time you took me up to Wisconsin?"

She was dressed all in white, in a clinging gown of silk, and her hair was loose on her shoulders. The lorgnette dangled from one hand, swaying gently back and forth like a hypnotist's watch. In her other hand, balanced delicately, a teacup held in abeyance. She was smiling, congenial, insouciant, the question no more charged than a query about the weather or what color hat he might like to see her in.

He never hesitated. From the moment he'd written her to come back to him he saw how selfish he'd been, demanding her full commitment and loyalty and yet all the while keeping her off-balance so that she was never certain of her status. Small wonder she had her moods. It was his fault. Entirely his. He set down the newspaper and gazed steadily into her eyes. "We'll drive up tomorrow," he said.*

The day was clear, the road untrammeled. He was whistling, fiddling with the gearshift, the choke, feeling as light as the puffs of cloud running high overhead across the pale blue roof of the world. Every bend in the road, every tree and cow, whether it be Holstein, Jersey or Swiss Brown, was the subject of a spontaneous discourse, and he couldn't help himself, his tongue running ahead

* I'm sorry, but no matter what O'Flaherty-San might say about sexual adhesion, this seems to me another of those suicidal leaps into oblivion Wrieto-San was repeatedly making. Certainly he must have known that the community—and the press—would universally condemn him for establishing a second mistress in the place of the first, as if he had learned little from the tragic consequences. Or worse: as if he cared less.

of him, the joy of possession working on him like the heady poteen the Irish laborers drank behind his back when he could smell it on their breath and see it in the delirious dance of their too-green eyes. Miriam sat beside him, uncharacteristically silent, a soft smile on her lips. How could she be so calm? he wondered. How could she not feel what he was feeling, this bubbling joy that made him want to burst into song? He stepped on the accelerator, rocketing past a tractor towing a cart piled high with corn, the wheels churning up twin tornadoes of dust and the back end wagging with the thrust of the engine, and suddenly he *was* singing, singing for her, singing for the joy of it. He sang "Clementine" twice through and then "Old Kent Road," and so what if the farmers stared and his voice floated on down the road behind him like the windblown squawk of the summer geese charging from one pond to another? He was happy. Purely happy.

They stopped for luncheon in Cross Plains, after which she grew calmer still, so much so she might have been comatose—or lost in a deep waking sleep. He kept shooting glances at her, her hair fluttering in the breeze, her eyes fixed straight ahead, her frame in perfect equipoise as if she were balancing on an invisible wire, and eventually he fell silent himself. A thought had occurred to him. A nagging unsettling thought, one he'd tried to suppress through the course of these running days. It had to do with what he knew of Miriam's temperament, how easily it could shift from light to dark, from this calm to sudden fury, and how that might accord with his mother's moods, not to mention Mrs. Breen's. Mrs. Breen ran the household the way the Kaiser ran his army. And his mother, no wilting flower herself, had taken exception to the housekeeper on any number of grounds ("Don't you dare call that woman Mother, not while I'm in this house").* Since the construction was progressing rapidly he'd moved her into the new wing—at her insistence—if only for an extended visit till the renovation was completed and the design fully realized, and that was fine. At least for the first day or so, until she and Mrs. Breen began feuding about everything from how to boil an egg to the proper way to make up a bed, set the table and polish silverware. How would they react to Miriam? More to the point: how would Miriam react to them? Distracted, he laid his hand atop hers and she turned to give him a vague smile as the wind took her hair and the sun tugged them forward and the road melted like butter under the glow of it. Like any gambling man, he could only hope for the best.

Miriam seemed to come to life as they made their approach along the Wisconsin River and Taliesin suddenly materialized on the brow of the hill before them. "Is that it?" she asked, straining forward in the seat as he rolled to a stop at the main gate so she could have a chance to admire the house in its proper perspective. "And this is the lake you've talked of? And the dam? And what's that over there to the left?"

"Tan-y-deri," he said. "My sister Jennie's place. And see beyond it? That's Romeo and Juliet."

Her face was flushed. She took hold of his arm at the biceps and pulled him to her for a kiss. "One of your earliest designs," she murmured. "How sweet."

"Sweet?" he said. "I don't know if I'd call it sweet."

"What I mean is the sentiment, of course, the sense of tradition. Your first windmill preserved here on your

* Even in old age, Anna Lloyd Jones Wright was an imposing woman, five feet eight and a half inches tall, a height to which her celebrated son could never quite rise, despite his elevated heels. It was she who decided on his profession while he was still in the cradle and she who made him her *okāsan ko.*

property and now this grand house, this palace of light and air. It's beautiful. More beautiful than I could have dreamed."

"You like it?"

"Like it? I adore it."

He left the car running as he got out to swing open the gate, seeing the small things, the way the ditch along the drive had eroded in the previous week's storms, the weeds crowding out the wildflowers, the iridescent blue of the damselflies threading the air, and then he was back in the car, shifting into gear and winding on up the hill, thinking he'd send Billy Weston or one of the others down to shut the gate behind him because he didn't want to spoil the moment, intent instead on watching Miriam's face as the house revealed itself by stages. Llewellyn, his youngest—twelve years old that summer and adapting to the life of the farm as if he'd been born to it—appeared out of nowhere to chase the car up the drive in a propulsion of flashing limbs, head down, elbows pumping and gaining on them even as Frank slowed to let him catch up. And that was a joy to him too, a pleasure Kitty had denied him as long as Mamah was mistress of the place, Mamah her sworn enemy, her nemesis, dead now and gone so that he could have his children back with him for the long stretch of summer, Lloyd and John married and settled but here to pitch in with the rebuilding, Frances home from college, Catherine and David running back and forth between Taliesin and Oak Park.

It was perfect. Ideal. The crowning moment of his life. Everyone together and Miriam here too and how could Kitty possibly object to a woman she'd never met and would never meet because she had to understand that things were dead between them and he had to live his own life in his own way? This was the start of something new, he could feel it, something better, and he pulled into the courtyard riding a wave of hope and optimism.

Everyone crowded round—the children, Billy Weston, even Mrs. Breen—and while the help unloaded their things he took Miriam out on the hilltop to give her a moment to breathe and take in the prospect. He didn't want to overwhelm her. She must have been exhausted from the journey—she wasn't well, he was aware of that—but she was superlatively calm and graceful and full of praise for the place and she had a hundred questions that took them through tea and a leisurely tour of the rooms and artwork before she felt she might want to rest prior to dinner.

Were there ominous signs? His mother claimed to be indisposed and wouldn't emerge from her room. The children—Catherine, especially, who was the neediest and most sensitive and so the one most poisoned by Kitty's invective—drew long faces all around. They were well-bred enough to conceal their feelings, of course, but he could see it would be a struggle to win them over—Miriam was an unknown quantity, perhaps not the ogre and housebreaker Kitty had made Mamah out to be, but she wasn't their mother either, and he would feel the sting of that in a thousand ways. But worst of all, right from the start, was Mrs. Breen. The minute Miriam had gone in to lie down, she was at his elbow, bellowing out a whole catalogue of questions to which she apparently required no answers, as her ear trumpet was nowhere in sight. She was stalwart, furious, her face compressed and her eyes jumping at him. Where was the lady to sleep? she wanted to know. Would she require anything special in the way of comestibles because she, Mother Breen, was as run-down and worn-out as a woman could be what with feeding all these workmen and the family too, and she was at the end of her tether. And why hadn't the lady removed her shoes at the door because who did she think would wipe up her muddy tracks after her? Did she speak French? Would she eat pork? Was she married? Did she expect maid's service?

He talked all through dinner, talked so steadily and with such a tailing edge of desperation he barely touched his food, and that wasn't like him—not to eat—and they all took notice. His mother sat across from him, icily silent, and while Paul Mueller tried heroically to make general conversation, Llewellyn chirped out an anecdote about the frogs in the upper pond and Miriam was on her best behavior, there was something distinctly off about the whole evening. After dinner he sat at the piano* and led them through a medley of songs, but Miriam wouldn't join in—was the scene too homely for her, a Parisian sophisticate, was that it?—and his mother lacked enthusiasm. Distinctly. In fact, she seemed to do nothing all night long but stare at Miriam so intently she might have been making a charcoal study of her. They went early to bed, Miriam settled in one of the guest rooms to maintain a sense of propriety, though he didn't give a damn for propriety, not under his own roof, and he had to find his way to her bed in the dark.

The following day began auspiciously enough, Miriam up early and looking alert at breakfast while Mrs. Breen confined herself to the kitchen and let one of the maids serve at table. Conversation mainly revolved around the weather—the dew lay heavy on the grass that morning and there was the breath of a breeze out of the north, which he took to mean that the heat wave of the past weeks was finally dispelling, though both Paul and Lloyd disagreed with him, citing some nonsense out of

* This was the famous Steinway, which had lost its legs when hauled through a window to spare it from the 1914 conflagration. Ever resourceful, Wrieto-San had adapted drafting stools as temporary supports.

the *Farmer's Almanac* about woolly bear caterpillars and the paucity of their coats. Still, to his mind it was undeniably cooler and that was a beneficence—Miriam would be more comfortable and if she was more comfortable she would find it easier to embrace the natural life in the countryside. That was what he was thinking, as she seemed abnormally sensitive to extremes of temperature—abnormally sensitive to practically everything, for that matter—but then that was only to be expected of a highly refined artistic temperament like hers.

He ate with a good appetite—he'd been up since four-thirty, busy in the studio, walking the grounds, tending to the garden and seeing to the horses, afire with energy and the flare of ideas that came to him almost unbidden, at the oddest times, as if inspiration were a vagary of the unconscious and not something to be earned through effort and focus and the application of pencil and T-square. The main house was largely finished now, but there was a whole lot of work yet to be done on the new wings and of course there were always projects on the boards, moneymaking projects, because the costs of rebuilding had exceeded even his wildest estimate and, as usual, he was woefully short*. . .

As the day wore on—and it did get hot, above ninety by noon, though he worked alongside the laborers, loudly insisting that it was cooler by far than yesterday—he lost track of Miriam. He'd taken her on his rounds in the morning, explaining as much as he could about the workings of the place, but she'd developed a headache or heat exhaustion or some such thing and had begged off. "You want me to walk you back?" he'd asked, and she'd

* Ultimately, Miriam would be tapped in this regard, contributing several thousand dollars of her own money to the reconstruction effort, a fact to which Mr. Fake would one day be intimately attuned.

given him a smile that shaded into a grimace. "I'm not an invalid," she said firmly, though her voice betrayed her. "I do think I can manage, what is it, three hundred yards on my own?" By the time he gave her another thought it was past five in the afternoon.

The minute he walked into the house he was confronted by his mother. "This woman," she said, all the lines round her mouth drawn tight. "I'm sorry to say it, but she's not a lady, Frank—she's not even civil. She's vulgar and foulmouthed, is what she is. It may be that that sort of language passes among the French—for all I know it's the fashion over there—but I won't have it here in my own household, not in the hearing of my grandchildren or the servants either. I won't. I tell you, Frank, I won't."

He wanted a bath—or no, a swim in the lake. His shirt was stuck to his back, his hands and forearms were filthy. He was exhausted. And in no mood. "I'm sorry, Mother, but we'll all have to . . . make adjustments. Miriam is under a great deal of strain, coming up here into the country, and—"

"She diminishes you. She's beneath you. She puts on airs."

And now Mrs. Breen appeared, her eyes savage, the ear trumpet clutched in one hand—and were they allies, had they declared a truce and joined forces to repel the invader in their midst? Had war been declared between lunch and dinner? He was stupefied and he stood there speechless, turning from one furious face to the other. "It's a sorry thing," Mrs. Breen roared, "to see such disrespect. Do you know what sort of vile names she's been calling your own mother? And in my hearing, no less?"

He'd come in the kitchen door, desiring only a glass of water before pulling on his bathing costume and calling Llewellyn to head down to the lake, and here he was in the docket. "I'm sure it's just a misunderstanding," he said. "Because Miriam—"

"Misunderstanding?" Mrs. Breen had elevated the hearing trumpet and now she dropped it to her side, her attenuated shoulder blades settling like bones in a sack. "To call your mother a meddling old hag? And me. To call me names I wouldn't call the devil himself? And just because I wouldn't jump at her every whim and command, because I have a household to run here if you don't know it and I'm not hired on to be anybody's handmaid—and who does she think she is to command me like I'm some slave out of her plantation in Tennessee or wherever her glorious ancestors hail from, and yes we all got a good earful of that too."

"Frank," his mother cut in. "Frank, now you listen to me—"

He held his hands up in surrender. "I'll speak with her," he said, irritated now, angry, all the satisfaction he'd taken in the day's work driven out of him as if he hadn't accomplished a thing—Sisyphus, this must be what Sisyphus felt like each time he got to the top of the hill. "Right now. Right this minute. Will that satisfy you? It's not enough that I've worked all day under that sun with the laboring men, slaved out there in this heat, and all I want is to have a swim and some quiet before dinner. No. I have to be the one to make peace, when both of you—" he checked himself. His mother was biting her lip. Her eyes were wet. "Where is she?"

"Where is she?" Mrs. Breen threw back at him. "Where she's been the whole day—in her room. And she won't let nobody in neither."

She didn't answer to his knock. He tried the knob but there seemed to be something blocking the door. "Miriam!" he called. "Miriam, are you in there?" Nothing. Not a whisper. He went round to the window, but she'd blocked that too, the casement locked, some sort of material—was that the bedspread?—tacked up so that he couldn't see inside. He felt a flash of irritation.* He pounded the glass with the flat of his hand, shouted her name again. People were watching him—two of the masons, on their way down the hill to the tavern, had paused by the garage to take in the spectacle, joined now by one of the housemaids swinging a pail of scraps for the hogs—and he cursed under his breath. Couldn't he have a little privacy? Was that too much to ask? In the next moment he was at the door again and this time he put his shoulder to it and felt something give—a piece of furniture sliding back and the door cracking open just enough to give him a view of the darkened room.

At first he could see nothing. Then, as his eyes adjusted, he saw that she'd nailed a series of shadowy objects to the walls, reckless with the plaster and the wood trim too—another flash of irritation—and what were they? Drawings? "Miriam!" he called again, and when she didn't answer he lunged at the door with everything he had till the barricade—a bureau with the desk and two chairs stacked atop it—spilled forward with a splintering crash that could have wakened the dead, and he was in the room. Which was empty. He flicked on the lamp and the walls sprang to life—drawings, yes, dozens of them, each a sketch of his head as seen from every conceivable angle, the features monumental and rugged, hair snaking beyond the margins and his orbits as deep as Beethoven's, but with the eyes left eerily null—and what was this? Clothes heaped on the bed as if laid out for a rummage sale, hats and shoes and undergarments scattered across the floor, a smashed teacup, a spill of roofing nails and the hammer with which she'd crucified each of the drawings. Her slippers. Her robe. The vertical plane of the bathroom door.

* Mildly put. As I've indicated, Wrieto-San's temper was a force all its own, incendiary, savage, excoriating, and all the worse for the caustic bite of his tongue.

"Miriam?"

He pushed open the door, the first stirrings of alarm working through him like a faint electric current, and there she was. Propped up in the tub. Asleep. Or meditating, perhaps she was meditating. Seeking the cool, the dark—she'd had a headache, hadn't she? That was it, that must have been it. "Miriam?" he tried again.

Her eyes were shut fast, the lids faintly blue, lashes entwined, her head thrown back against the wall—and her mouth, her mouth was slung open over the dark canal of her throat. She was asleep, of course she was, asleep, that was all. His first thought was that she'd been bathing and dozed off, but she was dressed in her nightgown—the material sodden, painted to her limbs—and there was no more than an inch of water in the tub, softly gurgling round the plug. It was then—and it came as a shock, as if he'd been slapped—that he noticed the needle.

A needle. A syringe. The sort of thing the doctor used for injections. It was clinging to the smooth white flesh of her upper thigh, out of place, wrong, deeply wrong, and all he could think of was a parasite, some bloated tick or leech fastened there where it didn't belong. Without thinking, he wrapped his fingers round the thing—cold metal and glass—and tugged it gently from her flesh, a speck of blood there, a yellowish contusion round the wound, and laid it on the sink. "Wake up," he said softly, taking her by the wrist. "Miriam, wake up."

She gave him nothing.

He pulled her toward him, slapped her once, twice, and then again, till her eyes began to flutter, and where were the smelling salts? Did they have smelling salts? Her breath was rank, flowering in his face with the odor of the swamp plants, the cattails and pickerelweed and the other things that grew with their feet in the water of the pond. He was frightened, his thoughts charging one way and then the other. Should he call the physician? His mother? Mrs. Breen? But this was a private matter, wasn't it? Between him and Miriam? Some mistake with her medicine, nothing to worry over, really, but shouldn't she be in bed?

He clasped her to him then and tried to lift her, dripping, from the tub, but she was surprisingly heavy, her limbs slippery, fish-cold, and it was a job to shift her weight and gather her up. Her head fell forward across his shoulder, her hair pressed wet to his cheek, and with a final sucking contortion she was in his arms and he was edging out the door and her lips were moving. "Frank," she murmured, "what is it? What are you doing?"

Something grabbed at his feet—one of her balled-up dresses—and he nearly stumbled.

"Frank." Her voice was stronger now, the voice he knew, Miriam's voice, piqued and challenging. "Put me down. What are you thinking?"

His lower back was on fire suddenly and he very nearly dropped her in that shambling half-hobbled moment, but he made it to the bed and let go of her even as she rolled away from him and the mattress gave with a long hissing groan.

"Miriam, for God's sake," he said, standing over her, breathing hard, his shirt wet and his eyes jumping in his head till they felt like ball bearings. "This, this *needle*—"

She'd sat up against the headboard, her arms wrapped round her knees. Wet, the hair fell across her face like strands of moss, like Spanish moss, and what was he thinking, where was he? "My medicine, Frank," she said. "You know how ill I am. You know I'm exhausted, mentally and physically, and that any, any"—her voice thickened, dredged with emotion—"*upset*, any cruelty or animosity is bound to, to . . . *destroy* me . . ."

He could only stare at her. He was utterly bewildered, adrift without oars or rudder, the seas piling and shifting beneath him. "I know it's difficult," he heard himself say, "but this heat won't last forever . . ."

"They have to go, Frank." Her voice was steady now, aimed true, homing on him. "Both of them."

For a moment the room was silent and he could hear the distant percussion of the axe on the chopping block, one of the workers splitting wood for the stove, and then the sudden harsh crackling shriek of a jay, so close it might have been in the room with them. He was grappling with the pronoun, third-person plural. *Them?*

"It's them or me, Frank. Them or me."

CHAPTER 5: THE LOVE BUNGALOW

If that was how they wanted to play, rough and tumble, cats with their claws drawn, well, she could play at that game too. For three full days she lay in that sweltering room, in the dark, while Frank pleaded with her and the little half-witted housemaid who couldn't have been more than sixteen, ugly as a turnip and graceless and stupid into the bargain, brought her iced tea, lemonade and cakes. Plenty of time to brood, and brood she did. The gall of that crone, Mrs. Breen, that bag, that sack of bones with her lace-curtain Irish accent tripping around as if *she* were the lady of the house—and what had she had the effrontery to say in response to the simplest request for a salad properly dressed and a sandwich of cold chicken with a bit of mayonnaise and a slice of cheese that didn't stink of the barnyard? "I'm nobody's handmaid, ma'am, and if you want your victuals outside of the regular dining hours you'll just have to help yourself like anybody else." *Victuals. Dining hours.* It was all she could do to stop herself from snatching the hearing trumpet out of the odious reptilian claw and snapping it over one knee.

And the mother. There was an old dragon crouching over her hoard if ever she'd seen one. From the very instant they'd laid eyes on each other, in that exquisite living room with all of Frank's things on display as if it were a museum—and it was, it was a museum, as fine and profoundly moving as any in the world—there'd been a mutual antipathy. A chill. As if a wall of ice, a thousand-year-old glacier, had sprung up between them. Frank had escorted her into the room on his arm and before she'd had a chance to catch her breath—all that rare beauty—his mother was there like one of the risen dead, tall, bony, white-haired, with a scouring look in her eye and a mouth that clamped shut so tightly it was a wonder she had any teeth left. "*Enchantée,*" Miriam had murmured, taking her hand, but the old woman said nothing in reply, merely looking to Frank and commenting, in the sort of tone she might have used while kicking the mud from her boots, "So this is the Parisian?" Only then did she look Miriam in the eye. "Or should I say, Parisian by way of Tennessee?"

Three days. To hell with them. To hell with everybody. She'd rather be back in Taos if it came to it, free of all this embroilment and animus, and she closed her eyes against the void of the ceiling and saw herself gamboling through a field of wildflowers in the cool pellucid sculptor's light of the high mountains, her arms outspread, the pure white silk dancing round her on the breeze. But Frank wasn't in Taos, Frank was here. This was his abode, his refuge, his poet's tower shining out over the wasteland of boorishness and diminished taste, and her place was beside him. And he was concerned for her, she could see that, his face heavy, his voice soft and chagrined, the most caring man in the world. He must have come twenty times a day to inquire after her—Did she need anything? Was she feeling better? Wouldn't she like to come in to dinner?—and at night he let all his need spill over her.

In the darkness, as they lay there side by side, she praised him, praised his vision and his genius and the way his great and giving soul was reflected in the beams that rose over them and the holy space he'd created within. She took his hand. Squeezed it. And gave praise, because praise was her main theme and her modus, but there was another theme here and it began to emerge even as his breathing slowed and the night wheeled overhead. "Frank," she whispered, "Frank, are you awake?"

Snatched from sleep, his voice thick: "I'm here."

"Your mother, Frank. And that dreadful housekeeper. I cannot"—her voice rising—"*will* not endure this sort of abuse much longer. Who is to be the mistress of this house? Tell me that, Frank. Tell me."

On the evening of the third day she emerged from her room in time for dinner, taking her place at the table beside Frank as if she'd been sitting there amongst them each night since the roof had been raised and the table brought in through the door. This time—and she didn't give a damn whether anybody liked it or not—she entangled herself in the conversation, letting no point pass unchallenged, whether it had to do with politics, pasturage, Paris fashion or the weather, and she let them know, all of them, Frank's mother and his grown children, his adolescent boy with the open honest look Frank must once have worn in the long-ago, the draftsmen, the visiting architect and his wife and whoever else was there, that she was the equal of anyone and that from now on the entire establishment would dance to a new tune, her tune, hers and hers only.

She knew something they didn't. She knew that Nellie Breen would be sent packing within a matter of days, as soon as Frank could find someone to replace her, and that in the morning he'd be having a long talk with his mother, emphasizing the fact that her rooms weren't yet completed—why, the building itself—and wondering, especially with the season changing and the cold sure to come on soon, if she wouldn't find it more comfortable back in Oak Park. At least temporarily. And she knew that when she went back into that pinched and darkened room this time it would be only to pack her things up and direct the maid to take them across the courtyard, through the loggia and into Frank's rooms.

What she hadn't taken into account was the tenacity of Nellie Breen. Nellie Breen wouldn't go quietly because Nellie Breen was a fire-breather of the first stripe, a shallow crude vituperative woman who'd somehow gotten her claws into Frank and wasn't about to let go. There was a scene, Frank's voice raised against the high rasping complaint of the old woman cornered in the kitchen like a badger in its den so that everybody on the estate must have heard it and the pig farmer down the hill too, and Miriam, lying abed with a pot of coffee and a novel propped up on the shelf of her abdomen, felt her own blood beginning to rise. This was a servant, for Christ's sake, a nobody. Give her the boot, that was what she was thinking, have her physically removed from the premises, and why should Frank have to bother? Why shouldn't his estate manager* take care of it? Or his mother? But then she checked herself—she wouldn't want *her* stepping into the line of succession, even for five minutes, even to do the dirty work.

"You're dismissed," she heard Frank shout suddenly, his voice echoing down the courtyard through the open kitchen window, in full roar. "Can't you understand that? You're no longer wanted. Period. Must I repeat myself over and over?" The old woman came

* At that time a young architect by the name of Russell Williamson. I have no record of his remuneration, but I suspect he worked for his bed and supper alone, prototype of the apprentices to come.

right back at him, her words chopping through the dull haze of the morning like so many swirling blades: "You think you can just toss me out? Without cause? So you can lie here with your—" Frank's voice swelled to drown hers, there was a sharp tumbling explosion shot through with metallic tones, a clatter and tintinnabulation of cook pans, implements, perhaps even cutlery, and then the thunderous slamming of the door. In the next moment she saw him stalking across the courtyard, his shoulders clenched in fury, and she rushed to the window, her emotions surging—*the bitch, the bitch, he was her hero, shining and golden, couldn't the whole world see it?*—and called his name as if her life depended on it.

He stopped in his tracks, spinning round to see where this new challenge was coming from. There was something about his posture, the shoulders, the fists, the gnomic big-headed stocky Welsh look of bellicosity, that brought her back to the scenes between them at 25 East Cedar Street before she'd gone off to New Mexico in capitulation, and that gave her pause. He was glaring at her, the compass of his fury expanding to include her now, as if she were to blame, and he cried out as if she'd just stuck a dart in his back. "What? What do you want from me?"

The moment was emblematic. She knew it, felt the knowledge run through her like a long shiver, but she was there at the open casement, not fifty feet from him, and without thinking, she just opened her arms to him. "Frank," she crooned, drawing out the single syllable in the continental way—"Frahhnnk"—and she saw his face change. "Come here. Come to me."

In the next moment he was there at the window, reaching out to wrap his arms around her, rigid with the residue of his anger. "Good, Frank," she murmured, hugging him to her, and it was as if they were on a stage, because wasn't that his mother's face hanging in the window across from them? Yes. Yes. The ghost of an image, already fading. She gripped him, squeezed him, pressed him to her. "Good," she said. "Good for you."

Six weeks later, the scandal broke, and everything had to be recalibrated.

They were in Chicago at the time, he on his business, she doing a bit of shopping, hoping to find something suitable for winter in this last dreary outpost of civilization, which was, at least, preferable to the sheer barbarism of rural Wisconsin, *Spring Green*, for God's sake—and no, she wouldn't go to see Norma, not on her life, because Norma was now apparently the moral guardian of the state of Illinois, excoriating her mother both by mail and over the telephone wires for living openly with a married man, as if such a child chained to such a joyless belittling marriage with a man who was her inferior in every regard could know anything about passion and the higher life of the mind. She'd just come back to the hotel after stops at the milliner, her tailor and half a dozen of the less absurd shops that nonetheless featured things they were wearing in Paris two years ago, when there was a knock at the door. It was Leora.* Looking flushed. "I must have missed you—I don't know how, I've been waiting in the lobby for *hours* . . ."

"But why? Whatever's the matter?"

She could only sigh and draw her face down, throwing a quick glance up the corridor to where two men in bright ties, their voices jocularly entwined, were just

* Then still living in Chicago prior to her husband's retirement from the stock exchange and their move to a more equitable climate on the West Coast. Cf. page 370.

stepping into the elevator, before she ducked through the door and fell into the nearest chair as if she'd been stricken on the spot. "He's not here, is he?" she whispered, puckering her lips in a show of concern, her eyes jumping to the bedroom door and back again.

"Who? Frank?"

"He's not, is he?"

"Why, no—he's at the office. Working. You know that—he works all the time, works like a stoker, day and night, the *vigor* of the man"—and here she had to smile a not-so-private smile because she'd already informed Leora, in some detail, about their nights together.

"Have you a cigarette?"

Without answering, she went to where her purse lay open on the table by the window, extracted her cigarette case with an absent glance at the mosaic of sun-splashed roofs below her and the great blue void of the lake beyond, and came back across the room with her hand extended, thinking of the hats she'd bought—and the shoes—and thinking she might model them for Leora, because she respected her opinion, though if truth be told Leora was hardly original in her dress. In the next moment, she'd lit Leora's cigarette and one of her own—Frank be damned: she'd smoke if she pleased, anytime, anywhere—and settled into the armchair beside Leora's. "So," she said, exhaling a rich blue cloud of Turkish tobacco, "what is all this about Frank? Something in the papers?"

"It's that maid," Leora said, her voice a whisper still, as if she were afraid someone might overhear her, though Frank was gone and the walls were as reasonably thick as one could expect from an American hotel. "Mrs. Breen?"

"Yes? What about her?"

"It seems she's got hold of some letters, letters you wrote to Frank when you were separated? And gone to the press with them."

"But how would she—?" The answer came to her before the question was out of her mouth—and, of course, she was thinking aloud in any case—the hateful pinched face of the puffed-up little woman invading her mind's eye even as she saw her rifling Frank's drawers under the pretext of dusting or mopping or whatever it was she did at Taliesin when she wasn't presiding over her reeking pots of greasy bland overcooked *victuals*. But the treachery of the woman—and how could Frank associate himself with people like that? Defend them, even? Mother Breen, he called her, and before she'd laid down the law for him he'd actually praised the woman for her efficiency and, astonishingly, her cuisine.

"I've got the clippings here for you, in the event you hadn't seen the papers." Leora, head bent beneath the stiff shelf of her hat, was digging through her purse. "Here they are," she said, handing her a neatly folded section of the morning paper and then focusing her big blinking eyes on her as if she expected her to collapse under the weight of a few lines of newsprint. "She's accusing Frank under the Mann Act.* And reporting you as an undesirable alien, if

* The Mann Act, passed into law just five years earlier as a means of prosecuting pimps, panders, fancy men and macquereau who transported women across state lines for the purpose of prostitution, would haunt Wrieto-San, as has been seen. Its intention was to combat the very real abuses of "white slavery," in which young immigrant girls were approached with offers of employment (in many cases as they stepped off the boat from Ellis Island), only to find themselves opiated, locked away in a room and gang-raped, starved and brutalized till all sense of dignity and individuality was destroyed, after which they were sold into prostitution. Mrs. Breen must have been among the first to attempt to use the law as a tool of harassment and intimidation.

you can believe the nerve of this woman—the newspaper says they want to deport you."

The fact was, she couldn't really make out much more than the headlines—NEW SCANDAL AT WRIGHT LOVE BUNGALOW—without her spectacles, but before she could rise from the chair to go search them out, she heard herself say, "Deport me? But my passport states quite clearly that I'm an American citizen. It's ridiculous. I might have got the thing at the consulate in France, but . . . you know I'm an American. Everybody does. What in God's name are they talking about, deport me?"*

Leora's voice went cold. "Frankly, Miriam, I don't know. But they're dragging your name through the mud. And your reputation too." She cleared her throat, tapped the ash from her cigarette and reached for the clipping. "They're saying that you and Frank—they call you 'the noted sculptress from Paris,' by the way—have been cohabiting at his 'love bungalow' in defiance of any conventional notions of morality and that Mrs. Breen felt she had to come forward as a matter of conscience. She's quite devout, it appears. Roman Catholic—the worst, the very worst. And she said—" Leora hesitated. Blinked her eyes. Blinked till Miriam thought she must have developed some sort of tic like the dropsical old man who used to sit all day at La Rotonde, contorting his face and spitting into a handkerchief, and who was very likely dead by now, dead of blinking and quivering and spitting. Or maybe exasperation. Maybe that was what killed him.

* A strange adumbration of what lay in the future. One can only speculate as to the extent this experience may have influenced Miriam's decision to report Olgivanna to the immigration authorities some ten years later on the same pretext.

She could feel the metallic burn of outrage in the back of her throat, though she was elated too—*the noted sculptress!*—and she rose up out of the chair in a shiver of anticipation and hate. "Said what?"

"Well"—another flurry of blinking—"that she felt she had to come forward because of the children."

"Children? What children?"

"Frank's children. She says they were there."

"*Frank's* children?" It took her a moment. A series of images ran through her head—Thomas in diapers, the girls nattering over their dolls, their hair in ringlets and their dresses spread out round them like parachutes fallen to earth, the glittering black eyes of a random infant in a perambulator, tiny immaculate fingers and toes, pink skin in a bubble bath—but none of them seemed to have anything to do with Frank. Children? Frank didn't have any children.

"That's what it says."

"But they're grown. They're adults. Two of them are married, for God's sake. And the youngest—he must be twelve or thirteen, at any rate—went back off to school the week I got there. In Chicago. Or Oak Park—at his mother's."

Leora gave an elaborate shrug. "You know that. I know it. But they're still his children."

Frank's response was to pack her into the car that very night and drive up to Wisconsin as if they were fugitives. The following day—it was early November now, the fields frost-burned, the windows aching with the cold—he gave a statement to the press denying everything. His attachment to Madame Noel, he said, was purely spiritual and to think of conducting a love affair under the eyes of his mother—who had been living at Taliesin for some months now—was preposterous. Madame Noel was a brilliant and highly sensitive soul who could only find solace in the company of her fellow artists and who was, accordingly, a member of the Taliesin atelier that included himself and a number of architects, draftsmen and artisans. Further, he and his attorney, Mr. Clarence Darrow, were looking into prosecuting Mrs. Breen—an embittered, discharged domestic who had written several letters threatening both Mr. Wright and Madame Noel—for the theft of his private property and misuse of the mails.

When the reporters had left, he sent his draftsmen out into the fields on the pretext of repairing the fences or raking up the stubble or some such thing and took her into the studio. "Miriam, I really do regret all this publicity," he said, sliding into the seat behind his desk as if he were easing into a bath. "It's the last thing we need, especially after—" he made a vague gesture. "And I'm sorry you've been dragged into it. But please, sit down, sit down, make yourself comfortable."

"No, I won't sit, Frank." She was irritated on a number of counts, not the least of which was having to cut short their Chicago sojourn in order to eat flapjacks and freeze her marrow out here in the dismal dull cloud-hung barn-stinking hind-end of nowhere. "And I won't hide myself away out of sight as if I have something to be ashamed of. I'm not ashamed of our love, Frank—are you?"

He picked up his spectacles and fiddled with them a moment before clamping them over the bridge of his nose as if to examine her more closely.* He looked like a

* Wrieto-San had been blessed with acute eyesight. However, according to his autobiography, he felt himself rapidly aging in the wake of the tragedy of August 1914 and acquired eyeglasses. I rarely saw him wear them, and never in public, a matter of personal vanity with him.

bank examiner, a livestock appraiser, his eyes distorted and rinsed of color. "Of course not, but that's not at issue, not at all."

She cut him off. "What is, then?"

"I simply cannot afford—and you know this as well as anyone, Miriam—another blowup. In this neighborhood especially, not after what happened here summer before last—"

"The dead woman again. It always comes down to her, doesn't it, Frank? Well, I tell you, I am not going to hide myself away. I'm going to proclaim the truth of what we are and I don't give two figs for what anybody thinks. Including you."

"Damn it, Miriam!" He stood so abruptly the chair pitched over behind him. In his excitement he began waving his arms as if he were trying to shoo a cow out of the garden and the gesture froze her inside. She wouldn't be intimidated. She wouldn't. "You don't understand. You talk about—"

"I love you, Frank."

"—love, yes, love, but that's not what this concerns. This concerns scandal, Miriam, the kind of scandal that will destroy all the goodwill I've patiently built up among my neighbors here . . ."

She held herself perfectly rigid. "That's the only truth, Frank. That's all anyone needs to know."

"No, Miriam, no, it's not. They're going to publish the letters and Clarence says it's too late to stop them."

The letters. To bloody hell with the letters. She never flinched. Never took her eyes from his. "Good," she spat. "Let them. Let the whole world know what I feel for you. Let them see what a true and good and noble love is, a love for the ages, a love that shines like the brightest star in the firmament."

And then (was she catching cold?) she brought her handkerchief to her face to dab at her eyes—and let him fume, let him rage at her—and very gently, very softly and delicately, blew her nose.*

* Despite his lifelong protestations to the contrary, I can't imagine but that Wrieto-San for the most part welcomed publicity, as it got his name out before the public and fed his sense of self-importance. So too with Miriam. Perhaps—and this occurs to me just now—they chose each other in a flare of mutual flamboyance, each reflecting all the brighter off the other.

CHAPTER 6: THE SERPENT OF HYPOCRISY

That night they ate a subdued meal, latterly shotgunned duck in its own oleaginous juices, with half a dozen insipid side dishes, the only recognizable one of which seemed to be some sort of potato concoction buried in strips of what looked to be roadside weed, prepared by the lumbering swollen wife of one of the workmen and served in uncovered tureens by the graceless little sixteen-year-old. There were just three place settings at the table, which would make this the smallest group she'd presided over since coming to Taliesin. Not that it mattered to her one way or the other, simply that a larger party made for gayer conversation, and gay conversation helped fight down the crushing tedium of the place. Frank's sons had long since returned to their wives, as the major part of the construction was completed now, and the visiting architect and his wife had gone back to Germany—or was it Austria? Paul Mueller was overseeing things in the Chicago offices and Russell Williamson and the other draftsmen had gone off to a concert in Madison. The third setting was for Frank's mother, but Frank's mother was in a funk over the newspaper reports and wouldn't come out of her room.

"Well, I guess it's just the two of us, then," Frank said, lifting his glass—of plain unadulterated eau de vie—for a toast. "To us," he offered, and she dutifully clinked her glass against his, making her best effort to hold on to a smile. In her glass, which she'd seen to personally before Frank came into the room, was a crisp dry Chablis she'd got from her wine merchant in Chicago, the palate and aroma of which momentarily took her back across the Atlantic to the vineyards of Burgundy on a long-ago autumn day when she was newly in love with René,* who'd been so wonderfully kind to her after Emil's death. Until he turned rotten, that is. And unfaithful. Like any man, if you gave him half the chance. The thought soured her and her smile abruptly vanished. She gave him a hard look.

"As I was saying earlier, we can't afford to stir up the press any more than we already have, thanks to Mrs. Breen—and damn that woman. I'm sorry to have to say it, but there it is. She's the one at fault, clearly, and these Mann charges will certainly be dismissed as the absurdity they are. What rankles me—no, what infuriates me—is this sordid effort to impeach your character, and it's got to stop." He looked up from his duck, the worry lines lashing at his eyes, and let out a sigh. "Which is why I've asked my mother to stay on. At least until this has blown over."

"It's false, Frank, and you know it."

"False or not, I won't have the press making sport of you—and me. Me, all over again. If I'm to get work, and you know perfectly well how tight things are for me right now, then there simply cannot be any more talk or even the breath of a scandal. God knows the letters will be embarrassment enough."

* Surname and provenance unknown. Perhaps he was the lover to whom Miriam would refer darkly when speaking of her "tragic love," perhaps even the very one she accosted with a drawn knife. See page 110n.

She was calm, utterly composed, and she sipped her wine and watched him over the rim of the glass until he was done. "I want to speak with them," she said, setting the glass down and taking up knife and fork. The duck lay there before her. She gave it a single glance—folds of luteous fat and dull dun flesh, steam rising, *gravy*—and laid down the fork, carefully realigning it with the plate, before going on. "I'll explain it all. I tell you: I will not hide."

"You will." His tone was curt and despotic and she didn't like it at all. He might have been speaking to one of his draftsmen over a poorly executed section or a farmhand who'd dared to express an opinion on the application of fertilizer. "You'll stay here at Taliesin, away from the reporters, until I say different. Do you understand me?"

Understand him? He was speaking English, wasn't he? But did he understand her? She didn't like to be dictated to. Emil had tried it and she was just a girl then. He lived to regret it. And René too. She lifted the glass to her lips, let the taste of the cold clear liquid—the taste of France, of civilization—soothe her throat and her nerves and her temper too. She didn't bother to answer.

The next morning they saddled up two of the horses and rode out over the hills together and everything seemed new-made and fine, the air and exercise dispelling the bad odor of the day before. He was a splendid horseman and that made her proud of him all over again. They cantered across the fields, the breeze in their faces, absolutely removed from the world, and they might have been Heathcliff and Catherine pounding over the turf in all the wild excess of their fraught and doomed love. It was bracing. Exhilarating. And when Frank's mother crawled out of her burrow to take luncheon with them she barely minded. The afternoon was pleasant too. She spent most of it reading before the fire while Frank and one of the men went into Madison to run errands, and she was so engaged with her book, so caught up in the momentum of the unfolding story (two men and a woman, the midnight assignation, blood and honor and the fierce crack of the vaquero's lariat as the lovers fled into the fastness of the Argentine night)* she hardly glanced up when he returned. It took a moment, a minor irritation, his shadow falling across the page as he stood there silently in front of the chair, before she acknowledged him. He was still in his hat and coat. His face was grim. "They've printed the letters," he said, dropping the newspaper in her lap. Then he turned on his heel and stalked out of the room without another word.

Irritated, she tried to read on, but the words began to meld and elongate so that she could make no sense of them, and after a moment she set down the book and took up the paper.

The headline—it exploded across the page, sending sparks and rockets high into the farthest reaches of her scrambled brain—made her catch her breath: "MIRIAM" LETTERS TO WRIGHT RANGE FROM JOY TO DESPAIR. It was like nothing she'd ever experienced. To see her name there, reproduced in canonical ink, was a shock—of course it was—but it was something more too, something indefinable, and even as she glanced over the subtitle (*The Shunned Woman: Her Cry, Her Pains*) she could feel the glow of it. Suddenly, overnight, in a single stroke, she was famous. Known to thousands, hundreds of thousands. She was Frank Lloyd Wright's love and all the world knew it, shunned no more. She thrilled with the knowledge, every cell and fiber alive with it, and if she was in exile, if the sky outside the window was as dull and dirty and depressing as

* O'Flaherty-San may be thinking here of *The Wild Pampas* (Boston: Lippincott, 1915) by H. (Harriet) R. R. Fleck, one of Miriam's favorite novelists.

an old tin pot in the kitchen sink, what did it matter? These were her words, her very words, broadcast to the world!

Of course, as she read on—and she *did* have a literary gift, a real way with the turn of a phrase, she had to credit herself there—she couldn't help regretting certain small infelicities. Had she really called Frank "a pathetic, bitter, aging man"? Had she actually said "I am going—the 'menace' to your safety no longer exists. Live your life as pitifully as you desire"? Or this: "You do not wish to be POSSESSED (OWNED) by love, by tenderness, kindness, devotion, but you ARE possessed by a tyranny whose sway is disastrous to the happiness of those who love you." The words hardly made sense. And she would have taken them back if she could. But she'd been overwrought at the time, spurned, cast out of the fold, people had to understand that—and the thought of it, of how beastly he'd been, how sharp-tongued and sarcastic and purely petty and mean, made her anger shine out all over again. She read through it all, column after column, weighing each word with a mixture of euphoria and heartache, and then she read it through a second time.

When she was finished she sat a long while staring into the fire, struggling to get hold of her emotions. The initial elation was gone now, replaced by doubt. This wasn't right—it wasn't right at all. The overall impression a casual reader of the *Tribune* would take away with him would be ungenerous, she could see that now. Instead of a true and noble cri de coeur from one great and giving soul to another—stars equally aligned and equally potent—these letters, these very private and personal letters, would be seen as the maunderings of a scorned woman, defeated in love, desperate and pitiful. Some people—the mean-spirited ones—might even laugh at them. And if that wasn't bad enough, she'd signed herself "Thine," and even worse, "Love me all you can."

Finally, the windows gone black with the fall of night

and the house settling into a quiet that dwindled down to nothing but the tick and crepitus of the fire, she pushed herself up and went looking for Frank. He wasn't in the bedroom and she traced her way back through the loggia to the dining alcove and on to the living room, but she didn't encounter him along the way. There was a smell of cabbage emanating from the kitchen—peasant fare, as poisonous as it was bland—and the cook and serving girl, busying themselves over chopping block and stove respectively, barely glanced up when she peered through the door. No one else seemed to be stirring. And that was odd—or maybe it wasn't. Maybe this was the way it was out here in the country, everyone battened down to survive the interminable winter, all human hopes and joys and aspirations buried under a heap of quilts, to bed at dark and up with the cows. The thought made her seize with anxiety, and where was Frank? Didn't he realize that she needed him, that the letters were all wrong, that she was the one who'd been exposed to public censure and maybe even ridicule—that it was she who bore the burden, not he?

She thought perhaps Frank had gone outside—whenever he was wrought up, no matter the weather, he'd pull on his boots and go tramping round the place, as if he were impervious to heat, cold, rain and snow alike. Frank the farmer, Frank the Welshman, the manure spreader and hog appraiser, a peasant for all his genius. She'd actually stuck her head outside in the intemperate air and bleated his name down the length of the courtyard before she thought of the studio. Which was where she found him, seated at one of the drafting tables beneath the oil portrait of his mother—the sole picture in the room—and the motto he'd affixed to the wall: WHAT A MAN DOES, THAT HE HAS. And what does a man do? she was thinking. Lock up his *amante* in a dungeon? Silence her? Let the newspapers make a mockery of her spirit, her love, her life? "This won't stand, Frank," she said.

He looked up from what he was doing—his eternal drawing, and he was like a child, exactly like a child, an infant, that was what he was—and gave her a sour look.* "I know it, Miriam. Believe me, we're doing everything we can to put a stop to it."

"A stop to it? It's too late already, isn't it? Do you know what those letters make me seem like?" He was watching her out of his shrewd little eyes, glaring at her, blaming her. "Like a ruined woman, Frank. Like a fool. A fool for loving you."

And what was his response? The little man, the cold fish who wouldn't even rise from the stool to take her in his arms and swear his love to her, who couldn't take a cue? "I can't help that, Miriam. What's done is done."

She woke next morning to a dull changeless light and a preternatural silence, as if the whole world had lost its hearing. The bed was empty beside her. Beyond the windows, a slant of gray wet snow, and of course there were no curtains to shut it out—Frank didn't believe in curtains—so that the outdoors plunged right into the room. She might as well have been camped in Alaska or some such place, the fire dead in the hearth, her breath suspended before her face and a rime on the water glass she'd set out on the bedside table. It was too cold even to get up and use the bathroom. Too depressing. The thought of the letters came to her suddenly, the shame, the stupidity, and then she thought of her pravaz, but she never moved, and if the housemaid came in to see to her she never knew it. Sleep was like a stone pressing down on her chest. She closed her eyes. When she woke again it was still snowing, still cold, but someone had lit the

* We can't know for certain, but it seems likely that he was then working on the plans for his revolutionary "American System Ready-Cut" standardized houses—what today would be called, in classic American shorthandese, pre-fab.

fire and her bodily needs spoke to her in a way she could no longer ignore. She found her slippers and her robe and made her way to the bathroom.

And this was primitive too, despite the bronze Buddha and the Han vases and the Oriental carpets, because the water from the tap was like liquid ice and if she wanted to bathe—and she did—she'd have to send someone out to fetch wood and fire up the boiler in the cellar. She made her toilette as best she could, feeling out of sorts, thinking she might have some tea and toast to settle her stomach, but as she brushed her hair before the mirror—a hundred strokes, morning and night, just as her mother had taught her—she felt the weakness in her bowels and had to sit down a moment. Almost accidentally—idly, certainly—her hand came into contact with the cosmetics case in which she kept her pravaz and it took only a moment to decide that what she needed was an injection to set her right. It was the cold, she told herself, the dreary unrelenting winter that gave everyone chilblains and ague, the same as in Paris, but at least there she could find refuge in a gallery or a concert hall or one of the cafés or *salons artistiques*. Paris, she was thinking, Paris, and felt the warmth spread through her.

It was then that she heard the voices. Frank's voice and another man's—or no, two others—twined and murmurous. They seemed to be drifting across the loggia from the direction of the living room, and that struck her as odd—Frank hadn't mentioned anything to her about guests arriving, though with one thing and another it may have slipped his mind. Suddenly her heart leapt up—here was the possibility of a reprieve, a release from the nullity of country life if only for an hour or two. But who could it be? Frank always surrounded himself with stimulating people, artists, musicians, architects and writers, many of them quite well-connected, and if his gatherings never quite approached the brilliance of the Parisian salons, they were often charming and diverting. And diversion was what she needed right now, above all else.

She cracked the door to hear better. Frank's voice predominated—he seemed to be delivering some sort of speech, but then he was always giving extempore speeches on an inexhaustible range of subjects, "pontificating," as one of his ex-draftsmen liked to say, and not very charitably she was sure—his fine mellow tenor sharpening now, even as the voices of the two men broke in to challenge him, and what was going on? Was he showing some of his prints for sale, was that it? Could Clarence Darrow have come all the way out from the city? A client? And then suddenly, through some trick of the air currents, one of the stranger's voices rang clear—"So what you're saying is that there is no romantic attachment whatever between you and Madame Noel? She's merely a spiritual affinity like Mrs. Borthwick?"—and she understood. Reporters. The reporters were here.

Frank said something that she couldn't quite catch—he must have been pacing up and down the room—and then his voice came clear too. "Yes, that's right, I've hired on Madame Noel in the capacity of housekeeper, as Mrs. Breen has been dismissed, as you know—"

Housekeeper? *She* a housekeeper? What was he thinking?

"But surely," the voice returned—a thin voice, reedy and wheedling—"you can't deny that these letters give quite the opposite impression."

She didn't hear what Frank had to say next because she was in motion suddenly, hurriedly dressing—the silk gown, the white one, a pearl choker and her rings—thinking that this was her chance to make them see the truth of the matter, to know what she was in her deepest self, in her heart, and to let the world know too. She felt almost as if she were dreaming as she drifted through the loggia with its windows giving onto the gray frozen drifts, her feet bare as a maid's and the gown flowing across her abdomen and her limbs with the simple elegance the Greeks had brought to perfection. Cytherea. She was violet-crowned Cytherea, the foam-risen, a goddess gliding across the carpet and into the living room where the two strangers, one bald and one not, their eyes flying to her, practically ruptured themselves jumping up out of their chairs to make obeisance to her, and "Yes," she was telling them, enchanted by the sound of her own voice. "Yes, it's all true: I love him!"

The denouement wasn't quite everything she'd expected. Frank was angry with her, at least at first, but he stood by her and the two of them, the fire leaping and the storm raging beyond the windows to produce an air of romance even the most gifted scenarist would have been hard-pressed to duplicate, made their defense of a love that defies the conventions, that dares strive for the sublime no matter the niggling concerns of the hidebound and unenlightened. First she made her thoughts known, then he, back and forth in counterpoint until they were both singing the same sweet song and the newspapermen scratched at their pads till their fingers went numb. Of course, the photograph they ran beneath the headline "I LOVE HIM!" SAYS MRS. MAUDE MIRIAM NOEL OF FRANK LLOYD WRIGHT, beautiful and doe-eyed though it was, revealing one bared and lovely shoulder and a faraway look of the most fetching appeal, left something to be desired. Namely, despite the fact that the caption read *This is her first published photograph,* it wasn't her likeness. Amazingly. Though she was certainly the equal of this model, whoever she was, and the accompanying article was flattering in the extreme.

But how could they have made such a gaffe? Anyone who knew her would see in an instant that this wasn't she—and yet, and yet, the picture was blown up to a full page and it might have been an idealized representation of her, a year or two younger, perhaps a bit firmer beneath the chin, and it was fine. Very fine. People would envy her and that was what she wanted more than anything at this point because she was no castoff and she was not in the least lovelorn—no, she had her man, one of the truly great figures of the age, and no one else did.

Two days later, on the tenth of November, the *Chicago Tribune* ran a story in which Nellie Breen denied attempting blackmail, but which seemed to catch her up in her own machinations.* Her back against the wall, the woman had apparently given the reporters a fair copy of her letter dated October 22 in which she warned Frank that he and Miriam were liable to arrest under the Mann Act on evidence in her possession (clearly the letters she'd stolen out of Frank's desk drawer), evidence so damning that it was unlikely they would even be released on bail. But she didn't stop there—she made demands. What did she want in return for suppressing this evidence? She wanted them to separate. Separate. And never see each other again. Oh, and she was very specific on this, the meddling arthritic broken-down old bitch: "That is, you cannot keep her at Taliesin or Cedar Street, nor have her to visit you or live with her."

If that wasn't blackmail, then what was? Miriam—and she was furious with Frank for having kept the letter from her, no matter how loving or charitable his intentions—could scarcely believe the audacity of the woman, who was, after all, no better than a common thief. In fact, when she first saw the article she was so enraged she flung the paper across the room, where it struck the wall in full flight and fell to the carpet like a crippled bird.

* Public sympathy turned against her at this juncture, and Wrieto-San was able to take the high road in declining to prosecute her for misappropriation of the mails. Still, the damage to his reputation was done and he was once again seen as philandering and venal, if not faintly ridiculous.

It was still there when she went to her writing desk, so absolutely rigid with hate and distaste and mortification that she'd taken a bit of sherry to calm herself—and if it had any effect at all she couldn't feel it, not in her present state. She was back in Chicago now, at least there was that—they'd taken the train in on the morning after the photograph of the wilting doppelganger had been printed ("No need to hide me away now, Frank," she'd remarked acidly, holding tight to his arm as they strode up the platform in a flurry of newspapermen and gaping passersby)—but the scene out the window was as close and gray and bleak as it had been in Wisconsin. Well, she welcomed it—it would only feed her mood. Which was dark, dark, dark. And thirsting for blood. How dare she, how dare that lace-curtain bitch set out rules for her—or for anyone, for that matter? Who appointed her moral guardian of the world?

In the lower drawer, locked away from Frank, was a sheaf of the stationery she'd ordered over his objections, the Hicks coat of arms glowing from the page beneath their conjoined initials. She produced a pristine sheet and smoothed it out on the blotting pad, taking another long sip of sherry as she brooded over it. Then she took up her pen, a new Waterman, a gift from Frank, so smooth and delicate and pretty a writing utensil it might have been a supernumerary finger, and without thinking let her ideas flow across the page as if she'd been writing letters to the newspaper all her life. The reporter—the bald one, and for the life of her she couldn't seem to recall his name—had taken her aside that day at Taliesin and encouraged her to give her side of the story. Her philosophy, her desires, something of herself the public could grasp hold of. Who was she behind the enigma, that sort of thing. It would be so much more gratifying than anything he or his colleagues could write because it was she who was at the center of things here, she who knew the real truth not only of Chicago and its ostensible mores but of the Continent too.

By the time she came back to herself she'd covered some five pages, hardly a letter blotted, her graceful hand undulating across the page with all the authority and elegance that had won her first prize in penmanship at the Thornleigh Academy for Women when she was a girl. She spoke of marriage as a worn-out dead letter, at least when it's loveless, a mere shadow of what a true and loving pact should be, but then she assured them—her audience, all the shining people of Chicago, and the little people too, the butchers and carters and whoever—that she and Frank weren't denouncing marriage per se, but simply obeying a higher law. For there was only one real loyalty and that was reflected in conduct consecrated to a living, lofty concept of life and love. That was what people should aim for, that and nothing less.

And then, with all the eloquence she could summon, she went about demolishing Nellie Breen, a hired domestic, a thief, an exemplar of false middle-class morality that stoops to dishonesty, to thievery, in order to uphold its own spuriousness, the very serpent of hypocrisy that was slowly dying out around the world as people listened to their hearts and not the dictates of men dead and gone. Finally, her pen moving so swiftly it was as if a spirit had risen from the grave to take her hand and guide it—Emil, with all his literary talents intact, or perhaps it was her father—she cried out to the world, "Do not pity me. I am no victim of unrequited love. Well might any woman proudly stand in my place and count the cost as nothing."

When she finished, she went to the window to stare out into what remained of the day. She felt unburdened at last, free of it all, and though she was bursting to show the letter to Frank (but he was at the office) or to Leora, to anyone, she sealed the envelope, affixed a stamp and went to the closet for her coat. She watched herself in the mirror as she did up the buttons, adjusted her hat and pulled on her gloves, staring into her own eyes, but not too deeply. There was a glow about her, certainly, and as she went out into the cold and made her way up the street to the postbox on the corner, she could feel people's eyes on her and she turned to them gracefully, men and women alike, and smiled.

CHAPTER 7: IN THE LONG SHADOW OF MOUNT FUJI

Frank was shouting, his voice booming out till the house rang with it, and everybody, not least Miriam herself, had been on tenterhooks for three days now and counting. Guests were coming. He was always impossible when people were expected, arranging and rearranging his prints and screens and pottery over and over, grouping the furniture first in one corner and then another and finally dragging it into the center of the room, where it would remain for all of fifteen minutes before he changed his mind yet again. He devoted hours alone to the floral arrangements or to draping his Chinese, Turkoman or Persian carpets over one chair or the other so that they fell just so, and on this occasion—the Japanese were coming and he was so wound up you would have thought the Emperor himself was about to breeze through the door—he went to a rosewood chest in the vault to dig out his eighteenth-century Japanese robes* so that he could

* *Kosode*, that is. Lightweight summer robes. Wrieto-San collected textiles as well as prints, screens, sculpture and pottery. Anything of the Far East seemed to hold a special fascination for him, most particularly, as has been seen, the art of Japan. Do I flatter myself to say that our folk art is the equal of any nation's?

display them beside his prints. But what was he bellowing about now?

Whatever it may have been—a spot of tarnish on a serving spoon, lint on the carpet, an insufficient fire in one of the guest rooms—it was no concern of hers. He had half a dozen of his lackeys running around the place as if they'd been scorched, the cook had her instructions and another housemaid had been taken on to oversee the arrangements. No, her concern—her only concern—was to see to her dress so that she could stand beside him and greet the guests with a pure ethereal serenity and the daintiest of Oriental bows. And certainly Frank had harangued her on this latter point—the form, duration and posture of the bow—till she wanted to scream.

Now, in the privacy of the bedroom, with a good bed of coals in the fireplace and two fresh splits of oak laid atop them because it was cold as a tomb in this rambling stone and stucco citadel with its leaks and drafts and the windows that might as well have been made of transparent paper for all the good they did at keeping the weather out, she practiced before the mirror, dipping her torso and rising again with her eyes radiant and a full-lipped smile spreading across her face till her dimples shone like a girl's, *How nice to meet you, Hayashi-San, enchantée*—or no, that wasn't the right note at all. She should keep silent, letting her eyes do the talking for her—wasn't that the way the Oriental women did it? Of course, they were nothing but chattel, no better than dogs, unless they were the painted courtesans who coquetted the night away with a passel of leering old men who had nothing more to recommend them than the yen in their pockets. And that horrible rice wine. She'd known a few Japanese in Paris—*Japonisme* was all the rage in those days; she imagined it still was—and they'd been decent enough, she supposed, with a good command of French, but then they were the artistes and by all accounts Hayashi-San was certainly not artistic in the least. No, he was a businessman. Manager of the old Imperial Hotel in Tokyo. And he was coming to be wooed. Well, all right, she thought, bowing before the mirror, she would woo him, then. For Frank's sake.*

She was just cinching her blue shantung silk wrapper over an emerald-green V-necked chemise that would show prettily at her throat, thinking with some satisfaction that this was the very quintessence of the Oriental look, perhaps with the addition of a string of pearls and the jade pin of a smiling tumescent Buddha she'd picked up as a curiosity in a stall on the avenue d'Ivry some years back, when Frank came hurtling through the door. He was in a state. His hair was standing out from his head like a collapsed halo and his eyes were so inflamed he looked as if he'd been up all night long. But he hadn't been. She could testify to that.

"My God, Miriam, what are you thinking?" he shouted, and he was so agitated she could see the flecks of spittle leaping from his lips. "Get dressed. They'll be at the station any minute now, don't you realize that? I give you one task only—to dress yourself so you don't look like a, a"—he couldn't seem to find the properly insulting term and ran on ahead of himself—"and what do you do? Are you intentionally trying to ruin this for me? Is that it?"

She tried to ignore him, slipping into the seat at her vanity to see to her hair, which she'd pulled back with a comb so as to mimic the pictures of the geisha in Frank's woodblock prints, and her eyes, which she'd extended

* Aisaku Hayashi had been sent by the Ōkura investment group (and the Emperor, who was providing sixty percent of the funding) to make a close study of Wrieto-San, whose reputation of working against the grain, not to mention providing regular scandals for the tabloids, bore examination before any contract for the new Imperial Hotel could be finalized.

vertically with two triangular slashes of kohl, but she felt herself hardening. "Look like a *what*, Frank?"

"I haven't time for this, Miriam," he warned, and as if he couldn't help himself, he went to the chair in the corner and moved it three inches closer to the writing table. "Just get yourself dressed. Now!"

She was watching him in the mirror, his erratic movements, the twitching of his limbs and the pent-up tarantella of his feet on the carpet, trying to sympathize—the Japanese were coming for an extended stay and he would have to be on his mark the entire time if he hoped to nail down the biggest commission of his life, she understood that and she wanted to give him all the love and support she could—but she didn't like his tone. Not one bit. "Ah *am* dressed, Frahhnk," she said, protracting each syllable in her best high-Memphis drawl.

He whirled round on her suddenly and took the room in three strides, dipping low so that his face loomed beside hers in the mirror. She was sure he was about to make some sort of nasty comment, his lips curling, eyes gone cold as day-old coffee, when there was a sudden crash from the other room, a muted curse and the clatter of running feet. Frank flinched, threw an angry look over his shoulder, and then came back to her, his hands sinking into her shoulders like the claws of a bird. "Don't you start," he hissed, his face right there, his breath hot in her ear. "You dress yourself and be there to greet them at the door—the door, do you hear me?—when I get back from the station. And for God's sake, maintain yourself."

Icily, with as much command as she could summon, she reached up to remove his hands, then twisted round and rose to face him. "I thought I would go along with the Oriental theme, this robe, my Buddha pin—I'm trying to please you, Frank, that's all. You should see that." A tearful note crept into her voice and she couldn't help it. "There's really no call for cruelty."

"You're ridiculous!" he shouted. "Look at yourself. A wrapper, for God's sake? And that preposterous makeup? You're like a parody— No, I mean what I say. Are you trying to insult these people?"

She observed, as quietly and steadily as she could, that *he* was in Oriental costume—the absurd linen trousers that billowed out from his thighs and clung tight to his ankles like something out of an illustration for *The Arabian Nights*, the wooden clogs, the cutaway tunic that fell to his knees and a risible hat that looked like a cross between a cardinal's biretta and a Russian *ushanka*—and so why shouldn't she follow suit?

"What I wear is none of your business."

"I could say the same."

And now a voice was calling from the other room, some fresh crisis erupting: "Mr. Wright, Mr. Wright, could you come here a moment, please?"

"Listen," he said, "Miriam, I beg of you—you're the most charming woman in the world, the most brilliant, and I just need for you to dress as you normally would, as if we were going out to the theater or to dine on Michigan Avenue. Not Tokyo. Not Yokohama Bay. But here, in the United States."

She was uncertain of herself now—perhaps the silk wrapper was too informal, perhaps he was right, and she supposed the eye shadow *was* a bit garish—but she couldn't help contradicting him nonetheless. "I'll dress any way I please," she said.

"Mr. Wright! Mr. Wright!"

"Yes, I'm coming," he shouted over one shoulder before turning back to her. "What I want, Miriam—what I require, what I need more than anything—is an adornment." He paused, glaring at her, trying to stare her down, intimidate her, and the insolence of him, the lordliness, was infuriating—as if he could preach to her, as if she would listen to one word. "An adornment, Miriam, not an anchor."

Still, when the carriage, followed by the automobile, came up the drive and into the courtyard half an hour later, she was there at the door, in her choker and beads and a gray peau de soie dress cut at mid-calf beneath her midnight-blue cape and a matinee hat that presented her perfect face as if it had been framed. And when she saw Hayashi-San in his Western suit, spats, mustache and slicked-back hair, she bowed as deeply as the hat would allow her and whispered "*Komban wa*" in the most delicate voice she could muster, just as Frank had taught her.

Dinner that night was nothing less than an ordeal, akin, she supposed, to what the flagellants must have experienced when they paraded themselves through the streets of Rome, blood drying in streaks, ritual humiliation, that sort of thing. At least for her, at any rate. For his part, Frank was having the time of his life, his voice rising and falling with the inevitability of waves beating at the shore as he regaled the assembled company with his views on the Japanese character, the parlous state of contemporary architecture, the use of natural materials, the samisen as opposed to the banjo and just about anything else that came into his head, along with a barrage of jokes, stories, snippets of song and limericks so hoary they would have fallen dead in the last century. The food was uniformly awful. The cook had attempted a Japanese theme, presenting the usual pork and gravy, fried fish and boiled cabbage with an accompaniment of little bleached mounds of white rice so impossibly adhesive it was as if she'd melted down a pot of Wrigley's chewing gum. And the chopsticks. Frank had had Billy Weston carve them from scraps of pine—as if Hayashi-San and the rest couldn't imagine how to perforate a bit of meat with the tines of a fork—and the Japanese just stared at them as if they'd never seen such a thing before in their lives. But it was hilarious, wasn't it?

Frank was at the head of the table, of course, and she was seated in her usual place, at his right, while Hayashi-San and his painted little wife sat across from her and Frank's mother commanded the far end of the table, where Russell Williamson and Paul Mueller and his wife tried to find common ground with the two mute students Hayashi-San had brought along with him as his entourage. Hayashi-San's consulting architect, a short slight man in his forties with an absolutely immobile face—Yoshitake-San—was on Miriam's immediate right, and throughout the meal he would turn to her at intervals and present her with brief guttural comments out of his English primer.

"Good evening," he said when first they'd sat down, and then he repeated the phrase several times in succession, and she, playing along, returned the greeting or observation or whatever it was, until, on the third or fourth repetition, it began to take on a new meaning altogether and it was all she could do to restrain herself when "Good night" would have been more appropriate. "The weather is pleasant, is it not?" he observed next. And then, after sitting silent through Frank's dissertation on the quarrying of native stone in its naturally occurring sedimentary layers so as to deliver it intact to the landscape, he cleared his throat and asked her if he might light her fire. "I beg your pardon?" she said, and he produced a cigarette case, offered her a cigarette and lit it for her even as Frank flashed his disapproval. She smiled then and Yoshitake-San, lighting his own cigarette, smiled back.

It was during dessert—by her count the eighth course of the evening—that Frank began to shift his focus to Hayashi-San's wife. He actually picked up his chair in the middle of the tea service and inserted it between Hayashi-San's and the wife's, and Miriam stiffened, she couldn't help herself. Of course, she was thinking, why wouldn't he fawn all over her like the beast he was—she was young, wasn't she? And pretty? Even if she was an Oriental. Oh, she was a little porcelain doll, the wife, wrapped in her black silk gown with the pale chrysanthemums climbing gracefully up the hem and across her abdomen and the swell of her pointed little Japanese breasts as if she were one of Frank's prints sprung to life, and when he spoke to her she batted her exaggerated lashes and smiled out of a mouth of uneven oversized teeth.* For the most part, she stared down at her lap, except when Frank was probing her with facetious queries about her kimono or her impressions of America, but at one point she turned to him and asked a question of her own, as if this were all part of the performance expected of her. "I wish to ask you, Wrieto-San"—and here she gave Miriam a look—"and Mrs. Wrieto-San, what is this word 'goddamn'?"

Frank laughed. And Miriam, despite herself—she detested it when he paid attention to another woman, any woman, as if he were dismissing her publicly, shaming her, *shunning* her, but the sound of that casual appellation, Mrs. Wrieto-San, was music to her ears—found that she was smiling as well. How adorable, she was thinking. How childlike. How pitiful.

* A sign of beauty in my country. O'Flaherty-San's wife, my granddaughter Noriko, has just such a dentition and a smile of rare and melting grace.

"'Goddamn'?" Frank repeated, levity lifting his voice, and everyone at the table was watching the wife now—Takako-San—and everyone was smiling in anticipation of the sequel. "Why do you ask? Have you heard this expression often since you've arrived in our country?"

A little pout, a widening of the eyes, and she was very young, Miriam saw, in her teens or early twenties, young and full of grace. And coquetry. But didn't they teach that in Japan? Wasn't that what women existed for over there?* "Oh, yes, Wrieto-San," the wife said in a diminished little puff of a voice, "every day. All the time. Here tonight. You have said it yourself."

And Frank, grinning, flirting—infuriatingly, as if she didn't exist, as if she weren't sitting across the table from him with the smile drying on her lips—gave a broad wink for the benefit of the table and for Hayashi-San in particular, no sense in ruffling *his* feathers, and replied that "goddamn" was a polite adverb meaning "very." "As in, oh, I don't know—Paul, help me out here—" But before Paul could answer, he went on, "—it's a goddamn fine evening. Or this is goddamn fresh butter. After a meal you might thank your host for a goddamn good dinner."

Takako-San shifted prettily in her chair, made her eyes big and looked round the table as if she were sitting in the catbird seat—*and she was, she was*—and chirped, "Then I thank you, Wrieto-San—and Mrs. Wrieto-San—for a goddamn good dinner."

* An unfair characterization, needless to say. My own late wife, Setsuko (née Takata), whom, sadly, O'Flaherty-San never met, was the very soul of the perfect mate, highly accomplished as a violinist, graphic designer and homemaker, graceful, intelligent, beautiful, my partner and equal in every endeavor. I shall miss her through all my days with an ache as deep and wide as the gulf that separates this life from the next.

Of course everyone laughed—it was a pretty performance—and Frank and Hayashi-San petted her as if she were a dog or monkey granted the power of speech, but Miriam, though she was grinning, felt a stab of hate run through her. Hate that carried over into the living room, where they sat before the fire and Frank paraded out his treasures—the prints in particular—to get Hayashi-San's studied opinion of them, and then there was the inevitable tour of the house that went on till it was past midnight and Hayashi-San, for all his rigid propriety, began to yawn.

"Well," Frank sighed, taking the cue at long last though she'd been signaling him with furious eyes for an hour and more, "you must be all tired out, rail travel can be so enervating, I know—but perhaps we'll take it up again in the morning. Perhaps you'd like to see something of the house from the grounds. Or from horseback. If you like we can saddle up the horses—or take the motorcar. But please, let me show you to your rooms . . ."

There were the elaborate good-nights, the ritual bowing, Hayashi-San's eyes all but melting into his head with exhaustion, the two students as silent and impassive as the carven statue of the Amida Buddha in the loggia and the little wife grinning her toothy farewells till finally they were alone in the bedroom and Miriam shut the door behind them and stalked to the closet. Frank had begun to whistle. He stood before the mirror, working loose the knot of his tie, a look of satisfaction on his face, and it was that look that set her off as much as anything. He was so pleased with himself, wasn't he? Frank Lloyd Wright, the great man, beguiler of foreigners, seducer of women, god of his own universe. The light at the bedside cast a soft glow. Shadows climbed the walls. She was one tick from combustion.

"That went well enough, don't you think?" he said,

shrugging out of the tunic with the trailing tails and open flapping arms that was like something you'd see on a Barnum & Bailey clown, and who was he to talk of parody? She snapped her neck round to glare at him, at his bare shoulders and the back of his inflated head. Did he actually expect her to reminisce over the evening? Over her own public humiliation? Was he that insensible?

"Hayashi-San, I mean," he went on, addressing the wall before him as he balanced first on one foot and then the other to remove his trousers. "He was reserved, of course, but that's the nature of the Japanese, their natural dignity, but I could see that he was visibly impressed with Taliesin and the beautiful things we've collected here . . . Yoshitake-San too, though it's Hayashi who makes the decisions, you can see that in an instant. No, I wouldn't be surprised if we don't come to a mutual agreement within the next few days. A ten percent commission, of course, and I'll want travel and accommodation in the old Imperial, for the two of us and three assistants at least. And I'll want a car and driver too, so that we can explore the countryside on our own, and the shops, of course . . ."

She made no answer. She turned away, removed her jewelry and set it on the tray, jerked the comb from her hair. Her hands were trembling. The blindness of him, the stupidity! And did he really think she was going to tramp all the way over to the Orient with him to be treated like this?

"And what did you think of Takako-San? Charming, wasn't she?"

And now it was too late, now the match had been struck, *now.* She flew at him across the room—he was just pulling the nightshirt over his head, oblivious, full of himself, swaggering, boasting, Lothario incarnate—and before she could think she'd slammed into him, both her hands extended, and he was staggering back against the wall, the garment caught over his head. There was a heavy fleshy thump and he cried out in surprise, working the neck of the nightshirt down over his face even as she shoved him again and he fell awkwardly to the floor. He was so stunned, so totally taken by surprise, that he just sat there staring up at her, not even angry yet, not even defending himself, as if he were the victim of some natural disaster, an earthquake, an avalanche. "What the—?" he stammered. "What are you—?"

"Your little Cho-Cho-San," she said, and she was standing over him, her fists clenched. She wanted to kick him like a dog. "Your little whore. Is that why you want to go over there, for your whores? *Wrieto-San?*"

"Miriam, damn you, damn you!" He scrambled to his feet, tugging at the folds of the nightgown as if it were a hair shirt, and she backed away from him—was he going to hit her? Well, let him. She didn't care. She'd show his precious Orientals the bruises in the morning, wear them like battle scars.

"No," she shouted, "damn *you*! But tell me, tell me, Frank, is it really true what the sailors say, because you ought to know, you're the one who deserted your first wife over there to go whoring with all the little buck-toothed fish-stinking geisha and if you think I'm going to tolerate that—"

"You don't know what you're saying."

"Tell me," she screamed, and she didn't care if they heard her all the way to Yokohama and back, "is it true? Do they really have their little slits on backwards?"*

* A crude *gaijin* notion that is beneath contempt, nothing more nor less than an attempt to belittle and dehumanize our people, a process that began with Commodore Perry and continues to this day. Would Miriam have stooped so low as to promulgate it? Sadly, in the derangement of her anger, I am afraid so. Which excuses nothing. (An editor wants to strike it, but we shall let it stand for the sake of realism. And O'Flaherty-San.)

* * *

In the light of day she began to see things more clearly. And calmly. She'd gone too far, she could see that now, but she'd been upset, she couldn't help herself. Still, Frank had been good about it—he was in the wrong, he knew it—and he'd taken her in his arms and held her to him till all the bad blood had flushed out of her and then he'd taken her to bed. And loved her like no man ever had, not even René at his best. She was left drained and she slept the night through without recourse to her pravaz and her dreams were fluid and rich, the bed undulating beneath her like a stateroom on the high seas, and if she couldn't have the SS *Paris* then she would have the *Empress of China*, and if the yokels of Wisconsin treated her like a leper, in Tokyo she would be Mrs. Wrieto-San, the daring and ravishing wife of the great man himself. They would marvel at her, at her style and her carriage and her Parisian manner and perhaps she'd turn back to sculpture, set up her own studio there, the materials cheap as water, and coolies—was that what you called them?—to do the onerous things for practically nothing, for yen, mere scraps of paper. Best of all, she would escape the narrowness of Chicago and the sterility of life in the countryside.

Edo. Old Edo. She lay in bed through the morning—long past breakfast—and stared at the prints on the walls until she felt she could enter them, climb into their richly colored depths and live there curled up in a ball of undiluted happiness. And what was all this—Frank's screens and vases and all the rest—if not preparation for the voyage of her life?

That night, when they sat down to dinner, she held fast to Frank throughout the meal and she did the talking, or the better part of it, and if Frank could enchant Hayashi-San, well so could she. By the time they retired to the living room to sit before the fire Hayashi-San wouldn't leave her side. His eyes—so dark they were nearly black—were fixated on her, roaming over her lips, her eyes, her tongue, her ears, her throat, and she recognized the look he trained on her from a hundred nights in the salons of Paris. All the while the little wife sat in the corner like a puppet with its strings cut while Frank lectured the architect and the earnestly nodding students—he barely glanced at the woman; he wouldn't dare—and his mother, with her bobbing old white-crowned head, served the tea herself. There was a record on the Victrola—strings pouring out of the speaker in pulsing waves of warmth that seemed to float over the room as if the orchestra were there with them. Hayashi-San looked into her eyes. All the beautiful things in the room glowed in the firelight. She took the wrap from her shoulders, leaned back in the chair and let herself relax. She was going to Tokyo. Better yet: she was already on her way.

CHAPTER 8: *DERU KUGI WA UTARERU*

He wasn't much of a sailor and he'd be the first to admit it. Give him a dingy or a canoe or even a sailboat out on the chop of Lake Mendota and he was fine, but the eternal pitching of the open sea took all the strength out of him. And, of course, leaving at the end of the year,* some ten months after Hayashi-San had visited Taliesin, only complicated matters. On the first day out of Seattle the ship was overtaken by a storm sweeping down out of the Gulf of Alaska, the decks as slick as a hockey rink, his bunk—which he was unable to crawl out of except in those intervals when he staggered to the head—floating in mid-air like a magic carpet for a giddy moment only to plunge violently as if all the magic had been sucked out of it before it floated up again and then plunged back down. And came up. And down. And up and down and up and down. He couldn't keep anything on his stomach, not even water, and when he was able to sleep his dreams were clotted with images of the *Titanic* and the *Lusitania* listing amid panic and chaos, and he woke, invariably, to the sensation of catapulting over Niagara in a barrel.

* 1916.

Miriam was a gem. She was as unaffected as a harpooner by the heavy seas, tucking away three hearty meals a day, walking the decks for exercise and lingering late in the first-class lounge, all the while urging him to take a spoonful of broth, China tea, brandy (purely as a *digestif*, of course), and sitting beside him in his agony for long stretches of time, reading aloud from the jumping pages of a kinetic book. She bathed him. Laid compresses on his brow. Massaged his cored-out muscles. She was at her best and sweetest and most motherly but nothing could awaken in him the slightest pulse of volition or the least tick of energy but the thought of the pier at Yokohama beneath his feet. It had been this way when he'd first come to Japan with Kitty* and when he'd crossed the Atlantic with Mamah too. He wasn't a sailor. He would never acquire his sea legs. If only they had transcontinental rail service, he thought, lying there miserably in his bunk, and he envisioned a bridge across the Bering Sea or maybe a tunnel as deep down as the core of the earth itself. Or what of those other Wrights and their airplane? Or a blimp. What about a blimp?

There were stretches during the two-week voyage in which he was able to sit at the drafting table and at least examine the preliminary plans, but it was impossible even to think of taking up a pencil, not with that infernal bounce and roll. Still, he was able to think things through all over again, the central problem one of engineering against the destructive force of the earthquakes that regularly ravaged the Japanese archipelago, another thing altogether from building on a stable lot in Chicago or Oak Park. He'd talked it over with his son John and Paul Mueller, both of whom had

* In 1905. Wrieto-San credits this trip with awakening his lifelong love for all things Japanese.

come along in the company of their wives to help set up shop, and with Antonin Raymond, the Czech architect he'd taken on as well, and his thinking was that he'd float the building on a series of piers,* relying for support on cantilevered beams, much in the way of a waiter balancing a laden tray on the adjustable axis of one hand. The Japanese wanted a new and spectacular hotel to replace the antiquated Imperial the Germans had designed for them in the last century, a structure that would symbolize Japan's ascent to the forefront of modern nations, and he was going to give it to them—a building that would be the glory of all Japan and stand proudly a hundred years and more even if the city around it was shivered to dust.†

They were met at the dock by Hayashi-San himself and an entourage of some fifty others, including various dignitaries, members of the Imperial Hotel board, Japanese architects, representatives of the press and any number of beaming young students who looked as if they were about to faint dead away with the anxiety of staring into a white face for what might have been the first time in their lives. A band began to play, something with trumpet fanfares and an erratic drumbeat he didn't recognize. Bows were exchanged. Gifts. Though there was a lingering chill over the ocean, the sun felt unnaturally hot on his face and he found himself sweating beneath the overcoat he'd slung casually over his shoulders. With Miriam at his side he went down the row of greeters, murmuring "*Ohayō gozaimasu*" and bowing to each of them in turn, feeling a burst of confidence and enthusiasm like nothing he'd ever known. He was free of it all, free of all the scandals, the bickering and tantrums of his

* Some two thousand concrete "fingers," as he styled them.
† It was demolished in 1968.

mother and his aunts, the struggle to maintain Taliesin and his practice and keep his head above water financially, and as he bent to the last of the greeters, a white-haired ancient in samurai costume, he caught a single scintillating whiff of Japan on the breeze riding up off Yokohama Bay—an ineffable amalgam of broiled eel, incense and human effluent, and knew he was home at last.

There followed a succession of dinners (running typically to more than two dozen courses), formal teas and ceremonial meetings with what seemed half the population of Tokyo, the greetings so elaborate and extended in those first heady days he barely had time to think about the hotel and the superhuman effort it would take to see it realized in three dimensions. After the drive in from Yokohama in a spanking new Mitsubishi sedan flying the flag of the rising sun, he and Miriam had been installed in a suite of rooms at the old Imperial, a three-story monstrosity of wood, brick and plaster in the heart of downtown Tokyo that featured neo-Renaissance facades and damp cavernous halls in the elaborate gimcrack style of the Second Empire. It was a molding, fermented sort of place that did no one the least lick of good, but at least their rooms opened out onto the courtyard below so that they would have access to fresh air and sunshine. His first order of business was to make himself comfortable, because, as he explained to Hayashi-San as best he could in the absence of a reliable interpreter, he simply could not work in a state of chaos, and as he always did no matter where he was or how temporary his residence, he quickly transformed the rooms into a flowing and elegant space. Before long, he'd acquired a grand piano (the sine qua non, along with a working fireplace, of any home), half a dozen suitable rugs and a few decent screens and hangings, and he positively haunted the shops of the print dealers.* Despite the language barrier—*Dōmo sumimasen, ukiyo-e arimasu-ka?* (Excuse me, do you sell prints?) he asked everyone he met—he was like a child in a candy shop. He'd come to the source and for the first few weeks the hotel seemed almost an afterthought.

But of course it wasn't. It was the commission of a lifetime. And once he'd settled in, once he'd made the rounds of the print shops three or four times each and set up an on-site office and got his assistants to work on the drawings, the rounds of dinners and teas began to wear on him.

One evening, he found himself in yet another teahouse, braced up against the wall on a pristine *tatami* mat while geisha fluttered about and his host—one of the ubiquitous bankers—made long *sake*-inflected speeches about matters that were entirely lost on him. He leaned forward over the low rosewood table, putting on his listening face and struggling to ignore the shooting pains in his knees and at the base of his spine, while Miriam, in a kimono and wearing an embroidered Turkish towel wrapped round her head, sat beside him with her back perfectly arched and her legs folded delicately beneath her, all the while nodding and smiling broadly, as if she not only understood but revered each nugget of wisdom with which Tanaka-San was showering them. They were on the sixteenth or seventeenth course, he couldn't recall which, one morsel of pickled ginger, seaweed and raw

* Wrieto-San was one of the foremost collectors in the world. As has been seen, he made use of his prints as a kind of currency, playing them off against his debts. He realized some $10,000 on the sale of prints just prior to leaving for Japan at the end of this year of 1917, and he was rapidly investing these monies in acquiring a far grander and more extensive collection than anyone in the United States had heretofore seen.

fish succeeding the next as if the chef had spent the entire morning combing the beach and breakwaters and was determined to represent every species in Yokohama Bay laid out on a ceramic saucer in its own drizzle of soya. He wanted a steak. Wanted to go back to the hotel and take up his protractor and T-square, wanted a hot bath, a mug of cider instead of the thin green tea, wanted to quarry stone and pour concrete and *for Christ's sake get on with it.* He wondered if he looked bored. If he was giving offense. His mind drifted.

And then, as if magically, a voice began speaking to him in a tone and accent so flawless he thought he'd been transported back to Wisconsin. Across the table from him, seated beside Yoshitake-San, was a young man in his late twenties, who had heretofore—through the elaborate greetings, the preliminary samisen playing, the *sake* toasts and the first sixteen or seventeen courses—held silence. He wore a mustache like Hayashi-San's and a thin pointed beard. "Wrieto-San, if I may," he was saying, and he bowed from a sitting position. "And Mrs. Wrieto-San." A second bow. "I am Endo Arata, and of course we have met in the confusion of the anteroom, but have not till this moment had the opportunity to communicate."

Startled, Frank simply smiled and nodded. Then he gave his own version of the sitting bow and murmured, "A pleasure, I'm sure."

At the head of the table, Tanaka-San had paused, his hands folded patiently before him. The young man said something to him then in his own language and Tanaka-San, a full-faced man in his fifties who managed to look as if he were attempting to swallow a perpetual goldfish, even when he was speaking, grunted "*Hai.*"

"I am, if you will allow me," Endo-San said, turning back to him with yet another bow, "able to act as an interpreter, as I have acquired some rudiments of your language. What Tanaka-San has said, and please do not take offense because he means only to provide you with an aphorism, one of our reverend sayings of the past: *Deru kugi wa utareru.* And"—a glance for Tanaka-San—"he means it not in reference to you specifically but to the Western style of architecture in general and the way in which he perceives *gaijin*, that is to say, foreigners, to do business—"

Beside him, her voice ringing out its richest tones, he heard Miriam say, "How charming, Endo-San. And what does this mean?"

"Literally?" He looked to Tanaka-San and back. "It means, roughly, 'The nail that sticks up will be hammered down.'"

Miriam, broadly Southern now, the belle in full display: "Oh, then I take it to be an architectural phrase?"

Frank stiffened. There was something afoot here, something lost in translation, a caution, a warning. He looked to Tanaka-San, who was clutching his *sake* cup and swallowing his goldfish, and nodded gravely before turning back to the younger man.

"Not actually," Endo-San said, bowing again as he maneuvered delicately round the question. "It is more a . . . general expression. You see, Tanaka-San"—a glance, a bow—"is commenting on the Japanese way of cooperation, in which the team is always held above the individual and all decisions are group decisions. He understands"—and here Tanaka-San clarified in a burst of guttural Japanese—"that some Westerners are what we call 'one-men'; that is, people who act on their own initiative without regard for the larger group. But that you are not such a man, Wrieto-San, begging forgiveness."

What were they saying? He kept his face neutral as he tried to make sense of it. Didn't they understand that the Imperial was his and his alone? That he'd been appointed because of his genius, because he stood head and shoulders above all the other architects of the world and that he would brook no interference? He looked from one man to the other—and to Yoshitake-San—and now Miriam was trying to fill the silence with her lyrical voice, assuring everyone that she and Frank were as thrilled to be present at this lovely gathering as anybody could imagine. And thanking them for their kindness. And generosity. And the exquisite and absolutely delectable cuisine. She paused, a bright pink morsel of fish roe eclipsing one of her front teeth, and let her smile radiate from one end of the table to the other.

"Which is to say, Wrieto-San, with your permission, I will offer my assistance at every step of the way"—Endo-San paused, struggled to find his own smile—"both as interpreter, and in my humble way, as consultant."*

If Frank was a bit huffy in the car on the way back to the hotel—"Good God, what do they think, they've hired a lackey to do their bidding? If they wanted a lackey why not have one of their own architects design the damned thing, Yoshitake or Endo or how about that man there in the straw hat and dirty *yukata*, he looks like he could use a job"—Miriam was floating on a cloud of serenity. She was Mrs. Wright in the eyes of an entire nation, given the respect and honor she deserved, invited everywhere in the highest circles of Japanese

* Arata Endo is, of course, the illustrious Japanese architect who went on to design the Minamisawa building of Jiyu Gakuen and the Koshien Hotel, among other prominent buildings. He became Wrieto-San's good friend and close associate and was invaluable as a liaison between Wrieto-San—who did tend to be somewhat imperious, to say the least—and the investors' group. Without him, I doubt very much that Wrieto-San, for all his charisma, would have survived the thousand misunderstandings and cost overruns the construction ultimately entailed.

and emigré society—and if she wasn't yet Mrs. Wright in her own country because Frank's pigheaded wife wouldn't grant a divorce, well, she would be, all in good time. And the hotel, though it was gloomy, did provide first-class service—and they had their car and driver and a pair of houseboys to see to their needs. Of course, the streets were of beaten dirt—mud when it rained—and that was something of a shock, and automobiles were as rare as shooting stars, and the food, noodles, miso, fish in one form or another three times a day, was a far cry from what she'd expected (and what she wouldn't give for a charcuterie or even a bistro). But the climate was acceptable and the company an enormous improvement over Chicago.

She was thinking of this—of the invitation for the succeeding evening from Count and Countess Lubiensky of Poland, who had the most charming little house and the most charming of friends, the Russian Princess Tscheremissinoff, Count Ablomov and his wife, a very pretty woman, actually, if her style was somewhat stodgy, and had she really been wearing a bustle?—when the car pulled up in front of the hotel and Frank sprang out in his usual impatient way, barely able to wait for her to gather herself before he had her by the arm, as if he meant to drag her up the walk.

The night was clear and cold. There was the sour odor of smoke on the air, of the braziers the Japanese warmed their feet with—paper walls and no central heating, every house as cold as an icehouse and no fireplaces, of course, else the whole place would burn to the ground every night of the week—and the pervasive tang of fish in all its essences. Red-paper lanterns everywhere, floating on the faintest breeze. The lights of the hotel. Stars overhead. As they made their way up the walk, she couldn't help noticing the cluster of sedan chairs in the street, fifty or more of them, and the coolies loitering beside them. Something must have been going on in the ballroom, Japanese high society having an evening on the town, dancing to the orchestra on the dais, just like people anywhere, in Paris, New York, Memphis. The thought arrested her and she pulled away from him just to stand there a moment and take in the strangeness of it all.

Music drifted down to her then, an odd tinkling sort of music with a rippling rhythmic undercurrent that seemed to tug the melody in another direction altogether, into the depths of a deep churning sea, but beautiful for all that, and so perfect and unexpected. She felt languid and free—all eyes were on her, every man turning to stare—and it came to her that she loved this place, this moment, these people. She could stay here forever, right here, in the gentle sway of the Japanese night.

"Miriam? What are you doing? Come on, will you?" Frank was five paces ahead of her, and he turned now to give her a look of exasperation. He was impatient, always in a hurry to move and make and do, the endless round of social engagements wearing on him, the forced smiles, his clumsiness with the language, the string of toasts with the rice wine he loathed and only pretended to drink.

"Are we in a hurry? Is this some sort of athletic competition? Can't I stop here a minute to take the air? Will that kill you?"

His face bloomed in all its complexity, the wondering frown, lines erupting at his hairline to pull deeper lines yet across his brow and into the creases at the corners of his eyes, and he would never sit for a bust, she saw that now, but no matter, she was busy with other things, helping him, guiding him through the shoals of inelegance and insensitivity and into the safe harbor of politesse, elegance, comportment. Because she could see through all the bowing and scraping, the tender solicitations and doe-eyed looks—these people were quick to take offense and no two ways about it. They would devour him if they could. But she wasn't going to let that happen.

"Please, Miriam. I have work to do."

"I want a cigarette."

Two couples passed them on the steps, the men openly gawking at her, the women riding rhythmically up off their lacquered clogs so that the movement of their haunches was exaggerated—they didn't walk so much as undulate, their every gesture a sexual advertisement.

"Can't you do it inside? People are staring. Come on, I want to go now," he insisted, his voice darkening.

"You don't like me smoking in the rooms."

He let out a sigh, then reached for her arm, but she drew it back.

"If you were a gentleman," she said, watching him as the lanterns washed his face in the gentlest shade of red, like a blush, "you would offer to light my cigarette. And you would stand here beside me for the whole night if that was what I wanted." She was toying with him now, enjoying herself. She took her time extracting her cigarette case and held it out to him so that he could remove a cigarette and offer it to her. When he leaned in close to light it, he murmured her name, twice, in resignation. Very gradually, bit by bit, through moments like this or at the teahouse earlier tonight when she'd eased over all the rough spots for him or at Princess Tscheremissinoff's when she taught him how to behave in society, how to kiss a lady's hand and murmur *"Enchanté"* or *"Je suis desolé de partir,"* she was taming him.

The wind stiffened, rattling the naked branches of the trees and setting the lanterns a-sway. She took her time, smoking the cigarette down to the nub, and then she turned to him—finally, when she was good and ready. "I'm getting cold, Frank," she said. "Let's go in. And by the way, I want you wearing your navy blue suit tomorrow night to the Lubienskys'—none of this Oriental business. It just won't do in polite society."

They stayed three and a half months that first time, leaving in mid-April, just as the weather turned mild and the cherry trees came into bloom. She hadn't been feeling well toward the end, some sort of intestinal disorder eating away at her—the diet, no doubt, eel and sea urchin and all the rest—and though she'd gone off on her own once or twice to make inquiries among the closemouthed, blunt-eyed physicians, she'd been unable to awaken in them even the most rudimentary apprehension of the problem or obtain any aid whatsoever and she'd had to ration her morphine tablets. The voyage back was something of a relief, however, the Western cuisine settling her—and who'd ever have thought that something as simple as an omelet could be so redemptive? And there were the wines, of course, and meats. She really tucked into the meats—she couldn't help herself. Filets mignons Lili, the sauté of chicken Lyonnaise, the roast duckling, the squab, beef sirloin and the pièce de résistance, real *pâté de foie gras* served on rounds cut from a real baguette with a nice *gelée de vin* and a sauterne to complement it.

Naturally, Frank was green-faced the entire time, poor man. He just didn't travel well. Especially on a rolling sea. She nursed him as best she could, but there was life on the ship, a whole society to beguile away the dull dank gray-crested days of the voyage, and she wound up spending a good deal of time simply enjoying herself, and why not? She'd devoted herself to him in Tokyo, giving up any notion of pursuing her own art in order to help him with everything from working out the designs for the textiles to be used throughout the hotel to the chinaware and cutlery (no chopsticks, absolutely, because what they were looking for here was strictly in the Continental mode), and keeping him on his toes and alert to the nuances in the presence of Hayashi-San, Baron Ōkura and the others. Mrs. Wrieto-San. She'd done her duty.

And then they were in Los Angeles, where Frank set up another office with yet another son—Lloyd—having left John behind in Tokyo to supervise as they prepared to break ground for construction the following year. Frank had taken a commission to build some sort of Aztec fortress on a hilltop there for a fat-faced heiress with theatrical pretensions,* and as long as she kept her hands off of him, that was fine with Miriam. There were palm trees in Los Angeles, ocean beaches, and, better yet, Leora's husband was retiring from the exchange business in Chicago and they were in the process of acquiring property in Santa Monica. Of course, Frank's concerns—he was always on the very lip of disaster, both financially and professionally—required a plethora of back-and-forth travel between Los Angeles, Chicago and Taliesin (and Oak Park, where the bank was threatening to foreclose on his wife's house and he was frantically selling off his precious prints to raise money). She tried to take it in stride. Inevitably it affected her nerves—she'd begun to think she put in more hours on the rails than the Negro porters—but her doctor examined her and comforted her and provided her with just the emollient she needed. And then, as soon as she'd begun to feel settled, it was back to Japan and the raw fish and the mincing little geisha and the bowing and scraping and the only honorific she ever cared to accept or adopt, Mrs. Wrieto-San.

* That would be Aline Barnsdall. Her residence, as any architectural buff will know, would come to be called Hollyhock House, after the flowers that grew on the hillside.

Somewhere in there—and in looking back on it she could never be quite sure which trip it was*—Frank fell seriously ill. It was springtime, that much she remembered, because they were out in the country with Baron Ōkura, the princess and some of the others (and here the name Olga Krynska rose up in her memory in a dark gnarl of hate and envy) viewing the cherry blossoms, which were then at the height of their beauty. For the Japanese, a quaint diminutive people so much in tune with nature and the change of the seasons they might have been a nation of satyrs and wood nymphs, the *sakura* bloom was one of the high points of the year, and everyone, from the murkiest slum dweller to the Emperor himself, made a point of celebrating the occasion. When the Baron proposed a blossom-viewing party at his country house, Frank—who'd been working himself to death in a din of noise and dust as his army of masons pounded away at the peculiar volcanic rock he insisted on using for the hotel's superstructure—agreed to take a hiatus. "How would you like a little ramble in the country?" was the way Frank put it to her. "Why not?" she said, because for all its brilliant company, Tokyo was an ugly squat over-bursting city, and its smells and sounds were beginning to weigh on her, especially now that she found herself compelled to leave the windows open in order to keep from stifling. A jaunt in the country sounded like just the thing.

The sky was brilliant that first day, the cherry trees marshaled in rows of pink clouds that softened the horizon as far as she could see or standing solitary on a sculpted slope where they seemed to concentrate the light, flaming

* In all, they made five trips to Japan between 1917 and 1922, staying for a total of thirty-four months. Sadly, the fifth trip marked the last time Wrieto-San would ever again set foot on our soil.

out against the dull grays and greens of the surrounding landscape as if on a stage, and the entire party made a picnic of the occasion, the Baron providing boxed lunches and champagne, various people sketching or reading, lying stretched out on mats in the sun, chatting in the soft revolving tones of perfect contentment. In short, it was an idyll. And she was enjoying herself despite Madame Krynska, the little unattached Pole the Lubienskys had brought along for what seemed the express purpose of separating her from Frank, as if she would ever allow that to happen, even for a minute . . . The champagne was chilled, the sandwiches were of white bread, butter and cucumber instead of rice and raw fish, the servants attentive. She was just communing with the Baron over their mutual love for things Gallic and reflecting aloud on how much the blossoms reminded her of spring in Paris, particularly in the urban oases, the Tuileries, the Jardin des Plantes, the Luxembourg Gardens (and he was as much under her spell as Hayashi-San, leaning forward over his tented knees, his black eyes fixed on her so as not to miss a single syllable), when Frank, who hadn't uttered a word in the past five minutes, suddenly let out a gasp as if the wind had been knocked out of him.

He'd been sitting beside her, or rather just behind her, in a circle that included the Lubienskys and Countess Ablomov, and as she turned round in alarm she could see immediately that he was in trouble—he seemed shrunken all of a sudden, deflated, his skin bleached and bloodless, his legs drawn up under him like a child's. He gasped again, but before she could reach out to him or even call his name he buckled over on his side, both hands clutching his abdomen, his face pressed awkwardly into the grass at the edge of the mat. Her first thought was that he must have had an attack of some kind—only that week Leora had written her in excruciating detail about her husband's heart problems—and even as she scrambled to him on her knees she felt the loss of him, the future closing over her like a dark engulfing cloud, and she would be nobody's widow because she was nobody's wife. She pulled him to her, already in tears, as he attempted, feebly, to push her away. "Frank, what's wrong, what is it?"

He was wincing. He kicked his legs out. Writhed on the grass. He was trying to say something, but she couldn't make out the words.

The others were on their feet now, gathered round in a constellation of apprehensive faces, and no one seemed to know what to do. Someone said it was appendicitis and then someone else said that if it was he'd have to be operated on, but weren't they getting ahead of themselves? Shouldn't someone call for a doctor? That was when La Krynska—slim, young, butter-haired, dressed in some sort of athletic costume and with a badminton racket still clutched in one hand—appeared on the scene, pushing her way through the circle to kneel beside him. "He needs water," she said. "Ice. Here"—and she rose to dip her handkerchief in the ice bucket and press it to Frank's brow—"try this. Does that feel better?"

Miriam felt the champagne float to her head. Here she was on her knees on the lawn of a baronial estate in the mountains overlooking the Kantō Plain and this Pole was kneeling beside her as if they were praying over a corpse, Frank's corpse, and it was the strangest thing in the world. Fear seized her. Loathing. Terror. He was going to die, she was sure of it.

"I need," Frank gasped, and she could see how weak he was, how reduced and mortified, "I want, if someone could help me . . ."

"What, Frank?" she heard herself cry out. "What do you need?"

Krynska let her fingers slip behind his ears a moment, to feel in the hollows there, then pulled back his eyelids to peer into the whites of his eyes. When finally she lifted her head, she let her gaze sweep over Miriam and take in the faces gathered round them. "I'm afraid he's got what we all contract here in Japan at one time or another, we non-Asiatics, that is"—a glance for the Baron, who was shouting over his shoulder for one of the servants to go and fetch the doctor—"and what he needs, most immediately, is a little privacy." She pressed one hand to the cloth on his forehead and looked back down at him. "And a bathroom."

Dysentery was common enough in the Far East, where primitive sanitary practices encouraged its spread, and the Japanese Isles were no exception. No matter how often Frank sang the praises of the cleanliness of the country and its people, the rituals involved in the washing of the hands, the scouring of the public baths, the simplicity and purity of the *tatami* mats and the robes they wore, there was no denying it. Plumbing was nonexistent. Flush toilets unheard of. For all the rustic charm of the lavatories in the inns and private homes—the bamboo screens, the ferns, pottery, flowers—you were nonetheless squatting over a hole in the ground, no different from the hillbillies in the mountains of Tennessee. Miriam could only account herself lucky that she hadn't come down with the scourge.

The Baron summoned the local physician, who tapped and auscultated and peered into Frank's ears and up his nose and confirmed Krynska's diagnosis, after which Frank slept for the better part of two days while Miriam sat beside him in a state of nervous exhaustion and the others took rambles over the hillside, observed the farmers at work in their paddies, played parlor games and watched the cherry blossoms shimmer in the breeze. Then it was back to Tokyo—the driver stopping at intervals so that poor Frank could be helped out to relieve himself—and on to the premier physician in all the country, who tapped and auscultated and peered into Frank's ears and up his nose and put him on a strict diet of water and rice balls and nothing else.

She was shocked. And she took the man aside and told him so. "Is that all you're going to do? Give him rice balls? Can't you see he has a fever?"

The man was tall for a Japanese, with a black brush of the chin whiskers they all seemed to affect. His English was minimal. They stood outside the door of the bedroom, surrounded by the artifacts Frank had collected. "*Hai*," he said, bowing. "Rice ball."

"But he's delirious, soaked in sweat. He's—he's been calling out in the night, talking nonsense." She had a sudden vision of her son Thomas, stricken with influenza when he was boy, the sticks of his legs beneath the sweated sheets, the hair pasted to his forehead, his lips cracked and dry. She'd been sure he was going to die and she was so paralyzed by the thought she couldn't nurse him, couldn't look at him, couldn't even pass by his door without breaking down.

The doctor glanced across the room to where Hayashi-San, who'd attempted to act as interpreter, but with limited success, clutched his hands before him and bowed. "Dysentery," the doctor said. "Very serious."

"But aren't you going to give him anything? Any treatment, any medicine? You do know medicine, don't you?" In exasperation, she turned to Hayashi-San. "Tell him medicine—what is the word for medicine?"

Hayashi-San bowed again and said something to the doctor in Japanese, to which the doctor replied with his own bow before turning back to her. "Rice ball," he said. "Only rice ball."

It must have been a month or so later when she came back from a shopping expedition, feeling as Japanese as she ever would, having haggled with various dealers over a brocade screen, a statue of the bodhisattva Guanyin

Frank had had his eye on and a beautiful little inlaid rosewood table, to find Frank sitting up in bed, looking pleased with himself. Over the past weeks he'd made a steady improvement, graduating from the rice balls to broth, tea and finally noodles with bits of fish and vegetables, but he'd been irritable, frustrated, cursing his foreman, the houseboy, the diet and the delay in construction this was costing him, and, of course, taking it out on her whenever he could. But now he was propped up against the headboard, the bed strewn with books and papers, whistling one of his music hall tunes.

"You look like you're feeling chipper," she said, removing her wrap and draping it over a chair.

He didn't answer. Just kept whistling.

"I got the most adorable little table"—she held off telling him of the bodhisattva, knowing what a fuss he'd make of it, criticizing the smallest flaws, badgering her over the price no matter what she'd paid—"and a screen I thought was quite . . . What's that I smell? Perfume?"

The whistling abruptly died.

There was a tray beside him, the tea things laid out, two cups, English biscuits, *mochi*. "And what's this? You didn't wait tea for me?"

His smile flashed and faded just as quickly. She saw that his hair had been carefully combed and that he was wearing his best robe and one of his stiff high-collared shirts. And a tie. "Oh, yes," he said, as if it were an afterthought, "Olga stopped by to see how I was doing, and we—"

"*Olga?*" she repeated.*

It was at that moment that the bathroom swung open

* Again, the ironies of Wrieto-San's life and attachments seem strangely cosmic, almost surreal, this Olga prefiguring the Olga who would become Miriam's bête noire some five years later.

and Madame Krynska—La Krynska, *Olga*—appeared, a washcloth in her hand. "Oh, Miriam," she chirped, "I didn't know you'd come back. How nice to see you." And she proceeded across the floor of the bedroom as if she were in her own Polish hovel to bend over Frank and lay the wet compress on his forehead, just as she had that day in the country. "Isn't it a marvel how well he's looking?" she said, still bent at the waist and glancing over one shoulder, her petite pretty manicured hand pressed to Frank's brow and Frank looking like a Pomeranian with a belly full of chopped liver.

Miriam was astonished. Slack-jawed. So stunned at the audacity of this woman—of Frank, the cheat, the liar, the adventurer—that she couldn't speak a word.

"There," La Krynska was cooing, her yellow hair burgeoning round her like some unnatural growth, like fur grafted to her head above the yellow paste of her Polish eyebrows, "does that feel better?"

In her own room, in the drawer where she kept her pravaz—right beside it—Miriam also kept a pistol. It was a small shiny thing that held two shots only and she'd bought it in Albuquerque the day she arrived, when she was feeling low, and she couldn't have said why she'd thought to buy it—she wasn't suicidal, not at all, no man could make her sink to that level and no man was worth it, not even the high and mighty Frank Lloyd Wright—except that having it near her, in her purse or in the desk drawer, gave her a sense of security, of power in reserve. She'd never fired it. Never even given it a thought. Till now.

"Miriam," Frank called out in the voice of a dog, the petted voice, false and callow, "come join us. The tea's hot still."

But she was already out the door, already crossing the hall to her own room and the drawer there. She was utterly calm. She fit the key in the lock and pulled out the drawer to reveal the pravaz and the pistol beside it and her hand never trembled the way it sometimes did when she was upset and needed a shot for relief. The pistol—it was called a derringer and she'd known women in Paris who carried such things in their purses in the most casual way—was cold to the touch, as if its shiny nickel plating had just been dug from the earth. She took it in one hand and crossed the hall to Frank's bedroom, all the world solidly in place, his prints and rugs and statues, and La Krynska just bending to the teapot, a thumb pressed to the lid as she lifted it and poured.

It took a moment. Frank's eyes leapt at her and retreated. "Miriam, what are you—?"

"I'll kill her, Frank," she said, and she was pointing the gun now, her finger on the miniature trigger, a sudden tide of emotion gushing up in her so that she was no longer calm, even as her voice rose and rose till it was a shriek, "and you. I'll kill you too. I'll kill both of you!" she screamed. "And myself! Myself too!"

Of course, she killed no one, least of all herself. But she would have—she knew it, she swore it—if that little Pole hadn't bolted out of the room and Frank hadn't come up out of the bed and wrestled the gun away from her. But it was finished in any case. He was a beast. A criminal. He didn't love her and he never had, no matter what he said. And even before she heard the news that his mother was on her way to Tokyo—the old dragon herself—to nurse him through his illness, as if she weren't perfectly capable, as if he hadn't recovered already and put the rice balls and all the rest behind him, she moved out. Bolted the door against him, packed up two suitcases—and no, she wouldn't shed a tear, not for him—and took the train back to the mountains and the dead cherry blossoms and any inn that would receive her. She was in Japan and she would live in Japan as she'd lived in Albuquerque, free of him, rid of him, in exile, one white face among all those yellow ones.

CHAPTER 9: THE AXIS OF BLISS

It was raining heavily as she walked up from the station to the squat wooden inn on the hillside, preceded by a porter carrying her suitcases. Her shoes were all but ruined in the rutted dirt street that resembled nothing so much as a streambed at this juncture, everything dripping and sizzling with the rain, but it didn't really matter—they could toss them on the ash pit for all she cared. She was going native. Throwing off worldly things. Dwelling within herself. And to hell with Frank. She concentrated on the porter's back as the planes of his muscles clenched and shifted under the weight of the suitcases, the water streaming from his straw hat that was like an inverted funnel, the hill rising ever more sharply. She put one foot in front of the other, trying her best to avoid the deeper puddles and thinking only of a bed and a hot bath. There was no one in the street. Nothing stirred. Just the rain.

She came up the single step into the anteroom, furled her umbrella and perched herself on the edge of a bamboo bench to ease into a pair of the slippers lined up on a rack for just that purpose. There was the smell of the charcoal and of *o-cha*, the acrid vinegary tea the Japanese seemed to put away by the gallon, and she had a moment's peace before an old woman in a robe and two bowing maids rushed out to greet her, their thin fixed smiles doing little to disguise their horror at encountering a white woman, a *gaijin*, soaked through and unaccompanied, washed up on their doorstep. They didn't speak English. No one in the entire village did, as she was soon to discover, but she could have been a deaf mute and got what she wanted nonetheless. She used a kind of pantomime to enlarge on her few disconnected phrases—*Dōzo, heya arimasu-ka, nemuri, yoku?**—showed the old woman a folded wad of yen and within minutes found herself barefoot in a tiny Spartan room, drying her hair in a towel while one of the maids served her tea.

Of course, she was wrought up, the scene in the apartment repeating itself over and over in her mind like a moving picture caught in a loop, but the pravaz calmed her and she took rice wine with her dinner—a *kaiseki* of twelve courses, faultlessly prepared, and was she beginning to appreciate the cuisine after all, or was she just starved?—and let the sound of the rain infiltrate her senses. Once the maid had cleared away the tray, she went into the little bamboo cubicle outside the bath and scrubbed herself all over, recording the process in the full-length mirror there, rubbing both hands slowly over her breasts, between her legs, into the small of her back, even lifting her feet one after the other to run the cloth over her soles and between her toes with the slow languorous ease of a bootblack, so that when she stepped through the door and onto the flagstones of the bath she felt as pure and regal as the Empress herself.

Two old men and what appeared to be a woman bobbed in the steaming water, only their heads and bony slick shoulders visible. There were flowers, ferns. Paper lanterns. She shivered, wondering if it was as chilly at the

* Literally, "Please, do you have room, sleep, bath?"

Imperial Palace as it was here on these wintry flagstones, and then she slipped into the water, the old men and the woman studiously averting their eyes, and it was heaven. The next thing she knew the place was deserted, the lanterns burned low, and the maid was there with her robe, murmuring something in her own language that sounded as lovely as the whisper of cherry blossoms in the breeze, and then she was in her room, on the futon, beneath the blankets, and the rain ran a thousand fingers across the roof.

There followed a succession of days during which she saw no one but the maid and the shocked and silent cohabitants of the bath—and oh, they looked at her, stealing a pinched sideways glance as she strode naked across the flagstones, and let them, let them see her as she was in her skin: she had nothing to hide. The bath was a miracle. She lay in the water for hours at a time, dreaming, till her body felt as limp as if the flesh had fallen from the bone. It rained constantly, day and night. She kept her pravaz close at hand. She ate fried rice, boiled rice, rice with salmon and cod roe, *udon* noodles, skewered tofu. She drank black tea. *Sake*. And, finally, a bottle of good scotch whiskey the maid brought her. And was there a pharmacy in town? There was. She sent the maid out with an empty tube of the morphine sulfate tablets and the maid came back with it full.

All the while, when she could summon the energy, the desire, she sat at the low mahogany table in her room and wrote letters to Frank on the thin rippled rice paper the maid left for her on the *tansu* in the closet. They were angry letters, letters that dredged up all the sourness and hate of the past and the present too—*Krynska, how could he?*—and yet they were sentimental at the same time, rising on the wings of poetry to illumine for him the reclamatory power of her love and the hallowed bond they shared that no amount of perfidy or venality or stinking filthy *philandering* on his part could ever break. The letters drained her. Crushed her. The rain fell. And the maid—pretty, perfect, a bowing kimono-clad extension of her will—took the letters to the post office and sent them away.

Within the week, Frank had written back. She came in from the bath and there the letter was, laid out on the mahogany table beside a finger bowl and a single lily in the slim white vessel of a ceramic vase. The first thing she noticed was the artistry with which he'd addressed the envelope—he'd used a brush rather than a pen, his *kanji* as pristine and elegant as any Buddhist master's or Shinto priest's—and that touched her. She pictured him sitting over his drafting table with his finest brush, a look of utter absorption on his face as he dipped the tip of it in the well of the ink stone, funneling his genius into it, creating something beautiful. For her. Even before she read through the letter inside, the nine pages of apologies, pleas and regrets—he was the one at fault, a selfish unthinking lowly impostor of a man who saw what he wanted and took it, and damn the consequences, and could she ever forgive him because Krynska was nothing to him and he'd never so much as kissed her, he swore—her heart went out to him. She read through the letter a second time, then a third, every nerve and fiber of her stirring with the highest regard for the nobility of this man, for his grace, his beauty, his truth and wisdom, and she immediately wrote back, and what she wrote was so deep and so true she might as well have opened a vein and written him in blood.

But she wasn't coming back to him. Ever. Or at least not until he made her his equal, not until the day he threw off the yoke of his prior attachment—his Pussy or Kitty or whatever she called herself—and pledged his troth before God and man alike so that no Krynska or Takako-San could ever threaten her again. That much she made clear. She had to. Just to preserve her own sanity.

His reply—more apologies, more pleas, more regrets—came by return mail, and the minute she'd read it through she clapped her hands and sent the maid for pen, paper and *sake* and wrote him back on the spot. Within the hour her letter was on the way to him and the following day another of his came to her, letters overlapping, reaching out, anticipating one another, so that over the course of the next two months they were able to hold an ongoing conversation through the slow but estimable Japanese mails, their pens assessing even the minutiae of their attachment, their love and esteem and mutual complaints—his snoring, eating habits, the way he sniffed his socks on removing them, his bossiness, his rusticity, and her faults too, though of course they were minor compared to his—and to branch out in the fullness of that conversation to easy companionable accounts of their day-to-day activities while they were apart.

His life was a frenzy of activity, of course. He was on the job site day and night, battling Hayashi-San and the Baron over every change and cost overrun, struggling with the permeability of the *oya* stone they'd quarried outside the city (it would forever leak, he feared, but it was beautiful beyond compare) and seeing to his mother's needs. Yes, she was there. Still. She'd come all the way across the board-flat plains and jagged mountains of the West, endured the two weeks at sea and rushed to her (formerly) ailing son's side only to come down with the very same complaint that had stricken him. It was low comedy, that was what it was, and Miriam, cleansed in the crucible of the bath and replete with the utter calm the pravaz gave her, laughed aloud at the thought of that gangling old lady—and how old was she, eighty, eighty-five?—towering over the Japanese like a freak of nature only to be stretched out on a too-short futon and fed rice balls and water till she could only wish she'd stayed in Wisconsin where she belonged.*

And for her part? She told him of the sound of the rain, of the emerald beauty of the stands of bamboo that clustered on the hillside like queues of silent people waiting for something that would never come and the strange tiny birds that visited them. Of her daily rituals, her reading and writing and the solace of the baths. Of the shaven-headed monks in the temple with its painted dragons and graceful *torii* and the way it made her feel as if she could touch the spirits with the pointed finger of her mind when they chanted, all in unison, and let the charred spice of their incense rise round them in empurpled clouds. She was at peace, that was what she told him, and she never mentioned the pravaz or the pharmacy or the adept maid who would lay down her life for her if she but asked. All she could want, she wrote, was for him to take her in his arms. That was all. That would make her world complete. But she wasn't holding her breath. And she wasn't coming back.

Two months. A gap in the calendar. Slow minutes, slower hours.

Each day was a replica of the last, but she was never bored. The everlasting tranquility of the saints came to dwell in her and she lived as if she were floating free out over the earth in some aeroplane or dirigible—or no, on her own fledged wings. Still, there was the impenetrability of the language, the harshness and abruptness of it, noth-

* Wrieto-San's mother was eighty-one when she came to Tokyo, where she was revered by everyone who came into contact with her. In Japan, unlike America, we honor the old for the passage of their years and the diachronic luxury of their thoughts. They are living artifacts and they are people, not abandoned husks to be shunted off to the purgatory of nursing home and hospice.

ing at all like the silken play of French. And the fish, the eternal fish, their opaque eyes staring up at her out of the multiplicity of the days, their sliced flesh raw as a wound, their tails, their lips, their appendages. And the mud. And the rain. Two months. She was ready for a change.

And so when, one evening after her bath, the maid's soft swishing footsteps stirred on the wooden planks of the anteroom, followed by a heavier tread, a man's tread, she sat up, fully alert. And when the *shoji* slid back with a soft click and he stood there grinning in the doorway, she was already on her feet, already moving across the *tatami* to him, her arms rising of their own volition to pull him to her. "Miriam," he said, as the maid ducked away like the shadow of a bird and she fell into his arms, her blood surging so violently she was afraid she was going to crush him. But oh, the smell of him! The touch of his lips at her throat! "Frank," she cried. "Oh, Frank, Frank, Frank."

They stayed on there together for five days. She showed him the trails on the hillside, the temple, the shops, pointed out the little yellow birds and the funny old man at the tobacconist's who'd cut a perfect pie slice out of his conical hat so he could see the sky above him. Frank found a trove of prints in an out-of-the-way shop even the Tokyo dealers didn't seem to know about, haggling over a dozen rare specimens, including at least one he immediately inaugurated into the pantheon of his favorites—it was a Shunshō, very colorful, dating from 1777, of the actor Ichikawa Danjūrō V in a red robe. When the money changed hands, he looked as if he wanted to get up and caper round the room, but she held him back because he had to save face for the dealer and his children and everyone else who came out to stare as they all but minced up the street, arm in arm.

They bathed together. Sat out in their *kosode* in the

evening and watched the sun plunge into the hills. They ate and laughed and made the futon rock on the *tatami* as if it were a creaking four-poster under the weight of the newest newlyweds in the oldest inn in Wisconsin. And when they left to go back to Tokyo—together—she had a shining promise to hold out before her, rarer and more beautiful than all the prints in the world: Kitty had relented after all these years and they were going to be married.

Just as soon as possible.

Three years later, as she sat fanning herself in the shade of an avocado tree in the back garden of Leora's little Spanish villa in Santa Monica, she was still waiting. Frank had been true to his word, she couldn't fault him there—or yes, she could, because he'd dragged his feet through every conceivable delay and evasion till she thought she was going to die unwed like some sad deluded cast-off little strumpet in a morality play. But at least he was free now, at least he'd seen to that. The divorce had been granted back in November and all that remained was to wait out the twelve-month probationary period before Frank could remarry, and the clock was ticking down on that too—in just over two and a half months she would be Mrs. Frank Lloyd Wright.

"What are you going to wear? For the wedding, I mean?" Leora tipped the ash from her cigarette against the lip of the urn Miriam had brought her from Japan and then looked away, as if they'd been discussing the length of the grass or the color of the drapes in the guesthouse. She was in her bathing costume, a blue woolen suit with a ruffled white skirt, her wet hair bound up in a towel, and she idly stretched her legs and flexed her toes to admire her pretty feet and freshly painted toenails. "You don't still have—?"

Miriam let out a laugh. "Lord, no. God, it's been so long. I was just a girl then. A child." She smiled at the memory. "No, I envision a small private ceremony, something unconventional, spiritual—midnight, maybe."

"Midnight? Well, I guess that *would* be unconventional. People will think—"

"That's just it—we don't care what people think. And I don't want the press there. You know what a nuisance the newspapers have been."

Leora didn't have anything to say to that. She set her legs back down on the wooden slats of the chaise, lifted her drink from the table. The wind—some sort of Californian sirocco, dry as dust—chased a scatter of spade-shaped avocado leaves across the patio and into the pool. She let out a sigh. "At least you don't have to worry about the mother," she said.

The old dragon's face rose up briefly in Miriam's consciousness—*Don't you dare call me by my given name: I'm Mrs. Wright to you and don't you ever forget it*—like a lump of driftwood bobbing in the murk of the Wolf River. "Yes," she said, "and thank God for small mercies."

Of course, now that the war had been won, she could be facetious about it, not that she'd ever disrespect the dead. But there was a time when it was no laughing matter. Taliesin had always been a trial to her, but when they came home from Japan for good* and Frank insisted on dragging her all the way across America to play at being the country grandee, his mother was entrenched there, undisputed mistress of the house, and she wasn't about to give an inch. From the minute they arrived, the old lady had started in, carping about her accent, her mannerisms, her dress, contradicting everything she said out of pure spite. If she said she'd like to open the windows to get a breath of air, the old dragon practically nailed them

* In the summer of 1922. They left Japan in July and were at Taliesin by mid-August.

shut. Mention the menu—hadn't anyone ever heard of a salad?—and she'd have the cook boil the lettuce. If Miriam wanted Frank to take her to Chicago or out to a restaurant or even into Spring Green to watch the dust settle in the street, the old lady suddenly developed the flu or her sciatica flared up and if her boy wasn't there to cluck his tongue over her she'd just about curl up and die. It was as if they'd never left. It was 1916 all over again.

And Miriam wouldn't tolerate it. She told Frank that point-blank. But this time she wasn't going to lie up in her room like some dog he'd abused—oh, no, she'd had enough. She directed Billy Weston to bring the car around and take her into Spring Green, where she was going to put up at the hotel until Frank could give her an answer to the question she'd put to him back then—"Who's it going to be: her or me?"—and hang the expense, because hitting him in the pocketbook was the only thing he could seem to understand. The mama's boy. The waffler. And before she left, with the car standing in the drive and the motor running and Frank wringing his hands in the studio or out in the stable or wherever he was, she marched right into the old lady's room to give her a piece of her mind.

It was mid-afternoon, hotter than the front porch of the devil's place down in Hades, and she took her by surprise, startling Anna up out of a nap in the armchair next to the bed. There were flies at the windows. A smell of camphor, ointment. Medicine bottles crowded the table beside her. Two of Frank's prints were propped up on the bureau, gifts he'd brought back for her. The old lady's head snapped up. "You get out of here," she growled, her voice caught low in her throat.

Miriam dispensed with the preliminaries, because this was it, the battle joined at long last. "You know you're destroying your son's last chance for happiness, don't you?" she demanded.

Anna made a shooing motion with the back of her

hand and tried to push herself up out of the chair but fell back again. "I won't talk to you. You're a cheap woman. A tramp."

"You will. You will talk to me. Because Frank is going to marry me whether you like it or not."

A glare. A tightening of the mouth, as if a noose had been pulled tight. "Not while I'm alive."

She loomed over the woman, so full of hate and rage and frustration it was all she could do to stop from snatching her up out of the chair and shaking her like a bundle of rags. The tremor ran up her spine and shivered the back of her neck. She felt as if she were going to faint but she fought it. She had to. Had to have this out once and for all. "Then you'll just have to die," she said. "Frank and I are engaged, do you understand that? Engaged to be married. As soon as the divorce is final—the very day, I promise you—*I'll* be Mrs. Wright and *I'll* be giving the orders around here. And I won't let you or anyone else stand in my way."

There was more. The old lady crying out like a parched peahen, struggling to get up out of the chair and nobody there to hear or help her either and Miriam acquainting her with the truth in all its unvarnished detail. Then it was the hotel and Frank running back and forth between the two of them, the biggest crisis of his life, the days burning into the sweated nights, and within the month Anna was gone and Miriam had Taliesin all to herself, triumphant at last.*

And now, sitting beneath the avocado tree in Leora's garden while Frank oversaw the construction of his block houses in Pasadena and Hollywood and Leora's husband

* But did she want it, truly? As for Wrieto-San's mother, her health fell off rapidly through that autumn and she died in a nursing home in the town of Oconomowoc, Wisconsin, in February of the following year, when Wrieto-San and Miriam were in Los Angeles. By all accounts, he did not return for the funeral.

slapped a little white ball around a golf course, she took a moment to let the weight of it sink in. Her nemesis was dead. And she wouldn't speak ill of the dead—or think ill of her either. All that was behind her, a bad dream dispelled in the light of day. "Yes," she said finally, "there's that, at least. And I was thinking of designing my own gown, something—oh, I don't know, artistic, Grecian, a simple little thing. Not satin. Crepe de chine maybe. And not white. White's for the first time around." She paused to lift her eyes to the rich foliate canopy above her, the leaves dancing on the breeze. "Something in taupe maybe. Or pearl. And my furs, of course."

Leora let out a little hoot of a laugh and treated her to her half smile, the one she used for intimacies, ironic or otherwise. "Amen," she said. "Outdoors, at night, in Wisconsin? In November, no less?"

Miriam was feeling insuperable, at peace with herself and Frank and the specter of his dead mother too. All the stars were aligned. Everything was in place. She could indulge in the luxury of anticipation. "Yes," she said, returning the smile, and she was almost giddy with the joy bubbling up in her, "it's not exactly Palm Beach, is it?"

Later, after a light luncheon and a girlish frolic in the pool, they sent the Chinese houseboy in to mix another round of cocktails and had separately turned back to the magazines they'd been flipping through off and on all afternoon, when the gate from the drive swung open and Leora's husband appeared in his golfing togs and crisp white cap, a bag of clubs slung over one shoulder. "Dwight!" Miriam sang out. "Come join us—we're just about to have cocktails." "Yes, do!" Leora called. "It's that kind of day, don't you think?" And for some reason, they both broke out in giggles.

Miriam watched him set down his clubs, prop them carefully against the fence and start across the lawn in his loose easy strides, his shoulders slumped in the conciliatory way of very tall men. She'd always liked Dwight. He was uncomplicated, stalwart, mild without being wishy-washy, and he treated Leora as if she were the only woman on earth.

"Don't mind if I do," he said, ducking in out of the sun. "Hot out there on the course, what with this devil's wind . . ." He stood a moment, arms akimbo, grinning down at them, and if Miriam had the sense that he was looking down the front of her bathing costume and admiring her bare legs, well, so much the better. He *was* a sweet man. And appreciative.

The conversation ran off on its own, light and amusing, the banter of three old friends united under an avocado tree on a late summer afternoon within sight of the distant sun-coppered crescent of the Santa Monica Bay, and the Chinese brought the beaded cocktails on a lacquered tray and Miriam felt her mood lift to yet a higher plane. They were midway through their second cocktail when Dwight suddenly leaned back in his chair and slapped his forehead. "Jeez," he said, letting out a hiss of air, "I nearly forgot—did you hear the news? Because I thought of you right away, and Frank, because you were over there—"

"News?" Leora's smile expanded till her lips drew tight. "How could we hear any news"—and she giggled again, this time in a thicker, throatier way, the gin at work—"when we've hardly moved between the chair and the pool all day?"

"The earthquake. In Tokyo. Everybody in the clubhouse was talking about it."

Miriam felt her own smile fade. Frank had been obsessed with earthquakes the whole time they were in Japan, and there was the one that struck when they were in their rooms at the hotel, terrifying in its suddenness, as if a freight train had come right on through the door and out the window all in a minute's time. "Was it—is it serious? I mean, do they know if there's been damage—?"

Dwight turned to her, the wind rattling the stiff leathery leaves overhead. His eyes faded a moment and then flickered back to life. "Oh, yeah," he said, "yeah. They're saying it's bad. Buildings down, fires, the whole works."

"And the hotel? Did they say about the hotel?"

In the next moment she was up out of her chair, the suit clinging damply to her as she hurried barefoot across the yard and into the house to call Frank. Her heart was pounding as she stood dripping on Leora's carpet in the dim hush of the front hallway and waited for the operator to connect her—she was imagining the worst, the Imperial in ruins, Frank's reputation destroyed, the Baron and the Ablomovs and Tscheremissinoff transformed into refugees, or worse, injured, killed—when Frank came on the line. "Hello? Miriam, is that you?"

She didn't have to ask if he'd heard—his voice betrayed him. "Yes," she said, and a calm came over her because she was going to stand by him no matter what, prove herself, defend him in the face of the whole world, "it's me. I've just heard the news."

There was a crackle of static. "They're saying"—his voice sank so low she could barely hear him—"that it's the worst earthquake in the history of Japan. And that Tokyo took the brunt of it."*

* I was in school in Washington at the time, but my parents had returned to Japan, so the reverberations of the great Kantō earthquake shook the ground beneath my feet nonetheless. All communications were down. Rumors ran wild. I don't think I slept for a week—impotent, terrified for my reverend parents and my countrymen too. Estimates of the dead ran to 150,000 as the fires reduced the city to cinders. When finally my father's telegram arrived—their apartment had been spared; they were both uninjured—I went out in a daze to sit by the Potomac and sob into my two cupped hands, living vessel of my relief.

"Any word of the hotel?"

"No. Nothing."

She couldn't seem to catch her breath. The receiver of the phone was dead weight in her hand—it took an effort of will just to hold it to her ear. "I don't care," she said, the words coming so fast she could scarcely get them out, "because I can see it standing there now, not a window shattered, a testament to you, to you, Frank, even if the whole city's destroyed around it, and I don't care what they say, I don't—"

They were in limbo for twelve interminable days.

The papers were full of the story, headlines trumpeting disaster, the least detail pried from the wreckage by the ghouls of the press, but nothing was certain, no one could be trusted till the full accounting was in. Frank was so distracted he couldn't seem to sit in a chair for more than two minutes at a time. He paced endlessly. Lost his appetite. Let his work lag while he twisted the radio dial and worried the newspapers. The cruelest moment was when they were awakened by the phone ringing in the middle of the night only to have a reporter from the *Examiner*, full of himself, full of the joy of Schadenfreude, crow over the line that the Imperial had been destroyed and wondering if Frank had a statement to make. Miriam came up out of the morass of sleep, groggy, drugged, buried in a river of oneiric mud, saying, "What? What?" And his voice was there, in the dark, crackling with outrage, truth against the world: "On what authority? How do you know? Have you been there and back on a magic carpet? No, no: you listen to me. The Imperial Theater might have gone down, the Imperial Hospital, the Imperial University and all the thousand other buildings that trumpet the Emperor's connection, but if there's a structure standing in all that torn country it will be my hotel. And you can print it!"

How she loved him for that—for his fierceness and

certainty. Get his back up against the wall and he'd fight like a lion. She lay there that night listening to his breathing decelerate, declining through the layers of consciousness till he was asleep beside her, her man, her fiancé, her very own personal genius, Frank Lloyd Wright, creator of the Imperial Hotel, may it stand ten thousand years. And even as she drifted off she heard the workers chanting all the way across the spill and tumult of the waves, *Wrieto-San, Wrieto-San, banzai!*

The telegram finally reached them on the evening of September 13. It had been forwarded through the Spring Green office to their apartment in Hollywood just as they were sitting down to dinner. Frank's hands quivered as he tore it open. And then his face flushed and he was reading it aloud:

> FOLLOWING WIRELESS RECEIVED FROM TOKIO TODAY HOTEL STANDS UNDAMAGED AS MONUMENT OF YOUR GENIUS HUNDREDS OF HOMELESS PROVIDED BY PERFECTLY MAINTAINED SERVICE SIGNED OKURA IMPEHO*

And now the press could feed on him to its heart's content. Now she and Frank could open the doors and stand there arm in arm for the photographer's flash and

* There has been a continuing controversy among scholars over the authenticity of this telegram, any number of whom question its provenance, claiming on the evidence that Wrieto-San himself composed it and contrived to have it sent to him from Spring Green rather than Tokyo, as a kind of rhetorical feather in his cap. Both O'Flaherty-San and I reject these claims. In any case, the telegram's sentiments are incontrovertible and the proof of it was the fact that when the dust cleared the Imperial stood proud and undamaged while all of Tokyo lay in ruins at its feet. Or, rather, its foundations.

Frank could prance and crow and sermonize and she, in the shadows no longer, could stand at his side and broadcast his genius to the wide world. She was so proud of him. And he—beaming, glowing like a one-hundred-watt bulb and offering up his grandest smile—he was proud of her.

In the wake of that—the tumult of the press and the international outpouring of awe and gratitude and congratulation that rocketed Frank so far ahead of his competitors and critics that he became, in a single heroic stroke, the most famous architect in the world and no one even to raise a whisper to deny it—the next two months slipped by so quickly she scarcely knew where they went. She kissed Leora on both cheeks, in the French way, her eyes full and her heart luminous, and then she and Frank returned to Wisconsin to make themselves ready, one more shriving of the soul and the flesh too. She was a new person altogether, newborn, and she stood at the tall living room windows looking down the long avenues of light and felt herself open up inside, lifting higher and higher till she was a bright fluttering pennant on a breeze that could never chill her again. The trees gave up their leaves. The weather turned bitter. The lake froze so hard it could have supported the weight of every automobile and tractor in the county. And the night sky was clear all the way to the rooftop of the universe, the stars strung from its beams in a cool white shatter of bliss. For her. For her and Frank.

They could have been married in Los Angeles or even Chicago (quietly, quietly, because whether they bowed to convention and he legitimated her with his ring and a kiss as if they were just any common Joe and Jane was nobody's business), but the symbolism of Taliesin was irresistible and when he proposed it she didn't demur or even hesitate. "Yes," she said, "there's no place

I'd rather be," and for once she meant it. This was where his heart was, this was where his mother lay buried and the ghost woman too, Mamah, the phantasm she'd had to compete with through all these gratuitous years at his side. It was perfect. She'd have it no other way. And if the wind screamed down out of Canada and the hogs threw up their stink and the rubes sat stupefied in their parlors while her light shone out over the ice-bound river in the witching hour of the night, then so much the better.

But now it was a question of shoes. Of her dress. Flowers. A midnight supper. The cake. Would there even be a cake? Did it make any sense? Who was going to eat it? If it were up to Frank they'd dine on cheese sandwiches and apple cider, but she would have champagne, crepes, caviar, and she wouldn't discuss it, not for a minute. If he thought she was going to get married without a champagne toast and at least the semblance of real cuisine, then he'd gone mad. Clear out of his mind. Cuckoo. She fought to stay calm as the day approached, though she wanted to fly out at the maid, the cook, at Billy Weston and anyone else who crossed her path, and she could see that Frank was wrought up too. More than once she heard his enraged voice echoing through the caverns of the house like the report of distant thunder, but he put on a face for her—and she for him. In fact—and it moved her so deeply she found herself dabbing her eyes to realize it—they were tenderer with each other than they'd been since that fraught and glorious week when they first met, when she was his ideal made flesh and her every movement bewitched him.

She hid herself away on the night of the wedding, bathing and dressing and making herself up with a precise measured care that took her through each step of the way as if she were rehearsing her catechism, and no, she didn't need the maid's help or the pravaz's either. She was purposeful, calm, utterly absorbed in the moment.

On her lips was the poem she'd committed to memory for him, the best translation she could make of the scroll that had hung in her *tatami* room in the green fastness of the mountains above the Kantō Plain when he came to take her away. It was from the hand of a woman who'd lived a thousand years ago at the court of the Empress, in a time devoted to the fulfillment of the senses, to beauty, poetry, art and love, and she would give it up to him there, in the cold of the primeval night as the stars wheeled overhead and the judge intoned the immemorial phrases and the ring slipped over her finger.

She spoke it aloud one final time, lingering over the rhythms and the aching sweet release of its sentiment. "'The memories of long love, / gather like drifting snow,'" she murmured, watching herself in the mirror—beautiful still, still unspoiled, still capable of ascending to the very highest plateau of love and grace abounding—even as her voice dropped to a whisper, "'poignant as the Mandarin ducks / who float side by side in sleep.'"

She held her own eyes a moment, looking as deeply into herself as she dared, and then she went out to marry him.

PART III MAMAH

INTRODUCTION TO PART III

Wrieto-San liked soft pencils. In his paternal—some would say tyrannical—way he banned hard pencils from the drafting room, but there were many among us who preferred them for the crispness and authority of the lines they produced, Herbert Mohl in particular. Herbert was sensitive to criticism, as we all were, but he'd been around Taliesin longer than any of us and we deferred to him, so that there was a period there during which people began to use hard 4H pencils for their drawings in defiance of Wrieto-San's dictates. (And *he* preferred soft pencils because their lines were easier to erase, as he was continually erasing while he drew and thought and revised and drew and revised again—"The eraser is the most important instrument of the architectural design," he used to say, making it one of his mantras.) One afternoon—it was cold, winter shrouding the windows, a certain post-luncheon lethargy casting a pall over the drafting room—he emerged suddenly from his office to stroll amongst us, as he did twenty times a day, and we all rose to our feet in deference. "Good God, it's like a meat locker in here!" he cried. "Can't any of you keep up the fire?"

We all looked to the fireplace. There was a fairly good blaze going, three tiers of logs stacked up and the flames licking upward from a healthy bed of coals—in fact, Wes had laid on another log not five minutes before—but of course all that mattered was the Master's perception, not ours. Dutifully, I left my desk and bent to the fire with the poker in hand so as to settle the logs, then laid on another neatly split length. "Ah-ha!" I heard Wrieto-San call out behind me even as the Lucullan heat scorched my face and hands. "Hard pencils! You, you're guilty, aren't you, Herbert? And you, Marian. And, Wes—not you, Wes, tell me it isn't true!"

He was being facetious, of course—you could hear the lilt in his voice and know he was in a capital mood—but there was a treacherous undercurrent here as well. By the time I'd swung round (I used soft pencils only, incidentally, both as a matter of preference and in homage to the Master) he'd snatched up all the hard pencils he could find, darting round the room like a leprechaun or whatever the Welsh equivalent might be, and tossed them into the heart of the blaze. Then he sprang up on a drafting stool and spread his arms wide. "I've just snatched victory from the jaws of defeat!" he sang (a phrase he usually reserved for the occasion of making alterations to our drawings), and we all, but for Herbert, laughed aloud.

I tell this story because it illustrates the kind of hold Wrieto-San exerted over us all whether we rebelled in an attempt to define our individual selves or not. Herbert continued to use hard pencils on the sly, just as I used soft ones—as I still do today—but the point is, every time we put pencil to paper Wrieto-San was in our thoughts. And, of course, as I've indicated, it wasn't just architectural matters over which he held sway, but everything else as well, from our diets to the clothes we wore and the automobiles we drove to whom we chose to date or marry.

Perhaps I did subvert his wishes here, on this last

point, but I feel to this day that I was justified—I didn't need to be treated like a child, nor did Daisy. If we came together in love and affection and a mutuality of taste and interest and outlook, that was nobody's business but our own. Or so I thought. Until Wrieto-San—and Mrs. Wright, who was equally culpable—disabused me of that notion.

I could see it coming, of course, from that very first day after Daisy's arrival when both the Wrights gave me a good dressing-down, but when the boom finally fell, I was unprepared for it nonetheless. Or, no (and why, at this distant remove, must I be so ridiculously proper?)—I was stunned. Heartbroken. Scalded by the sheer audacity and treachery of it. Still, I don't think it would have happened in quite the way it did—or perhaps at all—if they hadn't been hyper-sensitized around that time by Svetlana's elopement with Wes.

Of all the apprentices—and we each curried favor in his own way, even Herbert, who was the best draftsman amongst us—Wes was clearly the anointed one. If any job needed doing, Wes was there, always the first to anticipate the Master's needs, wants and moods (and this was a real trick—we had to be vigilant at all times, so that if, for instance, we spied Wrieto-San strolling off in the direction of the vegetable garden or the stables, we had to get there ahead of him and know what it was he wanted done before he did). And when Wrieto-San called out a name for preferment, consultation, companionship, it was nearly always Wes'. It hurts me to say it, but Wes was more a son to him than his own sons, and the affection he had for Wes was as easy to read as his body language and the quick sharp snap of his eyes when Wes entered the room. It hurts me to say it because I wanted to be that son with all my heart and soul—we all did.

Svet and Wes were thrown together at the outset, almost in the way of brother and sister, and yet they were anything but. Wes was in his early twenties when he appeared at Taliesin, the first member of the Fellowship (if you exclude Herbert Mohl, who'd begun as a paid draftsman and stayed on, with no more salary than the rest of us, during the tenuous years of the Depression), and Svet was just shy of sixteen. She'd grown up with a love of the outdoors and participated fully in the Taliesin life, taking her turn in the stables or the kitchen or out in the fields like any of us. Early on, she learned to drive, both the automobiles and the tractor, and she was especially adept on horseback. She was musical, and, as I've said, she was pretty, more often than not dressing in blue jeans and a simple blouse, with her hair in pigtails, and managing to look as captivating as any sophisticate out of Chicago or New York. Wes fell for her, just as I fell for Daisy, and who could blame him?

I don't know how Wrieto-San found out about it. He was so enveloped in his cloud of genius—and I wouldn't want to call it solipsism or privilege or *droit du roi*—that he didn't necessarily see the needs and emotions of others. My guess is that Mrs. Wright, constantly manipulating each of the threads of her web like a great painted spider, if you'll forgive the image, alerted him to what was going on under his very nose. At any rate, Wes was exiled to his parents' place in Evansville, Indiana, and Svetlana was sent to Winnetka, Illinois, to keep house for the family of the concertmaster of the Chicago Symphony Orchestra in exchange for musical instruction. They continued seeing each other during this period, however, and they were married two years later, after which Wrieto-San put out overtures and they returned to Taliesin. Shortly thereafter, Wes, having come into his inheritance on the death of his father, was able to rescue Taliesin from yet another attempt at foreclosure due to habitual non-payment of mortgage, taxes and fees accruing. He proved to be a boon as a son-in-law, enabling Wrieto-San to get back on his feet financially and begin to acquire a great deal of the surrounding acreage, including the parcels on which Reider's pig farm and Stuffy's Tavern stood, at fire-sale prices.

But the point of all this is Daisy. Daisy and me. We stole what time we could, so eager for the touch of each other's bodies that we engaged in the kind of reckless sexual behavior—the aforementioned trysts in the fields and at the top of Romeo and Juliet, slipping in and out of rooms and automobiles in the dark of night—that could have got us exiled as well, and of course there was always the risk of pregnancy. Which would have meant the intercession of her parents, frantic cables to my father in Tokyo, perhaps even arrest and prosecution for fornicating, miscegenating and God knew what else. Disgrace, certainly. The wrath of Wrieto-San. We had little choice but to lie low, and yet what we longed for was some time to ourselves, independent of Taliesin and the Wrights *in loco parentis*, and finally we got the opportunity. Wrieto-San and Mrs. Wright went off to Chicago for a week on business—this was at the height of summer, the year after Svet and Wes had left Taliesin—and Daisy and I counted off the minutes of one breathless hour, then threw a suitcase in the Bearcat and took off down the same road to the Windy City.

We could have gone to Milwaukee or Madison, I suppose, but we wanted a taste of the real thing, of jazz music, eclectic cuisine, the crush of people, and we never thought twice about it—Chicago was the only place to go. No one would recognize us there, and if we kept our displays of affection private, there was no reason to think that anyone would notice us either—or take exception to what we represented as a couple. They might think that I was a foreign exchange student (which, in a sense, I was) and Daisy the daughter of the family that had sponsored me (which, in a sense, she was) or perhaps a sister of mercy, an interpreter of Asiatic languages, a sightseeing guide with a soft spot for handsome, cultivated Japanese men.

"I want a beer—and a whiskey—in one of those speakeasies Al Capone shot up," was the first thing she said to me after we'd checked into our very modest hotel, separately, in our separate rooms, though it sickened me to have to pay double for the sake of appearances. "I want to see the holes in the walls. I want to run this little finger"—she held up her index finger—"round one of those holes. Just for the thrill of it."

"Sure," I said, "me too. I can be a gangster and you can be my moll—do you want to be my moll?"

We were waiting for the elevator. There was no one around. I leaned in close and kissed her even before she slid her skirt up one leg to expose an imaginary garter and said "*Sí, certo,* of course I'll be your moll, *signore,*" because we were like two kids playacting and I loved the way her eyes widened and her lips parted in expectation. We were in Chicago. We were free. And we had the whole afternoon and evening ahead of us, and two heady days beyond that.

I somehow got the notion that we should at least drive past the scene of the St. Valentine's Day massacre, which was on the north side, in the Lincoln Park area, and at that moment, truthfully, I'd forgotten all about Wrieto-San. Deep down, buried in some back room of my consciousness, I knew that he was somewhere out there in the confusion of pedestrians, streetcars, towering buildings and sun-striped boulevards, that he was very likely stopping at the Congress Hotel or paying a surprise visit to the Robie house or taking the air on Michigan Avenue, but I left the knowledge there. We climbed into the Cherokee-red Bearcat in the warm atomized sweetness of the late afternoon and let the breeze wash over us as I fought my way through the welter of cars and did my best to ignore the hooting horns and the double takes of one driver or another. The top was down. Of course it was down. It was summer. In Chicago. And we were out in the thick of it.

As I've said, I wasn't much of a driver, and though I'd gained confidence on the backroads of Wisconsin, negotiating big-city traffic was another thing altogether. We were lost almost immediately—we never did find the St. Valentine's garage or a tavern with holes in the walls, but we did manage a few beers in a bar and grill so murky and grime-encrusted it could have been the real thing. There were discolored flecks of some glutinous substance decorating the wall behind the table, which Daisy, lighting a cigarette in perfect nonchalance, claimed was blood but was more likely just catsup. Or marinara sauce, in keeping with the clientele. We ordered sandwiches, listened to the jukebox, kept our hands to ourselves. Nonetheless—I think we were on our third beer at the time—one of the patrons at the bar, who'd been speaking an animated Italian with his cronies, lurched over to our table and accused me of being a Chinaman, which I hotly denied. I didn't like his face. I didn't like his eyes. And things could have gotten violent very quickly if Daisy hadn't taken hold of my arm and jerked me through the door and out onto the street as if I were a limp fish she'd caught on the end of a very taut line.

At any rate, the beers didn't improve my sense of direction—or my sense of coordination with respect to gear shift, clutch and steering wheel, those essential tools of the road master—and we were lost on the way back too. I did manage to locate Lake Shore Drive and found a street heading west off of it that looked vaguely familiar even as Daisy insisted she'd never seen it before. It was then—and we weren't quarreling, not really, though we were both, I think, frustrated by the endless detouring, backtracking, lurching and bucking, and eager to get back to the hotel—that I spotted Wrieto-San. We were stuck in a line of cars at a stoplight, the fall of day thickening the shadows in the alleyways, exhaust rising hellishly round us, and he was on the far side of the street, swaggering along in his usual way, twirling his walking stick, chatting with Mrs. Wright and a round-shouldered man in a gray suit who followed half a step behind. In that moment, Daisy saw him too. She let out an expostulation—or more of a squeak, actually—then ducked her head down beneath the dash, compressing her shoulders and pinching her knees together so tightly I was afraid she was going to burrow down through the floorboards and into the pavement beneath.

I held absolutely rigid, as if by freezing myself in space and time I could render myself invisible or at least inconspicuous—daylight *was* closing down and there were cars and people everywhere to provide cover—but then how inconspicuous could the only Japanese on the street hope to be? Especially as he was presented center-stage in a Stutz Bearcat automobile in the one shade of color most likely to attract the Master's eye? Don't ask. Because I wouldn't want to have to answer the question myself. At any rate, the denouement had Wrieto-San and his party passing by, apparently oblivious, till he turned the corner and was gone.

I never had the courage to ask him if he'd seen me that day—seen us—even after the war when I came back to visit at Taliesin. He gave no sign of it when he and Mrs. Wright returned at the end of the week (and Daisy and I were hard at work on the upkeep of the place, taking our turns with the dishes and the hogs and all the other tasks the apprentices were assigned on a rotating schedule), but it was shortly thereafter that he strode into the drafting room one morning in his full regalia, beret, cape, jodhpurs and elevated shoes, and announced that he was leaving to inspect a building site in Wichita. "Wes," he called out, "and, uh, Tadashi—I'll need you to come along. Pack some things. We leave in five minutes."

When we returned four days later, Daisy was nowhere to be found.

At first I didn't understand—I went straight to her room, bursting with news of the trip, but no one answered my knock. Pushing the door open, I thrust my head in the room and saw, with a shock, that it had been stripped bare. Her books, her watercolors and hangings, her cosmetics, shoes, magazines and newspapers were gone—even the covers from her bed. Dumbfounded, I went to the wardrobe. There was nothing there but for one crumpled woolen sock in the back corner—and yes, I snatched it up and held it to my nose, desperate suddenly for the scent of her, thinking all the while that there must be some simple explanation, that she'd switched rooms, perhaps over to Hillside or even upstairs, where the views were more amenable. For all her cigarette smoking and urban tastes, Daisy loved the views down the long valley at Taliesin and on more than one occasion she'd told me how jealous she was of Gwendolyn because Gwendolyn had been assigned the room above hers, on the second floor.

I took the stairs two at time. It was late in the afternoon, windows open wide, ladybugs floating randomly up the stairwell, the sound of someone's gramophone running a naked wire through the atmosphere (Borodin's Second String Quartet, and I can never hear its sobbing strains without thinking of her, of Daisy, my Daisy, and the infinite sadness of that day). Gwendolyn was sprawled across her bed, still sweating from her exertions in the fields, and though I was so worked up I didn't think to knock, she didn't seem at all surprised to find me standing there in the doorway. "It was her father," she said, without bothering to get up. "Mrs. Wright called him—that's what everybody's saying—and he showed up in some sort of fancy car, maybe a Duesenberg or something like that. I barely got to say two words to her, let alone goodbye."

She was studying the look on my face as if she were a student of the human physiognomy, as if she were mentally measuring me for a marble bust. She'd never much liked me because I'd never much liked her. I tried to say something, but couldn't seem to get the words out. "What," she said, all innocence, "didn't she tell you?"

I skipped dinner that night and hiked out to Stuffy's to use the pay telephone there. I lost a pocketful of change before I finally got through to her, at her father's house in Pittsburgh. When she answered, her voice was dead and all I could think was that she'd been drugged. "It's me," I said. "I'm coming to you."

"No," she said, far away from me, very far, farther than I could have imagined. "You can't. My father—"

"To hell with your father." (I wasn't given to foul language, but I was beside myself.)

"He won't let me—and my mother either. They're threatening Mr. Wright with a lawsuit."

"A lawsuit? For what? Because we love each other?" I looked away absently as a man in overalls and a cloven hat swung through the door and into the tavern. The sun spread yolk over the glass of the phonebooth. It was so hot I felt like a candle burned down to the wick. "You're twenty years old. They can't stop us. Nobody can."

I listened to her breathing over the line. "Tadashi," she said finally, "you don't understand. I can't see you anymore. They're sending me to London, to stay with my Uncle Peter and Aunt Margaret—I'm going to study design at the Royal Academy. Or at least that's the idea."

"London?" I pictured a Dickensian scene, Daisy selling matchsticks on the street, huddled in a garret. My mind was racing. "When?" I said, and I was begging now, stalling for time, trying to calculate the distance from Taliesin to Pittsburgh, a place I'd never been to and of which I had only the vaguest geographic notion.

"Day after tomorrow."

"But why?" I demanded, yet I already knew the answer to that question, just as I'd known with the girl in college, just as I'd known from the minute Daisy and I laid eyes on each other. Japanese were personae non gratae in this country, the Issei forever barred from attaining citizenship on racial grounds alone, whereas Swedes, Germans, even Italians and Greeks were welcome. "Is it because I'm not white? Is that it?"

She was a long time answering, and all the while a hurricane of pops, scratches and whistles howled through the line, and when she did answer her voice was so reduced I scarcely knew she was speaking. She said, "Yes," in the way she might have dropped a pebble in the ocean. "Yes," she said. "Yes."

Of course, all this happened a very long time ago and I'm aware that it is peripheral to the task at hand, which is to give as full a portrait of Wrieto-San as I can, and I don't wish to dwell on the negative, not at all. Suffice to say that I stayed on at Taliesin, grudgingly at first (and perhaps I should have defied Wrieto-San and Daisy's father and all the rest of the world and driven through the night to Pittsburgh and held her to me so tightly no one could ever have torn us apart, but that sort of demonstrative behavior, is, I'm afraid, alien to me), and then, as the weeks, months and years wore on, in the way of humility and acceptance. Increasingly I came to an ever deeper understanding of the true meaning of apprenticeship and the sacrifice required in service of a great master, and I salved my wounds in the analgesic of work.

Which is precisely why I'd like to relate a happier

experience from this period, one in which Wrieto-San again called on me to travel with him on business. It must have been in 1937 or 1938—my memory and the notes I've saved from that time are in conflict here—but it was certainly before the great gulf of the war came between us. Wrieto-San, as it happened, was in need of a new automobile—or to be more precise, two new automobiles. We were by then caravanning annually to Taliesin West, which tended to take a toll on our vehicles, and this was the ostensible rationale for our trip to the automobile dealer's showroom in Chicago, but, in fact, as has been indicated above, Wrieto-San didn't concern himself so much with needs as he did with wants. He wanted the newest model of Lincoln automobile, the Lincoln Zephyr, and when Wrieto-San wanted something, he always—always, without fail—got it.

I suppose he brought me along that day as a sort of foil, a strange face to put the salesman off his guard, but of course I saw nothing of that—I was simply pleased and honored to be at his side, no matter my function. In any case, he strutted grandly through the door of the showroom, tricked out in all his Beaux-Arts finery, the ends of his senatorial tie flowing and his cane tapping at the gleaming tiles of the floor, while I brought up the rear. The salesman—a sort of Babbitt type, portly, glowing, pleased with himself—came sailing out of the office and across the floor like a liner out on the sea, his hand outstretched in greeting. He could see in a moment that Wrieto-San was someone great, a dynamo, a prince among men, but I'm not sure if he recognized him at first.

"Yes," Wrieto-San said, studying the man's hand a moment before clenching it in his own, "I've come for this car." He used his cane as a pointer. The Zephyr stood there in all its aerodynamic beauty, with its grill of chrome shining like the teeth of some fierce predatory animal, the skirts that extended the sculpted chassis and the long tapering wonder of the cab. It was a magnificent thing, elegant and brutal at the same time, its hood concealing the peerless V-12 engine that would tear up the road and transform its competitors into tiny gleams in the rearview mirror. I saw it and wanted it myself. Anyone would have. It was the pinnacle of automotive perfection.

"Good," the salesman said, rubbing his hands together in anticipation of his commission, and then he launched into a fulsome speech about the car's features and reliability, going on at such length that Wrieto-San, exasperated, finally cut him off.

"Can it be that you don't recognize me?" he said.

"Why, yes"—the salesman faltered—"of course I do."

I heard my own voice then, though I'd intended to remain silent—and watchful. "Mr. Frank Lloyd Wright," I said, and I had to restrain myself from bowing.

The man slapped his forehead. "Mr. Wright," he intoned, as if he were offering up a prayer, "of course, of course. It's an honor, sir, a great honor." And then he was pumping Wrieto-San's hand all over again.

When he was finished, when he got done wriggling and grinning and running a hand through his hair and straightening his tie, he stared expectantly at Wrieto-San, who gave me one of his patented looks (we apprentices liked to call it the boa-constrictor-swallowing-the-rat look), then turned back to the salesman. "I'll want two of them," he pronounced. "And I'll want them cut off here"—an abrupt slashing movement of the cane that sliced an imaginary line from the windshield to the rear window—"so that convertible tops can be installed." He paused. "They'll need to be painted, of course, in Cherokee red," he added, turning to me. "Tadashi, you have the color sample, do you not?"

"Yes, Wrieto-San," I said, and this time I did bow as I handed over the sheet of paper decorated with the red square.

And then, as that seemed to have concluded the business, Wrieto-San turned to leave, but stopped before he'd gone five steps. "Oh, yes," he said, his voice as self-assured as any senator's on the stump, "I'll want delivery within the month. And I won't be paying. You do understand that, don't you?"

We got a great deal of use out of those cars. They were every bit as powerful and rugged—not to mention elegant—as advertised. And they were especially useful for longer treks—to Arizona, to visit clients and construction sites in the late thirties and early forties, when we were busily engaged with the building of Florida Southern College, the Community Church in Kansas City, the Sturges House in California and any number of other far-flung projects. And, of course, their performance was all the more satisfying because Wrieto-San did not pay a nickel for them, nor was he expected to. Just as he'd calculated, the Lincoln Automotive Company was delighted to advertise just what make and model the world's greatest architect chose to drive.

This anecdote, illustrative as it is both of Wrieto-San's magnetism and his audacity, brings me to the darkest period of my time with him, if you except the contretemps over Daisy. I'm referring now to events that went far beyond the scale of what any of us at Taliesin or anywhere else in America could have imagined or foreseen—that is, the bombing of Pearl Harbor by my native people, and the consequences it had for me, a Japanese national living by dint of a student visa in the trammeled hills of Wisconsin. Nothing could have protected me from the backlash, not even the power and influence of Wrieto-San himself. Looking back on it, I don't know that any of us could have done anything differently.

The year prior to the "sneak attack," as the press liked to call it, I'd gone down to the local police department to register and have my fingerprints taken as required by Section 31 of the Alien Registration Act, but I really hadn't thought much about it. The militarists in my country had been rattling their sabers, as had their counterparts in Germany and Italy, and it seemed a reasonable precaution on the part of the U.S. government to attempt to keep an eye on citizens of the belligerent countries despite the fact that war had not yet been declared. I suppose I did feel a degree of shame over the posturing of my countrymen (not to mention the savage and dehumanizing way they were depicted in the American press, which, of course, lumped all Japanese in the same barbarian's boat regardless of outlook or cultural attainments), and yet the experience of registering alongside a dozen or so local Italians and Germans wasn't particularly troublesome or traumatic in any way. In fact, on that wintry afternoon nearly a year and a half later—December seventh, that is—I'd forgotten entirely about it.

I remember coming in to lunch just after the bell had rung, only to find the dining room deserted. Puzzled, I poked my head in the kitchen. No one was there, not even Mabel, who was as much a fixture of the place as its furniture. The stove was hot, a cauldron of soup steaming atop it, the room warm and redolent. Coffee was brewing. There was half a sliced ham on the countertop and several loaves of bread cooling beside it. Dishcloths, vegetable peels, ladles, knives and all the rest of the culinary appurtenances were scattered about in evidence of recent activity. But no Mabel. And no sign of the apprentice who was to serve as *sous*-chef and *plongeur*—or any of my colleagues, who should by that time have been bellying up to the counter with their plates in hand. I went to the window to peer out into the yard (this was at Hillside, where most of the apprentices were now living and working) to see if some disaster had struck in the time it had taken me to leave the drafting room, cross the property to the main house to fetch the set of plans Wrieto-San had sent me for and make my way back again.

It was then that the sound of the radio came to me across the intervening spaces of the building. Herbert's radio. He had a new Zenith in his room, a very powerful receiver with terrific sound quality and an extended aerial he'd fashioned himself, and we often gathered there to listen to programs at night, but here it was the middle of the day—lunchtime—and I could only wonder at that. I moved toward the sound as if in a trance. The sound grew louder. I heard voices raised in excitement and someone crying "Shush!" as the announcer thundered out the news and then I was there, framed in the doorway in astonishment: Herbert's room was a scrum of humanity, everyone—even Mabel, even Wrieto-San—wedged in as tightly as commuters on the subway.

The radio crackled ominously. Someone glanced up at me—Wes. "Did you hear?" he said, and they all looked up now, no trace of irony or even awareness in his voice—he was delivering information, that was all: *Did you hear?*

"Hear what?" I said. "What is it?"

"The Japs bombed Pearl Harbor."

Wrieto-San, as I'm sure so many readers are aware, was a pacifist. During the war years he advised his apprentices to declare themselves conscientious objectors and at least two of them that I know of—John Howe and Herbert Mohl—were imprisoned as a result. Wrieto-San stuck by them. He visited them in jail, sent them foodstuffs, letters, books and other amusements. So it was with me as well. Within an hour of the initial broadcasts, after we'd dined and got back to work in the drafting room, he took me aside. "Tadashi," he said, "I'm very sorry about all this, this—unfortunate—business." And he was sorry indeed, not only for the madness that was to come, the loss of life and destruction, but because he so genuinely admired the cultures of the powers the United States and its allies had aligned against. Certainly if the war had been with Australia or Indonesia or the Belgian Congo he would have opposed it, but this went even deeper, this saddened him so that his voice shook and lost its timbre. He looked up at me. We were standing just beyond the doorway to the drafting room, out of sight of the others. "You know what this means, don't you?"

I wasn't thinking. Call me naïve, but I never dreamed that the Americans among whom I'd lived and worked for so long now would see me as a threat to the national security. Or—more significantly—that I would be forced to leave Taliesin, the only sanctuary I'd fully embraced in all my life, the place that was more a home to me than Tokyo itself, and the man who was, at this juncture, as much my father as the man who'd sired me. I was about to slip the question back to him like the baton in a relay race, to say, *No, what does it mean?*, when his face told me. I was going into exile. Going to prison.

"They'll be coming for you," he said. "And by God"—his eyes flared—"I'll do everything in my power to keep them off of this property, but I'm afraid it's not going to do much good. Not in the end."

"But isn't it possible—?" I protested. I let my arm sweep forward to suggest all that was or should have been included in that realm of possibility, that they would see me as the harmless architectural apprentice I was, as a devotee of Taliesin and a follower of one Master only, and that against all reason or expectation I would be allowed to stay on and assist in the great work of Wrieto-San and humanity itself.

He took a moment. I could hear my fellow apprentices chattering away excitedly, war in the air, this place Pearl Harbor stamped suddenly in all our minds though none of us could have pinpointed it on a map the day before. "You might want to think about Canada."

A picture of that vast polar country came to me—a place I'd never been to, but which seemed an eternal wintry Wisconsin spread from one sea to the other—and my dubiety must have shown on my face.

Wrieto-San reached out his hand then and laid it on my shoulder, a gesture I will always remember for the spontaneous warmth of it, as Wrieto-San was never physical with anyone, always standing erect and proper and respecting what today would be called one's personal space. "Whatever you need," he said. "Anything. Just ask." He dropped his hand and shoved it deep into his pocket, then turned and strode back into the drafting room, crying out, "Good God, it's like a meat locker in here! Can't any of you keep up a fire?"

The next day, though it was snowing and Taliesin loomed amidst the frozen landscape like an ark locked in the fastness of an unreachable sea, they came for me. Two men from the Federal Bureau of Investigation, showing badges and faces as grim as boot heels. I'd thought of hiding in the stables, of asking Herbert or Wes to lie for me and say I'd fled to Canada, but that was the way of cowardice, not honor. That was the way that would have implicated them—and Wrieto-San—and I couldn't take it. Instead, though I was as close to tears as I've ever been in my adult life, I came forward, striding purposefully through that miracle of organic architecture and aesthetic purity, and bowed to the two men in the heavy twill suits and tan overcoats. *Shikata ga nai,* is what I said to myself—it can't be helped. And then I bowed to Wrieto-San, to Mrs. Wright and my fellow apprentices who'd gathered there in the living room as if for a Saturday night's entertainment, and gave myself up to the snow and my innocence and the two steely representatives of the country my country had wronged.

But I see, once again, that I've gone on too long here. Suffice to say that I experienced the usual abuses and deprivations, the local jail (or should I say hoosegow?) at first, then, after President Roosevelt issued his infamous executive order 9066, removal to a relocation center in Arkansas and finally to the Tule Lake camp in the north of California, where the most radical and suspect aliens were interned. I won't take time here to describe the appalling conditions of the uninsulated tarpaper barracks into which we were crowded, the lack of cooking facilities or waste and sewage disposal, the threats and insults of the guards or the anomalous and quite mad fact that hundreds of South American Japanese, many of whom no longer even spoke the language of Dai Nippon, were extradited and interned with us. Nor will I say anything about the national administrator of the internment program, Lieutenant General John L. DeWitt, except to repeat his rationale for all this suffering, humiliation and deprivation of basic human rights not only for resident aliens like myself but for the Nisei who were born in America—that is, "A Jap's a Jap."

Wrieto-San wrote me from time to time. My fellow apprentices, many of whom enlisted and went off to fight despite Wrieto-San's disapproval, sent me books and foodstuffs and for Christmas that first year a quart bottle of Canadian Club reserve whiskey that smelled, tasted and went down like the pure distillate of freedom itself. Still, for long stretches of time that seemed as vast as the desert scrub that fell away from the two knobs of desiccated rock that were all we had to stare at, I didn't care what became of me. I'd lost Taliesin. Lost Wrieto-San. Lost my dignity and status as a human being. If I'd known then how long the war would go on or that the scene in the courtyard would be the last time I'd lay eyes on Wrieto-San till after it was over, I don't think I would have been able to endure.

But of course I did endure—that is what we are put on this earth to do. We Japanese have a saying, *Ame futte ji katamaru:* the ground that is rained upon hardens. Or, if you like, adversity builds character. So it was with me. I read, learned to cook, worked the vegetable patches we planted that first spring, helped to insulate and fortify the barracks, putting to use everything I'd learned at Taliesin, from my farming skills to the hands-on construction techniques that Wrieto-San, in his casual way, expected us to develop sui generis. And I drew—drew a whole lifetime's worth of work. Plans for houses, industrial buildings, imaginary cities every bit as bold as Wrieto-San's Broadacre City (the model of which I had the honor and privilege of working on at Taliesin), anything to bank the fires of creation against the bleakness and destruction that was my life during those years.

After the war, radicalized by my treatment and fearful of the raw accumulation of racial hatred blistering the heartland, I didn't return to Taliesin as I'd initially hoped, but instead went back home from California to the devastation of my own country. There I met my wife, Setsuko, and worked on various projects—imagine an ancient and venerable civilization in ruins so hopeless and extensive they swallow the horizons like some nightmare vision out of the Book of Revelation—until the accumulated sorrow became too much to bear (Hiroshima! Nagasaki!) and my father arranged for me to go to Paris, where I spent ten productive years with the firm of Borchardt et fils, rehabilitating structures damaged during the war and designing a whole array of apartments, town houses and *maisons du pays.*

I mention my Parisian sojourn only as it relates to the story of Wrieto-San, which, I must keep reminding myself, is the object of these prefatory remarks. The connection resides in tragedy, a shared experience of a great and inconsolable loss, because here, I confess, O'Flaherty-San and I are somewhat out of our depth. Wrieto-San's first encounter with Mamah Borthwick Cheney occurred before I was born, and I was just seven years old when the cataclysm to which it ultimately gave rise occurred. And while this is hardly the place for apologies of any sort, I should say that O'Flaherty-San knows the material solely in an abstract way, though he is a marvel of imaginative re-creation—I can only thank the gods or the fates or whatever you want to call them that he has never had to experience a loss of this magnitude, and I hope, for his sake and my granddaughter's, that he never does.

But Wrieto-San did, and I believe it was the formative experience of his life, the deep well of sadness out of which all his later triumphs had to be drawn, and thus I warn you that the tone of the ensuing pages must necessarily grow more somber and reflective. I wasn't there. I didn't meet him until eighteen years after the murders at Taliesin. And yet, strangely, terribly, his tragedy echoed down the years in the sudden unfolding of my own, in the hammer blow of fate that struck me down as surely as any madman's axe, and my heart and spirit are with him, even now, two long decades after he has passed from this world.

Picture a rainy November evening, the streets gray against the accumulation of darkness and the thousand honeyed lights of the shops and cafés along the rue du Montparnasse, the soft hiss of the automobile tires, the sadness of the skies. I am at work still, head bent over a tricolored rendering and the graceful flowing lines of my soft pencils, thinking of dinner, Setsuko, my infant daughter asleep in the next room and my son, Seiji, a quiet night at home, *agedashi* tofu, *soba*, a cup of *sake*. Seiji is four years old. He wants a cat—a kitten—but the *propriétaire* will not allow it. Unless I make it worth her while. And I will—I will make it worth her while. This is what I am thinking as my hands and eyes work independently of my brain, bringing three dimensions to life in two—until the phone rings, that is. And the picture darkens: a young wife in kimono and clogs, one hand gripped tightly to her son's and an umbrella thrust over her head, running in the rain to catch her bus, and the taximan, whose breath reeks of *vin rouge*, and who is late in applying the brake of his automobile. Late. Very late. Too late.

Will you forgive me if I find my fingers trembling over these pages as I struggle to close out this scene once and for all? I merely want to communicate something, some deep knowledge that twists in my *hara* with an edge as sharp as any sword's, and, in a way, to present my bona fides, as morbid as that may sound. I've suffered. Wrieto-San suffered. We all have suffered. Even O'Flaherty-San, in his own way. But I simply cannot leave Wrieto-San here as if on some charnel heap of memory—I still hear his voice in my dreams, I continue to revere him and the recollection of him and all that he gave me in his supreme mathematics of addition, only addition. And so I present one final moment, my last memory of him.

It was in the late forties, after the war at any rate, and I was on my way to Paris. I got it in my head that I should show my wife the country where I'd spent so many years, the invincible land of the two-fisted giants who'd conquered us with their can-do spirit, their hot dogs and baseball, and the grand cities arising out of the plains and the factories that were like cities in themselves and all the wide-open untenanted reach of the lone prairie that could have swallowed our humble island country ten times over. And Taliesin, of course. Taliesin, above all. If I was honest with myself (and I was, or began to be, somewhere between Utah and Wyoming, as the night closed down over the lunar crags of the Uinta Mountains and Setsuko huddled beside me in terror of the *gaijin* porters and for the first and last time in my life I hoped people *would* take me for a Chinaman), I would have admitted that it was Wrieto-San and Wrieto-San alone who was drawing me all the way across the Pacific to his side as if he were the magnet and I the needle. I had to see him. Had to show him that I'd survived Tule Lake and the grisly business of rebuilding Japan. And more: I wanted him to admire Setsuko, wanted to trumpet my connection with Borchardt et fils, wanted him to pat me on the back and reassure me and tell me what a fine figure I'd made of myself.

I remember feeling overwhelmed as the train began to brake for the station at Spring Green, the hills dipping away to release us to the flatland where the town presented its forlorn cluster of buildings, everything different and somehow the same. My wife was watching me, her shoulders pressed so close to mine we might have been one flesh, though we had the entire compartment to ourselves. "Are you all right?" she asked, tilting her head to study me all the more closely. Were there tears in my eyes? Tears of joy, recollection, nostalgia, pain? I don't know. I suppose there were. And when the platform hove into view and I saw him standing there—Wrieto-San, come to greet us in person, in the midst of a knot of fresh-faced apprentices—I could barely hold myself back. I'd been half-afraid he would forget me or send an apprentice in his stead. But here he was, in the flesh, honoring me with his presence, reminding me of the indissoluble bond between Master and apprentice. "Yes," I said, struggling for control. "Yes, I'm fine."

The train lurched. There was the metallic wheeze of the brakes. My wife looked away from me to the platform and back again. "Is that him?"

"Yes," I said, and I could see that he was holding forth on one subject or another, his chin cocked back, the cane in motion, his cape fluttering with the quick chop of his advancing steps and the beret adhering to his brow as if by some force of its own. People gave way to him. Pigeons erupted. The apprentices scurried to keep up.

The moment we emerged from the train he came striding up the platform, barking out commands to the apprentices in his wake, his face easing into his open natural emollient smile, the smile that had beguiled a legion of reluctant clients round the world and every woman he'd ever met. My first impression? That he looked old, reduced, the hair gone white against the great riven monument of his head. But he *was* old, in his eighties now, as best I could calculate. "Tadashi," he called out when he was still ten feet from me, his voice as effervescent and youthful as ever, "you've gone gray!"

And then he was there and we were bowing, Setsuko and I, and he bowed first to me and then to her, a dip of his head only, and repeated the greeting I'd given him the first time we met all those years ago beside the still-hissing frame of my Bearcat: "*Hajimemashite.*"

"And you, Wrieto-San," I said, feeling as light as if I were filled with helium—"you've gone white." (I meant no disrespect, of course, but was simply playing off his mood, injecting a bit of the banter he was so fond of, though I could imagine his terrorizing the household staff all morning over the arrangements at Taliesin.) Despite the tidal wash of emotion I was experiencing—or perhaps because of it—I found that I was grinning.

"Ah, so you've noticed? Well, this is the color of venerability, Sato-San." His eyes were coruscating, flecks of glass incinerated under the sun. "No matter how soft your pencils nor how often you add tired to tired, that gray I see at your temples will fade on you so that you'll wake up one morning, look into the mirror and see an Oriental sage staring back at you." He seized a lock of his hair in one hand and laughed aloud.

On the way out to Taliesin, he hardly had a word for me—it was my wife to whom he devoted himself, Wrieto-San at his most impish and charming. She was young and pretty and she was an angel on the violin, a combination that must have proved irresistible to him. Though my wife's English was limited, Wrieto-San was very gentle with her, bathing her in the full glow of his charm, as I imagine he must have done with Nobu Tsuchiura and Takako Hayashi before her.

I stared out the window of the car, filled with such longing and nostalgia I thought my heart would break, a hundred questions for Wrieto-San on my lips—How was Wes? Had he heard from Yen? And Herbert was married, could that be true?—and then Taliesin separated itself from the hillside before us, as golden and sustaining as the picture I'd held of it in my mind's eye through the gray accumulation of weeks, months and years in the camps. Or no, deeper, richer even. The effect it had on me is hard to explain. It was, I suppose, like the feeling of wonder and revelation most people experienced when they first saw the images of the earth from the terra incognita of the moon's surface—only this wasn't terra incognita. Not for me. This was my home, my ideal home, if the world were a holier place and aesthetics ruled rather than necessity. And cruelty.

Wrieto-San was going on about the violin and music in general, how Iovanna had mastered that most subtle of instruments, the harp, and wondering if Setsuko would be so kind—so exquisitely thoughtful and indulgent—as to give him and Olgivanna a sample of her skills later on that evening, when we pulled into the courtyard and my wife turned to me, looking utterly bewildered, for a translation. I'm afraid I failed her there, at least for the moment, because suddenly a mélange of all-but-forgotten odors washed over me and triggered my olfactory memory—the cold ashes of the fire, the farthest corner of the hogpen, cabbage soup, sweet Wisconsin air and a trace of the poison bait the cook sprinkled round for the rats—and I was overcome all over again.

There followed a long and loving tour of the house, the late-afternoon sun awakening all its sacral nooks and corners, its dramatic dialogue of light and texture, the magical confluence of the horizontal and vertical, Wrieto-San reminding us of Lao-Tse's observation that architecture exists not for the sake of the structure but for the space it encloses, among other echoes of the past, and pausing to lecture most charmingly over each of his new acquisitions of Asian art. Then there was tea with Mrs. Wright, who perched formally on the edge of a chair and regarded me out of her Gurdjieffian eyes as if she couldn't quite place me, her face as drawn and mournful as these eight or nine accumulated years could make it. She was in the midst of grilling Setsuko over her musical tastes—were there Japanese composers she was interested in or was she strictly attuned to the Western canon?—when Wrieto-San set down his cup and clapped his hands like an impresario hovering over his audience. "Well, what do you think about taking in a little of the outdoors, Tadashi?" he said, rising to his feet. "It's a beautiful day, isn't it?" And he paused to give me a wink. "Just about perfect for a picnic, wouldn't you say?"

"A picnic?" I echoed, rising in concert with the Master, as if it were a tic.

"Yes, like in the old days."

I bowed by way of hiding my emotions. I was deeply moved. Not only had Wrieto-San come to the station for me and taken the time to show off the house and its treasures for my bride, but here he'd arranged a picnic in our honor as well. And of course Wrieto-San was a great champion of the outdoors, as sensitive to nature and its changes as the hermetic monks of my country who sit for days in contemplation of the cherry blossoms or the winged seeds of the maples, which made the gesture even more special and exquisite. In my years at Taliesin we'd picnicked up and down the fields and hillsides on dozens of occasions and in far-flung locations too, a group of apprentices going on ahead to make arrangements and the rest of us piling into the Taliesin cars and heading off to some locale Wrieto-San had chosen in advance for its beauty and serenity, a joy to us all—and now he was offering to rekindle the spirit. For me.

We were all on our feet now, apprentices darting about, the cars standing in the courtyard and Setsuko looking to me for assurance. I went to her, took her by the arm. Embraced the warmth of her.

"Oh, Tadashi," Wrieto-San said, as if the thought had just occurred to him, "you do remember Stuffy's Tavern"—and here a hint of slyness invaded his voice—"don't you?"

"Yes, Wrieto-San," I said, bowing again. "How could I forget it?"

"You might not know that Stuffy Vale is no longer involved in that particular establishment. It seems I'm the proprietor there now." He gave me a knowing look. "I seem to recall a certain adventure you had there in your first year—or was it the second? Excessive consumption of alcohol, eh? You've conquered that tendency, I can see." He glanced at Setsuko. "Well, bully for you. And for all my apprentices who've been tempted by the Demon

Rum. But today's a special day. And this is to be a very special picnic indeed, as you'll see."

And so it was. In the intervening years, Wrieto-San had resolutely gone about buying up all the surrounding property, as I've indicated, and he was in the habit of removing any structures that impeded the view from his windows or preyed on his mind in any way, however insignificant, rather like the warlords of the Shōgunate or the hermit heiress in the American poem who "buys up all / the eyesores facing her shore, / and lets them fall." Many have criticized him for this, as if wanting to live in purity were some sort of sin, but I've always defended him. Still, even I was taken aback by what ensued.

It was a fine summer evening, the air soft on our faces as we rode in a caravan over the short distance to where the tavern stood in its lot of weed and gently nodding trees. The apprentices had set out blankets and pillows for us and there was a table laden with salads and sliced meats, beans and bread and corn on the cob and great green bellies of watermelon, even as smoke rose from the fire of the barbecue pit. Wes was there—he'd suffered his own tragedy three years earlier when Svetlana and their young son were killed in an auto accident not five miles from Taliesin—and we embraced like brothers, no bows, no handshakes, but a kind of American bear hug that spoke volumes for what we'd meant to each other. I introduced Setsuko all round in a flurry of smiles and bows. When the spareribs, hot dogs and hamburgers were cooked through and piled high as a sacrificial offering on the table, we were led to a seat on the dais, in the place of honor beside Wrieto-San and Mrs. Wright. The sun made a painting of the clouds and settled in the treetops. We ate. I was as happy as I'd ever been in my life.

And then, at Wrieto-San's signal, one of the apprentices rose and began playing a jig on his violin, even as Wes and some of the others burst through the door of the tavern, great jerry cans of liquid clutched in their arms, and for a moment—naïve, forgetful, *thirsty*—I thought they were bringing beer. But it wasn't beer. It was kerosene. And I watched in astonishment as they tipped the cans and pooled the shimmering liquid round the foundation, the work already finished inside. We all caught the scent of it then, noxious, chemical, anticipatory.

The violin keened, every note singing at the high end of the frets. People had begun to tap their feet, a knee bouncing here, fingers tapping there, but no one rose till Wrieto-San did. Very slowly, with a nod to Mrs. Wright, he got to his feet and made his way to the barbecue pit. He bent for a moment to extract a flaming brand, then, in the most leisurely way, as if he were heading off for a stroll through the knee-high grass, he crossed the yard and dropped the brand where the kerosene had pooled on the front steps.

It was remarkable how quickly that wooden structure went up, the flames climbing the walls to the roof like pent-up things given their heads all in a moment, a swarm of gnawing animals with irradiated teeth. Within minutes the frantic leapings of the violin (or fiddle, I suppose) were lost to the clamor of the fire, the hiss and the roar, struts collapsing, bottles of liquor exploding in the depths like the bombs of war—and this was a war, Wrieto-San's war on the topers and wastrels and bumpkins who'd turned out to stand idle as Taliesin burned and burned again, cycling from renewal to ash, and here they were, sprinting through the weeds and jumping from automobiles with their features distorted and their shouts rising on the air. The fiddle skreeled. The fire raged.

Soon there was no roof to that place, and soon after, the skeleton of it, the frame that gave it life, was a fiery

X-ray of the interior. The skies darkened, the flames leapt and fell, and Wrieto-San, his face illuminated and his cane pumping, stood there and watched till it was full night and the stars shone and what had been erected and joined and carpentered fell away to coals.

CHAPTER 1: LADIES' MAN

Kitty was seated on the familiar hard-backed sofa before the Roman brick fireplace in the living room of the house that was so familiar it might have been her own, but of course it wasn't. It was Mamah's.* And Edwin's. Or perhaps she should call it Frank's, since all his interiors reflected one another as if he were simultaneously living in a hundred rooms, rooms scattered across the countryside but somehow, in the architecture of his mind, continuous. It was Frank's house, sure it was, just as the house they shared was his. Everything was his. He'd put his stamp on inanimate things and people alike—on her, his own wife, just as surely as he'd put it on Mamah and Mrs. Darwin Martin and all the rest of the women who came under his purview. He'd even gone so far as to design their clothes, as he'd designed hers, and until this moment, in this room, on an oppressive iron-clad Oak Park winter's afternoon, she'd never felt it strange or out of the way or even remarkable. That was just the way it was. The way Frank was.

* Pronounced *Maymah*, though, of course, the associations with the softer, more elemental "Mama" would be irresistible to a Freudian, given Wrieto-San's deeper needs. And what was, inevitably, to come.

And now she sat here watching the fire wrap its volatile fingers round the log set on the andirons, hearing it, hearing the sleet shush the neighborhood and the faintest murmur from little Martha in her crib in the bedroom below. It was very still. There were tea things on a low table before the fire, but no one had touched them. Mamah was perched on the edge of the seat opposite, trying not to look at her. Edwin—as mild and soft-voiced as a rector transported from the pages of an English novel—stood silently behind his wife, his eyes downcast, the broad bald stripe of his head glowing in the light of Frank's art-glass lamps. And Frank—he was hateful to her in that moment, execrable, hideous, an icon crushed beneath the wheel of a tractor—Frank had backed up against the mantel decorated with the Oriental statuary he'd bought with the Cheneys' money, the brass Buddhas and carved ivory figurines no civilized household should be deprived of. His arms were folded across his chest, his feet planted, his eyes hard and metallic, two darts pinning first Edwin and then her to the heavy fabric of the stiffened air. And what had he just said, what had he said? *Mamah and I are in love.*

In love. As if he would know anything of love. As if he hadn't trampled all over the memory of what they'd had together these past twenty years and pulled it up by the roots, so absorbed in his work—in his self—he hardly gave her a glance anymore, treating her like a servant and the children like strangers, a collective irritant and nothing more.* Love? She was the one who knew love and she loved him still, loved him in spite of herself, loved him so fiercely she wanted to leap to her feet and tear his hair out, gouge his eyes, batter him. And her. Her too, the vampire.

* From *An Autobiography*: "The architect absorbed the father in me . . . because I never got used to the word nor the idea of being one . . . I hated the sound of the word *papa*." It's not for me to comment, but if only I could hear that sound from my own son's lips just once more I would give everything I have.

He was in love. Her husband was in love. And with someone other than his wife, with a woman she'd always considered her special friend. Was it a revelation? Did he expect her to fall to her knees, beat her breast and rend her clothes? Or was she supposed to make the sign of the cross and bless them? This wasn't news—it wasn't even a surprise. He and Mamah had been skulking around for months now, wearing artificial smiles, ever discreet in public, except when he was squiring her about in the glaring yellow automobile that might as well have had a sign that screamed LOOK AT ME! pinned to the hood. But then her husband was a ladies' man, always was and always would be, and he even had a rationale to excuse it—he had to work his charms on the women of the neighborhood because the women were the ones who held the purse strings, the women were the ones who would nag their husbands into taking the leap and *how else did she imagine he earned a living to keep her and her six children clothed and fed and housed, and yes, yes, so there was the grocery bill and the livery bill and all the rest, which just went to prove how necessary it was to court these women, these clients.* She'd accepted that. She'd believed him. Trusted him. Hoped he would get over his infatuation, as he'd gotten over infatuations in the past. But now it was too late. Now he'd spoken the words aloud and there was no going back.

"We didn't mean for it to happen," he said, breaking the silence. "And we don't mean to hurt anyone, least of all you, Kitty—and you, Edwin. That's not what this concerns. Not at all."

Mamah—with her cat's eyes and showy movements—rose suddenly and crossed the room to stand beside him like some sort of ornament. Edwin glanced up sharply. "Then what does it concern?" he asked, his voice barely rising to a whisper.

Mamah's high fluting tones came back at him. "Freedom," she said.

"Freedom? To do what?" Edwin's eyes went to Frank. "To break up two households—and for him? For this architect? This sawed-off *genius?*"

All Kitty could think was that she wanted to be out of this, out in the cold, on the familiar streets, and she thought of Llewellyn, just five years old and in want of her, in want of his father, and dinner, his playthings and his coloring books. What about Llewellyn? What about the house? And Frank's mother, installed in the cottage out back? What of her? Was it all going to come crashing down?

Mamah stiffened. "There's no need to be uncivil, Edwin."

"Please," Frank was saying, and he actually took Mamah's hand in his own as if they were two children lining up for a school trip, "you have to understand how difficult this is for us, but there is no higher law than the freedom to love—"

"Ellen Key,"* Edwin said acidly. He hadn't moved save to clamp his hands together as if he were praying. Or crushing something.

"That's right," Mamah snapped. "Ellen Key. 'Love is moral even without legal marriage, but marriage is immoral without love.'" She delivered the line like an actress, as if it had been rehearsed, and it came to Kitty

* Ellen Karolina Sofia Key, 1849–1926. Swedish feminist, writer, educator, radical. Author of such titles as *Love and Marriage* (1911) and *The Woman Movement* (1912). Mamah was her acolyte, and, later, her translator. A typical passage from *Love and Marriage* reads as follows: "Just as alchemy became chemistry and astrology led to astronomy, it is possible that such a reading of signs might prepare the way for what we may call . . . erotoplastics: the doctrine of love as a consciously formative art, instead of a blind instinct of procreation."

then that it had, the whole scene, the two of them—she and Frank—iterating their lines in some back parlor or bedroom against the hour of performance. "I never loved you, Edwin, you should know that, and I never pretended to. Not in the way of a true and deep and binding love"—and here she gave Frank a fawning treacly look—"not in the way of soul mates. Or destiny."

There was nastiness on the air, a thrusting and parrying, cruelty suppurating out of an ordinary afternoon here in the teetotal suburb of Chicago known as Saints' Rest for its profusion of churches, its conventionalism and placidity—its normalcy and decency—and Kitty wanted no part of it. She was too humiliated even to speak. Without thinking, she rose to her feet and they all three gave her a look of astonishment, as if they'd forgotten she was there, one more wife and mother sacrificed on the altar of free love.

"Kitty," she heard Frank say. And Mamah, Mamah too: "Kitty." That was the extent of it, that was all they could summon, two worn syllables, as if by naming her they could bring her back to what she was when she came up the walk fifteen minutes ago.

She didn't answer. She went directly to the closet for her coat and shrugged away from Frank as he tried to help her on with it and in the next moment she was out in the stinging air, fighting her way round the maze of walls and turnings Frank had put up to protect the Cheneys from the life of the street out front. She heard him call after her, but she didn't turn. And when she got to the motorcar—the chromatic advertisement of self and self-love, because that was the only kind of love Frank was capable of, and she knew that now, would always know it—she kept on going.

Weeks went by, months, and nothing changed. Except that she couldn't see the Cheneys again—wouldn't—

despite the fact that they lived just blocks away and the social fabric of Oak Park was woven so tightly any loose thread would be sure to show. Had there been a rift? Her friends, perfectly respectable women she'd been acquainted with for years wanted to know, all of them sniffing round after the scent of scandal like vultures circling a corpse. No, she said, no, not at all—it was just that she was so busy with the children. Oh, she really had her hands full there, especially with Catherine a young lady now and Frances not far behind. Her smile was tired. And they knew, they all knew. Or guessed.

She kept up appearances as best she could, regularly attending the meetings of the Nineteenth Century Woman's Club as she always had, though with a wary eye out for Mamah—and she still couldn't believe it was she who'd befriended her and she who'd introduced her to her husband, the architect, thinking to do her part to drum up business. The irony of it, as grim as anything in a French novel. Did she hate Mamah, with her French and German and her college degrees and knowing air and the way she bossed everyone—or seduced them—and always got what she wanted, whether it was as trivial as the date of a card party or as momentous as choosing an architect to build her a house? Yes, yes, she did hate her, though she tried to put it out of her mind as much as possible. And she kept on washing and sewing and cooking and overseeing the servants and giving her every ounce of energy to the children, who seemed more needy than ever, as if they divined what was going on behind the scenes. She never could tell just how much they knew and so she couldn't help quizzing them in a roundabout way—especially the little ones, Llewellyn and Frances—but she wasn't very good at subterfuge. And Frances was smart, clever beyond her years—she was coming up on eleven in the fall—and Kitty had to be careful when she asked, as casually as she could, about John Cheney, if she'd seen him at school because it had been such a long while since the Cheneys were over, and how was he, a good boy, took after his father, didn't he? But yes, of course, he was only seven, just a baby. Llewellyn's age. Or no: a year and a half older. And why would such a big girl want to play with a baby—or even notice him?

It was all tentative, her life an unspooling string waiting for the blade to sever it, and each night when Frank came in from the studio he'd walled off from the house as if it were a bunker she felt a rush of relief and gratitude—and yes, love. True love. Not love of an object or love out of a book, but the deepest ache of wanting that had been there since she was sixteen years old and she'd collided with him at the costume party in his Uncle Jenkin's church, everyone in character from Victor Hugo's *Les Misérables*, she dressed as Cosette and he as Marius, and their two heads coming together so hard she wore the bruise for a week. You're too young to marry, they told her, everyone did, but he came for her with all his irresistible force and though her parents held back and his mother rose up like a harpy with her wings spread in opposition, she was Catherine Lee Tobin with the flaming hair and rocketing eyes and nothing could stop her. She wasn't yet eighteen when she was married. And now, two years short of forty, she was a castoff.

Spring that year—1909—brought a succession of cloudless days that stretched through late May and into the middle of June. Out in the countryside the farmers might have been scratching their heads, but in Oak Park, with its shade trees and enveloping lawns dotted with birdbaths and recliners, people welcomed the dry spell. The pace of things seemed to slow. Shopkeepers took the odd afternoon off, the children swam or played ball when school let out, flowers bloomed, cicadas sent up their soporific buzz from the dense nests of leaves. There were picnics, cookouts, horseshoe matches. Hammocks swung indolently in the backyards and the birds held their collective breath through the somnolence of the noon hour. One afternoon, when the boys were off somewhere and Catherine and Frances occupied with a play they were rehearsing, Kitty decided to get out of the house and take advantage of the weather—she needed a few things at the grocery and that was excuse enough. She made Llewellyn change his shirt and combed his hair for him, then put on a straw bonnet, gathered up her purse and parasol, and went down Forest, past all the grand houses Frank had designed and worked on there till it might have been his own private development, and out onto Lake, where the shops were.

The grocer wasn't rude, but he did mention the bill outstanding in the amount of some nine hundred dollars,* even as he toted up her purchases and she assured him Frank would be in that very night to pay on account, but the experience made her feel cheap, as if she were a shirker or a thief. She tried to put it out of her head, tried to enjoy the sunshine and the sustaining warmth of the day—it must have been eighty degrees, with the gentlest breeze off the lake, just perfect—and she looked at dresses, bought Llewellyn an ice cream and then started for home. She'd just turned the corner at Kenilworth, thinking to go home the back way if only to refresh the view, when the Cheneys' maid came down the walk opposite, both children in tow.

"Look," she said, bending to Llewellyn, whose hand was sticky in hers, "there's John and Martha. Should we say hello?" She gave a wave and the maid dutifully

* An astonishing figure, comparable to some $6,500, adjusted for inflation, in 1979 dollars. Both O'Flaherty-San and I have verified the amount from public records, as Wrieto-San was perennially being sued for payment. He once said to me, rather grandly, I think, given the contretemps over the Bearcat, that if one saw first to the luxuries, the necessities would take care of themselves.

crossed the street to her, John skipping on ahead, while Martha—she was three, or just about—clung to the woman's hand. She let go of Llewellyn and the two boys immediately converged and darted behind a tree, playing at some spontaneously invented game, and here was the maid. And Martha. "Good afternoon," Kitty said.

"Afternoon, ma'am." The maid was an Irish girl, slight and stooped, with black hair that blanched her face and two unblinking eyes. It had been a long while and Kitty couldn't seem to recall her name.

"My, how they've grown," she heard herself say, the conventional housewife, dealer in platitudes, and what else was there?

"Yes, ma'am," the maid said. "The two of them. And it's a blessing, isn't it."

She was about to observe that it was indeed, just a blessing, when she made the mistake of going down on one knee to look into little Martha's face and coo over how she was all grown up now, wasn't she? It was a mistake because when she got a good look at the child, at her coloring, the shape of her nose—and her ears, especially her ears—she saw Frank there and it gave her a jolt. But it couldn't be. There was too much of Edwin in the girl, wasn't there? Those were his eyes exactly. Or were they Mamah's? The way she held herself—even suspended from the maid's hand like an appurtenance—was like Mamah, the small-featured prettiness, the feasting eyes. But not Frank. Not Frank. They couldn't have been—could they? But then he'd built the Cheneys' house in 1904, there all day, every day, with his carpenters and workmen and his plans, and Martha wasn't born till two years later, as if that were evidence enough. She remembered Mamah pregnant, the gestating swell of her, and how she complained all the time as if she were a martyr, the first woman on earth to experience morning sickness and gas. She didn't care about children, that was what it was—not in the way Kitty did. She cared about ideas, her books, her precious *freedoms*.

"Yes," Martha said in her child's squeak, "all grown up. And I want a teddy bear. Lucy's going to get me a teddy bear. Did you know that?"

"That's very nice," she said absently. "I'm sure it's—" and then, overcome, she called out to Llewellyn in a kind of bleat, excused herself to the maid and went on up the street, silently adding up the months and the years and hating Mamah Cheney with all her heart.

At first glance, Frank seemed his old self that night. He joked with the children at dinner and afterward he sat at the piano a long while, reprising his stock of Gilbert and Sullivan songs, and the girls and Llewellyn sang along and she did too, though her spirit wasn't in it. And Frank's wasn't either. He was pretending—it was all a pretense, she could see that, see right through him—slipping into the role of father the way he would have slipped into a client's handshake or the latest suit he'd ordered from the tailor so he could shine and shine and let all the world marvel till the commissions piled up like drift and his name went round the world.

He was on his way back to the studio—he worked at night now, every night, later and later—when she caught up with him in the passageway, thinking to say something about the grocer, though she didn't want to nag and the financial matters were solely his concern, his and his alone, but couldn't he cut back on expenses just till they'd paid down some of the bills? That was what she meant to say, because it was on her mind and the look the grocer had given her made her feel common and she was upset in some way she couldn't name, but instead she blurted, "I saw the Cheney children today, little Martha and John, and I couldn't help thinking . . . of you."

She saw the look in his eyes—he wanted no part of

it, no confrontations, no arguments, and he had work to do, couldn't she understand that? Work. Work to sustain this whole tottering circus. He said, "Me? Why on earth—?"

"She looks just like you."

And suddenly he was furious, exasperated, rocking up off the balls of his feet and glaring till the flesh knotted between his eyes. "Who?" he spat. "Martha? Is that what you mean?"

She couldn't abide that moment, couldn't live through it and keep her sanity—because if it was true, and she was testing him, pressing him, forcing him out into the open—she'd kill herself. Shriek till the shingles fell off the house and run howling down the street to throw herself into the lake and stay there, deep down, till there was no trace of her left.

"You're a foolish woman, Kitty. No—you're delusional. That's what you are: delusional."

"Why? Because I expect my husband to love me or at least live up to his vows? Is that delusional? Is it?"

But he didn't answer her. He just turned his back on her and strode down the passage and into his studio that was all lit up like the break of day.

Nothing changed as the summer wore on and then school started up again and the weather turned abruptly damp. To keep herself occupied she started a kindergarten at the house, a development which only seemed to alienate Frank further, as if the exuberance—and sweetness, sweetness too—of a dozen young children for a few hours a day would annihilate his creativity and drive him penniless into the street. It was early October, the leaves beginning to turn, a smell of smoke on the air, when she heard the news that Mamah had taken John and Martha away with her and gone off to Colorado to nurse a friend who was gravely ill—or at least ill enough to be in need of nursing. They'd gone sometime over the summer, apparently, and hadn't come back for the start of school. Kitty didn't know the friend, didn't wish her ill or good or anything else, but she felt nothing but relief. Mamah was gone. The threat was past. And Edwin—she must have broken with Edwin, that was the only explanation, the story of the sick friend nothing more than a ruse. Or maybe not. Maybe it was legitimate. But in any case—and the thought lifted her like a sweet fresh breeze blowing all the way across the sodden plains from the painted peaks of the Rockies—Mamah was no more. Let Colorado keep her. Let her preach free love to the ranch hands and lasso all the husbands in the state right out of their saddles. Let her be a cowgirl. Let her wither.

Still, something wasn't quite right. She'd had it out with Frank—he said he'd never let go of Mamah, that he wanted a divorce, that their marriage was a sham and worse, a form of slavery—but she hadn't given in to him and he was still living under her roof and going about his business, even if his smile had died and he looked ten years older. He was grieving, that was what it was. So much the worse for him. He would get over it. And she would take him back to her heart and her bed, magnanimous and loving, a true wife, so that in time he would be transfigured into a semblance of his old self and everything would go on as before.

Was she delusional? He announced at dinner one evening that he was going into Chicago on business in the morning—he'd stay over a few days—and she didn't think a thing of it, beyond the fact that he was taking a suitcase with him and a raft of his prints to sell (could it be that he was actually going to pay off the grocery bill?) or that Union Station was an infestation of tracks that could have taken him anywhere—west, even, to Colorado. It was nothing. He put in more miles than a traveling man. He was in Chicago half the time as it was—and he ran off to South Bend, Buffalo, Rochester, Madison,

Mason City, anyplace his clients could be found. He'd even drawn up plans for a house in California.*

Delusional. Yes, she was delusional. She didn't see anything in his face that morning but a kind of numbness, and when he didn't call, didn't telegram, even from New York or the steamer that would take him across the Atlantic to Germany, she still couldn't seem to get a grasp on the situation, not till the reporters began to knock at the door and the grocer and the tailor and the liveryman crowded in behind.

* The George C. Stewart house, 1909.

CHAPTER 2: AUF WIEDERSEHEN, MEINE KINDER

At first, Mamah couldn't seem to lift her head from the pillow. She felt as if she were paralyzed from the neck down, strapped to the mattress like one of those ragged howling women in the madhouse, buried under an avalanche, a rockslide, the deepest waters of the deepest sea. If the house had suddenly gone up in flames she couldn't have moved, not to save her own life or Martha's or John's either. It must have been late in the afternoon now, judging from the light, and she'd been lying here through the stations of the sun since it rose up blazing out of the dun slab of the mountains and all the yellow-leafed poplars or aspens or whatever they were started to jump and twist in the breeze. She'd slept and dreamed and woken, the cycle repeating over and again, but nothing had changed. Julia* was dead and the baby dead too, and she hadn't been spared the bloody sheets and the hopeless frantic pacing of the hour before dawn or

* Invented name. History does not reveal to us the actual identity of the unfortunate woman, though a trip to Boulder, Colorado, and a search of the hospital records there might have produced it. Of course, we are comfortable here in Nagoya, O'Flaherty-San and I, and we strive only for a closely invested brand of verisimilitude. Cf. Albert Bleutick, page 29n.

the look in the eyes of the doctor with his masked face and invisible mouth.

She could hear the house settling in around her as the sun poised a moment on the fulcrum of the tallest mountain and then flickered out, the dry cold of elevation settling into the walls, the roof, the resisting panels of the windows. Soon it would be dark and then she'd have the night to lie through and another day after that. And what about the children? They would have been home from school by now—Julia's Teddy and Joe and her own son—but the maids would have seen to them, Julia's boys especially. And the husband. It came to her then that she was alone in the house with the husband, a man she'd never liked, a man like Edwin, closemouthed and inexpressive, as if to think and feel and reconnoiter the soul were a violation of some manly vow, as if to be insensate were the key to life. Well, she wasn't insensate. She was alive. And she'd come here to get away from a man with no more feeling than a stone and to be with Julia, her dearest friend, a graceful high-spirited woman in the prime of life whose last pregnancy had been such a trial and who needed someone to be with, to laugh with, to feel with, and was it a surprise that in these last months she'd felt at home, truly at home, for the first time in years?

And now Julia was dead and she was a stranger in another man's house.

The thought spurred her and she sat up abruptly. The moment of crisis had come. She had to move, act, see to the children. And her bags—she must get her bags packed, because she wouldn't stay here, not another moment. And Frank. She had to telegram to Frank. At the thought of it, of what she would say to him—how she could even begin to tell him what she felt, the shock of the words on the nurse's lips, Julia's blood that couldn't be stanched, a whole wide coursing river of it infusing every towel and sheet and garment till they were stained like the relics of the saints, the stillborn child as twisted and gray as a lump of wax propped against his dead mother's shoulder, the night she'd spent, the fear and hurt and anger—she could feel the grief rising in her till everything shaded to gray and the mountains beyond the window fell away into the void. But she wouldn't cry. She wouldn't. There was no time for that.

The first thing was to change out of her clothes—she was still in the dress she'd worn yesterday—and put something on her stomach. But then she didn't want to ring for one of the maids. The thought of that froze her. If she rang, they'd remember she was here still, they'd come to the door and enter the room and stare at her and speak and nod and put impossible questions to her—did she want soup, a sandwich, butter with her bread, jam?—and she couldn't allow that. And she certainly didn't want to go down to the dining room or the kitchen where she'd be exposed to him or the servants or the relatives who must have gathered by now or anyone else—and she realized, in that moment, that she didn't want to see the children either. The thought of them, John and Martha, with their multiplicity of needs, their wants and fears and the onus that was on her to meliorate whatever they'd been able to glean from the maids when they learned that Teddy and Joe were strictly enjoined from playing and that their own mother was indisposed and not under any circumstances to be disturbed, made her feel paralyzed all over again. She had a vivid fantasy of slipping out the window, shimmying down the nearest tree and stealing away across the grounds that led to the street into town and the sidewalk that led to the train that led . . . to where?

To Frank. That was where the train led. To Frank.

She unfastened the buttons of her dress, pulled it up

over her head and dropped it to the floor beside her, then went into the bathroom to run the water in the tub. The tiles were cold under her bare feet. She could smell herself, the dried sweat under her arms and between her legs, the odor of fear and uncertainty. When she reached for the faucet her hand trembled and she saw that and noted it and tried to look at it dispassionately as if this were someone else's hand, but she couldn't. Why was her hand trembling? she had to ask herself. Because of Julia? Because life had failed her and the shock of that was so insupportable she could scarcely stand to go on living herself? Because she couldn't stay here and couldn't go back to Edwin? Or was it something else, something she couldn't name, the dark climactic moment of her life clawing for release? She twisted off the faucet and stood up. What was she thinking? She had no time for a bath. A bath was insane, ludicrous. The indulgence of a woman who couldn't make up her mind.

She stepped out of her undergarments and sponged herself quickly, not daring to look into the mirror for fear of seeing someone else there, someone who would comfort the children and wait out the funeral, linger over her feelings as if they were beads on a rosary, subsume herself in someone else. Order flowers. Hide behind a black veil. That sort of person. As she dressed and began folding her clothes and arranging them in the suitcase, she was composing the telegram to Edwin in her mind—and the letter that would follow. *Julia's dead, Edwin.* Or no: *There has been a terrible tragedy. Julia died in childbirth. I cannot remain here in this house one minute longer. It is too painful. Come for the children on the next train. Your wife.*

When the suitcase was packed, she put on her hat and coat and went to the door to peer out into the hallway. Julia's husband had made his fortune in silver—he had his own mining company somewhere off in those labyrinthine mountains*—and the house was a testament to his parvenu yearnings, a great rambling cloyingly decorated Queen Anne with twenty bedrooms and a congeries of shadowy hallways. It was the antithesis of what Frank had achieved in her own house, and she'd always loathed it. Until now. Now it was just the thing, dim lights in sconces creeping along the walls, staircases to nowhere, a subterranean feel to the hallways as if the architect were trying to replicate the tunnels of the mines themselves. There was no one in the hall. All was quiet.

The children's room was on the second floor, just below hers. They would have had their dinner by this time and on an ordinary evening they might have been in the parlor, playing at games round the fire, reading, drawing, but with the house thrust into mourning, chances were they'd be in their room. It was getting dark, and in any case John wasn't especially enthusiastic about the outdoors and Martha was too little yet to be without supervision, which was why she'd brought Lucy along to look after them. Lucy would be with them. And they'd be in their room. Martha would already be tucked in and Lucy would be reading her a fairy story while John sat at the miniature desk before the darkened window, sketching, and pretending not to listen. The thought calmed her as she slipped down the staircase, her ears attuned to the slightest sound—there were whisperings, a door slammed somewhere—and made her way up the hall to the children's room.

To this point, she'd pushed herself forward, not daring to think beyond the impetus of the moment and the idée fixe that had taken hold of her, but now, her hand on the doorknob, she hesitated. For a long moment she stood there, listening, until Lucy's voice came to her in

* Call it Roaring Fork Mines and imagine that he got out—or at least diversified—before the collapse of 1893.

the soft undulating murmur of storytelling. There was a pause, then Martha's voice, a half-formed squeak of interrogation. Mamah pictured her, her daughter, not yet four and right there on the other side of the door, five seconds away from her arms, her miniature face pinched in concentration—*Why?* she always wanted to know. *Why do they live in a shoe? Why did the blackbirds? Why?*—and felt herself giving way. She was a disgrace as a mother, heartless, a failure, worse than any evil stepmother in any of the tales the Brothers Grimm could conceive. She was going away. Deserting her own children. Leaving them here, in this death-stricken house, with an Irish maid who wasn't much older than a child herself.

Very carefully, so as not to make the slightest sound, she set down the suitcase and positioned it flat to the wall just out of sight of the door. Lucy's voice went on, rich and sonorous, the sweetest sound in the world, the sound of comfort and security, maternal—*maternal*—and what was wrong with her? Why couldn't she push open the door and take her rightful place there with her children? Because she didn't love Edwin, that was why. Because she'd married him on the eve of the great precipice that marked her thirtieth birthday, even as both her parents had passed on that very year and he stepped back into her life and she thought she could bury herself in the ordinary and never know the difference. But Ellen Key knew the difference. Ellen Key, whom she knew by heart because Ellen Key was the true light and liberator and wisdom of the world and she was translating her work into English so that all women in America could know her and follow her to their own release. No one should live in a doll's house, no one. *And if a woman becomes a mother without knowing the full height of her being in love, she feels it as a degradation; for neither child nor marriage nor love are enough for her, only great love satis-*

fies her. And where was that great love? Where was that soul mate? In Oak Park. Waiting for her.

John said something then, his voice twining with Lucy's to make a song of the story, the nursery rhyme he'd grown beyond, and his tone was mocking and impatient, though he was listening, listening still, the colored pencil arrested in his hand. And Martha spoke up—*Why?*—but the door was thick, solid parvenu mahogany, and she couldn't hear the substance or the answer either. Just the murmur of it. Guiltily, shamefully, she withdrew her hand and examined the pale flesh and the scorings of her palm a moment in the dim subterranean light. It wasn't trembling. Not anymore. Her hand was as steady and decisive as any killer's, any woodcutter's with his axe poised over the belly of the wolf or witch's with the oven ablaze, and it went to the handle of the suitcase even as she whispered her valediction in the new language, the language of heroism and sacrifice, and slipped away down the hall.

The sky hadn't yet gone fully dark—it was a deep glowing tincture of cobalt shading to black in the east, a western sky, poked through with the glittering holes of the stars—but the grounds were dense with shadow. No one had seen her in the back hallway, though every time she heard a footstep or one of the servants' voices she froze in place. She had no desire to have to contrive explanations—she was beyond explanations now—and the suitcase would have given her away regardless. There was a moment at the back door when she thought all was lost, the housekeeper swinging through the kitchen doors with a tray of cut sandwiches and tea things for the husband and whatever mourners had gathered in the parlor, but she managed to duck behind one of the massive highboys along the wall till the woman, preoccupied with the tray and already garbed in funereal black, passed on by.

Then it was a quick dash for the door and out into the gathering night.

A motorcar and two carriages stood in the drive and she gave them a wide berth, though it wouldn't have mattered if the drivers had seen her. She was nothing to them—an anonymous woman with a suitcase, wrapped in her best coat and with her face shaded by the brim of her hat, bisecting the drive behind them and stepping out into the street. Her plan, and she was formulating it even as she shifted the weight of the suitcase from one hand to the other, was to go to the hotel and see if there was a car there to take her into Denver. From Denver she could catch a train east, to Chicago—and Frank would be there at the station to sweep her up in his arms. He'd have a suitcase with him too, and he'd board the train with the mob of passengers and ride with her through the hills and stubblefields of Indiana and Ohio and upstate New York, all the way down along the Hudson to Manhattan. They'd find a boat there, a great high-crowned steamer rising up out of the tide at one of the piers on the lower West Side, a boat to Bremen, and once they reached German soil they'd board a train to Berlin, where he was to meet with Herr Wasmuth to prepare his portfolio for publication and spread his fame throughout Europe. That was what they'd talked about, time and again: Berlin. And here it was, right before them.

She held that image, sidestepping the ruts of the street and passing from light to darkness beneath the streetlights as a wind off the mountains ruffled the collar of her coat: the two of them, together, turning their backs on all these . . . complications. If he was willing, that is. If he was brave enough. If he loved her the way he said he did. She was afraid for a moment—she was risking everything, every sort of censure and embarrassment, and what if he stalled? What if he wouldn't stand up and do what he had to? What if he couldn't raise the money?

What if Kitty's hold on him was stronger than she'd supposed? But no, no, none of that mattered. And if it did, it was too late now. She hurried down the street, feeling like a fugitive.

She stopped at the telegraph office to wire Edwin about the children and she forced herself to be cold and precise and to think of nothing but the matter at hand, and then she wired Frank. She told him she was coming. That everything they'd dreamed of in their letters was unfolding before them. That she was his. And that the time had come to prove that he was hers in return. Then she found a man to take her into Denver and when she got to Denver she bought a one-way ticket to New York via Omaha, Burlington, Chicago, Elkhart, Cleveland, Buffalo and Albany, and settled herself in at the station to wait.

It was just past nine in the evening and the station was all but deserted. She looked up at the lunar face of the clock and watched the second hand creep round, tick by tick, as if reluctant to let go of each of the hash marks in turn, her mind accelerating far beyond it, expanding in ever-widening coils that spiraled from one subject to another even as her stomach contracted round a shriveled nugget of fear and excitement. And hunger. Because she hadn't eaten. Couldn't eat. Didn't have the stomach or the time. The clock crawled. There was a woman standing at the ticket window clutching the hand of a girl of Martha's age. Two men, dressed identically in cheap gray suits, sat on the high-backed bench across from hers, cradling their hats in their laps and surreptitiously studying her. One of them absently stroked the nap of his hat as if it were a kitten, and what was he—a Pinkerton? A dry-goods man? A husband deserting his wife?

She had an hour and a half till the train came—or was scheduled to come—and she couldn't settle herself, couldn't stop the racing of her mind and the propulsive beat of her heart, and she wouldn't be able to relax or even think properly till the porter led her to her compartment and she shut herself in. She gazed beyond the two men to the doors leading to the street, half-expecting Lucy to burst in with the children on either side of her, all three of them sobbing aloud and imploring her to stay. Or Julia's husband. Or the sheriff. Wasn't she breaking some sort of law? She must have been.

Finally, just to do something, to distract herself, to rise up off the bench where it seemed she'd spent her entire lifetime though she saw with a sinking feeling that it had been no more than five minutes, she decided to go into the restaurant. She felt the eyes of the two men on her all the way across the expanse of the marble floor, her footsteps echoing in her ears like gunshots, each step a cry for solace, and then she was pushing through the door and into the restaurant. Which was a cavernous place, poorly lit. At first she couldn't see much beyond the door, but then a waiter emerged from the gloom and showed her to a table backed up against the wall. A scattering of people, mostly men, were seated at the other tables, drinking and gnawing away at sandwiches and chops, and a couple—middle-aged, gaudily dressed—were grinning at each other amidst a clutter of plates and sauce bottles at the table across from hers. Everyone looked up as she came in and set her suitcase down beside her, and the drama of the moment both shamed and exhilarated her. She wasn't used to going out in public alone. She'd always had Edwin there, breathing propriety at her side, the children shielding her, Frank strutting up and down as if he owned every square inch of every place he stepped into. Now she was on her own.

She'd thought she might have a cup of tea and a bun perhaps, but once she was seated and looking over the menu, she realized how hungry she was. The waiter set down a plate of celery and olives, then a basket of bread with butter. She dispatched it all without thinking and then ordered a steak, medium-rare, with fried potatoes, a vegetable medley and a green salad with Roquefort dressing. Did she care for anything to drink? Beer, perhaps? A glass of wine?

The waiter—a man in middle age with a paunch swelling against the buttons of his jacket and hair that looked as if it had been barbered in the dark—stood over her. He was dressed in a well-worn and faintly greasy suit he might have borrowed from an undertaker and he was giving her a knowing, even insolent look, as if he knew all about her, as if every night married women who were deserting their children to run off with their lovers paraded before him, one after the other, drinking deeply to deaden their thoughts and the guilt that weighed them down like a leaden jacket. She held his eyes—she wouldn't be intimidated. The man was an oaf, a servant, no one she'd seen before or would ever see again. "Wine," she said. "A bottle of Moselle."

She'd learned to appreciate wine the first time she'd gone to Europe, on her honeymoon, when she and Edwin had toured Germany, and while she was hardly a sophisticate, she knew enough to rely on the German wines with which she was familiar. And this one, as cool and cleansing as the issue of an alpine spring, had an immediate effect on her, taking the tenseness from her shoulders and warming her where she was coldest, in her heart. And if she was a woman drinking alone in a public place, what of it? She was independent, wasn't she? Would Ellen Key have thought twice about it? Or any European woman, for that matter? She was having wine with her meal, absolved of guilt, worry, the panic that had gripped her earlier, and she cut her meat and tipped back her glass and never once dropped her eyes. Let them look at her. Let them have a good look. Because soon she would be on the train, hurtling through the night, and all this would be behind her.

* * *

When the train pulled into the station at Chicago, Frank was waiting for her on the platform. Despite herself, despite the wine and the gentle swaying of the compartment and the purely positive and loving thoughts she'd struggled to summon, she'd spent a restless night and a day that enervated her with a thousand pinpricks of conscience and uncertainty, and when she saw him there, sturdy and shining and undeniable, she felt the relief wash over her. They would be together now and tonight she would sleep the sleep of the possessed, her skin pressed to his so that every cell and pore of her could drink him in from head to toe . . . The brakes hissed. The station rocked and steadied itself. She caught his eye then and he gave her his world-conquering grin and started across the platform for her and she was so overcome with the tumult of her feelings that it took her a moment to realize that his hands were empty.

He didn't take her in his arms—there was no telling who might be watching, she understood that—but he seemed so stiff and formal she very nearly lost her nerve. "Mamah," was all he said and then she felt his hand at her elbow and he was guiding her through the crush of people, down a corridor and into an office of some sort, a single room with desk and filing cabinets and a fan fixed overhead, and she realized with a start that he must have hired the room for an hour so that they could have a private interview. But why? Why didn't he have a suitcase with him? Why hadn't he boarded the train with her?

He shut the door behind her and she felt afraid suddenly, certain he was going to deny her, construct a wall of excuses, abandon her as she'd abandoned Edwin and her own motherless children. "Frank, what is it?" she demanded, breathless now, her blood surging with the chemical sting of panic, iodine running through her veins, acid, liquid fire. "Where's your suitcase? What's going on?"

"It's all right," he said, pulling her to him. He kissed her. Held her so tightly she could barely breathe. "I just need more time, that's all, just two days, three at the most—to, to raise the money. Good God, this is all so sudden . . ."

She held to him, her chin resting on his shoulder, the smell of him—of his hair, his clothes, the body she knew so well—working on her like a tranquilizer. She trusted him. Absolutely. He was hers, she was his. But still, she pulled back. "Sudden? We've been talking about this for a year now and more. I left Edwin in June."

"Your telegram, I mean. I've been—I was, well, since you telegrammed all I've done is run from one place to another, selling prints, soliciting clients for advance funds, trying to do something, anything, with the projects on the boards. I need more time, that's all."*

She softened momentarily, then hardened all over again. "And what of me? What am I to do?"

"Go on to New York as planned. There's a hotel there I know—I've already reserved rooms. And I've booked passage for two on the *Deutschland* for Friday. Don't

* Wrieto-San's behavior in this regard can hardly be viewed as anything less than irresponsible, perhaps even criminal. He seemed always to assume an adversarial relationship with his clients, for whom he felt he had to cheapen himself in some essential way simply to have the means to practice his art, and so if he were to "burn" them, as the saying goes, with cost overruns and advances upon advances, he felt it was only his due. Needless to say, he was abandoning these people and the projects he had no intention of completing except by proxy. What is the expression—take the money and run?

worry. Don't worry about anything—I'll be there as soon as I can. Do you need money?"

"Yes," she said, "yes, I do," and the implications roared in her ears with all the opprobrium of a cheap novel, and what did that make her, a woman who takes money in exchange for her favor?

"Here," he said, and he opened his wallet to her and they kissed till she felt the rigid heat of him ready to run right up inside of her and then he was sitting with her in her compartment on the train, holding her hand in his, and the conductor gave his shout and Frank stepped back on the platform and waved at the glass as the wheels jerked and the station fell away behind her.

If there was a moment that made it all worthwhile, a single moment she might have captured with a photograph and pressed into an album of memories, it was when she stepped through the door of the stateroom high out over the roiling sun-coppered waters of the Hudson and saw him standing there, his arms open wide to receive her. He'd kept her waiting three days in that hotel in New York and she'd never left the room, not once, for fear of discovery. Her thoughts had weighed on her. She missed the children. She slept poorly. Edwin would have been back in Oak Park by that point and the alarm would have gone up, every gossip and scandalmonger in town putting two and two together, and would he send a detective out after her? Would he be that petty, that vindictive? Even Kitty, poor dull Kitty, must have known the truth by now. And, of course, though Frank had come to her the night before, they were constrained to go aboard separately—to take separate taxis even—so as not to show their hand. She'd been in a state all morning, everyone she laid eyes on a potential betrayer, the desk clerk, the doorman who showed her to the cab, the driver himself, and she felt all but naked as she stood there on the pier waiting for them to see to her luggage before she could go up the gangplank and vanish amidst the crowd. Until she was there, until she felt the ship plunge and rise majestically beneath her feet, she kept bracing for the moment that someone would shout, *There she is! The deserter! The adulteress! Stop her!*

Frank had decorated the room, flowers everywhere, pottery, a selection of his Japanese prints propped artfully in the corners. She saw the sunlight caught in the portholes as if in a private universe, the scent of the flowers supercharging her senses, the geisha in their elaborate robes smiling benevolently on her from the confines of their frames and Mount Fuji, distant and white-clad,* lending its aura of solidity to the delirium of happiness that washed over her. "There's no stopping us now," Frank said, his smile widening. He snatched her arm before she could think and whirled her round the room to the strains of an imaginary orchestra, all the while humming in her ear. Then he showed off the appointments as if he'd designed them himself, fretted over her as she put her things away, insisted on a promenade of the decks while the horn sounded and the ship pulled back from the pier and the gulls rode a fresh breeze out over the river. "And let's eat," he cried. "Let's have a feast to celebrate. Anything, anything your heart desires. Because this is the first day of all the days to come, the first day of freedom to do as we please. Isn't it grand?"

And she felt it too, thinking of Goethe, the translation she'd been making for him as the hours ground themselves out like cinders in that lonely hotel room,

* As rendered by Katsushika Hokusai, 1760–1849, from his series *Thirty-six Views of Mount Fuji*. Wrieto-San possessed at least one premier example, *Fuji from Honganji Temple in Asakusa, Edo.*

Faust, thinking of Faust: "'Call it happiness!'" she recited, holding tight to his arm, "'Heart! Love! God! / I have no name / For it! Feeling is everything!'"

And it was, till the second day out when Frank turned the color of liverwurst and couldn't get out of bed. "I'll never make a pirate," he told her, his voice faint and throttled. She watched him hang dazed over an enameled pan, his stomach heaving, watched him contort his limbs and walk shakily to the toilet, watched him sleep and groan and pull the blankets up over his head as if he could hide away from the pitch and yaw of the heavy seas that blew up around them for the entire two weeks of the journey. She sat by him all the while, nursing him, reading aloud, drilling him on basic German phrases—*Ich spreche ein wenig Deutsch; Ein Tisch für twei, bitte; Moment! Es fehlt ein Handkoffer!*—and he was utterly childlike, like John when he had the grippe, like Martha. He would take broth only. He was always cold, wrapped miserably in his blankets. He complained incessantly. Edwin—that stone, that block—was like an admiral compared to him. But none of that mattered, because feeling was all and Frank was a repository of feeling, a bank of feeling, fully invested. She read to him till the words went numb on her tongue, she laid a wet compress on his brow, massaged his shoulders and the cramped tight muscles of his calves. He was miserable, but she was strong and each day getting stronger.

When they arrived in Bremen, he recovered himself. He ate so much in one sitting—dumplings, Spätzle, Sauerbraten, Schmierkäse, pickles and kraut and rich thick slices of pumpernickel slathered with butter—she thought he would burst. By the time they got to Berlin, he was his old self, prancing at her side, his cane twirling and the tails of his cape flapping in the brisk breeze he generated all on his own, and when they entered the Hotel Adlon on Unter den Linden, everyone turned to stare as if the Chancellor himself had arrived. He strode up to the desk, pulling her along in his wake, spun the register round with a flourish, and in his slashing geometric hand signed *Frank Lloyd Wright and Wife* without thinking twice about it.

CHAPTER 3: THE SOUL OF HONOR

That it had to have been one of the children who answered the door—Catherine, with her young lady's poise and eagerness, expecting good news, a letter from her father, a parcel she'd sent away for, a friend from school come to gossip over the boys—only made the situation all the worse. "Mama," Catherine had called, making her way through the house to the kitchen. "Mama, there's a man here to see you. Says he's from the *Tribune*."

She'd been busy with dinner, trimming the roast, mashing potatoes, peeling carrots and onions and running from the icebox to the sink and stove and back again, and she was in her housedress and apron, her hair pinned up hastily to keep it out of her way. She wasn't expecting guests. Certainly not a stranger. And certainly not a man from the newspaper.

"What does he want? It's not the subscription, is it?" And then, as if she were talking to herself, "Are we behind on that too?"

Catherine stood in the doorway, an expectant look on her face. She shrugged. "He didn't say."

Kitty looked at her for a long moment, her daughter leaning against the doorjamb now, insouciant, pretty, with her mother's eyes and her father's stature, in her school clothes still, a ribbon in her hair, the locket at her throat catching the last fading streak of sunlight through the window. She was fifteen years old, almost sixteen—nearly as old as she'd been when she met Frank. The thought arrested her a moment, made her feel nostalgic and protective all at once, and then Frank was ringing in her thoughts like a tocsin. Was it Frank? Was this about Frank?

The man was waiting for her in the entranceway, just inside the door. He was in his twenties or perhaps early thirties, in an ill-fitting suit in some sort of checked pattern, and his tie was sloppily knotted. He gave her the smile of a small child presented with a rare gift. "Mrs. Wright?" he said.

"Yes," she answered, giving him a puzzled look in return. And though she had a premonition that whatever he wanted would be unwelcome—she could see it in his eyes, a flutter of superiority, as if he knew something she didn't—she heard herself say, "Won't you come in?" She led him to the inglenook and the fire laid there. The light was dulling outside. A wind scattered leaves across the yellowed remnants of the lawn. It was November seventh, a date she would never in all her life forget.

"Well," he said, moving forward to warm his hands over the fire while she stood there rigid and Catherine edged into the room, lifting her eyebrows in consternation, "I don't want but a minute of your time." He extracted a notepad and pencil from his pocket and turned to her. "My name is Adler, Frederick Adler, and I'm from the *Tribune*." He paused a moment to let the weight of the association sink in. "And I was just curious—we were; that is, my editors and I—if you had anything to say. For the record, that is."*

* An eerie adumbration of what Olgivanna would one day face. Cf. page 124.

"To say?" she echoed. "Concerning what?"

"Your husband."

The smallest tick of unease began asserting itself somewhere deep inside her. She felt a vein pulse at her throat. "My husband? What about him?" And then—she couldn't help herself—she made a leap of intuition and knew that he was dead. Or injured. Gravely injured. She saw the crushed bone, blood on the pavement. Her eyes jumped to her daughter's. "He isn't—?"

The man's expression hardened. "Is he at home?"

"Why, no. He's away on business. Has been these past . . . why, is anything the matter?"

"No," he said, "no, nothing at all," and Catherine, poor Catherine, gave her a look that made her feel as if she were being roasted over the coals by a party of savages with bones stuck through their noses. "I was just hoping for some"—and here he reached into the folds of his coat and extracted a newspaper, the *Chicago Tribune*, and handed it to her as if it were a copy of the Bible to swear on before the judge—"clarification."

The headline screamed at her, mute letters, black and white, but screaming all the same, loud as the siren at the firehouse: ARCHITECT WRIGHT IN BERLIN HOTEL WITH AFFINITY. And the subheading, in a louder pitch yet: *Mrs. Cheney Registered as Wife.*

Just then the telephone rang. It was all she could do to hold on to the paper, to keep from dropping it to the floor, flinging it into the fire, shrieking out her rage and hate. "Catherine," she said, struggling to control her voice, "would you please see who that is." And she watched her daughter's every step as she crossed the room, made her way to the telephone in the hall and lifted the receiver. Only when Catherine was gone, when she was out of range—and harm's way too—did Kitty turn back to the reporter. She lifted her head even as she unconsciously retreated a step so that her back was to the mantel and the inscription Frank had carved above it, TRUTH IS LIFE,* because what she was about to say wasn't the truth at all. "Yes," she said, "yes, he wrote us just last week from his publisher, Wasmuth Verlag, to say that he would be detained there in Berlin while working up the drawings for his portfolio."

She drew in a breath. The man was scribbling something in his pad, eternal words, her official statement, her testimony. But she wasn't done yet. "Of course," she went on, "there must be some sort of mistake. You see, Mrs. Cheney—she's his client, you know—Mrs. Cheney is in Colorado."

Two days later, the phone ringing so continuously she had to disconnect the wires to keep from going mad and the children slinking about as if they'd been whipped, afraid to show their faces in their own house and as glum and pale and put-upon as she was herself, she agreed to meet with the newspapermen. If only to put an end to the siege they'd laid. They were everywhere, as ubiquitous as flies, a whole host of them swarming over the property no matter how many times she sent the maid out to ask them to leave—she'd glance up from the stove to see some stranger gesticulating from the street, cross the living room and find herself staring into the face of a man waving a notepad and mouthing speeches from the flowerbed. People

* The full panel, inscribed in three-inch-high letters beneath the motto, reads: *Good Friend, Around These Hearth-Stones Speak No Evil of Any Creature.* In his early years, devoted nineteenth-century aesthete that he was, Wrieto-San was enamored of such aphoristic expressions, as well as antiquated decorative touches like the classical frieze in the entry hall. He soon abandoned them for the cleaner, modern style he pioneered. Which, needless to say, required no verbal amplification.

were peering in at windows and ringing the bell day and night till she thought she would have to disconnect that too just to silence the buzzing in her head.

She'd canceled her kindergarten. Kept her own children out of school to spare them—and that was the cruelest thing. To think that her children had to be sullied in this way was intolerable—how could he have done this to them? How could he have been so selfish? Frances was in tears—the whole class was reciting "Hiawatha" and the teacher had warned that each of them, no matter how shy or reluctant, had to be present and have his or her lines committed to memory or let the whole group down. "But, Mama, I have to go," she kept insisting. "I have to be Minnehaha. And, and"—she broke down, twelve years old and sobbing her heart out, "Roger McKendrick is Pau-Puk-Keewis!" Catherine's life was disrupted. And John's and David's too, the school abuzz with whispers, and she could picture it all, the cruelty of youth, conversations dying as they entered the room, fingers pointing, eyes snatching at them . . .

But she had to put those thoughts strictly out of mind because the reporters were gathering downstairs and she wouldn't fall into their trap, she promised herself that. They wanted scandal, they wanted the vituperative housewife, the madwoman scene, but she wasn't going to give it to them. She combed out her hair—and it was her glory still, the color of a new copper penny and without a single streak of gray to tarnish it—and dressed herself in one of the straight-lined gowns with the Dutch collar he'd designed for her, the blue one, to complement her eyes. It was his dress, his mark on her, and she would wear it proudly, modestly, and answer their questions without bitterness or irony. He was her husband and she would defend him, no matter what it cost her.

The bell—the infernal bell—rang and rang again while she dressed and it kept on ringing until Reverend Kehoe came to knock softly at the bedroom door. He'd been kind enough to offer his services as intermediary, greeting the reporters at the front door and leading them austerely down the hallway and into the playroom, the largest public space in the house and its domestic heart.* She'd decided on facing them here, rather than the living room or Frank's studio—it was a playroom, after all, devoted to family and built for the children by their loving father, who was no philanderer, no deserter, but a soul led astray by the forces of temptation. Though she was sick at heart and sick in her stomach too—she'd brought up her breakfast not an hour ago—that was the line she was going to take.

She pulled back the door and the reverend stood aside for her. "They're ready for you," he said, his eyes flaring with conviction in the darkness of the hall even as the clerical collar cut a ghostly slash beneath his chin. He was the father of eight, deeply pious, rigid as iron. She'd sat through his dull droning sermons over a decade of Sundays as he picked away at the fine points of biblical exegesis, gave to his charities, attended various stifling teas and bake sales at his behest—or his wife's—and now he was here to repay her. He was a minister of God and he was going to stand by her side throughout this ordeal, because she had no husband to support her, not any longer. Was this the way it was going to be, living like a widow the rest of her days? Or would Frank tire of Mamah and come back to her? She had a fleeting vision of him bent over a plate of dumplings in some Prussian palace with bear rugs on the floors and stags' heads arrayed over the fireplace, Mamah sipping champagne from a crys-

* This is, of course, one of Wrieto-San's most celebrated early designs, added to his residence in 1893 to accommodate his growing brood. It is an impressive, grand space, with its high, barrel-vaulted ceiling, a fireplace surround of Roman brick and brick wainscoting that carries into the window embrasures. I imagine a hearty fire burning in the hearth as a symbolic backdrop to the first Mrs. Wright's travail.

tal flute and throwing her chin back to laugh her rippling carefree laugh that was calculated to freeze every woman to the core and make every man turn his head.

"Are you quite all right, Catherine? Are you prepared for this?"

"Yes," she said, so softly she wasn't sure if he'd heard her.

"Because we can cancel it. Just say the word and I'll send them all home."

But she had to go through with it, had to do what she could to meliorate the situation, put an end to the rumors and speculation—for her children's sake and her own too. And for Frank's. The children needed to go back to school. She needed to go about her business. And though she felt like an outcast, felt as if she were walking into a public stoning and wanted to be anyplace else in the world, she told him no and strode into that room with her spine straight and her head held high.*

"Mrs. Wright!" one of them called out, but the reverend silenced him with a glare and she wouldn't look at them, so many of them, utter strangers gathered here in the inner sanctum of her house with the sole purpose of destroying her and her family, and they were hateful to her, no better than murderers, all of them. She took a minute to compose herself—whiskers, all she saw was whiskers, a rolling sea of facial hair—and in a clear unflagging voice began reading from the statement she'd spent the better part of the past two days composing.

"My heart is with my husband now," she began. "He will come back as soon as he can. I have a faith in Frank Lloyd Wright that passeth understanding, perhaps, but I know him as no one else knows him. In this instance he

* Press conferences. One wonders when they were first conceived of—and wonders too at Wrieto-San's curious propensity to inflict them carelessly on the women he professed to love.

is as innocent of wrongdoing as I am." Was her heart slamming at her ribs like a spoon run round the bottom of a pot? Were they all, to a man, giving her looks of incredulity, distrust even? It didn't matter. Because these were her words and they would report them, that was what they were there for, that was their purpose, their function in life—to report. They'd reported the dirt gleefully enough and now they could report the sweeping clean of it too.

The room was very quiet. One man tamped his pipe against the palm of his hand and made as if to rise and dispose of the ashes in the fireplace, but thought better of it. She glanced to the windows, wishing she could float up across the room and escape like a vapor, but they were shut and locked, dense with a strange trembling light, as if a biblical flood had inundated Oak Park while she'd been speaking, the silent waters seeping in till they were all of them sunk here forever. Perhaps it was that thought—the thought of water abounding—that made her realize how thirsty she suddenly was. She swallowed involuntarily, swallowed everything, fear, hope, shame, and went on.

She talked about Frank's struggles as a young architect who'd come to Chicago with nothing and become the great man he was through hard work and application, about how his present predicament was simply another bump along the road, one he was fighting to overcome with all the fierceness of his will. "Frank Wright has never deceived me in all his life," she said, and believed it too, at least in the grip of the moment. "He is honest in everything he does. He is the soul of honor."

There was a silence. She could see that they were all trying to digest this last bit of information, their faces strained and flummoxed. And then they started in with their questions, Reverend Kehoe recognizing first one and then another. “Are you planning to start divorce proceedings?” a man in front wanted to know, and she answered him spontaneously, passionately, with real conviction, as if she’d become a convert in the course of these past ten minutes and had never in her life had an untoward thought for her husband. “Whatever I am as a woman,” she averred, “aside from my good birth, I owe to the example of my husband. I do not hesitate to confess it. Is it likely then that I should want to commence court action?” And she assured them that he’d be back once he was able to master himself and win the battle he was now heroically fighting on her behalf and on behalf of his children. And that when he returned—and this she truly believed, the passion of the moment aside—all would be as it had been before.

“But what of Mrs. Cheney?” a rangy insolent young man in the rear wanted to know, and who was he? Mr. Adler. The one who’d broken the story and caught her unawares in her own house. Well, she wouldn’t be caught twice, that was for certain.

“Yes, what of her?”

“When he comes back—your husband, that is—how will she fit into the picture?”

Here it was: the moment of truth. She could see them all take in a breath. There was a collective flipping back of note pages, a tightening grip on the stubs of pencils. This was what they’d come for.

Mamah, showy Mamah, with her dance hall laugh and high tight girlish figure, rose up and tripped through her consciousness, and she very nearly slipped up, but she didn’t. “With regard to Mrs. Cheney,” she said, and Reverend Kehoe gave her a sharp glance, which she ignored, “I have striven to put her out of my thoughts. It is simply a force against which we have had to contend. I never felt I breathed the same air with her. It was simply a case of a vampire—you have heard of such things?”

They had. Of course they had. They made their living off of them, scoured the alleys and brothels and the dirtiest, lowliest dens to dig them up and show them in the light of day—for profit. For a good story. And here it was, as good a story as they were going to get: Frank was innocent of anything more than falling under the spell of a vamp, and she, Catherine, Kitty, his wife, stood behind him with all her heart.

For all that, though, she'd been abandoned, and she knew it. Frank didn't write her. Didn't cable or communicate in any way, though he must have known about the newspapers, must have known the position she'd been put in—but apparently she was a stranger to him now, worse than a stranger, because he wrote strangers all the time on one matter of business or another, bartering his precious prints or ordering so many custom-made suits or hats or board feet of cypress or a new saddle for the horse he couldn't ride because he was away in Europe. What had she done to deserve such treatment? Such disdain? And this silence—above all, this maddening silence?

It was just after Christmas when he did finally write—to Lloyd, begging him to come over to Europe and help him work on the drawings for his portfolio—and Lloyd came directly to her because he was dutiful and loyal and took her side (all the children did, and Frank, when he returned to them, would just have to face the consequences of that). At first she was opposed to the idea. Outraged, in fact. Frank had run out on her and now he wanted to take her eldest son away from her too? What next, ship the whole family to Germany or Italy or wherever he was and install Mamah Cheney as their mother in her stead? No, she told him, absolutely not, and she spent a dismal afternoon in bed, alternately sobbing into the pillow and staring at the ceiling, feeling as lost and desolate as she ever had in her life. She might have stayed there the rest of the week if Llewellyn hadn't come to the door dragging one of his battered toys behind him and asking her in one breath why she was so sad and informing her in the next that he was hungry. "Mama, will dinner be ready soon?" he asked her, and he was Frank entirely, not a trace of Tobin in him, Frank's image exactly. "Because I'm hungry. I want a piece of cake. Can I have a piece of cake?"

After a while—dinner helped settle her, seeing the children gathered round the table chattering on about the events of their own lives, lives that had nothing to do with marital discord and the empty place at the head of the table—she began to see things in a different light. This was a positive sign, wasn't it? At least Frank was reaching out—he must have been missing his family as much as they were missing him, their first Christmas apart, the house cheerless without him, every gift and song a sham, every ornament hung on the tree weighted with absence. Lloyd was nineteen, the age Frank was when he first apprenticed as an architect, and this would be his chance for employment, advancement, an association with his father and an opportunity to see the world—she couldn't deny him that.* And another thought

* Lloyd Wright, 1890–1978, eventually became an adept and celebrated architect himself, despite having to work in the shadow of his father. He collaborated on and oversaw a number of Wrieto-San's projects, including Hollyhock House, and designed a great many buildings independently, among the most admired of which are the Samuel-Novarro House in the Hollywood Hills and the Wayfarers Chapel in Palos Verdes, California. If we apprentices often felt the burden of Wrieto-San's mastery, I can only imagine how heavy that burden must have been for his firstborn son. But then, genius is never light of weight, is it?

occurred to her too, and if it was purely selfish, who could blame her? Lloyd would be her spy. He would bridge the silence, become her ears and eyes, shrink the gulf that lay between her and Frank, give her reason to hope again because Mamah was nothing, a fancy and nothing more, and he would be coming home, she knew he would. And Lloyd—how could he resist him, his own son?—would be the one to bring him back.

Lloyd left in mid-January, on a day so bleak and gray the sky might have been the lid of a coffin for all the light that shone through. How the newspapers found out about it she would never know, but there was a reporter waiting for them at the Oak Park station, insinuating himself between her and her son, *Just a few questions if you don't mind.* Well, she did mind, of course she did, and so did the children, standing there on the platform looking stricken while she dabbed at her eyes and Lloyd sagged under the weight of his suitcases. She told him to wire her when he got to New York and then again when he reached Florence, because that was where Frank was apparently, basking under the Italian sun with his mistress while his family shivered through a thankless Chicago winter.

The article in the following day's paper—FRANK LLOYD WRIGHT'S SON MAY REPAIR FAMILY BREACH; *Boy Sails for Italy Today at Request of Father, Who Eloped with Mrs. Edwin Cheney*—was one more intrusion, yet another humiliation in an ongoing series. She felt dirty. Felt as if she were the guilty one. And what would that be like, to take another man, feel him between her legs, his lips at her throat, her breasts? She couldn't imagine. As hard as she tried to picture it, she could imagine only Frank, her husband, the only man she'd ever known. But then she thought of him with Mamah, and the whole scene dissolved in shame. She couldn't face her neighbors, couldn't bear the thought of encountering them on the street or at church or the grocery, of seeing the way they fabricated their pitying faces or shifted their eyes away from her as if she were contaminated, and so she stopped going out.

Very gradually, as the weeks and months began to accumulate, she found herself adjusting to his absence. Spring crept softly into the trees, the days warming and the sun painting stripes across the lawn, and she went out and turned over her flower garden like any other widow or spinster or deserted woman—and there must have been thousands of them out there somewhere, legions, a whole army, only not in Oak Park, not in Saints' Rest where every woman had a man on her arm and every pew was filled with the upright and the true—and then it was June and the children matriculated and the long high-crowned days of summer settled in. She had regular letters from Lloyd, but even he seemed distant to her now, someone she'd known in a previous life. Like Frank. Who was living in Fiesole with his son and a hired draftsman, working steadily on converting his designs to the format required by the publisher, while Mamah had stayed on in Berlin, teaching English at a school there. Could it be that he'd tired of her already? She wouldn't let herself hope because before she knew it, it was fall again, the children returned to school and her husband gone out of her life for nearly a year now. A year. A year entire. And how many years did anyone have, any couple, that they could be squandered like that?

She wouldn't hope, wouldn't believe, but here came the letter from her son to say that Frank was coming home, alone, first to New York and then to Chicago and the house he'd built in Oak Park for her and the children, his children, his and hers. He was coming home. He was already on his way. He'd be back before the leaves changed and the frost rimed the lawn. She had to catch her breath—the frost had already built up inside of her, ice, a rigid wall of it, and the letter, two thin sheets of paper, melted it in a rush that swept everything away before it, the sweetest abstersion. *Home. He was coming home.* And when he did arrive, finally, in the automobile of one of his clients who tried to hide his face for shame and wouldn't get out of the car,* he strode up the walk as if he'd never been away and the children rushed to him, Llewellyn clinging to his waist and Frances dancing in his arms as the reporters scribbled on their ragged sheets and she held her smile till it burned.

If she had any illusions they were soon crushed, because once he was out of sight of the reporters he barely glanced at her, and after dinner—their first family dinner in a year—he set himself up to sleep in the studio. Not in her bed—not *their* bed—but the studio. She'd thought about that for a long while, about the sleeping arrangements, because she wasn't just going to roll over and let him have his way with her after taking that slut to his bed—she was going to give him a good piece of her mind, a real verbal thrashing, and it would take time to heal the wounds, of course it would—but this was her husband, the man she loved, and in time there would be reconciliation, tenderness, forgiveness. She foresaw taking him to her, the old Frank, and he'd be contrite, needy—he'd

* W.E. Martin, brother of Darwin, who was one of Wrieto-San's foremost patrons and patsies. Scandalized, Martin's wife refused to ride with them, and Martin took the back streets, hoping no one would recognize him. Wrieto-San, however, with his hair down to his collar and dressed like "the man on the Quaker Oats package" in knee breeches and drover's hat, caused a commotion on the platform, crying out in a stentorian voice for his luggage and shouting, "All aboard, all the way to Oak Park by auto!" No skulking for Wrieto-San, no shuffling or pulling a long face—he was the returning hero. Always.

beg her, beg for it. But she was delusional, wasn't she? He wasn't the old Frank and never would be. He was like an enemy combatant, cold as death in the winter, and if he stayed under her roof it was for show only. And while the newspapers crowed out their headlines—WRIGHT RETURNS TO OAK PARK WIFE, *Family Welcomes Architect Who Went to Europe with Neighbor's Spouse*—it was all an imposture. He used the children as a buffer, wouldn't look her in the eye. And every time she tried to dig deeper, assay the ground, look into his face to see where she stood, he'd jump up and leave the room.

There came a night a week into it when the first cold spell blew down out of Canada and they all sat round the hearth after dinner to listen to his fine voice as he spun out one story after another, now rhapsodizing the play of the morning light on the olive trees at Fiesole or describing the way the fishermen flung their nets into the waves for sardines at Piombino, now breaking into song and making up a nursery rhyme on the spot for Llewellyn. She never took her eyes from him. She smiled a false smile, laughed for the sake of the children, but the look of him—the mobile face, the easy grin, the posturing of a confidence man, utterly at his ease, unrepentant, murderous in his intent—infuriated her. She would have it out with him. She was determined. And she wasn't going to leave the room, not even to put Llewellyn to bed, until she caught him alone.

Eventually, the party began to break up, the children drifting off to their rooms, to their books and lessons, till only Llewellyn remained. Her youngest seemed both puzzled and fascinated by his father, this apparition he'd heard so much about over the course of the past year, six years old and trying his best to reconcile the shadowy figment of his memory with the real presence of this self-consciously zany figure in the inglenook, and why wouldn't he be confused? He insisted on sitting in

Frank's lap the whole time, demanding his attention, touching his face and hands and pressing his head to his chest again and again as if to make sure of him—she could see that Frank was finding it a strain, and under other circumstances she might have spoken out. "Stop fussing," she would have said. Or: "Isn't it time for bed?" But she said nothing. Just watched. Until Frank, exasperated, gave her a look. "Shouldn't he be in bed by now?"

"Yes, he should be," she said, but she didn't get up to lift the child in her arms like the dutiful wife and mother, didn't coo or cajole or even crack a smile.

"I don't want to go to bed," Llewellyn put in. "I want to stay here with Papa."

Frank let out a sigh. "Well, why don't you take him, then?"

"Why don't you? You're his father, aren't you?"

"Don't start in," he said, and she wanted to laugh in his face. Who was he to tell her what to do? She was the one stuck with the bills, stuck with the house, the children, his mother.

"Llewellyn," she snapped, "get to bed. Now!"

The child looked startled—sleepy, cranky—but startled too. He wanted to raise a fuss, she could see that, but the tone of her voice warned him off. Very slowly, as if he were climbing down from an impossibly high and treacherous place, feeling for footholds all the way, he left his father's lap and started across the room, head down and shoulders slumped in defeat. "I'll be up shortly," she said, softening. And she looked at Frank. "I must speak with your father a minute."

But Frank was already on his feet, shying away from her, and she had to come up out of the chair and take hold of his arm to keep him there in the room with her. "You tell me," she said, trying to keep her voice under control, "just what's going on here. And you tell me now."

The look he gave her was absolutely empty. He wasn't annoyed or angry, only indifferent. "As soon as I can make the arrangements, I'm leaving," he said.

"Leaving? What do you mean? You just got here—"

She thought she heard footsteps in the hallway. There was a thump from the floor above. The house ticked and hummed around her like some alien space, a place she'd never inhabited, never been happy in.

He jerked his arm away from her. "I want a divorce," he said.

She ignored him. She wouldn't listen. Wouldn't hear him. "But where will you go?" she heard herself say. "Where will you live?"

His face went secret. She saw that he'd been planning this a long time—the break, the final break, all the fanfare of his homecoming just a pretense so he could appear properly contrite for the public so the public would give him commissions and go on lionizing him rather than suffer him like the pariah he was. "My mother," he said.

"Your mother? You're going to move in with your mother? Are you mad? Have you lost your mind?"

"She's selling her house. She doesn't want to be here anymore. She"—and he hesitated over the lie—"she wants to go back to the country, to Wisconsin. To be close to her people, her sisters and brothers."

She was silent a moment, trying to take it all in. There was a calculation here, an algebra of the emotions as abstruse as anything in any of the textbooks on her children's desks. Stupidly, she said, "You're not serious. You're joking. Tell me this is some kind of cruel joke."

"There's a plot of land she's buying there—near the Hillside School. She's asked me to build her a house on it"—and he repeated himself, the surest sign of a liar—"so she can be close to her people. In her old age. She wants a place for her old age."

And now, suddenly, the equation came clear: solve for *y* when *x* equals Mamah. "It's for her, isn't it? You're going to build a place for her, for your, your—"

"Go ahead, say it. Call her what you will. Because she's something you could never in your life imagine, and I'm sorry to say it, Catherine, but that's how it is."

She could feel everything turning inside of her as if she were caught in a mangle and she was flushing red, she knew it, and her face was ugly, hot and ugly and hateful. "What is she, then? Huh? You're the great saint, the great spirit—you tell me!"

He was calm now and that calmness frightened her more than anything—it meant he didn't care, meant he was already gone. "I'm sorry," he said.

Her voice flew out away from her and she didn't want to make a scene, didn't want the children to hear, but she couldn't help herself: "No, no. You tell me, what is she that I'm not? Tell me!"

The house went silent. The night came down and lay across the roof like a presence out of the forest primeval that had once stood here, on this lot, while Indians beat their squaws and stripped the flesh from their enemies with knives of stone. He drew himself up. Leveled his eyes on her. "She's my soul mate, Catherine. Can't you understand that? My soul mate."

CHAPTER 4: TALIESIN

It was the same old conundrum: how to build what he saw in his mind's eye, how to raise a thing of beauty from the earth so that people would look at it and marvel for a century to come, without first raising the money to see it to fruition. Money. It was always a question of money. He'd borrowed from Sullivan to buy the lot for the Oak Park place all those years ago,* and while he couldn't very well sell it out from under Catherine, he'd already hit on the expedient of remodeling the place so she could rent out half of it and at least have a reliable income. He would provide for her and the children too, that was his responsibility and he would meet it—no one could say he was neglectful there, though they might whip him over Mamah all they wanted, pinching their noses and crossing the street to avoid him as if he were a leper. And he'd just have to find a means of raising money, not only for the remodel-

* Louis H. Sullivan, the great Chicago architect, for whom Wrieto-San worked as a draftsman from 1888 to 1893, after which he was fired for designing homes on a freelance basis (though Wrieto-San, in typical proprietary mode, claims that he quit). At any rate, he was a keen borrower, as has been seen, but at the same time seemed to have difficulty with the concept of repayment.

ing, but for the new house that was already taking shape in his dreams and his waking hours too, a place away from all this confusion, a place where he could live and work in peace till it all blew over.

And that was something he just couldn't understand, the way the whole community had gone after him as if he were an axe-murderer or Kropotkinite or some such. He'd left a prosperous practice a year ago to go off to Europe and improve himself and now he had nothing, and how was he to get work if no one would negotiate with him in good faith or even look him in the eye for fear of catching his moral contagion? How did they expect him to live, these moral paragons trapped in their own miserable little lives and marriages as dead and loveless as the rugs on the floors of the insipid boxes they called home? There was no Christian charity—a sad joke, that was all it was—and no forgiveness either. He hadn't been home three days when the Reverend George M. Luccock of the First Presbyterian Church, a man he scarcely knew, preached a sermon against him, which was, of course, duly reported in the papers. He still had it seared in his memory—*When a man leaves his wife and family and goes over to this other woman, such a man has lost all sense of morality and religion and is damnably to be blamed*—though he'd crumpled up the paper and tossed it in the fire like the rag it was. *Damnably to be blamed.* Why couldn't they leave him alone to live his life as he saw fit? Who made the rules to contain him? Rules were for other people, ordinary people, people who had neither insight nor originality or any sense of the world but what they'd been force-fed by the Reverend Luccocks and their ilk.

Well, he'd played out the charade in Oak Park as long as he could stand it, the loving father and repentant husband come home to his family, manfully unfurling the Christmas tree, splitting wood for the hearth, throttling the goose and gathering his children to his bosom, but he saw much further than any of them could ever imagine. And as the year turned and he put out inquiries everywhere for work, commissions or outright loans and his mother's house went up for sale and Kitty burned and the newspapers flapped away over some fresh scandal, he could think of nothing but that property in Wisconsin, the hill there, his vantage and his refuge. He'd roamed its flanks as a boy, sat atop the crest of it to contemplate the valley spread out below him while the clouds ran across the sun and the insects chirred and deer slipped out of the shadows to browse in the long grass at the edge of the woods. It was a magical place, as serene and uncluttered and pure as the open skies above and the glacial till underfoot, with views to the Wisconsin River on one side and the far end of Paradise on the other. And it was set squarely in the middle of the valley his grandparents had settled, just over the slope from his aunts' school and the home he'd built for his sister, the most perfect site in all the world for the house and farm and workshop he saw rising there, a place of native wood and amber stucco and stone, yellow dolomite limestone laid rough, just as it had come from nature. A place to catch the light. To surround with orchards and gardens. To dwell in as if it had been there forever.

Darwin, good old Darwin, had come up with the money—a loan, that is, secured by a trust deed on the Oak Park property. Twenty-five thousand dollars' worth, enough to redeem the print collection he'd left with Little,* pay for the work in Oak Park, buy back the

* Francis W. Wrieto-San borrowed $10,000 from him to finance his trip to Germany, leaving the bulk of his *ukiyo-e* collection with him as collateral. He'd built a house for Little in 1902 and Little would become one of his few repeat clients, hiring him to build Northome on Lake Minnetonka, the Minnesota lake that would later provide the scene for Wrieto-San's arrest in the company of Olgivanna. Wheels within wheels.

American rights for the Wasmuth portfolio and free him to break ground at Hillside. On the house for his mother. Or that was what he told Darwin, at any rate. And he swore too to give up Mamah, because Darwin was every bit as condemning as the rest of them, though he should have known better. Still, he was a fine and generous man and good-hearted too. And he recognized genius when he saw it.

But Mamah. Give up Mamah? No one could begin to understand what existed between him and Mamah, certainly not Darwin Martin staring blearily across the dining room table at his all but extinguished hausfrau, or Kitty, whose concept of marriage never seemed to rise above the kitchen and the laundry and the children's clothes and looks and moods. All the while he was back he missed her with an ache that was irremediable, a steady burn of regret as omnipresent and physical as the loss of a limb—he couldn't step outside the door or breathe the air without thinking of her, longing for her, worrying over her—and as soon as he had the money in hand he fled back to Germany to be with her. Of course, he couldn't admit this to Darwin or Kitty or anyone else for that matter—he was returning to Berlin to shepherd the portfolio into print, a purely onerous task but absolutely necessary if a whole year's work wasn't going to go up in smoke, and God knew how he detested ocean travel . . .

This time they were discreet. He met her in a hotel near the Tiergarten that was as unfashionable and private as the Adlon was chic and public. It took him the better part of an hour even to find the place, stopping passersby to ask directions in his tortured and rapidly dwindling German while the rank animal odor seeped down the alleys and various creatures chirped and howled in the distance, and when he finally arrived, when he marched into the lobby and announced himself at the desk, he was so wrought up, so impatient and angry with himself—and lustful, mad for the touch of her—that he had to take a minute to collect himself before following the bellman up the three flights of stairs to her door. To lift his hand and knock, to fumble with the unfamiliar currency and grease the man's palm—what was the fool staring at and why the sick parody of a grin, or was it a grimace?—was nearly impossible. But he did it. And the door opened. And she was there.

"Frank," she said, and he said her name too, but there was a moment's hesitation before he took her in his arms, a strangeness they both felt, an airiness, as if there were no walls to the building and the wind was blowing right through it and the sky shifting crazily overhead—she looked different, so different, her color high, her hair lighter than he'd remembered it . . . All the way across the Atlantic he'd pictured this moment, the scent and feel of her, the look of her face and the way she tilted her head back when she laughed, how he'd lead her to bed, straight to bed, but that wasn't the way it was. He felt disoriented, uncertain of himself. A shudder of suspicion ran through him—she'd been seeing somebody else, of course she had, an attractive woman, a sensuous woman, alone in a European capital and flying the banner of free love . . .

What did she say, what was the first thing? *It's good to see you,* yes, of course. *I've missed you. How I've missed you.* Sure, likewise. But then, out of nowhere, she said, "I've been learning Swedish."

They were standing awkwardly in the middle of the room, still holding on to each other, but now she led him to the couch and the low table there, where she'd arranged flowers, sandwiches, a bottle of wine, though he wasn't thirsty and he didn't drink, or hardly ever. "Swedish?" he echoed. And then it hit him: "For Ellen Key?"

Her eyes shone. "I've met her. And she's the most astonishing—did I tell you she's calling me her American daughter? Can you imagine that?"

It was dusk when he'd arrived, the gray weathered city grayer yet under a winter sky, and the darkness of night crept gradually over the room until she had to get up and turn on the lamps. She came and sat beside him on the couch then and took his hand in hers and they talked about the small things, catching up, keeping all the rest at bay. Free love had been convenient for him, hadn't it, but if it was convenient for him, why not for some other man, some Lothar or Henning or Heinrich?

She was laughing her rich laugh over a story he'd been telling her about his mother and her ongoing feud with Kitty and Kitty's mother and even her grandmother, her throat thrown back and her eyes rolling with the pleasure of it, when he said, "You haven't been seeing anyone, have you?"

Her face went cold. "What are you talking about? Seeing who? Who do you expect me to see? I go from my rooms to the library and back. I see my students. The concierge—Frau Eisermann, did you notice her? The little woman with the mustache?"

"I didn't mean that. I meant—"

"Men?"

"No," he said, "no. I was just—inquiring. After your social life. You must be lonely. I worry about you."

She leaned away from him as if to get a better look. "I have no social life." He watched her lift the wineglass to her lips, take a sip of the pale yellow liquid—it was a Johannisberger, she'd said, a special wine for a special occasion, though it was all the same to him—and set it down again. "I'm waiting for my divorce, if that's what you mean," she said, measuring out each word. "And for you." She held him with her eyes. "Only you."*

"I don't want you to wait, not here, anyway." He leaned forward in his seat. Now was the time for affirmation, now was the time to kiss her, but he held back. "I want you to come home. As soon as possible."

Her smile was fragmentary, bitter round the edges. She dropped her voice. "Have you seen my children?"

"No. I can't bring myself even to drive past the street—"

"They don't answer my letters. It's Edwin. He's turned them against me. I'm sure of it." She looked off into space a moment, then came back to him. "And where am I to go when I do come back? I can't—I'll never set foot in Oak Park again, I'll swear to it."

"I've taken care of that," he heard himself say, and suddenly it was all right—it was a building problem, that was all, salvaged by design, materials, plans. "That hill in Wisconsin? It's ours. Two hundred acres, free and clear. I'm building for you—a place that'll put to shame anything I've done to this point. Something new, entirely new."

"I miss them. The little one especially, little Martha. I keep asking myself what they must be thinking—that I'm in prison or something? Or dead? That I don't love them anymore?"

He had the solution, all the solutions. "Bring them to Hillside. Anytime you want."

* Edwin was suing for divorce on grounds of desertion. State law prescribed a two-year absence before the divorce could become final. Since Kitty refused to grant Wrieto-San a divorce on any grounds, Mamah must have felt she had no choice but to remain behind in Europe, far from the prying eyes of the American press. But far from her lover too. And her children. And her life.

"Edwin wouldn't allow it. Never. He'd die first. I know him."

"For school vacations. For the summer. They'll adore it there—and you will too."

There was a silence. No one was going anywhere. Everything was in stasis, and the moment—their reunion—began to sag under the weight of it. He felt lost all over again. Two weeks across on the boat and two weeks back for these few days, these precious minutes that were slipping away and Mamah all but a stranger to him. It was hopeless. The room shrank. He didn't know what to say. But then—and it was the strangest thing, a thing he'd remember all his life with a mixture of gratitude and wonder—a lion began to roar from the grounds of the Tiergarten, a furious belligerent racketing noise that tore through the night in defiance of walls, bars, cages and all the safe people sitting down to dinner in their safe apartments along the tree-hung boulevard. Truth against the world. "Mamah," he said, and all at once he felt supercharged with energy, with power—and love, love too. "Think of it, think of how it'll be, the two of us together again . . ." His hands spun before him, as if he were trying to capture the image before it fluttered away.

"Listen to me," he said, insistent now. "Think of the Villa Medici in Fiesole. Remember how the walls looked as if they'd grown up out of the ground like the trees and the feeling we had there, the contentment, the way the light struck them and everywhere you looked there were vistas, and they were different through each turning of the sun, eleven o'clock a miracle, three o'clock, six in the evening? That's what I'm going to give you. That's your refuge. With me. And who gives a damn what anybody says." He was trembling, burning up with it, the vision of that place to come rising before him in a luminous shimmer of conception. "I want you back," he said, and if his tone was sharp and peremptory it was because he wasn't pleading anymore, wasn't making excuses—excuses were for little people, frightened people, people without command or direction. "This is ridiculous, this separation. I want you there. Soon. As soon as the roof's up. Promise me. Enough of this."

She didn't answer. She just stared at him a long moment. Then she rose, took him by the hand and led him into the bedroom.

Two and a half weeks later he was back in Oak Park, back to the charade, and nothing and everything had changed. Kitty was as furious as ever, rattling things in the kitchen, squaring her shoulders when she came through the door like a boxer stepping into the ring, scalding him with one look or another—a whole repertoire of frowns and scowls and visual crucifixions—and berating him every chance she got. Why had he had to go back to Germany? Were the problems so insurmountable that Herr Wasmuth couldn't have handled them on his own, because he was the publisher, after all, wasn't he? Was *she* there? Had he run to her, slept with her, made her promises? And where was the money for the bills? Could he even begin to imagine the humiliation she had to go through just to put food on the table? And then there were the children with their needs and demands and their incessant clomping up and down the stairs, the whole mad cartwheeling circus, creditors popping up like so many jacks-in-the-box, no work coming in, nothing.

All that, yes, but it was worth it, it was endurable, because he was sure of Mamah now, sure she was coming back to him, and he was only waiting for the snow to recede and the ground to thaw so that he could do what he lived to do: build. In the meanwhile, he oversaw the work at Oak Park, petitioned for clients, mollified his mother and avoided Kitty as much as possible, taking long walks with only his stick for company, riding horseback, driving the streets like a daredevil and not giving two damns whether anybody got out of the way of him or not. And, of course, he drew—sketches, elevations, sections, floor plans—until the house, his and Mamah's house, began to disclose its form. He looked out the window on the gray streets, snow giving way to sleet and then a cold rain that fell through the end of March and into April, mud, the season of mud, but then the wind shifted to the north and the snow fell again and every trace of spring was obliterated.

He'd begun to think a new ice age had come to haunt him—he even joked about it with Billy Little, the carpenter he brought up to Spring Green with him to contemplate the snow fields—but finally the days began to stretch out, the birds came back, the trees flamed with buds and the crocuses pushed up out of the tatters of the receding snow. He let it be known that he was assembling a crew to build a modest little house—for his mother, strictly for his mother, because if word got out the press would be all over him, suspecting the truth of the matter, and God only knew but that the community would rise up into the bargain—and he hired an Irishman, Johnnie Vaughn, as chief carpenter. Johnnie had the ability to talk, chew and swing a hammer for hours on end without appearing to draw breath—and while a talker rarely made a good worker,* Johnnie was the

* We had a talker among the apprentices in the mid-thirties, a man just out of college by the name of Ken Milligan. He talked so compulsively—and distractingly—that Wrieto-San insisted he work alone. One morning, Wrieto-San appeared on the site with a local plasterer, who happened to be deaf, and, in his sly way, singled out Ken to work with him. Three days later Ken came into dinner, looked up from his plate and announced to the table at large, "You know, I don't think that new guy understands a word I say—what is he, a Polack or something?"

exception, a brilliant organizer who worked without stint and knew every artisan and laborer within a twenty-mile radius. He brought in Ben Davis, the single most creative cusser the world has ever known, to oversee the stonework and the wagons to haul the slabs from the quarry, and Ben in turn recommended the two best men in the county, old Dad Signola, the Czech, and Father Larsen, the Norwegian, and no one could say which was the older. Their fingers were splayed and bludgeoned, their backs stooped, their hair a pure patriarchal white. Dad and Father. They knew stone, knew nothing but, and they were unerring and true, and Frank felt lucky to have them. Good men, good men all, and day by day the camaraderie of purpose growing into the joy and mission of the work.

It was June, the foundations laid and the stone running on up into the chimneys and walling off the four courtyards so that the skeleton of the house was visible, all stone, nothing but stone, Druidic, antediluvian, organic in the best and original sense, and he worked right alongside the men, singing the body electric and as full of joy as he'd ever been. This was what he was born for. This was what made sense. The only thing.

He was directing the man from the lumberyard one early morning, the cart overloaded and the horses fighting for traction on the muddy slope up from the road, unable for the life of him to fathom why they couldn't have hired somebody at least halfway competent to sit there and hold on to the reins and watch the big sweating fly-speckled rumps do the work for him, when there was a tap at his shoulder and he swung round to see Johnnie Vaughn standing there, grinning wide, and another man beside him. This second man looked to be about thirty or so, tall and round-shouldered, with the brim of his pork-pie hat pulled down over the frames of his spectacles and his arm in a sling and a white plaster cast projecting from it like a ramrod. "Mr. Wright," Johnnie was saying, "Boss,

I want you to meet the new man, best carpenter in the state of Wisconsin, better than me even, better than anybody. Wait till you see the way he goes at it. Right? Right, Billy?"

You had to trust your instincts—that was what he always told himself and told everybody else too. He'd hired and fired and goaded and pleaded with and laid down the law to a thousand men over the years, and he prided himself on taking in a man at a single glance. He liked what he saw, the worn overalls washed till the fibers showed through, the flannel shirt with the sleeves rolled up and the cotton undershirt showing white at the collar, everything about him neat and clean, even the sling, even the cast. But how could the man expect to work with his arm broken? He wanted to ask, but instead he grinned and said, "Another Billy?"

The man reached out his hand—the left—for an awkward handshake and flicked his chin so that the brim of the hat rode up and his eyes, as gray as the water in the cistern, glanced out from behind the spectacles. "Billy Weston," he said, and then added, "master carpenter."

"I know what you're thinking, Mr. Wright," Johnnie put in. "But the cast comes off in two weeks and I'll swear to you Billy'll outwork any man on this place with one arm tied behind him—or, well, you know what I mean. He's a good man. I'm vouching for him."

Just then, Ben Davis, who'd started down the hill to castigate the idiot in the wagon, let out a string of polysyllabic curses questioning the fellow's sanity, his mother's mores and his grip on the concept of delivering his cargo to where it was needed—"On the motherfucking top of the motherfucking fucking hill!"—and the man responded in kind.

"Ease off there!" Frank heard himself call out. "You—take that wagon back down and make another run at it—there, where we've laid the gravel. And if that doesn't work, unload it at the bottom." He paused to give him a significant look. "No sense in killing those animals over a load of lumber."

When he turned back round, the two men were still standing there patiently beside him, but Billy had removed his hat and held it down at his side, clutched in his good hand. "He's equal with either hand, Mr. Wright," Johnnie went on as if there had been no interruption, "—what they call ambi, uh, ambi—"

"Dextrous."

"Yup, that's right. That's what he is. Hell, he'll drive nails with a hammer in both hands, *bang-bang-bang*."

The wagon slid back with an abrasive squeal and Ben Davis let out another skein of curses. The horses stood rigid. Very slowly, an inch at a time, the teamster eased them back until the weight of the wagon rocked the wheels free of the ruts and got them moving forward again.

"You think you can work with that arm?" Frank asked, addressing Billy for the first time.

Billy looked down at the toe of his boot and traced a pattern in the wet earth. "I can manage."*

It took a day or two to appreciate how much an understatement that was. Billy worked as hard as any two men—every time you looked up, there he was, the plaster arm flashing in the sun, hauling lumber, juggling tools, lending a hand wherever it was needed. He tossed the sling aside the first day and by the end of the week

* Years later, Billy confided to me that he had no idea why they'd hired him, unless it was for his tools. "I think they were short," he said, "and I had everything from my father—braces, bitstops, augers, chisels, drawknives and spokeshaves, planes, squares, bevels, every kind of saw ever made—plus what I'd been collecting over the years on one job or another. I guess I was tool-rich and they were tool-poor."

the cast seemed as much a natural extension of his body as the arm it contained and the strong sure hand and fingers sprouting from the end of it. Every saw cut he made and every nail he drove passed muster—left-handed, no less—and he worked with such an intensity of concentration it was hard to get him to sit down for lunch or even a coffee break and when he did sit down it wasn't for long. He'd fidget and shuffle his feet and stare off across the yard to where the frame had begun to rise above the floor joists as if he could see the whole thing complete and wouldn't rest till it was done. And he'd climb like an acrobat, his tool belt dangling in the air, the cast hooked over one stud while he hammered home another. He was the first one there in the morning and the last to leave at night, and after a while Frank asked him if his wife didn't miss him, and Billy, looking down at the toe of his shoe rotating in the sawdust, said, "Not much. I guess."

By the end of the month, there were all sorts of people coming round to look at the place—Frank's bungalow, they were calling it—and Frank tried to accommodate them all because he was going to have to live here amongst them and, of course, his reputation had preceded him. He supposed they expected him to breathe fire and speak with a cloven tongue after what the newspapers had said about him and certainly the local farmers and their wives had come to sit in judgment, but they would have reacted the same no matter who was buying up two hundred acres in their midst and putting up a house and barn and expecting to farm the place and make a living out of it. That he was one of the Lloyd Joneses, Anna's boy, the nephew of James and Jenkin and the rest, cut him no slack. If anything, it made matters worse because they were going to hold him to a higher standard—he could see it in their eyes as he squired one hidebound old Welsh farmer after another round the place, explaining as patiently as he could the theory behind the design and painting the hills full of orchards and gardens and pastures. And what did they have to say once he'd walked them through the place and expended all the breath he could draw? "Awful big for just your mother, ain't it?" And: "Must be costin' a fortune."

Snooping. Endless snooping. He was a public figure and this was a public undertaking, no matter how much he tried to keep it quiet. The workmen went home to their wives at night. They talked at the lumberyard, at the quarry, at the feed store, the grocer's and the church. The truth was that the whole community knew what he was up to whether he liked it or not and though no one mentioned Mamah—no one would dare—the rumor of her settled over the place in a vast glutinous web spun by every busybody in the county and all of them tugging simultaneously at the threads. It was only a matter of time before the first reporter came slinking around.

He happened to be beneath the house, in the basement room where the boiler would be set in place to provide hot water and steam heat for the winter, listening to the metronomic *tap-tap-tap* of Billy Weston's hammer just above him and giving the place a final look-over, when the moment came. Footsteps on the floor. A man's voice insinuating itself in the interregna between the beats of the hammer. "Hello, there . . . Say, *hello*!"

The hammer paused. "Yeah?"

"I'm just here to, well, I'm from the *Trib.* Name's Adler. You work here, for Wright?"

"Yeah."

"Well, it's a pretty elaborate place, isn't it? Kind of a bohemian design, wouldn't you say? What would you call this, modern architecture, is that it?"

No response. Frank could hear the hammers of the other carpenters at work, a sound as multi-voiced and steady as a driving rain. There was the smell of the earth, of the stone, of boards fresh-cut.

"Seems like Wright has big plans for the place." A pause. "He ever mention the Cheney woman?"

No response.

"But if he did, you wouldn't tell me, would you?"

"Can't say as I would."

"Well, what's it cost, you think? So far, I mean? Must be a pretty fair piece of change." Silence. Banging aloft. "I don't guess I've ever seen so much stone for one little house—or such a mob of workmen. You'd think he was building one of those Chicago skyscrapers here, wouldn't you?"

"I wouldn't think that, not especially."

"What would you think then?"

There was another silence, then the steady beat of Billy Weston's hammer, speaking for him: *tap-tap, tap-tap-tap.*

Frank never spoke with the man—no one did, as far as he knew. And if he found anybody opening his mouth—and he let them all know it, from Ben Davis and Johnnie Vaughn right on down to the casual laborers hired to haul things up the hill and fetch on demand—then that man would be looking for another job. No excuses. He expected loyalty, absolute and unwavering, and loyalty meant keeping your mouth shut, just like Billy Weston. Still—and it goaded him the way they goaded the Brahma bulls in the chute at the rodeo—the newspaper came out the next day with a page-one story under the header ARCHITECT WRIGHT BUILDING LOVE NEST FOR MRS. CHENEY.

It always amazed him how fast the days swept by when a job was going right, the mornings coming sweet and hot, the sun arching overhead by degrees to bake them all the color of mulattoes, thunderstorms rolling in of a late afternoon to drench the studs and make soup of the earth and all the while the house fleshing out over its ribs and growing into the snug low roofs and cantilevered eaves that would hang thick with icicles once winter came. He'd never needed much sleep to sustain him—five or six hours a night and leave the rest to the slugabeds—and he found himself up at first light, pacing the hillside, getting the feel and the smell of the place, eager to get going and Sundays off a kind of deprivation. He listened to the crows, the jays, the orioles, bent to the earth and sifted it through his fingers, picturing the flower gardens he'd plant in the spring, the cherries and peaches and apples, asparagus, rhubarb, melons.

As often as not Billy Weston was there to greet him with a laconic "Mornin'," his stoop-shouldered figure emerging from the mist of the fields, the cast gone now and his right arm tanning and strengthening under the sun, the tool belt dangling from his left hand and his hat cocked down over his spectacles. They talked quietly over coffee and fresh-baked rolls until the others began to file in—or he talked and Billy listened—and it was the best sort of talk, the kind that freed his mind to see, and it wasn't long before Billy began to see too. Taliesin was rising and it wasn't just for him and his mother and Mamah but for Billy and all the rest of the community, a thing of beauty that would tip the balance sheet of the great buildings of the world and make people line up and marvel for years to come. He looked out over the misted fields and felt his own genius wrap round him like a cloak. He *was* the world's greatest architect. He *was*.*

The major part of the exterior was finished—or at least as finished as it was going to be for a work in prog-

* This brings to mind the story of one of the many civil cases in which Wrieto-San was involved. The judge asked him his profession and he stated that he was an architect—in fact, the world's greatest architect. "The greatest?" the judge echoed. "How can you make that claim?" "Well, Your Honor," Wrieto-San replied, "I *am* under oath."

ress—by the time Mamah's divorce came through at the end of the first week of August. The roof was up, the shinglers pounding away. The two Billys climbed like monkeys. The men shouted and joked and Johnnie Vaughn kept up a running patter over the curses of Ben Davis down below. Somebody produced the newspaper, which he declined even to glance at—more lies, innuendo, character assassination—and he had a few round things to say about the press at lunch that noon to the amusement of Billy Weston and some of the others, but after everyone had gone home he couldn't help unfolding the thing and at least taking in the page at a glance. And there was Mamah, in profile, with some sort of amateurish Valentine's heart sketched into the upper corner of the photo above a cameo of Edwin with his drawn mouth and scalped bulbous head. *Her Spiritual Hegira Ends in His Divorce*, the article announced, and then went on with all the authority of a blind seer to assure the diligent and disinterested reader that Mamah's "affinity" had grown tired of her even as he'd vindicated his wife's faith in him and returned happily to the bosom of his family.

He took dinner that night at Tan-y-deri with his sister and he never mentioned a word about it, nor did she. Dinner was exceptionally good and Jennie was good too—good company—and her husband, Andrew, as well, the conversation leapfrogging delightfully from one subject to another, just the way he loved it, repartee, thesis and antithesis, easy smiles and strong opinions, and the view of Taliesin on the ridge opposite was as fine a thing as he'd ever seen. But the newspaper was claptrap and the thought of it flared inside him like a bout of heartburn and he wanted to thrash the men who made their living sorting through people's dirty laundry, these so-called journalists, because they were nothing more than panders. The cretins. They knew nothing and never would.

The painful thing was the thought of what it did to Mamah and her reputation—or whatever they'd left of it intact. Bad enough that they should drag her through the mud over her divorce, but to make it seem as if she'd been nothing more than a passing fancy to him was just plain cruel. And false, false to the core. For a moment, sitting there on the porch of Jennie's place and looking out over the hills draped in shadow, he entertained the idea of hiring an attorney—one of these real balls of fire—and suing them for defamation. Let them crawl to him. Let them writhe and suffer and wring their hands. Let them print a retraction, tell the truth for a change. Of course, Mamah insisted that it meant nothing to her, that she—and he—stood so far above the gossipmongers it was as if they didn't exist at all, but still he could hear the hurt and uncertainty in her voice when they spoke on the telephone on a line open all the way to Chicago. (And if the mighty men of the press were so prescient and all-seeing, how could they not have known she was there, a mere two hundred miles from him? Being discreet. And private. And biding her time.)

Three weeks later he left Taliesin and went into Chicago in the roadster, alone, maneuvering round the streets as inconspicuously as he could, given the coloration of the automobile and the way the tires seemed to cry out in surprise every time he negotiated a turn. He'd tried to dress inconspicuously as well, leaving the cape and jodhpurs at home and selecting the sort of narrow-brimmed hat and constricting tie he imagined any American Joe would have worn to a baseball game or fireworks display, but still he glanced round guiltily every time he had to stop for a pedestrian and twice he reversed direction for fear he was being followed. Eventually, after a series of evasive moves, he found his way to a nameless little boardinghouse where he was certain no one would recognize him—or the former Mrs. Cheney, who was registered there under her maiden name.

The street was all but deserted. A big soapy white cloud danced over the roof, sparrows clung to various appurtenances and a pair of rubber plants peeped out from behind the ground-floor windowpanes. If the house itself was a tricked-out eyesore that should have gone down in the great fire and the world a better place for it, he didn't care about that, not today. He even whistled a little song to himself as he went up the walk, and he was the most discreet and innocuous man alive as he loaded her bags into the car, escorted her out the door and settled her into the seat beside him. Then he put the machine in gear and drove with elaborate care through the familiar grid of streets, as restrained and circumspect as a judge—until he reached the city limits, that is, when he opened the throttle wide and let the Yellow Devil live up to its reputation all the way back to Wisconsin.

CHAPTER 5: MADE FOR THE AVERAGE

It was snowing. Had been snowing, off and on, for most of the day. Frank was delighted, his face lit with the purest pleasure every time he sailed in and out of the room—boyish, brisk, talking of coasting, how they'd go coasting that night once the workmen had left, and was she warm enough, should he build up the fire for her?—and there was an easy slow languor to the course of the day that made her feel like a petted thing, like a cat in a spreading lap, though if it were up to her she'd rather be back in Italy, with the sun warming her shoulders and the trumpet flowers playing their bright colors off the wall behind her. It was cold. Cold outside and cold in here too. The carpenters and plasterers and all the rest were banging away in one of the back rooms—eternally banging—and the wind out of the north that carried those romantic snowflakes in suspension blew up between the cracks of the floorboards and passed right through the windows as if there were no glass in them at all. She sat by the fire, a rug over her knees, and warmed herself through the day with tea, cocoa, coffee and hot broth, Ellen Key's *The Torpedo Under the Ark* in one hand, her lined notebook in the other, doggedly untangling the sense of the Swedish and letting her mind run free to find its English equivalent.*

At some point—it was late in the afternoon, the light fading, the clamor of the workmen gradually dying away till for long intervals the house fell mercifully silent—she found her attention flagging. She kept lifting her eyes from the page to stare out the window to where the snow obliterated the walls Frank had put so much time and effort into constructing, all that linearity—that maleness, the science of the object—smoothed out under the soft contours of the feminine. The fields were gone too. The black spikes of the trees dulled and softened. Roundness. The world had achieved roundness overnight.

A day earlier—just yesterday afternoon, though it seemed like an age—everything had looked harsh and sharp-edged, the grass a stiff hacked brown, the trees like daggers, and she'd asked Billy Weston to bring the car round and take her into Spring Green because she wanted to get out of the house for a few hours if only to see something new, anything. And of course Christmas was coming and she needed to find something for the children—that was the rationale, at any rate. She'd kept to herself most of the fall, striving to live quietly, productively, out of the glare of the press and out of sight of any

* This is a feminist text, a gloss on Ibsen and his female characters. Women, Ibsen felt—certain liberated women, at any rate—were less regimented by society and more a natural force than men. Of course, while we make no claims here to be feminists or sociologists or anything of the like, I can say that Daisy Hartnett was certainly a natural force, and I too much constrained by expectation—and by Wrieto-San—to fully grasp it. Oh, Daisy. Daisy, Daisy, Daisy. Where are your creamy white thighs and your butterfly mouth now?

of the rustic moralists who might tend to view her as a threat to decency. A scarlet woman. A husband hunter. A feminist. They had a hundred stock phrases at their command, as if they had the right to pass judgment, but she tried not to be bitter. For Frank's sake. He had his heart set on living here amongst them, living self-sufficiently, growing his own food and raising his own animals for slaughter, generating electricity from the dam he intended to build at the base of the hill where the creek passed under the road, felling trees, diverting a stream for water and building, always building, and she wouldn't be the one to upset the balance.

She had Billy drop her on the outskirts of town—every man, woman and child within a hundred miles knew Frank's automobile as well as they knew their own buggies and farm wagons, and she wanted, above all, to be anonymous. A woman in ordinary clothes, wrapped up against the cold, taking tea at the hotel and browsing the shops for Christmas gifts. It wasn't to be. The minute she stepped out of the car the curtains parted in the house across the way and by the time she'd walked the three blocks to the general store every head was turned up and down the street. She selected a bow and a quiver of arrows for John, thinking he could practice target shooting in Oak Park and, looking ahead to the summer to come, perhaps hunt things in the fields at Taliesin—rabbits, she supposed, gophers, that sort of thing. She found a paint set and an easel for Martha, to encourage her in her artwork—she did seem to have a gift for composition, even Frank said so. That was fine. That was all right and pleasant enough in its way. But the woman who waited on her kept clenching her jaws as if it were a tic and wouldn't look her in the eye. There was no pretense of small talk or even civility. And while she did take tea and a sandwich at the hotel, keeping strictly to herself, there were whispers and guarded glances and every time she looked up someone seemed to be staring at her.

She didn't mention it to Frank—no need to upset him over nothing. But the experience made her more determined than ever to push forward with her work. The world was in desperate need of Ellen Key—not simply these pig-headed farmers and their prudish wives, but the world at large. People—women, especially—absolutely must learn to think for themselves instead of blindly following the dictates of a patriarchal society that would deny them not only the right to vote but the right to love in their own instinctual way. She had a fleeting fantasy of herself as a sort of Joan of Arc of erotoplastics, wielding a radiant sword and cutting them all down to size, and then, though she was exhausted and the house was as cold as an igloo, she turned back to the book in her lap and there it was, right before her, in Ellen Key's native tongue: *till älska*, to love. To love. There was no higher purpose in life, no greater duty—why couldn't they understand that? She was just reaching for her pen to note it down, the house gone still, the snow at the windows and Ellen Key on her lips, when she heard Frank's voice, raised in exasperation, drifting to her from the door that gave onto the courtyard. "No," he was saying, "no, she isn't."

There was the sound of stamping feet, someone knocking the snow from his boots in the anteroom, then a man's voice, a stranger's, rang clear: "But isn't it true that she's living here? Rumor has it—or more than rumor, reports, eyewitness reports—that she is. Just yesterday—"

"That's none of your business. Or anyone else's."

"But will you at least confirm or deny it?"

"I won't say a word."

"The fact is that Mrs. Cheney is living here under this roof even as we speak, is it not?"

There was a sudden sharp whine as the door pulled

back on its hinges and Frank's voice riding over it, firm but consolatory: "I'm very sorry you had to come all the way out here in this weather for nothing, but I'll remind you that it wasn't at my invitation and I'm sorry too that I can't ask you in—I do hope you'll find your way back to town in the midst of this glorious winter weather. Spirit of the season and all that, eh? Old Charles Dickens' sort of weather."

"There isn't anything I can do to induce you to—?"

"I won't say a word."

Then the door slammed shut and she heard a single set of footsteps coming down the hall—Frank's, the rhythmic clack of his elevated heels giving him away. She set aside her work and got up from the chair as he strode into the room and bent automatically for the poker to stir up the fire, though she'd been tending it all afternoon and it was more than sufficient. "Did you hear any of that tripe?" he asked over his shoulder.

She didn't know why she should be upset, but she was. All at once she felt lost and abandoned, filled with a sorrow that ate right through her, Julia dead, her children estranged from her, her marriage wrecked, and for what? For this cowardice? This hiding behind a locked door? "Why can't they just leave us alone?" she said, her voice catching in her throat. She was waiting for him to wrap her in his arms, but he didn't, so she went to him and held him awkwardly, one arm draped round his shoulder, the other at his waist. "I feel like a criminal, like I'm being hunted. Persecuted. Like Jean Valjean."

"I know," he said. "I'm sorry."

He was sorry. Well, so was she, but what did they have to be sorry about? They were together, living true to their principles. It was the reporters—they were the ones fomenting this atmosphere of hate, and on Christmas nonetheless; they wouldn't even let them celebrate Christmas in peace. She wasn't thinking, didn't even know what she was saying till the words were out of her mouth: "Why don't we just tell them the truth?"

She felt him stiffen and then he slid out from under her arm and bent again to poke needlessly at the fire. "I don't know," he said. "We should. God knows we should. But the neighbors . . . they're such . . . they're so locked into their self-righteousness, so rigid and just plain ornery—there's no telling what they'd do."

She snatched at his wrist, made him look at her. "But don't you see—that's exactly the attitude that's kept women down all these centuries. We have nothing to be ashamed of—are you ashamed? Because I'm not."*

His face lost its expression. He shifted his eyes away from her. "No, of course not. It's just that—we need to be cautious, go slow. Give the neighbors time to adjust."

But she wasn't listening. She was in the grip of an idea. "Why not, I don't know, why not call them here—the reporters, all of them—make a statement, a formal statement? That way we could at least get our version in the papers, let Ellen Key speak for us, lay out the principles we stand for. Educate them. Isn't that what this is about, at root?" She was elated. Her eyes were burning. "You do love me, don't you?"

He nodded.

"Well, let's do it, then. Let's trumpet it to the world."

He nodded again, but she could see he wasn't convinced. For a long moment he stood there with the poker in his hand, as if he'd forgotten what to do with it, then he set it down carefully and excused himself to wash up for dinner.

She wasn't daunted. The feeling of euphoria carried

* Precisely the tack Miriam would take under similar circumstances. See her speech, pages 327–28.

her through the meal, Frank chattering away, the incident with the reporter already forgotten as he spun out his plans for half a dozen projects and Christmas dinner too—and they would go coasting, that very night, they would—but she was only half-listening. She knew what she was going to do now, what she had to do—she was going to take the initiative, step from the shadows, reveal herself to the world. She was already making speeches in her mind, addressing an audience that wasn't there, shadowy men, their legs crossed, notepads balanced on their knees . . .

The cook served dessert. Frank was still talking. Outside, the snow spun down out of the sky. It was a moment to treasure, domestic and true and loving and peaceful—until it was broken by the sudden sharp bleat of the phone. "You sit, Frank," she said. "I'll get it."

She made her way across the room, lifted the receiver from the hook and answered, "Hello?"

"Mrs. Cheney?" The voice on the other end of the line purred at her, an oddly familiar voice, a man's voice, and before she responded she identified it—this was the man who'd been to the house earlier, the newspaperman playing a little trick on them. She could have said "no" or "there is no such person here," could have played right along. But there was no point in that, not anymore. "Yes," she said, "this is she."*

* * *

* It may seem surprising just how much respect was accorded the press during Wrieto-San's time, given its reputation today. But journalism was considered a high calling in those bygone days and the public's right to know seemed to trump even a true American original's right to privacy. Still, I fail to see why Wrieto-San didn't give the reporter what is commonly known as "the bum's rush" and jerk the telephone cable from the wall. Could anyone have blamed him if he had?

On Christmas morning they were up early, stoking the fires, sweeping the rugs and dusting the statuary. She made breakfast herself, though the culinary arts were something of a mystery to her (eggs, ham and fried potatoes, the eggs runny, the ham seared and the potatoes blackened), and when the cook came at eight she helped her roll out the dough for three pies and then followed a recipe for two trays of raisin cookies. They'd had their Christmas at dawn, a simple exchange of gifts beneath the tree—a jade pin set in platinum for her and a new hat and scarf for him—and while it wasn't exactly perfunctory, their first Christmas together in their new home, they were both hard at work within the hour. Frank must have spent half the morning arranging and rearranging the living room, twice stamping off through the snow to cut yet one more holly sprig or evergreen branch, and he was in a state, she could see that, flying from one room to the other, very nearly barking at her every time he tore through the kitchen. He was a perfectionist, she knew that—it was one of the things she loved about him, a testament to his artistic sensibility—but there were times when he could be just a bit excessive. Like this morning. Which only made things more difficult for her. And then there was the matter of what to wear, Frank settling finally on his country gentleman's outfit of tweed jacket and matching knee breeches, with his artist's tie and a pair of heavy woolen stockings, and she choosing a simple embroidered blouse in a shade of ecru over a skirt just a tone darker—she wanted to appear fashionable, of course, but proper too. Sober. Relaxed. The gracious hostess at ease in her own home.

The first of the reporters came up the drive in a buggy from the Spring Green station just before eleven and she tried to make him feel welcome as Frank paced up and down the length of the room and the fire sparked and jumped and the fields lay icebound beyond the windows. Then two more appeared, sliding along the county road like skaters before edging their way gingerly up the slick incline of the drive. She served the cookies and fresh-brewed coffee, asked them about their families—Christmas morning, and here they were away from them, but it was all in the line of duty, wasn't it?—and before long the entire contingent had arrived, eight men in all, of varying ages and temperaments, and each of them drinking in every detail of the place they'd be pressed to re-create from memory back at their desks in Chicago, Madison, Spring Green.

When they were all gathered and comfortably seated, Frank, who'd been dissertating on some of his art pieces in his usual disarming way while she played the hostess and the exquisite beauty of the room exerted its spell, called them to attention and began reading from a prepared statement in his fine clear voice. It was a statement of principle, without apology, beautifully reasoned and presented and laying out the ideas of Ellen Key in the most practical way, as a method of living and loving truly. They'd worked it out together through half a dozen drafts the previous night, Christmas Eve dissolving in an intense fugue of diction, syntax and revolutionary rhetoric—he was a beautiful writer, really, and he would have made a striking politician too—and they both agreed that he would speak for the two of them and that what they had to say would once and for all put an end to the rumor and speculation. As she stood by his side, watching the reporters' faces as he spoke, she felt so full of pride and vindication she could have led a parade from one end of the country to the other.

He spoke frankly of his first marriage—how he'd married too young, how he'd grown apart from his wife intellectually as he matured into his art and how he'd always tried to live honestly and by the highest precepts. One of the men—and she immediately fastened on him, the narrow-shouldered one in the sagging blue-serge jacket with the soaked-through boots and running nose—nodded in approval. *Good*, she was thinking, *bravo!* And then Frank talked of her and the principles on which their love was founded—"Mrs. E.H. Cheney never existed for me; she was always Mamah Borthwick to me, an individual separate and distinct, who was not any man's possession"—and she felt a thrill run through her, because this was it, this was it exactly: no man's possession but an individual in her own right and the equal of any man on earth. And Frank standing there in public and declaring it. He used his walking stick to underscore his points, as fierce and assertive as any orator on the floor of the senate. Finally, in conclusion, he talked at some length of his art and what it meant to be held up before the public and judged by standards he'd never made or agreed to adhere to.

Afterward—and they were interested, oh, they were, in the most engaged and broad-minded way, every one of them a potential advocate for Ellen Key—there were questions, both for Frank and her, probing, earnest calls for clarification and instruction. She felt these men wanted to understand, wanted to help, wanted, above all, to send her message out to the world, and she let herself go till she was speaking purely from the heart. And so did Frank. He grew more magnificent by the moment, extemporizing now on the rigidity of the loveless marriage and the strictures society attempts to impose on the middling and the great spirits alike. "On the general aspect of the thing," he said at one point, striding up and down the length of the room while all their eyes followed him as one, "I want to say this: laws and rules are made for the average. The ordinary man cannot live without rules to guide his conduct. It is infinitely more difficult to live without rules, but that is what the really honest, sincere, thinking man is compelled to do."

And now the little blue-serge man raised his hand and interjected a question—blew his nose piteously, wrung and wiped it in his handkerchief, and asked in a thick dredging voice, "But what of your families, your children, separated from you on Christmas day, of all the days of the year?" He paused to blow his nose once more while everyone waited patiently for him to go on. "Is this the way 'the honest, sincere, thinking man' creates rules for himself? What of them? What of the little ones?"

There was a silence. One man stood up abruptly. Another, his voice ragged with emotion, echoed, "Yes, what of them?"

She felt something clench inside her. Suddenly she saw John in his pajamas and Martha in her nightgown, tumbling out of bed to race through the house chirping like birds and the tree standing there in all its array and the looks on their faces as they saw revealed what Saint Nick and the magic manipulations of his airborne sled and flying reindeer had brought them. Her children. Christmas. She didn't know what to say.

"We're in contact with them, of course," she heard Frank say at her shoulder.

"*In contact?*" the blue-serge man threw back at him and there was no mistaking the sarcastic thrust of it.

"And we've sent them gifts. And cards and the like. And my sons, my two eldest, Lloyd and John, will be coming to work in the Chicago studio with me before long—and Mrs. Borthwick's children, uh—"

Another of the reporters, a fleshy man with disarranged hair and a face the color of week-old grits, supplied the names for him: "John and Martha."

"Yes, John and Martha," Frank went on and she felt stricken all over again. "We plan to have them up here to Taliesin this summer once school lets out. For a month, a month at least. Isn't that right, Mamah?"

Somehow—and she was having difficulty breathing

all of a sudden—she managed to answer in the affirmative, but even as she did she could see that every man in the room was studying her as coldly as they might have studied a corpse laid out for dissection at the morgue.

As soon as they'd left, Frank retreated to his studio and she buried herself in the kitchen, working side by side with the cook to prepare the goose, the gravy, stuffing, pudding and side dishes, determined to make a holiday of it despite the disaster of the morning. And it was a disaster, she had no doubt of that. She let the cook go at five to be with her own family and willingly took on the burden of the meal herself—she was glad for the activity, for anything to take her mind off the way those men had looked at her as if she were some sort of female Scrooge. Or worse, another species altogether—the mother who couldn't seem to muster any affection for her children, even on the most sacrosanct day of the year. She took out her frustration on the chopping block, on the cutlery and the cookware. She rinsed and chopped and mashed and prodded the goose and poured the wine and did her best to braise the vegetables in the pan without burning them, and when they sat down to dinner, Christmas dinner (they were twelve, with the Porters and their children, Frank's mother, a few of the workmen and a couple from Chicago who seemed to be the last of Frank's friends who would have anything to do with him under his present circumstances), she tried her best to be equable and pleasant and to let her laugh conquer all, but it was the most miserable Christmas she'd ever spent.

She tossed through a sleepless night, dreading the outcome—she was a fool to have gone to the press, an idiot, a dreamer; she should have hidden in the cellar, should have poisoned their coffee—while Frank, as unconcerned and artistically removed as ever, snored in his own distinctive way, as if a great wall of water were tumbling into a pit and then rising up to inundate a solitary man breathing through a piccolo. The next day's papers gave a full accounting, and it was worse even than she'd imagined. The Spring Green *Weekly Home News* was savage, inflammatory, labeling Frank and her "a menace to the morals of the community and an insult to every family therein," and the *Tribune*, right from the maddening qualifiers inserted into the headline—SPEND CHRISTMAS MAKING 'DEFENSE' OF 'SPIRIT HEGIRA'*—managed to combine a tone of high dudgeon with outright mockery. They were seen as ridiculous. Pompous. Self-serving. And worse: unfit and uncaring parents.

By the following day, it had turned ugly.

She'd been working on her translation since early in the morning, working so intently she skipped lunch altogether and very nearly let the fire burn itself out, when Frank came through the door with her ice skates dangling from one hand. "Enough work for today," he announced. "Time for some physical activity, something robust, eh? How about a little turn on the ice? What do you say?"

It took her no more than ten minutes to dress and then they were out the door and crunching their way along the path Billy Weston had shoveled down the center of the courtyard. Everything was still, the air newmade, the house as settled and comfortable under its spreading eaves as a chalet in Kitzbühel. Smoke spiraled from the chimneys. A crow beat heavily overhead, its wings creaking like unoiled hinges. Frank led the way,

* An unfortunate term the newspapers picked up from Wrieto-San himself, who'd made use of it the previous year in an attempt to justify his elopement to Germany. Anent the ongoing and spiraling catastrophe of Wrieto-San's press conferences: we Japanese have an expression, *Nakitsura ni hachi*, very roughly, When it rains, it pours.

dressed in lederhosen and a Tyrolean cap, the great trailing swath of his scarf slicing right and left with the sway of his shoulders, and he was in such high spirits he dodged away into the drifts to break off one of the great rippling icicles depending from the roof and prop it over his shoulder like a mock artillery piece.

They made their way down the drive, crabwise, ice underfoot, the pale disk of the sun settling into the trees at their backs and the river opening out before them, and then they crossed the road and went down the narrow path on the other side, everything pristine and perfect under the sculpted banks of snow. She breathed in the scent of the pines, saw the way they stood ranged along the river like sentinels, rugged and alive and giving up their color to a monochromatic world, and felt a surge of joy. This was it exactly, the life she'd envisioned, work and play united, self-sufficiency, the out-of-doors, Ellen Key, Frank. It was too perfect. The ideal of any woman, of every woman. Every woman should feel like this.

She paused a moment to brace herself against the bole of a tree and kick the snow from her boots, wanting only to shout out her joy to the world, and Frank stopped to look back at her. "Are you all right?" he called. "Out of breath already?" He was a picture, a framed picture, and where was the camera to record it?

"No," she said, "not at all. In fact, I can scarcely wait to get down there on the ice and challenge you to a race, twice round the rink, and let no man—or woman—stand between us." Her blood was singing. Her eyes jumped at him.

"You're on," he said, and here was his grin. "It's a bet. The winner—and I'm sorry to say it's sure to be me—will receive one back rub, gratis, at the hands of the loser. Agreed?"

Oh, yes, yes: even if she lost she couldn't lose. "Agreed," she said, and let her laugh carry the freight.

As they came down the slope and through the trees she could see the figures of the skaters out on the river, dark forms sailing free or locked in tandem, their cries echoing across the ice. There was a bonfire going on the far bank, families gathered there with wieners, soda pop, flasks of something stronger. An Irish setter spun round in circles in the middle of the rink they'd cleared, yapping, while two boys flew past and then doubled back, urging it to chase them. It was a scene out of Brueghel. Or maybe Currier and Ives. She was just strapping on her skates when a black-haired man with fierce black eyebrows, in a bulky homemade sweater and patched trousers, sailed in close to the bank and growled something at her before shooting off again. And what had he said? Who was he?

Frank was off to her left, as eager as a child to get out on the ice, entirely oblivious, one skate already on and now the other, and in the next moment he was gliding past her, crowing, "Come on, come on, what are you waiting for?" Then she was up on her skates, unsteady yet, and he had her by the hand and the wind was in her face and here they were, weaving through the crowd, one grand circuit of the rink and then she began to understand—or no, she was made to understand. People—and she recognized some of them—were skating to the far shore, singly and in groups, bunching there on the foot-worn snow to remove their skates before climbing up the bank to the road. They were leaving, en masse. Turning their backs on them. Snubbing them. And then, just as the apprehension of it began to sink into Frank's features, the black-haired man glided up to them and said, quite distinctly this time, "You should be ashamed."

"Ashamed of what?" Frank shot back at him, but the man looped away from them and sailed far out across the river, only to come rocketing back a moment later, moving so fast she was afraid he meant to collide with her—

she'd actually raised her hands to cushion the blow—until he pulled up at the last moment in a slashing spray of ice. "Go back where you come from, you old pervert," he shouted, his face red and his eyes bugged with rage. "You and your conkabine both." Everything evaporated then, all the joy she'd felt in the simple pleasure of the day and all her hopes too, and though Frank cursed him and left her side to chase after him in a fury of his own, the man danced on ahead of him, just out of reach—by far the superior skater. "Pervert, pervert!" his voice rang out till the fire fell into itself and the banks were deserted and the two boys took their dog and ambled up the road and out of sight.

When she and Frank got back—he'd insisted on skating till he'd had his fill, just the two of them alone on the ice with the scowling man—Billy Weston was waiting for them, looking like Doom and his brother. He had the newspaper in his hand and he laid it out on the kitchen table for them. ASK SHERIFF'S AID TO OUST WRIGHT, the headline read, and though she tried to ignore it, tried to recapture the feeling she'd had going down the drive and through the woods with Frank at her side, she couldn't help herself and took it off into the bedroom to confirm what she already knew: the whole community had risen up against them. And worse: they'd petitioned the sheriff to arrest her and Frank on a morals charge. A morals charge, for God's sake. It was like something out of the Dark Ages. Or Salem. A Salem witch hunt.

She was devastated. She sat there in the armchair by the window, a blanket pulled up to her throat, staring at the cheap newsprint till the words no longer made any sense. The house ticked and groaned. The wind came up through the floorboards. Cold, so cold, the fire nothing more than a glow against the blackened stones of the hearth and the boiler in the cellar below might as well have been in another country for all the good it did.

So much for Ellen Key. So much for enlightenment. She and Frank turned in early that night, listening for the errant footfall in the courtyard. For the second night running she couldn't sleep. She lay awake for hours, staring into the darkness, thinking of that man on the ice, seeing him, the twisted lips, the burn of hate. Finally, at first light, she fell into a deep and dreamless sleep.

There were no backrubs. Not that night. Or for many nights to come.

As it turned out, the sheriff never did come for them.* Nor did anyone else. The winter crawled on, Taliesin married its design and grew beyond it and Mamah remained quiet and productive and she gave up newspapers in all their complexity of motive and purpose and vowed that if she ever laid eyes on a reporter again she'd cross the street to avoid him. As for the townspeople, she drew back there too, scarcely leaving Taliesin for any purpose, even to go to the market. If they weren't ready for advanced thought, if they felt compelled to insult her in the local paper and fulminate against her from the pulpits of their churches, well, so much the worse for them. They were the ones losing out to the forces of fear and ignorance and there was little she could do about it but pursue her work and let Ellen Key speak for herself—

* This is the very same singularly reluctant man, Sheriff W.R. Pengally, of Iowa County, whom Miriam would later seek to employ on the same pretext. Fruitlessly, as has been seen. Could it be that this public servant wanted no part of making such fine moral distinctions as to who was sleeping with whom? Or was he just averse to stirring the pot further? The newspaper article, which both O'Flaherty-San and I have examined, quotes him, rather comically, I think, as saying, "I told them I would do my best to thwart any attempt at tarring and feathering."

in as accurate and direct a translation as she could manage to produce.

Very gradually, as the new year broke and wore on, people began to concern themselves with other things, their own families, the weather, with the lives of their farms, with milking and calving and the tilling of the fields and raising of the crops. She began to meet in a quiet way with a few of the more receptive women—an invitation to tea or to go for a hike over the hills, to pick wildflowers or portray them in watercolors—and though she might mention Ellen Key in the most casual way, she tried not to proselytize and no one, not even Diana Milquist, married to the dentist and her closest friend in the neighborhood, ever mentioned her living arrangements. John and Martha came for a month that summer—of 1912—and she tried her best to be a mother to them, though it was clear that Edwin had done his all to turn them against her and that they had little interest in country life. As she confessed to Diana, as much as she loved having them at Taliesin it was something of a relief to see them go, and did she think she was an awful mother for feeling that way? No, Diana said (childless Diana, whose reproductive organs had been damaged as a result of a childhood accident), no, not at all.

In August, *The Torpedo Under the Ark* was published in an exquisite little edition by Ralph Fletcher Seymour of Chicago, and the press was largely favorable, though a number of papers invariably recycled the old news of her elopement with Frank and all the rest of the bilge that went with it *(Former Mrs. Cheney, Who Eloped with Wright, Has New Book; Adopts Views of Ibsen and Swedish Author on Loveless Marriage)*. Still, the repercussions were relatively minor and Ellen Key went out into the English-speaking world all the same. She and Frank celebrated with a trip to Milwaukee and raised a toast (she with a glass of Liebfraumilch, he with a glass of *eau vive*, straight from the tap) to the success of the book and to the translations to come—and the book of her own, the ideas of which were just beginning to coalesce, a volume that would address questions of love, marriage and freedom in a plainspoken American way. For American women, women like herself and Diana and all the beleaguered Oak Park housewives forced into living a lie day after day through the fruitless course of their empty lives. And while she didn't consider herself heroic or ambitious or even especially radical, the more she thought about it the more it grew in her mind. She couldn't see the book's title yet—it was just a blur of letters, like a word puzzle—but she saw her own name beneath it, Mamah Borthwick, or maybe Mamah Borthwick Wright, and she pictured a shifting series of ageless women in fashionable dresses absorbing her words in their parlors, kitchens and screened-in porches, their eyes shining, their faces rapt.

The dog days set in. Haying time came and went. Color struck the trees. She found herself falling easily into the routine of life at Taliesin, writing at her desk in the morning, joining in the work of the household through the afternoon and early evening—trying to assume as much of the load as she could in order to free Frank to pursue his architectural projects*—and contenting herself with quiet evenings at home. With Frank. With the man she loved. In fact, it got to the point, through that fall and into the winter, where she felt so at home she no longer had any desire to leave Taliesin at all.

When Frank came to her about a trip to Japan in the

* She was no Olgivanna. From all accounts, Mamah was naturally gracious and undemanding, content to let the estate manager and housekeeper run things as they saw fit. And yet, if she perceived something amiss, she could be quite determined in rectifying it. As we shall see.

spring, her first instinct was to deny him, not that she had anything against the Japanese. Quite the contrary: the Oriental culture intrigued her, with its iconography of dragon and crane and the exquisite sensitivity of its artistic design set against the fierceness of its samurai tradition and the bizarre subjugation of its women in their lacquered clogs and clinging robes till they were nothing more than playthings for men (and certainly *they* could use a dose of Ellen Key).* It was just that she was settled finally. And content. She tried to tell Frank that but he wouldn't listen. He needed the work, that was what it was. Needed to acquire his prints and screens and statuary in order to trade in them and make a profit to channel back into Taliesin because there were precious few commissions coming in. Because of her. He gave a long speech—a series of speeches—tiptoeing around the issue of blame, which was mutual, of course, and he assured her he had no regrets but there was the fact of it: he was being passed over, boycotted. And there was the promise of the biggest commission yet, the biggest of his life, a project that would erase all their financial concerns forever—a hotel, a Tokyo hotel to dwarf anything in Asia—and he simply had to go. Had to. And he wasn't going anywhere without her. Ever again.

The whole time they were away she missed Taliesin with an ache nothing would soothe, though the Japanese women were far different from what she'd supposed—the society very nearly matriarchal in some respects, the wives and mothers firmly in control while the men went off like so many schoolboys to play with their painted little geisha and drink rice wine till they lost consciousness—and the food, especially the fried dish they called tempura, appealed to her more than she'd thought it would. She was open-minded. She even asked

* I will refrain from comment.

for the recipe and tried to duplicate it once they got back home to Taliesin, but the coated vegetables and strips of fish she dropped into hot oil in the cavern of her deepest pot seemed only to bloat up and absorb grease like miniature sponges till the blandest fritter or heaviest doughnut would have been a gourmet item in comparison.

"The Asiatic experience was intensely interesting," she said, summing it up for Diana Milquist over soggy fragments of what was meant to be tempura, "truly enlightening—if you could only see the way those people live. Nothing like here. Or Europe." She poked at a limp bit of carrot that had shed its batter, thinking how primitive conditions were, especially in the countryside. She thought of the wooden pallets, paper walls, the toilet that was little more than a hole in the ground. "Nothing at all."

Still, if she'd found Japan a bit of a trial, Frank was invigorated. He bought up prints till their rooms were filled with them, working with money he seemed to draw out of a hat like a magician,* and when they returned he began making preliminary sketches for the hotel project, though nothing had been confirmed. Another year—a blissful year—rolled by at Taliesin, and then, from an unexpected source, a major project for Chicago pleasure gardens modeled on those in Germany and Scandinavia came his way and he plunged into it with all his characteristic ferocity of purpose and vision. Spring came that year on a dizzying wave of perfume from the blossoms of the hundreds of fruit trees he'd planted, pear, apple, peach, apricot, plum, and if the pleasure gardens—Midway, they were calling the place Midway—kept him

* He was, in large part, using funds advanced him by several prominent U.S. connoisseurs of Asian art, most particularly the Spaulding brothers, William S. and John T., of Boston. We can only guess at the magnitude of his commissions on sale. And his schemes for expanding his own collection.

away from Taliesin a good proportion of the time, it was only for the better. Truly. It was. Because she loved him all the more now that he needed her in a practical way, not merely as soul mate and avatar, but as mistress of the house—she was in charge now that he was away so much of the time, and she consulted with the employees and worked to her utmost to make the place shine as it rightfully should, as a testament to him.

It was glorious. She was his right hand and his left hand too and everything fell into place as the days lengthened and warmed and the vines climbed up the sunstruck walls and the honeybees charged the air with a current so alive she could feel it in her veins. Glorious. Just glorious. Until the housekeeper abruptly quit. And then the cook.

"I won't come to work here no longer," the cook told her, "not for no pay—or pay whenever *he* feels like giving it out. And not with what people are saying." The woman stood there before her in the kitchen that had been her exclusive domain, arms akimbo, big-bosomed and thick-waisted, with her sagging chins and loveless marriage, thankless and heedless both. "It's sinful, that's what it is. And sin and pay is one thing, but sin and no pay I just can't abide, and I'm sorry, ma'am, I truly am."

Mamah went straight to her desk and scraped together every coin and bill she could find there, wrapped it all up in a handkerchief and dropped it into the woman's hands, but still she wouldn't stay and she wasn't about to beg her, that was for certain. But now suddenly she was the servant, she was the drudge—the daily accumulation of tasks far beyond her—and though she put out a call to the community, to Diana Milquist and the few women she could call friends, no one came up the drive to work for Slow-Pay Frank and his tarnished mistress.

She did the best she could, but she began to feel as if

she were out of breath all the time, as if dusk followed dawn without an interval, without surcease, and the first thing to suffer was her writing. She simply didn't have time for it. Or for reading either. Or reflection. Or even walks over the hills or a swim in the lake or anything else, her every waking moment focused on keeping the household from collapse while Frank ran to Chicago and back again. Somehow she managed to make it through the month of June, wielding mop, broom and scrub brush in a fury that took her right out of her body and doing her utmost to maneuver around the big pots in the kitchen and prepare the meals for Frank and the men he had working the place. But she was no cook and she'd be the first to admit it, her bread as flat as her flapjacks and her flapjacks charred and rubbery at the same time and the weather too hot for standing over the oven so that the chops were reduced to jerky and all the color seared out of the steak and rump roast. And then one evening in the middle of July, when she'd begun to despair, her hands coarsening, her skin darkening like a peasant's, every joint and muscle aching day and night and the sweat thick at her hairline and gummed up under her arms and between her legs till she was permanently chafed and simply to move was an agony, Frank came in off the train from Chicago with his grin alight and said, "You know, I think I just may have a solution to this little domestic problem."

She'd gone down to the station to meet him in the automobile, with Billy Weston at the wheel, and it seemed to her even hotter at seven in the evening than it had been at noon. She brushed her hair away from her face, trying to look fresh for Frank—and she'd changed her dress, though it was already wet through where she'd leaned back in the seat. Frank was handing his suitcase into the car while Billy saw to his baggage—pottery wrapped in brown paper, yet another carved

Buddha, the broad plane of the Oriental brow and the flat unresisting nose poking through the package. He was lively and full of himself and though he hadn't embraced her—he wouldn't till they were out of sight of prying eyes—he'd already managed to brush up against her twice and she could see he was in urgent need of her. He was grinning. Ducking his head and shuffling his feet on the pavement and tugging at the brim of his hat as if he meant to snatch it right out from under the crown.

"Yes," she said, letting out a long slow breath while fanning herself with the palm of one hand, "and what is it? What's your solution?"

"Say, Billy," he called, turning his head away a minute just to keep her in suspense, "I think I might want to drive tonight and you can climb in back or just go on home to your wife if you like. She's missing you, you know she is. And that boy of yours too. Doesn't he ever wonder where's his daddy?"

Billy was bent over one of the statues and he stood up now and gave an elaborate rolling shrug. "Sure, whatever you say, Mr. Wright. An evening at home? Well, I guess that'll just about hit the spot, then." He was grinning too now. "And Mother"—why did married men of a certain age insist on calling their wives *Mother*?—"I don't suppose she'll mind seeing me around. Or not too much, anyway."

"All right, then. Good," Frank said. "Careful with that, careful!"

It wasn't until they were in the car and he had the machine in gear and started hurtling up the street with a great tromboning blast of the exhaust that he returned to the subject at hand. "You remember John Vogelsang, the caterer down there at Midway?"

She did. Vaguely.

"Big fellow. Heavy build. Blond hair, cropped close?"

She made a noise of assent, but it didn't really matter. He could have been talking about the emperor of China and it was the surest thing in the world that he would fill in the details, all the details, without stint.

"Well"—his hand at the shift, the wind beating like a hurricane and she holding on to her hat for dear life—"I told him about your little problem, *our* problem, that is, and he recommended a couple to me, good workers, husband and wife. She cooks and he serves at table and does repairs and what have you. A kind of handyman/butler all in one."

"They're in Chicago?"

"Yes. They're Negroes. From somewhere in the Caribbean, he says. One of the islands."

"And they're willing to come up here and"—she let out a laugh—"cultivate the Emersonian virtues of country living?"

The roar of the engine, the startled looks on the faces of the cows, the clouds shredding overhead. He shrugged. "Apparently. But they're educated people—at least he is. Very well-spoken for a Negro. Name's Julius, I think it was. Or no, no: Julian. Julian something."

CHAPTER 6: ENTER CARLETON

The man who met them at the station, all elbows and knees and dressed in denim trousers and an open-collared shirt, wore a mask for a face. No smile, no frown, no expression of any kind. He had dishwater eyes, and that was no surprise—all of them had that washed-out look to them up here in the country, like so many duppies, as if the gloomy dead ashpit of the sky had sucked all the life out of them, and this one hid his behind a pair of wire-rim spectacles. He wore a little sand-colored mustache under the jut of his nose and short-clipped hair the same color and all Julian could think of was river sand, dirty with the rains. At least it wasn't yellow. Yellow hair was an aberration on a human being and he swore he'd never seen so much yellow hair in his life all the way up on the train and everybody staring at *him* as if he was the freak and he never raised his eyes once except to look out on the unbroken scroll of green, too much green, green enough to bury anybody—they should have called this place Greenland and not that Eskimo island in Canada. But here he was, the dishwater man. He didn't say hello or welcome or anything at all civil or even human other than "You must be the new help" and "I've come to fetch you up to Taliesin," and he stood apart from them at the station, as if he was afraid the color of their skin would rub off on him.

In the rain that seemed to have started up the minute the train left them on the platform in a volcano of smoke and cinders, Julian struggled with the weight of the steamer trunk and Gertrude's overstuffed suitcase and when she went to help him, with that struck-dumb frog-eyed look of sympathy and hopefulness on her face, that look he hated because it demeaned him, made him into a puny slack little boy all over again, he shrugged her off. "I can handle it myself, woman. I don't need a bit of your help. Now you just stand over there at the wagon and then you climb in and see if you can't open that umbrella." That was what he heard himself say, simple instructions, but his voice was choked with a kind of awakening rage she recognized in the space of one second and she stepped lively and that was that.

And what had this dishwater man come to fetch them in when any fool could see it was going to rain like the deluge itself? An open wagon pulled by a little sorrel team that looked as spoiled as household pets—a wagon, as if this was the nineteenth century still, and here he'd been telling Gertrude how they were improving themselves by going to work for a rich man in the country. He'd had enough of Chicago, where the black people acted just like they were slaves still and the whites were as ignorant and tightfisted and blunted as the Hunkies and Polacks and dumb doughy Irish Micks they were. The country. That was what he'd yearned for, thinking of the island, where at least you could get away into a field of sugarcane and talk to the sky when you had to.

But this country was different, he could see that already, see it before he climbed down off the train and hauled the trunk and suitcase to the wagon and settled in beside the dishwater man and watched the horses grind their pretty flanks. This country was desperate.

Wild. They'd tried to break it with their mules and plows and axes, but it was a very hell pit of trees and bristling hilltops that ran all the way back as far as you could see, a place where bears roamed and wolves howled and the spirits of the red Indians murmured through the ghost hours of the night. And where the only black face he'd see besides Gertrude's was when he looked into the mirror and he never looked into the mirror because he didn't particularly like what he saw there.

So they went up the road past the blood-colored barns and planted fields in the rain that chopped and drove and hissed against the inadequacy of the umbrella, across a bridge with the river spread out under it like a mother's lap and right into the reek of hogs. He saw the place before she did, a collection of stained sheds and a little clapboard house, a man out there in the downpour with his shovel trying to open up a ditch so the discolored waste of the animals could flow out of the pen, and he felt his heart sink when the dishwater man tugged at the reins and they started through the yard. "Is this the place?" he heard himself say, and he wouldn't turn his head to the dishwater man but just let the words tumble out of his mouth like something he was afraid of losing.

Here were the hogs poking their mud-crusted snouts through the slats of the fence, the stink cataclysmic, Gertrude looking woebegone and trying to keep herself from taking in a single breath, and the dishwater man let out a laugh. A laugh. As if any of this was comical. "No," the man said. "No, this is Reider's place." And he pointed on up the hill through the web of the trees and there it was, the biggest house in the world creeping out of the hillside like a wounded beast, like the tail of a big golden dragon, and then they rocked through the ruts and the house came at them and Julian stepped out into the mud boiling up round the flagstones of the courtyard and ruined the shine of his new leather shoes even as his best suit of clothes drank in the wet and clung to his flanks and lay bloated and heavy across his shoulders.

"Hey, Billy!" A voice stabbed at them out of the shadows of an open stall and he saw the man whose voice it was and the motorcar at the same time, a fine expensive machine pulled up safe from the rain and painted just exactly the color of a boatload of bananas. The man was tall, with broad shoulders and a waist narrow as a girl's, with the swollen lips and wet eyes of a sensualist. Maybe he was thirty, maybe that, no more. "Mrs. Borthwick told me to tell you to take them to their quarters to get settled and then have them come into the house so she can show them what needs to be done."

The dishwater man was standing in the mud himself now, as unhurried as if he were bathed in sunshine. "Yeah, sure, Brodelle, just as soon as we unload here and I can get the horses unhitched—but it's a hell of a glorious day, isn't it?"

"Oh, yeah," the other man said and he never moved to lend a hand, never even acknowledged that there were two people here, a man and his wife, strangers in need of assistance, "I guess so—as long as you're a duck."

They both of them had a laugh over that, Gertrude trying to climb down out of the wagon without getting her skirts wet and what did she think, he was going to carry her? Well, he would have, just to show them, but then she was down in the mud, trying to shield him with the umbrella, and he had hold of the trunk with everything they owned inside and they were following the dishwater man across the courtyard and into a room that smelled of old lye soap the mold had got the better of and he was so furious with himself for ruining his shoes and letting his wife down he just dumped the trunk on the floor and stalked back out across the courtyard for the suitcase and when he got back the dishwater man was gone out into the rain to see to the horses and still nobody had offered a word of kindness or welcome or even bothered to introduce themselves. They were cold haughty people, that was what they were—even the lowliest cum rum-shop Bajan idler would have got up and lent a hand. And nobody on the island would have let a stranger walk by without calling out a good day to him. Nobody. It was the smallest courtesy and if you didn't have courtesy then you were no better than an animal.*

"Ah, Julian, honey, you all soaked t'rough." Gertrude was standing in the middle of the room, her muddy shoes already wiped clean and set neatly against the wall. She'd found a towel in the drawer of a bureau that stood half-open and was working it at the nape of her neck where her hair had fallen loose. "Here, honey, you take it and dry yourself," she murmured, handing him the limp towel, which he took without seeing it or feeling the nap of the cloth because for just an instant there the novelty of the situation took him out of himself and he was thinking *I don't know this place or these people and nothing smells right here, nothing smells, nothing smells at all except for lye soap and mold and the dead cold ashes in the hearth*, and then he was running it over the crown of his head so furiously it was as if he was trying to rub the hair right off his scalp.

There was a white service jacket hanging on a hook on the inside of the bathroom door—rich man's plumb-

* We don't know if it was, in fact, raining that day, as all the principals are now dead and I never did ask Billy Weston about it when I had the chance. But O'Flaherty-San likes the echoes here of my own experience of fetching Daisy Hartnett and Gwendolyn Greiner from that very same station on an afternoon on which I can assure you it was raining with all the merciless ferocity rural Wisconsin could summon.

ing, toilet and sink, at least there was that—and if it was two sizes too big for him, he didn't give a damn. "Let me put de iron to dat," Gertrude said, fussing over him, and first he said no but then he relented because he was going to go in there ramrod straight and no wrinkle on him and show this rich mistress of the house that he was no shuffling black fool like half the niggers in Chicago but an educated man with his diploma from Combermere School in Bridgetown, Island of Barbados—Little England, they called it, *Little England*—and an accent as cultivated as the late King himself, even if his wife did speak like a barefoot Bajan peasant and that was no fault of his. They wanted a proper butler, he would give them a proper butler. So yes, put *de* iron to it, woman.

It wasn't fifteen minutes and there was a knock at the door and the dishwater man standing there to lead them through the maze of that house and into the presence. Gertrude kept her eyes down the whole way. She'd changed into her best dress and the white apron she'd found hanging beside the jacket and she had her lips bunched in that monkey way of hers that showed she was nervous and he called her out on it, hissing "Monkey, monkey" till she shot her eyes at him. They went back out into the rain, across the courtyard, quick-stepping to keep out of the mud—cows lowing, and a smell of them too—then into a door on the other side, which led through a sitting room for the workers. Then there was the long expanse of the studio and two men—he recognized the one from the courtyard—seated there at their big desks with their drawings on sheets of paper the size of tablecloths spread out before them and neither one even bothered to look up. Outside again, but with a roof over their heads—the loggia—and on into the main house and a big pot-cluttered kitchen there with a greasy wood range and a mess of plates and dirty silverware in the sink and the lazy fat bluebottle flies clinging to the walls and windows as if they didn't have a care in the world. "This is the kitchen," the dishwater man said and they made one rotation of the room and followed the bony twitch of his shoulders out the door and through a dining alcove festooned with enough artworks, statues, rugs and animal skins—and what *was* that, a badger?—to stock a museum, and then took a sharp left turn into a great grand room crammed with even more foolery and bric-a-brac and the lake livid as a bruise out there beneath the windows.

They saw her before she saw them. She was sitting at the window in a strange kind of high-backed chair slatted like a lobster trap, her rum-colored hair pinned up in a coil so that her ears stood out like scallop shells, white as white. There were books stacked round her, both on the low table to her left and on the floor at her feet, and she seemed to be inscribing something in the ledger in her lap. He shifted his eyes to Gertrude and there she was making those monkey lips again, her hands knitted in front of her as if she were in the side pew of the church, her eyes gaped wide at the sight of all the fine things in the room—the grand piano, the fabrics and paintings and colored-glass lamps and the books in their polished wooden cases that fit them just so—and he wanted to hiss at her but he didn't.

He was feeling the same thing she was: they were inside, in the inner sanctum, the place where the white elite lived at their leisure, and it was a new world to both of them, as fantastic as Captain Nemo's submarine or that spaceship H.G. Wells sent off to the moon. What did they know? They were Bajans. Ignorant and small. And even as the thought came to him he saw himself as a boy filled with shame and excitement as he crouched in the horse nicker and thatch palm outside the grand big house of the landowner, Mr. Brighton, and half the village there ducking down shamefaced to see how he and his white guests took their tea out on the patio, how they lifted their little fingers over the thimble-sized teacups and how the ladies arched their backs and cooed in their little birds' voices and took their tea cakes up to nibble at them without dropping a crumb or staining their perfect white gloves with even the smallest single spot of sweet cream butter or a granule of sugar. So *that* was how it was done, they were all thinking and thinking too of their banged-together wood-slat houses listing over the white limestone foundations and picturing their neighbors sitting there, all black, black as the night of the hurricane, lifting their little fingers over the cups that were no bigger than the ones in a dollhouse.

The dishwater man cleared his throat. "Uh, Mrs. Borthwick," he said, and he was shuffling the toe of his shoe on the carpet as if he was all nerves too, "I'm sorry to disturb you but you said to bring the new help around, and I—"

She started—a quick jump of the shoulders and the blood flushing those scallop-shell ears—and it was as if they'd burst in on her in the bath or in her bed, and she swiveled round in the seat and dropped the heavy book to the floor with a dull reverberant thump he could feel all the way across the room through the soles of his shoes (which he'd wiped up as best he was able, though the shine was dead and gone, maybe forever). "Oh, yes," she said, up on her feet now, smoothing down her dress, two white hands fluttering to her hair, "hello." And then again: "Hello." She paused, drew in a breath. "But how you startled me—I was so deep in my work . . ." Her smile swept all three of them like a lighthouse beacon until it landed on the dishwater man. "But, Billy Weston, how you do creep up on a body."

They stood at the edge of the carpet. No one moved. Then she laughed in a way that was loose and unbridled, almost flirtatious, and let her gaze fall first on Gertrude and then on him. He watched to see her smile fade, but it didn't. "And you must be the new people."

He heard himself say, "Yes, ma'am," but he wasn't fully present, or not yet, anyway. He was trying to gauge her, mental arithmetic, trying to add the sum of her parts and reach some sort of accounting because she was a young woman, younger by a good measure than the architect with his big head of gray hair who'd expended a whole three minutes of his precious time questioning them about the island before he hired them on . . . but she was old too, a kind of chameleon, he saw that now in the light that leached in through the window and trembled along her cheekbone—old as his mother but with the face and figure of a girl yet to bear children. And that was another conundrum, because she had borne children, that's what he'd heard—two of them, by another man altogether—and she was standing here in her pretty dress and her silky pinned-up hair as if she were something high when she was nothing more than common, common and worn-out and *old*.

And what sort of comment was that, or question or whatever it was: *You must be the new people?* Who else would they be, standing there on the edge of her carpet, their black faces shining with sweat above the servants' costumes she'd hung on a hook in the bathroom?

"Well," she said, "good," and she took a step forward as if to see them better. "You must be Julius, then—"

"Julian," he corrected her.

"Julian, yes. And you are—?" She'd turned to Gertrude and she was young again, graceful, sweet.

Gertrude was bunching her lips. For a minute he thought she was going to curtsey. "Gertrude, ma'am."

"Oh, yes, yes, of course, *Gertrude.*" The way she said

it, the way she pronounced his wife's name as if she'd taken it up like a pewter pin she'd found in the dirt and then polished it on her sleeve so it glowed like silver, made something seize in him. "And you'll be cooking for us, then. You've seen the kitchen?"

Gertrude nodded, then dropped her eyes.

"You do understand that you'll be expected to serve as many as ten to twelve people at meals, three times a day—Mr. Wright told you as much, I take it?" She didn't wait for an answer. "And that you'll have to handle the meats and the produce and make use of what we're growing here on the farm, as well as take on all the housekeeping, you and your husband, that is. Do you think you're capable of all that?"

"Oh, she's capable, ma'am." He was standing there at the edge of the rug as if it were a precipice—and for a second it was, waves crashing on the rocks below, gulls screaming in the void. He held himself absolutely rigid. "She may be young, but she's the best cook in all of Bridgetown, a real paragon."

The mistress—and what should he call her, certainly not Mrs. Wright, because she wasn't married, was she?—ignored him. Her eyes were the color of week-old cider with the green flecks of mold still floating on the top of it. They never left his wife's face. "What sort of things do you like to cook, Gertrude—what do you specialize in?"

He tried to answer for her but he barely got the first word out of his mouth before the woman cut him off. And still she wouldn't look at him. "I want to hear from you, Gertrude. What do you cook?" A dip of the shoulders, a laugh. "Practically anything'd be better than what I'm capable of . . ."

Monkey lips, monkey lips. Gertrude gave him a look, squared her shoulders and lifted her eyes. "Jug-jug, pepper pot, fish any way you like it. And conkies.

I make conkies they famous all up down Baxter Road."*

He couldn't help himself. "And white people's food," he blurted, "—she makes white people's food too. Of course."

"Mash potato," Gertrude sang out. "Ham hock and black-eye pea, pig he feet, bee'steak in de pan, frittah, dat sort t'ing."

And here he was, not five minutes into that house and that job of work, and he was hotter than any iron in any smithy's shop in the whole godforsaken country—peasant talk, low ignorance and the smart of humiliation like a stingaree lashed across his face—and he couldn't contain himself to save his life. "Hush," he hissed, jerking his face to hers, every line knitted, "you just shut that, woman! You don't talk like that. You don't ever." He was going to add, *Is that the way I taught you?*, his right hand, his slapping hand, trembling so hard he had to shove it in his pocket, but he caught himself. This wasn't the place. But what place was it? Where was he?

The dishwater man rotated his toe. Gertrude stared at the carpet. In his head, sailing high in quick blooming bursts, were the rockets people sent up arcing over the night-black void of the sea on Empire Day, *pop-pop, pop-pop*. And the mistress—Borthwick, Mrs. Borthwick, was

* I rely on O'Flaherty-San here. He spent some time in the islands while ricocheting round the ports of South and Central America on a merchant ship before transecting the Pacific to grace our lives in Nagoya. Jug-jug is a mixture of guinea corn, green peas and salted meat; pepper pot, as the name implies, is a spicy stew made with a variety of meats; and conkies a blend of cornmeal, raisins, coconut and sundry vegetables, served up in a banana leaf. I'm told the Barbadians—or Bajans, as they seem to call themselves—also love to eat flying fish on a bun, much in the way Americans eat hamburger.

that what the dishwater man had called her?—puffed herself up like a crapaud frog and let her voice rise two levels. "And, *you*," she said, pinning him with her eyes while the words rattled like steel blades in her throat, "you will not talk to her in that tone of voice, not in my presence, not in this house." There was a silence. The earth stopped dead, transfixed on its axis. "Is that understood?"

He could have said anything, could have lost all he'd wanted and dreamed of right then and there and found himself back on that yellow-haired train again, disgraced and disrespected, his poor black peasant Bajan wife crying on his shoulder, but all he said was, "Yes, ma'am."

Out beyond her, beyond the carpet and the bookcase and the lobster-trap chair and all the rest, the sun suddenly exploded through the clouds in a fiery pillar that silhouetted her like some unearthly being, and he saw that sun and that room and the look on her face and fought himself down. He could never be sure afterward but he might even have bowed his head in the way those people in the bushes bowed and ducked away into the shadows when Mr. Brighton or one of the gentlemen or ladies sitting there under their parasols looked out across the lawn. He might have bowed his head. And for what? For what?

He watched her face, saw her arm rise and fall in a dismissive sweep as she ordered the dishwater man to take them off to the kitchen, and then they were moving, he and his wife, following the twitch of the dishwater man's shoulders across the floor and out of the room. And what did she say, Mrs. Borthwick-Wright, Mrs. High-and-Mighty, in her voice of scorn? "*Woman*," she spat, two syllables flung at his back as he retreated and all the while the rockets going off in his head, *pop-pop, pop-pop*.

* * *

She took a dislike to him the minute she laid eyes on him, and she hated to admit it to herself, hated to admit any kind of prejudice, but there it was. It wasn't his looks. He was a good-looking Negro, light-skinned, with proportional lips and deep chocolate eyes, of medium height, slim and self-contained. No, it was something in his demeanor, the way he held himself, rigid as a pole, as if he'd just been shocked with an electric wire and was waiting for his torturer to throw the switch and shock him again. And the way he looked at her with a kind of cool insolence, as if she were the one applying for the job, as if she had to meet his expectations. She'd never seen anything quite like it, though admittedly her experience of Negroes was limited—she'd seen them in people's homes serving at table and the like, and she'd encountered a handful of them when she was a librarian in Port Huron in the days before Edwin, but those Negroes were the ones she approved of, hard-working people educating themselves on their own time. Or at least trying.

And yes, this one—Carleton, Julian Carleton—was well-spoken, as Frank had said, and he seemed intelligent, perhaps too intelligent for his own good, but that he attempted to speak for his wife, to take the words out of her mouth, bully her right there in his first interview in the house, simply infuriated her. She had half a mind to telegram to Frank and tell him to find her someone else because she was sending them right back to Chicago on the morning train, but she didn't. She needed them, needed somebody, anybody, to get her out of the kitchen and back to Ellen Key and her studies and her writing—the life of the mind instead of the scrub brush and the washboard—and perhaps she was being hasty in her judgment. The wife—Gertrude—had seemed sweet and shy. And so young. If Carleton was twenty-five or thereabout, she must have been five years younger, a girl still, eager to please, with real kindness in her eyes—there was a moment there when she actually thought the girl was going to curtsey to her. Her features were regular, almost pretty but for the exaggerated lips, her skin so dark and exotic it seemed to drink up the light. And the way she spoke, with the broad open vowels and the tripping syncopated rhythm that flowed like a song, like a sweet tropical melody played out spontaneously just for her, was perfectly charming.

But could she cook? That would be the test. If she could cook—and the husband serve the way Frank had assured her he could, serve at table and take up the household chores with some of the rigor that had held him frozen there on the carpet—then she was sure she'd be able to get over the awkwardness of that first impression. It was probably nothing, she told herself. He was uneasy, that was all. Trying to make a good impression. She couldn't really blame him for that, could she?

She settled back in her chair. Took up her book again. Before long, she was immersed in her work, the afternoon absorbed in the flow of her hand and the rush of sentiments crowding her mind, and if she thought of the new help at all it was in the silences. Somewhere, at the margins of her consciousness, she might have heard a door open and shut again, might have detected the smallest sounds drifting in from the kitchen—a drawer sliding out, a knife at the whetstone, water running in the sink—but it was the long intervals of silence that made her feel that the house was in good hands, nothing amiss, the routine establishing itself by increments from one tranquil moment to the next. She took her dinner privately that evening, out on the little screened-in porch overlooking the lake, and he set the table and served her properly, without any fuss or a single wasted word. And the food—vegetable soup, tomato salad, a steak the wife had rubbed with a combination of exotic spices that managed to be piquant and savory at the same time, cob corn, potatoes braised in the pan with rosemary from the garden and a dessert of custard flavored with vanilla bean and cinnamon—was better than anything she'd tasted since she'd come back from Europe. She took two glasses of wine with her meal and had a brandy afterward, and for the longest while she just sat there staring off into the distance while the ducks and geese settled in on the lake and the shadows deepened and the fireflies traced their punctuated patterns across the night.

The next morning she went to the kitchen after breakfast (which had been equally delicious and just as thoughtfully prepared as the previous night's dinner), thinking to praise the cook and encourage her too—perhaps even engage in a little small talk. She was curious. She wanted to hear what the girl had to say, listen to her opinions, discover something of her life and where she'd come from. Barbados. It sounded so exotic. And the way she talked—*bee'steak*, *pig he feet*—was like a tonic to her, sweet and refreshing. And different. Above all, different.

She eased open the door, a little speech forming in her head—*Gertrude, I can't begin to tell you how pleased I am*—and stopped dead. The place had been transformed. Where before the room had been close and rancid with the must of last year's bacon and drippings immemorial, a real farm kitchen, now the windows were thrust open onto the courtyard and there was a scent of that piquant spice, of fresh fruit and vanilla. And everything had been rearranged, the cluttered oak table gone, the pots sorted by size, the fry pans hanging from hooks over the stove and shining like jewels, every last plate and saucer and piece of cutlery washed and dried and tucked away in the cupboard and not a fly to be seen anywhere. Gertrude was down on her knees, polishing the brass handles of the stove, and Carleton, up on a stepladder, was scrubbing the ceiling—the ceiling!—with long sweeping strokes of his arms, as if he were dancing in place with an invisible partner. She didn't know what to say. Both of them were aware of her—they had to be—but they gave no notice of it. They went on with what they were doing, utterly engrossed, and she stood there a moment, feeling like a stranger in her own house, until she softly pulled the door to and went on down the hall to her books.

That evening, she had Diana Milquist and her husband, Alvin, to dinner and asked Frank's draftsmen, Emil Brodelle and Herbert Fritz, if they would join them to round out the party. She'd struggled with her work through the morning and into the afternoon, unable to concentrate, her thoughts repeatedly drifting away from Ellen Key and the woman movement to the Barbadians in the kitchen, the wonder of them, the strangeness, *Negroes in the house and who were they, what were they thinking, what sort of bond held* their *marriage together?* Though she wouldn't have admitted it to anyone, the fact was that with Frank gone she was growing bored. She'd begun her book with a thrill of anticipation, in full command of her materials and with an outline so considered and thorough it had stretched to some thirty pages, and yet now that she'd progressed from her introduction through the opening chapters, a certain sameness had begun to creep into the writing—and worse, each sentence seemed to erect a wall against the next, so that she found herself manipulating phrases instead of ideas till all the freshness had gone out of the task.

The irony wasn't lost on her. Here she'd chafed against the burden of the housework and cooking, and now that the Carletons were in charge and she had all the time in the world to devote to herself she couldn't seem to recapture her enthusiasm. But, of course, all writers—even Ellen Key—had to struggle through the dry spots, and she would persist, absolutely, there was no question about that, and she had Frank to look forward to. Frank always enlivened things. Day after tomorrow, that was when he said he'd be back, for a few days at least. And in a matter of weeks, Martha and John would be there with her and everything would be new again.

If anything, the meal was even better than the previous night's. She'd suggested a menu—roast chicken stuffed with cornbread, white biscuits and gravy, boiled ham, deviled eggs, potato salad and vegetables, sliced melon, perhaps a peach cobbler or blackberry pie—and Gertrude had played her own variations on it. Masterfully. And her husband had impressed everyone with the way he'd served at table, holding himself with the unassailable dignity you'd expect from the head waiter at the finest restaurant in Chicago or New York, attentive to the smallest needs, silently whisking one dish away even as the next was set down in its place. Herbert Fritz—just nineteen and living at home with his widowed mother before Frank brought him and Emil Brodelle out from Chicago and Milwaukee, respectively*—had obviously never experienced anything like it. He was on his best behavior, shooting a quick glance round the table each time he was served as if afraid someone would find him out and snatch the plate away, and he ate with a growing and barely concealed enthusiasm, compulsively bringing the napkin to his lips beneath the trace of mustache he was straining to cultivate. "This is simply delicious," he kept saying throughout the meal, first to himself and then to the table at large. "Extraordinary. Really extraordinary. I don't think I've ever tasted—"

"Ever?" Brodelle put in. Emil was just thirty, but he liked to think of himself as a man of experience—he

* To prepare the drawings for an exhibition of his work in San Francisco, projected for the fall. It was, alas, not to be.

tended to lord it above the others when Frank was absent, and she could hardly blame him. There wasn't much for him out here in the country, apart from a trip to the tavern or a solemn horseback ride along the dusty roads. He had a ready wit and a range of learning rare among draftsmen, who tended to be narrowly focused and—well, to her mind at any rate—dull. There was a moment of silence. When he was sure he had everyone's attention, he went on. "Aren't you afraid that comment just might possibly be construed as an implied criticism of our hostess"—and here he smiled at her—"who's done such a heroic job in the kitchen ever since the last—not a whit lamented—*chef de cuisine* left us?"

The boy ducked his head. When he glanced up at her, he was blushing. "I didn't mean—I was only—"

And it was all right. Everyone laughed. Except Carleton, of course, who remained in character, hovering against the wall like a revenant in his white jacket.

"Yes," she said, laughing still, "I know what you mean. Our new cook is such a paragon"—she was conscious of using Carleton's term, wondering vaguely if it would please him—"I'm afraid we can all look forward to putting on weight up here at Taliesin." She raised her glass. "Compliments to the chef!" she said, and everyone, even Alvin, whose profession seemed to have made him dubious about all things oral, lifted a glass in homage. She felt expansive, contented. "Well," she said, setting down the empty glass, "is anyone ready for dessert?"

She took a long walk next morning, then settled into work. Despite the heat—it must have been ninety by half-past ten—she found she was able to see the book afresh and resolve some of the problems that had dogged her the day before. She read over the completed pages, making small emendations—and they truly *were* good, the prose sharper and clearer than anything she'd been able to extract from Ellen Key, whose language had a tendency to bog down in a Swedish morass of misplaced modifiers and parenthetical phrases. She was in another place altogether, moving forward with a subtle refinement of Key's ideas on the evolution of love and the way men often desire a woman before they know her while women are too often obligated to develop sexual desire after the fact, thinking of Frank, Frank and her, and how she'd been the one to reveal herself first, a rainy autumn day, the children in school and Edwin at the office and she in her robe and nothing under it—when she became aware that someone else was in the room with her.

There was a smell of some caustic solution—muriatic acid? gasoline?—and when she looked up she saw Carleton bent over the fireplace with a bucket and scrub brush. He was wearing a blue work shirt with the sleeves rolled up and a pair of heavy trousers, far too heavy for this heat. His back was to her. She watched him go down on one knee, the brush working rhythmically over the upper surface of the stone where the soot stains reached almost to the ceiling like long grasping fingers, but was it wise to use a flammable solution? Even if it would have evaporated, whatever it was, by the time fall came around and the fireplace was in use again? She wanted to say something, wanted to interfere, but she didn't. Let him show some initiative. Certainly Mrs. Swenson, the housekeeper who'd preceded him, wouldn't have dreamed of scrubbing the fireplace—or anything else, for that matter, except at distant intervals and then only under compulsion. Just the night before, as Diana was gathering up her things to leave, she'd taken Mamah aside and told her how lucky she was. "These Negroes of yours are just too good to be true. I'm envious. I am. If I could only get Alvin to loosen his purse strings I'd march right over here and steal them away."

For a long moment she simply sat there, watching him. There was something intrinsically fascinating about the Negro's movements—he was so fluid and athletic—and he wasn't so much dancing, she realized, as conducting, as if the brush were his baton and the stone of the fireplace his orchestra. But that was a foolish thought, *the stone an orchestra*. What was she thinking? She had work to do. She turned back to the page before her *(For many men, too many men, sexual attraction precedes any notion of love, and this too often leads to . . .)*, but the rhythmic swish of the wire brush distracted her and before long she was staring out the window. He truly was a good worker, she thought, glancing up at him again. She watched his shoulders dip and rise, the brush sweeping to and fro like a hypnotist's watch, thinking she'd been too harsh on him that first day, too judgmental, too quick to take offense . . . but then she saw the rage in his face all over again, the way he'd snapped at his wife, and thought how wrong it was, how inadmissible, how *primitive*.

He needed education, that was all. There were cultural differences at work here, just as there were in Japan and even Germany, but still, beneath it all, the attitudes were the same. Male attitudes. Archaic. Barbaric. Suddenly she felt herself go out to him—she could help, she could, not simply him but Gertrude too. Her eyes fell on the low table before her, and there, amidst a scatter of books and notepaper, was one of her presentation copies of *The Woman Movement*, still in its wrapper.* She took it up on an impulse and rose to her feet. He was an intelligent man, she was sure of it, the sort of man who would welcome the gift of knowledge, thank her a thousand times over, because now, for the first time, he would see

* Translated by Mamah Bouton Borthwick, A.M., with an introduction by Havelock Ellis. New York: G. P. Putnam's Sons, 1912.

the other side of the coin, the woman's side, see how his wife felt and should be made to feel.

The only problem was that she didn't know what to call him, not under the circumstances—Julian was too familiar and Carleton too formal. She saw the muscles clench in his shoulders as the sound of her footsteps drew closer, noticed the briefest hesitation before both arms swung back into motion, and then she was standing over him, the reek of the gasoline fumes in her face, clearing her throat. "Excuse me," she said, "Mr. Carleton, *Julian*."

He turned at the sound of his name, a slow rotation of his head, the hair there cut short so that it clung to his skin in dark whorls like some extraneous growth wheeling out across the expanse of his skull, but he remained in his crouch, one knee braced against the coping, the brush arrested. And here were his eyes coming into play, dark eyes, so dark she could scarcely distinguish iris from pupil. He stared up at her, his eyes fixed, his features immobile.

She held the book in both hands as if it were a missal, her fingers playing over the wrapper. "I just wanted to say," she began, "what a splendid job you and your wife are doing. I'm very pleased. Very pleased indeed. And I'll be sure to tell Mr. Wright." She hesitated. His eyes were dead, his lips pressed tight. "I'm sure he'll be—well, he'll be pleased too. I'm sure."

If the moment was awkward it was made even more so by the fact that he was kneeling, as if he were bowing to her in subjugation, as if he were a slave in the old South—a darkie—and she the overseer's wife. Mrs. Legree, Mrs. Mamah Borthwick Legree, her whipping boy at her beck and call. He didn't smile, he didn't nod, didn't utter a word. He didn't even seem to be breathing.

"I'm sorry," she said, though she didn't know why or

what she had to apologize for, "—to, to interrupt you like this. You're doing a very fine job there. But I just wanted to say—about that first interview—well, I'd like you to have this." She held out the book to him, and without coming up out of his crouch, he shifted the brush to his left hand and took it from her with his right, his gestures so slow and deliberate he might have been moving underwater. He didn't even glance at the book. Just held her eyes, as if to await further instructions. Or any instructions.

"I think you'll find this rewarding," she went on. "Enlightening too, I hope. You see, no matter what our various cultures proclaim, marriage is almost everywhere the same. And, by and large, the women are the ones to suffer—under the current system, the system under which we've had to live from time immemorial, from the time of Moses and beyond, the Egyptians, I suppose, the Mesopotamians—women have been unequal partners and must live out their lives unfulfilled, in either love or work. Do you understand what I'm saying?"

Nothing. He knelt there in his fumes.

"I'm speaking of Gertrude. Of your wife."

Suddenly his face opened up. "Oh, don't you worry about her," he said, and he was grinning now. "I've got that under control."

"No, I don't think you understand—she needs to express herself."

The grin faded. He was shaking his head side to side. "I know that, ma'am, and that's why I work her day and night to stop her talking like a bush nigger and use the King's English. And she will. She *will.*" His eyes stared out past her, as if he were addressing someone across the room. His voice went cold. "I promise you that."

When Frank came home for two days at the weekend, he was every bit as pleased as she was with the new help.

Billy Weston fetched him from the station an hour before dinner, and he blew into the house like a cool breeze, taking her in his arms and dancing round the room with her before thrusting a foil-wrapped box of chocolates at her and disappearing into the drafting room to confer with Emil and Herbert. Of course, he couldn't help shifting a vase from one shelf to another along the way or sliding a chair six inches to the right before deciding to move it back again—it was a compulsion with him—but the house seemed to have passed muster. The next she saw him was when she went out to her garden to cut flowers for the table and he was striding across the courtyard with Billy Weston in tow, firing off instructions to Lindblom, the landscaper, and his foreman, Thomas Brunker (a big-bellied man with a corona of white hair who always gave her a sour look, as if he disapproved of her, and so much the worse for him because she was the mistress of this house now and she was here to stay). "Dinner in ten minutes, Frank," she sang out, and he smiled and waved and went on round the corner, never breaking stride.

When they finally did sit down to dinner she saw that he seemed to have lost weight—fretting over the loose ends at Midway, sleeping irregularly and to all appearances dining on the fly or not at all—but he tucked into everything Carleton brought out of the kitchen on the silver tray he held high over one shoulder and manipulated with a flourish that managed to be neither subservient nor showy, but just precisely right. Gertrude surpassed herself with the cuisine, serving up one of her spicy stews ("'Hotter de day, hotter de spice,' dat what my mama say. 'You got to sweat to cool off'"), with cornbread, cucumber salad and mint yogurt made from a culture she'd brought with her from Barbados via Chicago, fresh-picked melon and a berry tart. The next day she spent the whole morning preparing a picnic lunch, which Carleton, ever proper in his white jacket, served them on blankets down by the lake. Frank was enraptured, declaring the day a holiday from work and inviting all his employees, right on down to the field hands, to join in the festivities. The plates circulated. Carleton went up and down the hill a dozen times and every time he came back the platter was laden and everybody agreed that they'd never tasted better fried chicken or potato salad or pork chops and greens. They were lying there on their blankets, content, when one of the men pulled out a mouth organ and Frank started the singing and before anyone knew it the stars were showing overhead.

The next day Frank went back to Chicago, but not before putting away a two-fisted farmer's breakfast and raising such a hosanna of praise to Gertrude's buttermilk pancakes that she sidled out of the kitchen to give him a shy smile and one of her Barbadian homilies ("Nothin' better den you eat well and purge clean"), and when he came back in the middle of the following week, she slaughtered a turkey for him and stuffed it with a mixture of smoked sausage and something she called cou-cou. And then Frank was gone again and the work of the farm went on and Mamah found herself counting down the days till the first of August, when John and Martha were due for their visit.

She was there at the station an hour early on the appointed day. Billy Weston parked the automobile at the curb and made use of the time to bring out the sheen of its finish with a nappy cloth and a can of wax, always thinking of Frank and how particular he was about the condition of his machines, while she paced up and down the platform in the rising still heat of midmorning. She hadn't seen the children since Christmas when she and Frank had gone into Chicago to a hotel and she tried to make up for the past two Christmases by taking them out to a restaurant and the symphony and burying them in gifts they seemed entirely indifferent to. Ellen Key had liberated her and she knew she should feel nothing but joy in her present circumstances—she was one of the chosen ones, a woman living her life in love's freedom*—and yet still, the looks on their faces, wary and hopeful at the same time, always seemed to flood her with guilt. Each time she saw them she expected them to deny her, to lash out and declare their independence—or worse, to tell her about Edwin's new bride and how she was their mother now. Because their old mother wasn't fit. Had never been fit and never would be.

The train pulled into the station, one more arrival, and there they were, looking like strangers, John too adult now at twelve to take her hand and Martha gazing up at her in bewilderment, as if she were having difficulty placing her. "Children," she cried, "John, Martha, come to your mother," and they did come, with some prompting by their nanny (Edwin's employee and no love lost there), because they had no choice. "How was your trip?" she asked as they waved their goodbyes to the nanny and settled themselves in the automobile, and both immediately answered "Fine," in unison, as if they'd rehearsed it. "Well, good," she said. "We've got all sorts of things planned for you—horseback riding, swimming, of

* "Love's Freedom" is one of the chapter headings in Key's *Love and Marriage*, also published in the United States in 1912. The chapter that precedes it is titled "The Evolution of Love," and it is succeeded by "Love's Selection," an application of Darwinian terminology to manners and mores, building toward the final chapters on free divorce and a new marriage law. One can't help seeing Mamah's passionate embrace of the Swedish author as a means of self-justification, if not ritual cleansing.

course, and, John, did I tell you there's a new rowboat for the lake? And, Martha—we've got peacocks now, two of them, and they have the most wonderful call or squawk or whatever it is . . ."

It was hot. The children were withdrawn. She found herself nattering on inanely, hoping to spark some sort of reaction in them, but they seemed joyless, as if coming to the country were a rare form of punishment. John perked up a bit over the details of Frank's motorcar, comparing it (unfavorably) to the new red Abadal Stephen Pennybacker's father had just bought, and Martha seemed gratified to discover the dolls she'd left behind last summer lined up all in a row on the shelf beside the bed, and yet it wasn't until after they'd gone down to the lake for a swim that they began to resemble the children Mamah remembered. There was something in that scene—bare legs and feet, the skipping of stones and chasing after the geese, frogs erupting in their chorus, the smell of hair gone wet and dry and wet again—that had a deeply calming effect. By suppertime, both children were complacent, replete with their hamburger sandwiches, Coca-Cola and paper-thin Barbadian potato crisps. By bedtime, she was able to look in on them and offer a goodnight kiss, and Martha, though she announced that she was almost nine now and perfectly capable of reading on her own, allowed her to sit in the rocker by the bed and read aloud from *The Wind in the Willows* as if the past five years had been merely an interruption.

In the days that followed, as the children gradually acclimated themselves to Taliesin and she began to feel more at ease with them, her work seemed to come easier to her, because she was a mother—their mother—and no use in denying it or avoiding it or whatever she'd been doing. When they were away from her, home in Oak Park with their nanny and their schoolfellows and the new wife Edwin had been so quick to acquire, she pictured them as incorporeal, ghost images on a photographic plate.* They were distant and so was she. But now that they were here, she realized how much she enjoyed seeing them ambling about the rooms or draped over Frank's furniture, handsome open-faced children who made her proud. Of course, the situation wasn't ideal and never would be—they were forever bursting in on her, squabbling over one thing or another, pale children, indoor children who had no appreciation of the countryside and little capacity for entertaining themselves, but that wasn't their fault, it was Edwin's.

More than anything, she looked forward to seeing them at meals, where there were no distractions and she could tease out their thoughts. She was amazed at the change in them in just a year's time. They seemed so mature, especially John, who was on the verge of young manhood, but Martha too, Martha who should have been Frank's child, but wasn't and anyone could see that in the set of her eyes—even Kitty, as grasping, jealous and vindictive as she was, should have been able to recognize that in an instant and allow Frank to have his divorce without hesitation. Very gradually, Mamah began to acquaint them with the ideas of Ellen Key—and Frank was a help here, when he was home, the two of them holding a sort of Socratic dialogue for the benefit of the children, never lecturing, but rather letting the subject of the conversation shift naturally from the events of the

* Edwin Cheney was remarried in 1912, a year after his divorce, to Miss Elsie Millor. They were to have three children and a placid life, a small mercy after the conflagration into which Mamah and Wrieto-San unwittingly tossed him. He prospered in business, doted on his children and never missed a college reunion.

day to love and the soul and the right—the compulsion—of women everywhere to stand up and take charge of their lives.

She wasn't going to remake the children in a single summer, she knew that, but her hope was to educate them in the way she was educating Carleton, with the ultimate aim of making the world a better and more equitable place. And, on another level, to ease her guilt, to offer a rationale for what had happened on that awful night in Colorado when she'd stolen away without a word because she had to save her own life before she could save theirs. At any rate, the children were there and Frank was there (when he wasn't in Chicago) and the Carletons were in the kitchen and Billy Weston came up the hill each morning to see that every little detail fell in place, the peacocks gave out with their desolate cries, the cattle lowed and the horses nickered at the rail because they wanted an apple and they wanted to be mounted and spurred through the fields and out over the hills, and she was there too, as deeply and fully as she could ever remember being anywhere.

Then there came a morning, breakfast done with and the children quietly occupied in their rooms—reading, she supposed, or hoped, at any rate—when she settled down to work with a cup of coffee and realized she'd forgotten something, and what was it? She gazed out on the yard, trying to recollect, the dense moist air drifting in through the open casement windows along with the faintly acid scent of the lady ferns Frank had clustered against the yellow stone of the foundation. For contrast. And there was genius in that too, his vigilance for the telling detail, the flowerbeds of the courtyard alive with color—coreopsis, phlox, hollyhocks and tiger lilies, and she really did need to get out more and tend them—even as the outer walls denied it, the simplest chromatic scheme there, green against yellow and the yellow fading to gold. She saw Billy Weston down below at the base of the hill conferring with Brunker over the lawn mower, the sun shearing them so that their features were annulled, two irregular shining spheres cut loose from the dark shadow of their gestures, and beyond them the lake and the road and the distant smudge of grazing cattle. She took a sip of coffee. Glanced down at her notes.

And then she remembered: she'd meant to speak to the cook, to Gertrude, about baking something special that afternoon for Martha. Or rather Martha's friend Edna, who was planning on riding her pony over so the two of them could put on their party dresses and have tea like little ladies out on the screened-in porch. Some finger cakes, maybe, something with coconut and cream—Gertrude was a marvel with coconut. And if John promised not to pester the girls, she supposed he could join the party at some point—and Billy Weston's son, Ernest, who was a year older than John and more rough and tumble, more a country boy, but who at least gave John someone to tag along with. Or maybe that wasn't such a good idea—the boys could have a separate party, yes, that would be better, perhaps down by the lake where they could work off some of their high spirits.

She got up from the chair—Billy had taken the mower himself now and was cutting a swath away from Brunker, who hadn't moved save to shove his hands in his pockets—and crossed through the dining room to the kitchen. She rarely came into the kitchen anymore—there was no need to really, and when she did she felt almost as if she were intruding. Especially when both the Carletons were there. It was nothing they said or did particularly, but they seemed to tense when she entered the room, which was only natural, she supposed. Though Mrs. Swenson never seemed to mind. She wouldn't have cared if Mamah had camped out under the sink—would have preferred it, for that matter, so she'd have someone to complain to all day long in her high ratcheting whine. But the Carletons were different and she respected that.

It wasn't till she was there, her hand on the doorknob, that she sensed something wasn't right. A noise alerted her, a sharp wet sound, as of meat pounded with a mallet, succeeded by a curse—a man's voice, Carleton's, rising up the scale. She pushed open the door. And entered a room that was like an oven, like a furnace, the windows drawn shut and smoke in the air, something burning in a pan on the stove. She saw Carleton then, his back to her, standing over what looked to be a pile of washing on the floor, but wasn't washing at all. It was Gertrude. Her left eye was swollen shut and there was a bright finger of blood at the corner of her mouth. She crouched in the corner, shrinking away from him, her head bowed, her arms clutched to her chest.

"You stupid fucking cow!" Carleton shouted. "I've told you a thousand times if I've told you once: I want my meat cooked rare. Rare, do you hear me?"

The door was ajar. The smoke erupted from the pan. Carleton didn't seem to notice. Or care. He was secure. He'd pulled the windows shut on the scene, closed the room off so he could assault his wife and no one to interfere. Mamah stood there in the doorway, paralyzed.

Carleton's shoulders jumped beneath the fabric of his shirt. He dropped his voice. "You stupid, stupid Bajan slut," he whispered, and lashed out with the toe of his tarnished tan boot, once, twice, as if he were trying to kick through the wall, and Gertrude drew in two sharp breaths in succession and he kicked her again. "What does it take to get some respect around here? Huh? What do I have to do, kill you? Is that what you want? Is it, woman? Is it?"

That was when Mamah stepped in. She was terrified, panicked, her every instinct to turn and run, but she took hold of the enameled edge of the wash basin and flung herself between them, raising it up like a shield. He was right there, right in her face, the smell of him as raw and unrelieved as anything she'd ever experienced, as death, as mangled flesh, rotten flesh, flesh set afire and burning up in the pan. He didn't move, didn't flinch or back off or acknowledge her, and for the fraction of a moment she thought he was going to come at her next, but then she saw that he was as shocked as she was, his eyes retreating from the scene as if he'd just awakened from a dream to this nightmare of abuse and outraged whiteness and the flame under the pan and the smoke rising, rising. "Don't you dare," she said.

He took a step back, dropped his arms to his sides.

Mamah could barely control her voice. She was shaking. "You get out of here!" she shouted. "Get out!"

And then the strangest thing happened: he grinned at her. His eyes went cold and up came that automatic grin. But he wasn't moving. And his hands were clenched. "You speak to me like that?" he said, without a trace of emotion. "Who do you think you are? You're nothing but a—"

"No," Gertrude groaned, trying to get to her feet. "Julian, no—"

"Nothing but—" And then, only then, did he turn away, jerking the handle of the cast-iron pan so that it skittered away from the flame and clattered to the floor, pausing only to give it a savage kick before he made his way to the door. But he wasn't finished, not yet. He swung back round on her. "You people," he spat, "with your *books*. This woman is my wife here. My *wife*. Can you understand that?"

"I'm giving you your notice, right here and now, as of

this minute," she said, but the words sounded hollow in her ears, and she knew it and so did he.

He shook his head slowly, as if the motion of it pained him—"And you call *us* niggers," he said—and then he was gone.

CHAPTER 7: POP-POP

He was lost and he knew it, hot blood beating in his temples with the certain knowledge of every degraded inconsolable thing to come, the hurt, the yellow-haired train, Chicago, the island, back to the island with his tail between his legs like a whipped cur, and who was to blame? Who else? Gertrude. That bitch. That cow. And how he'd ever got mixed up with a woman like that was a mystery to him—the ignorance of her and the insipidity, the barefooted low peasant drivel that came out of her mouth—but it was his fault too, he knew that, the fault of his lust that was like a dog's lust. He saw her naked breasts in the eye of his mind, and the tight sweet insuck of her belly, the place between her legs, the way she swayed beneath the maubey pot perched up on the flat crown of her head sashaying her derriere through the marketplace in Bridgetown, and it was *Maubey, maubey for sale, and you t'ink you be wantin' somet'in' else, little sir?*, she seventeen and he too weak to deny himself. That's right. And now it was over. Now it was ruined. One slip and he had his notice and where would he go now? *Women.* They squeezed you, oh, they did. Squeezed you. Squeezed you. Till there was no juice left.

Only then did he realize that he was talking to himself, that he'd spoken aloud for anybody to hear, and he took a moment to lean forward and spit on the corner of the rug he'd brushed himself and brushed again till the nap stood up and laid itself down twice over. But the door. The door was right there beside him, still half-open, because he'd stalked out of that room and stopped in his traces, his back pressed to the wall, too worked up and twisted with the sick clutch of despair to make his legs work. Through the gap of the door came the smoke, black as skin, twisted like a pot of eels, eelskin, rising in a column to fan across the ceiling. He could hear her in there sobbing as if she had something to sob about—he had half a mind to go back through that door and finish what he'd started, finish both of them, both of the bitches, one black and one white. Mamah. Mamah Bouton Borthwick. Translator. Suffragist. Soul mate. He'd read in that book and it was nothing but cant and heresy. Who was she to interfere between a man and his wife? She might have been free with her love but even the whores on Baxter Road had the sense to charge for it.

His legs were moving. He was going up the hall, that was what he was doing, thinking to get into the cornfield and work the rage down out of his head and into his legs, his feet, down into the ground where he could bury it, and he was twisting his hands, one inside the clench of the other—the heel of his right hand stinging where he'd slapped her, or had he burned it when he jerked the pan from the stove? No matter. He could barely control the right one or the left either, all the fine things of the house mocking him with what they were and he wasn't, but he fought them with all his will and then he was out the door and freed into the air he could breathe with its veritable stink of cattle and their hindquarters, the sun sudden on his face, and a flutter of movement against the sky. He saw the peacocks perched on the low line of the roof like displaced things and that was all right because they were cocks and not hens and the hens were little pecking creatures going around in the shadows because they were ashamed of themselves.

Things had been coming to a boil for the past week and more, these whites—Brodelle and the dishwater man and the rest of them, the fat-faced fools in the village, shopkeepers, horsetraders, farmers in their buggies and black Ford automobiles—giving him no more notice than they would a bug. Or less.* At least they could see a bug, but they didn't see him at all because they didn't like what they saw any more than he did. Unless they wanted something. Then it was *Carleton, fetch me this; Carleton, polish my boots; Carleton, the soup's cold.* And Gertrude. Gertrude gave him her look of dole day and night, fretting over him, begging him not to upset the mistress—or the children or the precious holy houseguests or the squinting idiot at the grocery, as if every one of them was a king and queen in his own right—and always it was the same low peasant talk. Biddy wisdom and platitudes. Diarrhea out the wrong end.

She'd got up that morning in the pulsing gray tumble of dawn and the first thing out of her mouth was, "Julian, Julian, I dream de sucking pig." He ignored her. He was slapping water on his face, feeling his way with the razor because he wouldn't look in the mirror. "Not jus' de pig." She came round him from behind, thrust her sorrowful face in his. Her voice had turned ominous—more of her Bajan claptrap and superstition, that was

* Certainly I can appreciate what the Barbadian must have been feeling, given my own experiences in the lily-white state, but O'Flaherty-San, as a *gaijin* in Japan, brings his own sentiments to the table as well. He can scarcely walk down the street without people whispering "long nose" and "butter stinker" and the like behind his back. Our own family embraces him, of course, without prejudice, in respect to his qualities. Even if he is a *gaijin*.

what it was, more ignorance. Tears started up in her eyes. "I dreamin' de wedding too, don't you see? Pork. Pork and de wedding all in one dream—"

"Oh, hush it," he snapped and turned his back on her again, the towel rough as sandpaper against his face. "There isn't going to be any wedding. Not here, not with these people. They're too good for the forms and rituals of civilization. For the Bible. For anything but themselves."

Her eyes bled out at him. She turned up her palms and she was pleading now, her voice slipped down and gone, no more than a gargle in her throat. "Don't you know what that means?"

He knew. If you dreamed of pork and a wedding, all in one dream, it meant the cataclysm was coming, *pop-pop*, the bloodletting, the horror. And maybe it was, but he didn't want to hear about it. Not now. Not at this hour of the morning, when he had to put on his service jacket and go in amongst the white people and bow and scrape like a plantation nigger, not ever. "Shut that ignorance," he said, whirling round on her.

She shrank away from him, dwindling into her bones, but she was still there. Still talking. Still pushing him. She said: "What you do wid dat hatchet?"

"Hatchet? What hatchet? I don't know anything about any hatchet."

"Under de pillow. For de shingle. Dat one."

He shrugged, caught out in a lie, and what was she now, his keeper? "I don't care," he said, and he was just floating the words out there. "Protection. I keep it for protection."

"From what? Bears?" Her eyes had sharpened. She was on the offensive and he didn't like it one whit. "De redskin Indian wid dere tomahawk? T'ieves? Or maybe Jesus. Maybe Jesus gone come for you and you gone chop 'im up in little pieces." She backed up a step, just out of reach, in her shift still, with her eyes like two coals shining in the stove, two red-hot fiery coals that nothing in this world could extinguish. "Julian," she whispered. "Julian."

"What? What is it? Can't you see I've got work to do—?"

"I heard you. Las' night. Night before dat too. You was sittin' by the window dere, talkin' to dat hatchet you was holdin' in your lap like a baby child, like a hex doll. Dat what it is—dat your hex doll?"

There was no answering that kind of willful stupidity and she knew it before the words were out of her mouth because he'd taught her to know it and he was going to keep on teaching her till she learned it for good and he took two quick steps forward and caught her face in his right hand, pinching it there in the hollows of her jawbone so her mouth was distorted, and then he shoved that lewd hateful cringing black fish face as hard as he could so she fell away from him like one of her rag-and-bone voodoo poppets and that put him in a mood, it surely did.

But here he was in the courtyard, striding along with his head down and the peacocks wailing and the sun beating at him like a hammer, as full of pure rage as he'd ever been. One foot in front of the other, the cornfield down there like a tall green stand of cane, the closest thing to cane, and maybe she'd relent, maybe she'd step back and keep him on if he could just get down there into that field and let it all run out of him like the poison from a snakebite wound till his heart slowed and the beating stopped in his head. He was so intent he didn't see the figure poised there in the shadows of the stable till the figure emerged into the chop of the light in one swift motion—a giant's step—and took hold of his arm.

Brodelle. Brodelle in jodhpurs and riding boots, narrowing his wet blue eyes and pursing his lips round whatever it was he had to say, and what was it going to be this time? Lick my boots, kiss my arse, go fuck yourself? But no. "Saddle my horse, will you?" That was what it was. Saddle my horse. "I'm in a hurry."

He didn't have time to be astonished, the sequence of events as swift and sure and unstoppable as a row of dominoes all falling in a line, and he jerked his arm back as if he'd been stung, squared his shoulders under that sun and stared the man in the face, the fool, the interfering white fool who couldn't have known what he was doing. He stared. Just stared. And here came the change, because Brodelle saw him now, really saw him, one man to another, the tight-jawed look of the deliverer of commands shading to something else, something puerile and powerless, because a command presupposes a response—scrape and bow, *Yassuh, Massah*—and Julian was giving him nothing. "What's the matter with you—are you deaf? I said saddle the goddamn horse."

One more full beat, holding fast to those soft sinking useless wet eyes and not a word needed, not a word to waste, and then he turned his back on him and went down the courtyard to where the green corn sprang up even as Brodelle cursed him—"You black nigger son of a bitch!"—knowing even then that there was no help now, not in the fields or anywhere else, because there were two voices speaking in his head, the one that said maybe, maybe I will, maybe she will, maybe, and the one that said never, never again, never, never, never.

She wasn't much use as a nurse—she didn't have the sympathy for it or the patience either and the sight of blood made her feel faint—but she bent to Gertrude, helped her to her feet and threw a frantic glance round the kitchen, looking for a scrap of cloth, a towel, anything to use as a compress. The pan was on the floor, a blackened slab of meat hissing beside it, the smoke faltering now, bellying and receding till it began to dissolve in transparent wisps. She went to the sink, ran cold water over the washrag she found hanging on a hook there and tried to press it to Gertrude's eye, but Gertrude shied away. Wouldn't look at her. "No, no, ma'am," she kept saying. "No, no, don't you bother. I jus' fine. Julian too. Julian fine. Please, ma'am, please don't go blamin' Julian, 'cause half de time he don't know what he do."

"Doesn't know?" She was outraged. How could this woman even begin to defend her husband when she herself had seen him kick her as remorselessly as he might have kicked an animal? "He beat you."

"No, I slip on de wet spot and take a tumble, dass all." The eyes came up now in a sidelong glance. Her hair had fallen loose in a solid kinked wedge that floated over one eyebrow in a glisten of the purest black. She had a blunted look to her, the look of suffering in all its forms and array, but there was something else there too, something distant and calculating.

It took a moment before Mamah realized it wasn't fear of her husband that was driving her—this pretty young girl who only meant well—but fear of her, of the white woman who'd invaded the kitchen, the mistress of the house who could snap her fingers and hire and fire three times over. It was a shock. She'd seen women cowed by their husbands, living behind them, through them, as if they were mere instruments or tools, but this was sadder still, the saddest thing in the world. "You know I have to let you go," she said. "I'm sorry."

"Give 'im one more chance. He de good mon. You say so youself."

But she was shaking her head, awash with emotion, soaked in it, trembling still with the dregs of the fear and rage that had thrown her up against that hateful black beast who'd beaten his wife as if she weren't even human and was one step from turning on her too. It was impossible, intolerable to have that sort of thing in her own house as if they were in some foreign slum, some shanty crawling with every kind of violence and ignorance and fever. "I'm sorry," she said again. "I know it's not your fault—you're a good woman, I'm sure of it, a good dutiful young woman and a first-rate cook . . . but don't you see? It's just wrong. Wrong."

She realized then that she still had the wet compress in her hand and she held it out before her with an insistent shake of her wrist till Gertrude stepped forward and took it. Then she went to the door, thinking of Frank because Frank would know what to do, Frank would handle this, and she didn't care how hectic his work was or how much they needed him because he'd have to come home that very afternoon, on the next train, and she wouldn't feel safe till he did. She'd get her bag and go right straight out the door and have Billy drive her to the telegraph office, that was what she was thinking, but she paused just a moment in the doorway to look back at Gertrude standing stock-still amidst the wreckage with the dripping rag clenched in one hand while she absently lifted the other to her lip and the dark stain of blood there. "You've got two weeks," she said. And once more, one final time: "I'm sorry."

Her first impulse was to go to the drafting room and rouse Brodelle or Herbert Fritz to go find Billy and she'd actually started off in that direction before she reversed herself and went instead to the bedroom for her purse and hat. She barely glanced at herself in the mirror—she was wrought up, her heart in her mouth, and there was no time to waste—and then she was striding through the house, past the kitchen, out the door to the loggia and into the drafting room. Herbert was there, bent over his desk, but Brodelle was nowhere to be seen.

"Herbert, I don't mean to interrupt," she said, and she could hear the agitation in her own voice, "but I was wondering if you've seen Billy—or, I mean, if you could go and fetch him, please. I've got to—it's urgent."

The boy was wearing a loose black satin tie and long trailing smock, in imitation of Frank, though it promised to be another hot day. He'd been deep in his work and he gave her a look of utter bewilderment, as if he'd suddenly lost the capacity to speak, snatching a quick glance at his drawing before he flushed and got to his feet. "He was here earlier, with Brodelle, an hour ago maybe—"

"Where *is* Emil?"

A duck of the head. "He said he was going to go riding before lunch—and work late, of course, to make up for it—"

She waved a hand in dismissal. "If you'd tell Billy to bring the motorcar round—I need to go into the village and I won't be gone an hour. It's very urgent." He was already at the door, a scramble of limbs and the scrape of his shoes, when she called out to him. "I won't be taking the children." She hesitated a moment, watching his face—he was still flustered but anxious to please, a good boy, malleable, likable. "Would you look in on them—if it's not too much trouble?"

The sun was already baking the flagstones of the courtyard as Billy held the door for her and she climbed into the car, everything still and peaceful and not the hint of a breeze. Billy was in his work clothes, as clean and precise and neat as he always was, no matter the job or its demands or how grease-stained and mud-caked his fellow workers might have been. He tipped his hat to her as he slid behind the wheel—"Looks to be another scorcher," he said and she answered that it certainly did—and that was the last thing she said until he pulled up in front of the Western Union office and she instructed him to wait there for her. She'd wanted to confide in him, but the thought of the scene in the kitchen was too humiliating, too overwhelming, to confide to anyone. She'd had a shock, that was it. And she wasn't over it yet.

It took her two minutes to compose the telegram—COME AS QUICKLY AS POSSIBLE STOP SOMETHING TERRIBLE HAS HAPPENED—and then she paid the man, got in the car and had Billy drive her back to Taliesin, trying to stay calm, telling herself that this crisis would pass as they all invariably did and that Frank would be there to support her, as he'd always been and always would be.*

When Billy turned in off the main road, she watched the house emerge from its frame of trees, a house more precious and exquisite than anything in Tuscany or Umbria or anywhere else—the sky above and Frank's creation below, every detail spun out of his head and for her, for her—and it made her glad and proud too. And it calmed her, just the sight of it, because there was no place she'd rather be. It was home. She was home. And as Billy shifted gears to climb the hill she felt a stab of nostalgia so powerful the tears came to her eyes, but she was quick to dab them with her handkerchief and avert her face so Billy wouldn't notice. It was nerves, that was all.

She sent Herbert to tell the cook that she and the children would be taking lunch separately out on the screened-in porch and that the workmen would be served in the dining room, and Herbert bobbed back almost immediately to say that the cook was asking how many they'd be. She was seated at her desk, rereading a paragraph she'd already read twelve times over, feigning normalcy—everything was on an even keel, nothing

* The telegram was duly delivered at two o'clock that afternoon at Midway Gardens, but Wrieto-San was not there to receive it. He was already on the train. With his son John. And Edwin Cheney. And with a heart pounding so violently I can hear it pounding still.

amiss, and she wanted them all to believe that, even Carleton—and she looked up and counted them off on her fingers. "Well, let's see," she said, "Brodelle's here somewhere, isn't he?"

"He's back at his desk, yes."

"All right: Emil and you, and Brunker and Lindblom—that makes four. And Billy makes five."

"And Billy's kid."

"Ernest." She smiled. "He's busy learning his father's trade, is he? I hope he'll keep up his studies when school starts up again in the fall—there's no substitute for a good education, wouldn't you agree?"

He shuffled and stammered a bit, but certainly he agreed—that was the whole point of his being here at Taliesin under the hand of Mr. Wright—and of course, he'd appreciated the gift of *The Woman Movement*, which he was finding very . . . stimulating.

She thanked him. Told him he was very kind. And thanked him too for acting as go-between for her and the cook—she wasn't feeling very well and her work had reached a critical stage . . .

He nodded. He was standing at the door, looking only to escape.

"Oh, by the way," she added, "I think we can expect Mr. Wright back this evening." She picked up her pen, idly tracing over a notation in the margin of the page. "I just thought you and Emil might want to know."

Then it was lunch. She'd steeled herself—the thought of seeing Carleton, let alone have him there serving at table, made her stomach turn, but she had to appear as if everything was normal. For everyone's sake. There was no point in upsetting the children—or the workmen either. Or the Carletons, for that matter. She'd had enough upset for one day and she was determined to get through with the meal without exacerbating the situation.

She led John and Martha out onto the porch—"I want to eat with Ernest," John kept whining. "Why can't I eat with Ernest?"—seated them at the table and then took her own place. "Not today," was all she said in response, and she didn't mean to be curt but she saw no need to involve the children in this—she wanted them with her, she *needed* them there, and that was enough—and so she turned to Martha and said, "You know, Martha, that truly is a pretty dress. And so lightweight too, perfect for this weather. Aren't you glad now that we picked it out together?"

And then Carleton was there with his face of iron and his inflexible posture and his gaze on the furniture, the floor, the tray he set down with the faintest mockery of his usual flourish, never daring to lift his eyes to hers or the children's or to utter one single word. There was soup to start, a vegetable broth into which Gertrude had diced red peppers from the garden, along with paper-thin slices of pork she'd rubbed with sage and then marinated in vinegar and lime oil. It was delicious. But John, always a choosy eater, turned up his nose at it. "Mama," he said, pinching his voice, "do I have to eat this?"*

* * *

* This gets very difficult for me. If Wrieto-San had four women in his life—four chances at happiness—I had but two. After Setsuko's death, I thought of contacting Daisy, but I heard—through Wes—that she'd found an Englishman to marry in London, and though I never did discover how that turned out, I didn't have the heart to pursue it. But she was taken from me, just as surely as Mamah was taken from Wrieto-San, and I, like my estimable Master, was able to find solace and love, true love, in another woman, my wife, Setsuko. We came to love and esteem each other more and more through each day, I think—at least until that French cabbie came along. With his *vin rouge*. And his pulse of doom.

Well, corn wasn't cane and this place was no island you could walk across in a day from shore to shore but a glowering dark limitless prison he wanted no part of, not anymore, and he came up out of that cornfield where he could smell the hot reek of the earth that was nothing but spilled blood and shit and the bone meal of all the men and animals that had ever lived atop it and went into the house and washed his hands and slipped into his white service jacket as if he'd been born to it. *Service.* He'd show them service. The kind they never expected. Because they didn't know a thing about him and they didn't know how he'd squatted over his heels and smelled the raw earth while the cornstalks stabbed all around him like ten thousand spears and he learned and studied and talked to the sky and the voice in his head until he had no choice.

The first thing was the windows to the courtyard where the men would be.

Fifteen minutes to twelve noon and he ghosted round outside, nobody in sight, and nailed those windows to the sills with a fistful of two-penny nails and the mallet end of the hatchet he'd found on a shelf in the automobile stall where the roofers had left it behind for him. He recognized it as something he required as soon as he saw it lying there in a whole farrago of forgotten things, a ball of twine, half a dozen rusted cans full of nails and bolts and woodscrews, a dried-up tin of shoe polish and a jar with the talons of a hawk preserved in it and the whole business sprinkled over with bits of straw and a black rice of rat turds. Or mouse. He'd brushed it off with a flick of his hand and then tried it for balance and it was just right, the closest thing to a tomahawk he could find. Brodelle. He thought of Brodelle with the blade of it cleaving his head just the way the naked Indians would have given it to him when they were in possession of the land and whole boatloads of Brodelles came with their whey-faced women to take it away from them and build their big yellow houses and drive down everything and everybody till there was nothing left but hate and want and sickness. It was his. And he kept it under his pillow. For a time like this.

Next was the kitchen and Gertrude with her puffed-up eye and crusted-over lip giving him a wary look and telling him *de mistress and her chillun gone take dey refreshment down de screen porch* and she already ladling out the soup and the aroma of it rising to his nostrils so that he had to swallow down the saliva, thinking how right they were to separate themselves like that. "Be quick about it, woman," he said, and then the three white china bowls were balanced on the silver tray and he was elevating the tray on the platform of his spread black fingers, all the while imagining the three white faces—the woman movement herself and her pale little grubs—bent over their good Bajan soup. Slurping. Commenting on the weather. The books they were reading. Dolls and horses and the geese by the lake and the peacocks caught on the eaves like individual bursts of God-given flame. And the boy like a grub. And the girl. And her. *Get out!* she'd screamed. *You get out! I'm giving you your notice.*

He steeled himself because he had to be hard and this was the hardest part of it, going in there on that screened porch and facing her after what she'd said to him, what she'd done, interfering, meddling, thrusting in her cheap whorish opinions when they weren't wanted or needed or called for in any way save the devil's way, but he balanced the tray on one hand all down the corridor and out across the paving stones and pulled open the door with the other and set down the white ceramic bowls without drawing a spare breath and then he went back to the kitchen and balanced six more bowls on the tray and went into the close little twelve-foot-square dining room with its big wooden table and lobster-trap chairs and that was hard too. Because Brodelle was there. Brodelle, who'd called him a black nigger son of a bitch to his face and who was ready to laugh at him, who *was* laughing at him even as he set down the bowls and never looked a one of them in the eye and backed out the door to go see to the mistress for the last and final time.

He wouldn't be needing the serving tray, not this time, and he let it fall to the flagstones of the loggia with a clapclatter of silver metal and took up the only tool he'd ever need again. Were his thoughts racing? Yes, sure they were, but not in the way of a thinker or mathematician or an architect in the helter-skelter of conception or even a rabbit with the fox at its throat, but in the detached way of a soldier under fire. He saw every detail as if it had been segregated just for him. He saw the cracks between the stones and the weeds struggling there, saw the yellow stucco like the stippled skin of the beast that was the house, saw the screened porch at the end of the passage and the three figures held in abeyance there behind the dark grid of the screen even as a hand rose like a dream hand or a head bobbed on the verge of invisibility. He heard their voices, her voice: "There," she was saying, "that wasn't so awful, was it?" And his: "Was so." And her: "You liked it, John. Admit it—"

And then he came through the door, moving so swiftly he surprised himself, and she looked up this time, this time she saw him, this time her eyes locked on his at the very moment the hatchet came in one savage furious stroke that went in at the hairline and let loose all the red grease of her brains, gray grease and pink grease, and it was on his bleached white jacket like a kind of devil's rain. The boy was next. Before he could react, before the knowledge of what was happening there in front of him could settle into his eyes, the hatchet came down again, twice, and he was dead and twitching even as the girl jumped up and ran till he hit her just behind the right ear, one time, two, three, until she was down on the stone crawling like a grub and her face turned to him now, grub-pale, with her eyes open so that he had to hit there again with the flat of it to crush the cheekbone and shut them for good.

The gasoline. He had the big canister of it right there, ready to hand—"Mr. Weston," he'd said to the dishwater man not thirty minutes ago, "may I have some of that automobile fuel to work the spots out of the rug in the living room, that one with all the swirls and patterns on it?" and the dishwater man had said yes, go ahead, he didn't care—and he sloshed that gasoline over the two of them at the table and the one that had made it out the door and was still alive and working, her legs against the stone floor, and dropped a lit match on it and heard the sudden harsh sucking sound it made.

Quick now, quick—make a job of it. He ran as fast as his lungs and legs would take him to where the men were boasting and laughing and sucking the soup his wife had cooked between their teeth and he bolted into the kitchen through the courtyard door and jammed a wedge of wood under it so no man, even Achilles himself, could have pushed it open. Gertrude might have called out his name, but he gave her one look—one look and two words through his clenched teeth: "Save yourself"—and then he let the gasoline flow out under the door, the whole canister of it and the rugs in the hall already soaked through with it and here was the match, cousin to the last one, and he dashing out his door to the courtyard and the single exit he'd already shut and barred against any man or boy with his clothes aflame and trying to escape. Quick. Quick. The second canister propped there beside the door and gone up in an instant. He could hear them inside, cursing, screaming, shouting like the damned in their hellfire, hear them pounding at the immovable door—shrieks, raw shrieks as alive as the skin that was blistering off their flaming white faces—and then there was the sharp celebratory explosion of the glass of the window and the first of them to come hurtling through it to meet the hatchet, which rose high and higher and fell on them each in turn with all the force of his killing arm and the gravity behind it and it was no more troublesome than splitting shingles.

They were dead as they came through the window and now the flaming rectangle of the door, dead or stunned, the stunned ones rolling on the ground with their clothes aflame, as if that would do them the least lick of good, and he struck them again and again as they rolled and dodged and put up their hands to try to protect themselves where they were most vulnerable. There was a method to this. An order. An efficiency. And he wanted, above all, to be efficient. Three blows for the dishwater man, the hatchet spinning so that it was the flat that brought him down and not the blade, and the boy too, but Brodelle—*black nigger son of a bitch*—he split him open like a wiener on the grill, the same as Mamah, and the fat man too and he went after the other boy, Fritz, but Fritz was rolling, rolling, and every board and fiber of the house in an uproaring lit-bright pandemonium of flame.

Later, he was sick. Later, it burst out of both ends of him and he knew they'd be coming for him with their dogs and the noose braided for lynching and if he ran out into the fields he'd have no say in the matter because he would just be their bait. How he got down into the cellar beneath the inferno of the house he couldn't have said. And he couldn't have said either why he didn't just stand there and let the burning joists fall to crush him and the flames to devour him, because he was done now, all the rage purged out of him as if it had never been there at all. He gave a thought for Gertrude—they'd make her pay and she didn't deserve any part in it—but it was a thought that flitted by and vanished in the instant her sorrowful face materialized in his brain. A flame was as light as air, and yet the frame of that architect's house couldn't withstand the weight. Brands fell round him. Everything shrieked and groaned, unholy noise, the structure rattling and striking out against the death that had come to embrace it. He opened the door of the furnace that had boiled the water for the dead of the house. It was cool inside. Or cooler, anyway. He got in there with the thick glass bottle he'd saved for last, the caustic to kill him before they did, muriatic acid and the triple X and the skull and crossbones to warn them off. He pulled the steel door closed against the roar and the chaos. It was black, purely black, not the thinnest tracery of light to be seen in any direction. They would never find him here.

CHAPTER 8: ALL FALL DOWN

Lunch. A sandwich from the restaurant, a moment to relax with the newspaper—umbrage in the Balkans and the guns thundering across the Continent, and what next, the Archduke rising up out of his coffin on angel's wings?—before he went back to wrangling with Waller over money and Iannelli over the sprites, because the Italian, understandably but maddeningly, was balking at delivering the rest of the statuary without payment in hand or at least guaranteed. The sandwich was good, first-rate—Volgelsang really knew his business, give him credit there—and the newspaper was sufficiently lurid and bloody for even the most jaded reader, but Frank couldn't help keeping one eye on John,*

* I don't know if this is the time or place for it, but in keeping with precedent, I think I should identify the reference here. John is, of course, John Lloyd Wright (1892–1972), Wrieto-San's second son, who was apprenticing during the building of Midway Gardens. Like his older brother, Lloyd, he went on to become a well-known architect in his own right, but was perhaps even more celebrated (and remunerated) for another mode of construction altogether—he was the inventor of the toys known to children worldwide as Lincoln Logs. There may be a ripe irony in here somewhere, but I'm afraid I don't feel up to plucking it. Not now, at any rate.

who was at the far end of the room, up on the scaffolding, applying a wet brush to the polychromatic mural behind the bar. A pretty picture that, and John as precise and unerring a worker as his father himself. Details, details. This room, the tavern, was Waller's number one priority and never mind the glories of opening night with Max Bendix and his hundred-piece orchestra sawing gloriously away and Pavlova pirouetting across the stage and all the rest, he was bleeding money through his pores till the beer started flowing right here, out of these dry and thirsty taps. ("I don't give a damn about murals or sprites or anything else," Waller kept telling him. "I just want the place finished and the tables full. Beer. I just want beer.")

Of course, it was an insult, and he was determined to see the design realized in its every last particular if he was going to draw another breath on this earth, but he could hardly be blamed for the delays at this point. He took another bite of the sandwich. Lifted the glass of ice water to his lips. It was hot. Damnably hot. He thought of Taliesin then, of the lake, and how he'd give anything to throw off his shirt, trousers and shoes and plunge into the cool opaque depths of it and maybe give the fish a run for the money. He was thinking of that, of the fish and how Billy Weston's son had pulled a catfish as long as his arm out of there just a week ago—an amazing thing, really, with its big yellow mouth gaping wide as if to suck in all the air in the valley and the barbels twitching and the tiny dots of its blue-black eyes that hardly seemed sufficient to take in the incandescent world that had loomed up on it so precipitately—when the stenographer from the main office suddenly burst through the door, looking as if she'd had all the blood drained out of her in a scientific experiment. He was going to comment on that, make a joke of it, a quip about the heat and how it was a leading cause of anemia in women under thirty, but her face warned him off. "Mr. Wright," she said, out of breath, running sweat, paler than the stack of paper she kept to hand beside her typewriter, "you're wanted on the telephone. Long distance. From Spring Green."

Once, when he was young, younger than John was now, he'd seen a building collapse. It was a massive brick structure still under construction, men aloft, hod carriers rushing to and fro, the workmen all separately focused on their tasks but communicating as if by some extrasensory intelligence, the whole thing—men, materials and machines alike—a kind of living organism. He'd stopped to watch as he often had over the course of the weeks past, fascinated by the frenzy of activity and the way the building rose in discernable increments—different each day and yet the same too—and he was there watching when all that changed in an instant. More than anything he remembered the sound of it, the explosive snap of the beams buckling and the cannonade of one floor tearing through another, a roar of the inanimate animated, withering, unforgiving. And the screams. The screams that rose up out of a clenched fist of silence and the harsh soughing of the dust. He'd stood there for hours, the dread rising in him with a bitter metallic taste that constricted his throat—one man had been crushed till he was little more than extruded pulp; another had to be sawed, living, from the wreckage, two raw stumps palpitating there in place of his legs—and he'd wanted only to put it all right again, to build it back up so it would never fall. But Taliesin had fallen, was falling now, and it was worse, far worse, because this was fire and fire not only crushed you, it consumed you too.

The roar was in his ears as John pushed him into the cab and the cab hurtled through the streets, and it was there still as they pulled up to the curb and John jerked open the door and led him out of the cramped automotive interior and into the marble vault of Union Station. He held to his son's arm through the crush of people and across the floor to the ticket window, his throat dry, his legs stripped of muscle and bone alike so that he could barely stand upright. And here were the reporters, their faces rabid and their mouths working—"Mr. Wright! Mr. Wright!"—and John shouldering past them and through the door and onto the platform where the local would haul them over the rails for five agonizing hours before the station in Spring Green rose up like a gravestone beyond the windows. And couldn't they hurry? Couldn't they call it an emergency and cancel all the other stops? Rush on through, red flags flapping and whistle shrieking as if the president himself were on board?

He shut his eyes and heard the roar. And it was a merciful thing because the roar drowned out the shouts of the newsboys who were there now and who would change faces and jackets and hats and mob every station stop along the way to hawk the very latest up-to-date special edition: *Murder at Taliesin, read all about it!; Taliesin Burning to the Ground, Seven Slain, Seven Slain, Seven Slain!* It was John who kept them off and John who took the conductor aside and arranged for a private compartment, John who spotted poor Edwin Cheney standing there stricken in a circle of reporters and spirited him into the compartment before they could work their beaks in him and their talons too. Five hours. Five hours on that train staring at Ed Cheney's shoes while Ed Cheney stared at his. Five hours. Seven slain.

He didn't pray. He hadn't prayed since he was a boy. But each minute of that journey was a slow crawl to Calvary and the moment when they'd stretch him on the Christ tree and drive the nails in, and all the while he imagined the worst and hoped for the best, and maybe this was prayer, maybe this was what prayer was after all. What he didn't know was that Mamah was dead, her corpse so incinerated as to be unrecognizable. What he didn't know was that John Cheney was dead too and that Martha, with her graceful limbs and her mother's ready smile, was writhing under the wet towels they'd laid over her, her hair and eyebrows gone and her skin fried like sidemeat in a pan, or that she would die by the time he got there. He didn't know that Brunker was dead, didn't know that Lindblom would soon follow him or that Brodelle was already gone. And he didn't know that Billy Weston, concussed, burned and bleeding from the scalp, had grappled with the Barbadian and chased him off before running to Reider for help and then come back to unfurl the garden hose and play it on the fire while the victims lay there stretched out on the paving stones of the courtyard like so many sacks of grain. Burned-up grain. Rotten grain. Grain fit only to turn into the earth. Or that Ernest, the very make and model of his father, lay there among them, unconscious and dying from his wounds while one of the neighbor women tended him and Billy struggled with the hose, numb to everything but the infernal scorching heat on his face.

Then it was night. The dead were laid out on the porch at Tan-y-deri, the stink of incineration riding the air till it overwhelmed everything, till there was no use for the organ of smell except to admit it. There were no mosquitoes. No fireflies. Even the lake seemed dead save for the faint traces of movement there where the firemen and the neighbors had formed a bucket brigade to quench the coals. He couldn't look at Mamah—there was no use in that. It was shock enough to see the form of her, laid out in her twisted sheets, and the blood-color there like rust stains.

People thrust things at him, his sister fussing over him, black coffee, a plate of food, but he didn't want any of it. He wanted to lash out, wanted revenge, wanted to meet violence with violence. If he could have laid hands on Carleton, he swore he'd tear him apart, just as if he were some beast in the jungle. They'd found the man at five-thirty that evening, hidden in the furnace where the fire wouldn't touch him and he'd tried to kill himself by swallowing acid, the burns of it there like long pale fingers clawing at his lips and spots of it scorched through his shirt. By then, all of Taliesin was an armed camp, people beating the woods, searching the cornfield stalk by stalk, the sheriff loosing his hounds and shouts and alarums going up everywhere.

They were going to lynch him, that was what Andrew Porter had said, the noose already dangling from the limb of one of the oaks in the courtyard and all the farmers in high color and itching at the triggers of their .22s and shotguns and deer rifles, but the sheriff stood against them, and he and his deputy dragged the Negro out and handcuffed him and spirited him off to the Dodgeville jail, a mob of men chasing the car and cursing him all the way down the hill. He was there now, in a jail cell, unable to speak or to give any reason for what he'd done, for this hate and mayhem and devastation that had laid everything to ruin and grievously injured the souls of so many good people, because his vocal apparatus was destroyed and he wouldn't take up a pen to write a word though the sheriff stood over him and the reporters clustered three deep on the courthouse steps. Frank never did get to see him, and that was just as well, because it would have been like staring into the face of the devil himself—that sooty abandoned face, that blackness without surface or limit—but at some point they ushered the wife into the room and he looked up from the chair he was sunk in and saw her standing there before him.*

There was a sheriff's deputy in the hall. Boards creaked. Footsteps echoed on the stairs. The coroner was there, the undertaker, the house alive with comings and goings, doors creaking shut and open again, voices drifting from room to room. They were nervous—Jennie was nervous, Andrew, the servants, the whole community—and they would have a scapegoat, a black scapegoat, and here she was.

What he saw was a very young woman, a girl not much older than his own daughters. If he'd noticed her before, when he'd hired her or glanced up to see her flitting in and out of the kitchen or hurrying across the courtyard with a basketful of tomatoes and greens from the garden, it was only in passing. She worked for him. She was doing her job. Mamah praised her. And, of course, he had other things on his mind. She was an employee and you only noticed employees—really looked at them—when they were late to work or drunk or sleeping on the job. When they stole. When they murdered people.

The lamps were low. A moth sailed lazily across the room. But for John—who'd never before laid eyes on Taliesin because his mother, in her jealousy and her rage, wouldn't hear of it—they were alone. The girl stood just inside the door where the deputy had left her and soon

* As it turned out, the Barbadian was never brought to trial. He succumbed in his jail cell some two months later, not from the effects of the acid he'd ingurgitated, but of a hunger strike. Billy Weston told me that Carleton couldn't have been more than a hundred-forty or -fifty pounds, and that he'd lost nearly half of that weight by the time of his death. From the moment he raised that shingling hatchet, nothing passed his lips but water. Nor did he talk. Strange man, stranger fate.

she'd be in the jailhouse too, because she was the Negro's wife, a Negro herself, and everybody in the county knew they'd plotted this horror together. Her dress was plain. She was thin. And her face, when she lifted her chin to show it to him, was gaunt, hollow-cheeked, smudged with traces of dirt where she'd wiped back the tears, and the socket of her right eye seemed to be bruised, as if someone had taken a poke at her, but for all that she was beautiful. Beautiful in her simplicity and her innocence. He saw that right away—she'd had nothing to do with this. It was the husband, the husband alone.

John had stood when she'd been led into the room. He was leaning against the near wall, his arms folded across his chest, shifting his weight from foot to foot in a spasm of nervous energy. He was his father's protector now and the tug of that responsibility jerked at him and jerked again. "Well," he said, "what have you got to say for yourself?"

She shook her head, a long slow meditative roll from one shoulder to the other, and she held out her palms, splayed her thin fingers and opened up her face—not to John, but to him. "A judgment," she whispered. "It a judgment. Dat what it is."

He could see John go rigid. His son was about to throw it back at her, bully her, but he cut him off. "Hush, John," he said. "Enough."

Gertrude—that was her name, wasn't it?—was staring down at her feet, bare feet, the nails neatly trimmed and glowing against the shadow of her skin, canescent almost, and there were traces of wet ash on her ankles and the pale underside of her arches. What she'd said had shocked him and he was struggling to recover himself. A judgment? That was what the press was calling it, the sermonizers and tub-thumpers, and for one hard moment he saw how wrong he'd been, how cruel and selfish. He'd lusted after Mamah. Thrown everything over. Ruined Kitty, ruined Edwin, alienated a whole community and spat in their faces. And here was the result of it, seven slain and a scared young black woman going to jail and maybe worse, Taliesin in ashes, Billy's son dead and gone. And Mamah. And both her children. He wanted to deny it, wanted to call it fate, bad luck, anything, but the words wouldn't come.

John couldn't restrain himself any longer. "How dare you say that?" he demanded, his voice fracturing with the rush of his emotions, his father's protector, the golden walls, the forbidden city. "It was your husband. A maniac. A black—"

"No," she said, and she was shaking her head again, long-faced and slow and mournful. "On *me.* It a judgment on me." She lifted her eyes to him as if John weren't even there. "That I should marry wit' such a man—"

There was the sound of voices raised out in the yard, the heavy tramp of feet on the floorboards of the porch. A dog began to bark. He felt himself closing up again, angry suddenly—he was the victim here and it was all these others who were in the wrong because they wouldn't allow a man to live in peace the way he saw fit. He wasn't going to let God or his ministers or this scrawny Negro woman or anybody else dole out guilt because the onus was on them—they were the murderers, not he.

Her voice had broken. Her eyes clawed at him. "He was a good mon, sir, so good to me. We—I jus' seventeen in Bridgetown and he say he love me, all the time he say he love me, and I don't know what dat is, I don't know, I still don't know . . ."

She was sobbing now, her chest heaving and both hands gone to her eyes. "A good mon," she kept saying, "he was a good mon," till John stepped forward to open the door on the deputy's furious red face and the people crowding in behind him, strangers come to share in the outrage, and all he could think to say, the aggrieved victim, bereft and inconsolable, was "Take her away."*

At some point, his sister was there with something in a cup for him to drink and then she took him upstairs to the bedroom and laid him down on the bed by the darkened window, and for some strange reason, as she turned off the lamp and stood silhouetted in the light of the door, murmuring the sorts of things only women can command in times of heartache and affliction, he called her Kitty. "I'll be all right, Kitty," he said, though he knew he wouldn't be, and as he lay there sleepless, listening to the voices in the dark and the breathless haunted groans of the two survivors laid out in the parlor (Fritz, who would recover from his burns and a forearm shattered in his plunge through the window, and Lindblom, who would die by morning), she began to emerge from the shadows, Kitty, not Mamah, and wasn't that the strangest thing? He saw her whirling away from him in the blue satin gown her mother had made her, Cosette to

* As I reread these pages, I can't help imagining how different the world would be if Wrieto-San had sat down to lunch on that fatal day. He'd realized some 135 buildings to that point, a prodigious output for any architect, but the world would hardly know him as the monument he is today if he'd been buried beside his mistress in that little family cemetery in the outer reaches of nowhere. Think of what we would have lost—the Imperial Hotel, Fallingwater, the Guggenheim and all the rest of his constantly evolving and magisterial mature designs. Taliesin wouldn't exist except as a charred ruin in somebody's cow pasture. And I'd never have apprenticed with him or known his friendship and guidance. This book wouldn't be. O'Flaherty-San, brilliant as he is, might never have risen above the facile gratifications of fiction. One man—Wrieto-San—and what a banner he has carried for us all. A judgment indeed.

his Marius, and half the girls there were Cosette while the boys favored Valjean and Javert, Kitty, with the elastic limbs and the red-gold hair that piled up like waves on a beach . . .

In the morning, the sun rose out of the hills in a dark bruise of clouds and the clouds spread over the valley like a stain in water. By noon, it was like dusk. He felt the humidity the moment he rose from his sweated sheets, heavy air bearing him down and his shirt wet before he put it on. He'd fallen into a dreamless sleep sometime in the early hours, listening to a solitary bird—a whip-poor-will—riding up and down the glissando of its liquid notes till he'd gone unconscious along with it. He didn't know how long he'd slept, but when he woke he was fully and immediately present. He knew where he was and why he'd come and that his loss and misery were continuous and that he wouldn't taste his breakfast or his lunch or his dinner either.

He tried to comb his hair, but it was a snarl, and when he lifted his arms to smooth it back he was assaulted by his own odor. He smelled of yesterday's sweat, a deep working stench of fear and uncertainty that no soap or eau de cologne could ever drive down. For a moment he thought of going down to the lake for a swim, but that wouldn't be right either, not if Mamah couldn't join him or her John and her Martha—no, he would wear his odor, deepen it with the sweat of digging, the pickaxe riding high over his head as he stabbed at the earth and loosened the teeth of the yellow rock that lay clustered there along the black gums of the soil, because every grave was a mouth that opened and closed and swallowed till there was nothing left.

There was breakfast. A hush of voices, people tiptoeing round the house like ghosts of the departed. He sat for a moment with Fritz—the hair gone, the scalded scalp, gauze pillowed up like a spring snowstorm—but the boy didn't seem to recognize him. Then he went out into the yard to smell the thin poisonous odor of the smoke that still rose from the ruins across the way, and there were people here as well, too many people, and so he walked down the hill and back up again to Taliesin and into the burned-out courtyard. That was where Billy Weston was, both his hands bandaged and a white surgical strip wrapped round his skull so that he looked like a casualty of the war. Frank saw the blood there, a slow seep of it accumulating at the temple, a wound that would never heal. "Billy," was all he could say, and Billy, a rake in one hand, the streaming hose in the other, could only nod in return. For a long while they just stood there, side by side, and then they bent forward and began to rake the ashes.

In another place, all the way across the world in Paris, where the talk was of nothing but the war—the insuperability of Plan 17, the fierceness of the French cavalry and the defects of the German character—Maude Miriam Noel was just sitting down to breakfast at the Café Lilac. She'd chosen a table under the awning, out of the sun, though the day was lovely, so tranquil and warm you'd never know a war was going on not a hundred and fifty kilometers away. It was her skin. She'd been out for a walk along the Seine the day before, and though she was wearing her hat and carrying a parasol, she hadn't bothered with gloves because of the heat, and now the backs of her hands were red—or worse, brown. She'd rubbed cold cream on them, but she couldn't help noticing the faint rippling of the flesh there—wrinkles, they were wrinkles—and that worried her, worried her deeply. Old women had wrinkled hands, parchment hands ("Lizard skin," as Leora used to joke all those years ago when they were both young and could barely conceive of what a wrinkle was, at least in relation to themselves), and she wasn't an old woman. Not in fact or by any stretch of the imagination. Men stopped to stare at her as she went down the street, and not simply men of middle age, but young men too.

But here was the waiter. A little man—so many of them were little men, not simply among waiters or the French, but men in general, so very pinched in spirit and disappointing when you most needed them. This particular waiter—Jean-Pierre Something-or-Other—had stared into her face on innumerable mornings through all the seasons of the year, at least since she'd moved into her little apartment at 21 rue des Saints-Pères, with the window boxes trailing blood-red geraniums above the *antiquités* shop so crammed with marble and pictures in gilded frames it could have been a museum itself, and yet each time he presented the menu with a "*Bonjour, madame,*" it was as if it were the first, as if he'd never laid eyes on her before, as if she were a mere tourist and interloper. Which infuriated her. She'd complained about him to the management on more than one occasion, but the management, which consisted of a terminally weary old lady in a stained blue kerchief (yes, with lizard hands and an eternally dripping nose) and her entirely deaf husband, hadn't seemed moved to do anything about it. And so here he was. And here she was. Because she'd be damned if she'd go even half a block out of her way to the next café—this one was hers, her *territoire,* and she was willing to fight for it. Or at least endure a certain degree of rudeness, day after day, meal after meal.

The waiter handed her the menu as if he'd just found it in the street, and she waved it away—they both knew perfectly well that she'd all but memorized it and wanted only *deux oeufs*, poached, accompanied by a pair of those little English sausages and the sauté of tomatoes, *avec café noir sans sucre.* They both knew, and yet every encounter was played out as if it were the first, as if they were players in an Oscar Wilde farce. Then the waiter was gone and at some point the coffee appeared and she reached beneath the table for her bag and the newspapers Leora had sent her from Chicago. She liked to keep up on events in the States, especially now that the war had broken out, but she always had, because as Frenchified as she'd become she was still an American girl at heart, Maude Miriam Noel, the Belle of Memphis. Just the other night, at a gathering in her flat over a very nice Beaujolais and croquettes of crab she'd produced herself, an Englishman by the name of Noel Rutherford—*Noel*, and wasn't that a cozy coincidence?—had told her how utterly charming her accent was. "You're from the South, I presume," he'd said—"Richmond, perhaps? Or perhaps deeper? Let me guess: Charlotte? Savannah?" And she'd smiled up at him—he was tall, lean, with that constricted muscular energy so many of the English seemed to cultivate, his hair as sleek and dark as an otter's, and she'd begun to see real possibilities in him—and positively drawled, "Oh, no, honey, you've got me awl wrong. I'm a Memphis girl."

She spread the papers out before her. Took a sip of her coffee. Of course, the past year had been hard on her, what with the way she'd been thrown over by René and that unfortunate incident with the carving knife—and she would have stabbed him, she really and truly would have and gladly gone to the Santé Prison for it, if he'd only stood still long enough. And there was her cat. Mr. Ribbons—or Monsieur Ribbons, as she liked to call out from the door and watch him scamper across the street, his tail held erect above him. When he'd begun to spit up blood, she immediately suspected the crabbed odious horse-faced woman downstairs of poisoning him, and there'd been another regrettable incident over that, though the veterinarian assured her that the animal had died of natural causes. Yes. Certainly. *Natural causes.*

What else could it be? At the thought of it she looked up sharply over her reading glasses, riveting the waiter with a look, which he ignored, and where were her eggs? Had they sent out to the provinces for them? Did it take a Cordon Bleu chef to set a pot of water boiling and dice a few tomatoes over a pan?

She was irritable, and she would have been the first to admit it. It was the war, the uncertainty, the rumors. Everyone said it would be over in six months, but what if it wasn't? What if the Germans pushed through and marched into Paris? What if there were shortages, rationing? Would the cafés be deserted? Would her landlady raise her rent? She'd thought of going back to Chicago, to Norma, but that was distasteful to her in so many ways she could hardly count them. So many of her friends—the Americans and English, at any rate—had already left, the Belknaps, Clarissa Hodge, the Payne Whitneys. Even her closest friend and confidante, Marie-Thérèse, had gone away to the country, deserting her when she most needed someone to confide in, and not just over René but the creeping fear that started as a kind of upset of her stomach and radiated all the way down to her toes and back up her spine to the nape of her neck, the fear that everything she knew and loved was wearing down and coming to some awful end.

The waiter sauntered up with the heavy ceramic plate and slipped it onto the table as if he were placing a bet at Auteuil before vanishing like a magician, only to reappear in the depths of the café, a freshly lit cigarette jutting from his mouth. She spread her napkin across her lap, adjusted the newspaper and her reading glasses, and cut into one of the sausages. It was then that the headline caught her eye: SEVEN SLAIN AT TALIESIN. And under it: *Love Bungalow Murders.* She set down the fork and began reading—the story was so horrific, so compelling and awful, she couldn't help herself; it was like a novel, a romance, and here was the hero of the affair, Mr. Frank Lloyd Wright, in half-profile, staring out nobly across the continent and the sea too. Her breakfast went cold. The coffee sat untouched. The waiter never so much as glanced at her.

She read through the article twice and then sat for a long while studying the photograph. Very slowly, as if she couldn't control it, she began to shake her head from side to side even as the tremor crept up her spine one vertebra at a time, as if a series of individual fingertips were poking at her in succession.

The poor man, she was thinking. *The poor, poor man.*

FOR MORE FROM T. C. BOYLE, LOOK FOR THE

Budding Prospects
All Felix Nasmyth and friends have to do is harvest a crop of Cannabis sativa and half a million tax-free dollars will be theirs. But they haven't reckoned on nosy neighbors, torrential rain, demands of the flesh, and Felix's improbable new love. As their deal escalates through crises into nightmare, their dreams of easy money get nipped in the bud. *ISBN 978-0-14-029996-0*

Descent of Man
A primate-center researcher becomes romantically involved with a chimp. A Norse poet overcomes bard-block. These and other strange occurrences come together in Boyle's first collection of stories. *ISBN 978-0-14-029994-6*

Drop City
Rich and allusive, T. C. Boyle's ninth novel is about a California commune devoted to peace, free love, and the simple life that decides to relocate to unforgiving Alaska in the ultimate expression of going back to the land.
A *New York Times* bestseller and Finalist for the National Book Award *ISBN 978-0-14-200380-0*

East Is East
Young Japanese seaman Hiro Tanaka jumps ship off the coast of Georgia and swims into a net of rabid rednecks, genteel ladies, descendants of slaves, and the denizens of an artists' colony.
ISBN 978-0-14-013167-3

A Friend of the Earth
It is 2025. Ty Tierwater, a failed eco-terrorist and ex-con, ekes out a bleak living managing a rock star's private menagerie of scruffy hyenas, warthogs, and three down-at-the-mouth lions, some of the only species remaining after the collapse of the earth's biosphere. *ISBN 978-0-14-100205-7*

Greasy Lake and Other Stories
Mythic and realistic, these masterful stories are, according to *The New York Times*, "satirical fables of contemporary life, so funny and acutely observed that they might have been written by Evelyn Waugh as sketches for . . . *Saturday Night Live*."
ISBN 978-0-14-007781-0

If the River Was Whiskey
Boyle tears through the walls of contemporary society to reveal a world at once comic and tragic, droll and horrific, in these sixteen magical and provocative stories.
ISBN 978-0-14-011950-3

The Inner Circle
As a member of Alfred "Dr. Sex" Kinsey's "inner circle," John Milk is called upon to participate in sexual experiments that become increasingly uninhibited—and problematic for his marriage—as Kinsey ever more recklessly pushes the boundaries both personally and professionally. *ISBN 978-0-14-303586-2*

Riven Rock
Millionaire Stanley McCormick, diagnosed as a schizophrenic and sexual maniac shortly after his marriage, is forbidden the sight of women, but his strong-willed, virginal wife Katherine Dexter is determined to cure him. *ISBN 978-0-14-027166-9*

The Road to Wellville
Centering on John Harvey Kellogg and his turn-of-the-century Battle Creek Spa, this wickedly comic novel brims with Dickensian characters and wildly wonderful plot twists.
ISBN 978-0-14-016718-4

Talk Talk
Dana Halter, a young deaf woman, is in a courtroom as a list of charges is read out—assault with a deadly weapon, auto theft, passing bad checks. There has been a terrible mistake—someone has stolen her identity. As Dana and her new boyfriend set out to find him, they begin to test the limits of the life they have started to build together. *Talk Talk* is both a suspenseful road trip across America and a moving story about language, love, and identity.
ISBN 978-0-14-311215-0

T. C. Boyle Stories
A virtual feast of the short story, this volume collects all of the work from Boyle's first four collections, as well as seven tales that have never before appeared in book form.
ISBN 978-0-14-028091-3

Tooth and Claw
In T. C. Boyle's dazzling seventh collection of stories ". . . men are fools, women hold the sexual cards, and nature is full of surprises, few of them pleasant." —*Entertainment Weekly*
ISBN 978-0-14-303743-9

The Tortilla Curtain
Illegal immigrants Cándido and América cling to life at the bottom of Topanga Canyon, dreaming of a privileged existence of the sort enjoyed by L.A. liberals Delaney and Kyra. When a freak accident brings these two couples together, darkly comic events leave them wondering what the world is coming to.
ISBN 978-0-14-023828-0

Water Music
Water Music, Boyle's first novel, follows the wild adventures of Ned Rise, thief and whoremaster, and Mungo Park, explorer, through London's seamy gutters and Scotland's scenic Highlands—to their grand meeting in the heart of Africa. There they join forces and wend their hilarious way to the source of the Niger.
ISBN 978-0-14-006550-3

Without a Hero
With fierce, comic wit, Boyle zooms in on an astonishingly wide range of American phenomena such as a couple in search of the last toads on earth and a real estate wonder boy on a dude safari near Bakersfield, California, in this critically applauded collection of stories.
ISBN 978-0-14-017839-5

World's End
Set in New York's Hudson Valley in three time periods—the late seventeenth century, the 1940s, and the late 1960s—this fascinating novel, for which Boyle won the prestigious PEN/Faulkner Award for American Fiction, follows the interwoven destinies of three families.
ISBN 978-0-14-029993-9